Memory and Modern British Politics

Memory and Modern British Politics

Commemoration, Tradition, Legacy

Edited by Matthew Roberts

BLOOMSBURY ACADEMIC
LONDON • NEW YORK • OXFORD • NEW DELHI • SYDNEY

BLOOMSBURY ACADEMIC
Bloomsbury Publishing Plc, 50 Bedford Square, London, WC1B 3DP, UK
Bloomsbury Publishing Inc, 1385 Broadway, New York, NY 10018, USA
Bloomsbury Publishing Ireland, 29 Earlsfort Terrace, Dublin 2, D02 AY28, Ireland

BLOOMSBURY, BLOOMSBURY ACADEMIC and the Diana logo
are trademarks of Bloomsbury Publishing Plc

First published in Great Britain 2024
This paperback edition published in 2025

Copyright © Matthew Roberts, 2024

Matthew Roberts has asserted his right under the Copyright,
Designs and Patents Act, 1988, to be identified as Editor of this work.

For legal purposes the Acknowledgements on p. viii constitute
an extension of this copyright page.

Cover image © Thomas Paine Statue, Thetford, by Sir Charles Thomas Wheeler.
Photograph by Robert Evans/ Alamy Stock Photo.

All rights reserved. No part of this publication may be: i) reproduced or transmitted in any form, electronic or mechanical, including photocopying, recording or by means of any information storage or retrieval system without prior permission in writing from the publishers; or ii) used or reproduced in any way for the training, development or operation of artificial intelligence (AI) technologies, including generative AI technologies. The rights holders expressly reserve this publication from the text and data mining exception as per Article 4(3) of the Digital Single Market Directive (EU) 2019/790.

Bloomsbury Publishing Plc does not have any control over, or responsibility for, any third-party websites referred to or in this book. All internet addresses given in this book were correct at the time of going to press. The author and publisher regret any inconvenience caused if addresses have changed or sites have ceased to exist, but can accept no responsibility for any such changes.

A catalogue record for this book is available from the British Library.

A catalog record for this book is available from the Library of Congress.

ISBN:	HB:	978-1-3501-9046-7
	PB:	978-1-3501-9071-9
	ePDF:	978-1-3501-9047-4
	eBook:	978-1-3501-9048-1

Typeset by Integra Software Services Pvt. Ltd.

For product safety related questions contact productsafety@bloomsbury.com.

To find out more about our authors and books visit www.bloomsbury.com
and sign up for our newsletters.

Contents

List of contributors		vi
Acknowledgements		viii
1	From Colston to canons: Memory, tradition and the political use of the past in modern Britain *Matthew Roberts*	1
2	A practical English past: Commemorating the Glorious Revolution in England from Tom Paine to T. B. Macaulay (1792–1848) *Rémy Duthille*	15
3	'Generation 1789': Welsh Dissenters and radicals lost in translation *Marion Löffler*	35
4	The canon of Irish republicanism: Constructing a separatist 'tradition' *Colin W. Reid*	67
5	Romantic memory? Forgetting, remembering and feeling in the Chartist pantheon of heroes, c.1790–1840 *Matthew Roberts*	93
6	'A new political baptism': Memorializing the Reform Acts in 1832 *Gordon Pentland*	121
7	Living in stone or marble: The public commemoration of Victorian MPs *Kathryn Rix*	139
8	Peel's death as family tragedy: Remembering Sir Robert Peel in public and in private *Richard A. Gaunt*	171
9	'Whatever happened to all the heroes?': The monumental failure of British plebeian radicalism, c.1850–1920 *Antony Taylor*	193
10	Making Martyrs: Contested histories and the British labour and Socialist movements' commemoration of the Dorchester labourers *Marcus Morris*	217
11	Magna Carta, memory diplomacy, and the use of the past in Anglo-American relations, c.1915–65 *Sam Edwards*	235
12	Remembering British rule: The uses of colonial memory in Hong Kong protest movements, 1997–2019 *Mark Hampton and Florence Mok*	257
Index		274

Contributors

Rémy Duthille is Reader in British Studies at Université Bordeaux Montaigne, France. His first book, *Le Discours radical, 1768–1789* (Voltaire Foundation, 2017), is an intellectual history study of the radicalism of the dissenting milieu of Richard Price, John Cartwright and their circle. He has since worked on British political sociability, from *c.*1760 to *c.*1850, and especially on the cultures of political dining and drinking, on sociability and male feminists. He is currently preparing a book on British celebrations of foreign revolutions from 1789 to 1848.

Sam Edwards is Reader in Modern Political History at Loughborough University. His research engages with transatlantic relations, commemoration and memory, and the cultural history of conflict. His publications include *Allies in Memory: World War II and the Politics of Transatlantic Commemoration, c.1941–2001* (Cambridge University Press, 2018); *Histories on Screen: The Past and Present in Anglo-American Cinema and Television* (Bloomsbury, 2017); and *The Legacy of Thomas Paine in the Transatlantic World*, ed. (with Marcus Morris, Routledge, 2018).

Richard A. Gaunt is Associate Professor in British History at the University of Nottingham and a specialist in the period between *c.*1780 and *c.*1850. He is the author, among other publications, of *Sir Robert Peel. The Life and Legacy* (London, 2010) and *Sir Robert Peel. Contemporary Perspectives* (Abingdon, 2022), 3 vols. Since 2013, he has co-edited the journal *Parliamentary History*.

Mark Hampton is Associate Professor of History at Lingnan University, where he is also Warden of the Jockey Club New Hall (H). He is the author of *Visions of the Press in Britain, 1850–1950* (2004), and *Hong Kong and British Culture, 1945–97* (2016). He is a co-editor of the journal *Media History* and general co-editor and Volume 5 co-editor of the forthcoming *Cultural History of Media*, in Bloomsbury's Cultural Histories series.

Marion Löffler is Reader in Welsh History and History at Cardiff University. Her research focuses on the cultural and economic entanglements of nineteenth-century Wales with Europe, Empire and the world. Among her monographs are *The Literary and Historical Legacy of Iolo Morganwg, 1826–1926* (2007), and *Political Pamphlets and Sermons from Wales, 1790–1806* (2014). She is a regular expert media contributor on Welsh culture and identities, especially Wales's relationship with the British monarchy, appearing on BBC landmark series like *Art That Made Us* (2022) and *The Union* (2023).

Florence Mok is Nanyang Assistant Professor of History at Nanyang Technological University, Singapore. She is a historian of colonial Hong Kong and modern China, with an interest in environmental history, the Cold War and state-society relations. She has published peer-reviewed articles in well-respected interdisciplinary and historical journals; her *China Information* article won the Eduard B. Vermeer Best Article Prize in 2019 and ICAS Best Article Prize on Global Hong Kong Studies in 2021.

Marcus Morris is Senior Lecturer in Modern European History at Manchester Metropolitan University. His research is primarily centred on British and European history in the late nineteenth and early twentieth centuries. In particular, he focuses on the labour and socialist movements of Britain and Europe and has published widely on a variety of themes in relation to those.

Gordon Pentland is Professor of History at Monash University. He has published widely on the history of Scotland and Britain since the eighteenth century and his most recent book (edited with Michael T. Davis and Emma Macleod) is *Political Trials in an Age of Revolution: Britain and the North Atlantic, 1793–1848* (2019).

Colin Reid is Senior Lecturer in British and Irish History at the University of Sheffield. He is the author of *The Lost Ireland of Stephen Gwynn: Constitutional Nationalism and Cultural Politics, 1864–1950* (2011), and a number of articles and chapters on Irish political thought.

Kathryn Rix is Assistant Editor of the House of Commons, 1832–1945 project at the History of Parliament Trust. Her research interests focus on nineteenth- and early-twentieth-century British electoral and parliamentary history. She has written in particular on the themes of electoral corruption and party organization, including her book, *Parties, Agents and Electoral Culture in England, 1880–1910* (2016).

Matthew Roberts is Associate Professor of Modern British History at Sheffield Hallam University. He works on the history of popular politics, protest, commemoration and the history of emotions. He is the author of *Chartism, Commemoration and the Cult of the Radical Hero* (2019) and *Democratic Passions: The Politics of Feeling in British Popular Radicalism, 1809–48* (2022).

Antony Taylor Emeritus Professor of Modern British History at Sheffield Hallam University in the UK. He is the author of *'Down with the Crown': British Anti-monarchism and Debates about Royalty since 1790* (1999); *Lords of Misrule: Hostility to Aristocracy in Late Nineteenth and Early Twentieth-Century Britain* (2004) and *London's Burning: Pulp Fiction, the Politics of Terrorism and the Destruction of the Capital in British Popular Culture, 1840–2005* (2012).

Acknowledgements

The idea for this volume emerged from previous research undertaking by the editor on Chartism and commemoration, and in many conversations and email exchanges with contributors and others. Events at Bristol in June 2020 acted as another prompt as the project was beginning to take shape. The editor would like to thank the contributors for agreeing to write chapters for this volume. Little did we all realize back in early 2019 what the next few years would have in store. I am especially grateful to my fellow contributors that the pandemic only delayed rather than derailed the completion of the project. Bloomsbury have been exemplary publishers, in particular Abigail Lane and Megan Harris, who have helpfully shepherded the project from the beginning through to publication.

1

From Colston to canons: Memory, tradition and the political use of the past in modern Britain

Matthew Roberts

On 7 June 2020 Black Lives Matter protesters in Bristol toppled the statue of the slaver and civic worthy Edward Colston. This was a powerful reminder that political activists and the public care about the past – over 10,000 people were present at the demonstration – and that heritage can be intensely political. The backlash to that day's events, long in the making, gave rise to a protracted debate in the media about Britain's heritage landscape. The question of who is commemorated, and who is not, and – perhaps more significantly – who decides, can be intensely political decisions. For Black Lives Matter campaigners and other groups, those historic figures with connections to the slave trade do not merit any place in the civic landscapes of modern Britain.[1] In some respects, what took place at Bristol was unusual, in particular, the lengths that the protesters went to. While previous monuments have been defaced as acts of political protest – some of them regularly, such as the statue of Winston Churchill in Parliament Square – rarely have British protesters resorted to such audacious acts of iconoclasm, at least since the Reformation.[2] Colston's statue was not just forcibly toppled; it was defaced and thrown into Bristol Harbour. This action was an example of what the historian Alan Rice has termed 'guerrilla memorialization', which he defines as instances where people take direct action to reshape the heritage landscape.[3] In other respects, what happened at Bristol was only the latest chapter in an evolving campaign to remove statues and other forms of commemoration deemed offensive and elitist and to reshape Britain's heritage so that it reflects the multicultural past and present.[4]

And yet the fallout over Colston – as some rushed to defend and exonerate the protesters, while others censured them and called for prosecution – revealed a paradox in relation to the historiography. For all the political and public debate, the fact remains that pantheonization, the invention of tradition, political canonization, heritage politics and the broader political uses of the past are under-explored aspects of modern British political culture, at least when compared to the sizeable scholarship on European and North American commemoration.[5] In part, this relates to the broader place of cultures of remembrance in the national past and present. As Antony Taylor reminds us in his chapter, Britain is a much older nation, and thus it remained comparatively untouched by the period of frenetic monument building, 'statuemania' and mass memorialization in the nineteenth century that was such a central part in the birth of new nations or dramatic regime changes which necessitated the invention of legitimating traditions.

Another linked reason why these aspects remain relatively under-explored is that much of the rich literature on commemoration and the invention of tradition – beyond Britain – has focused on nation-building, state-sponsored memory, war and genocide, while the little scholarship that does exist on Britain has understandably focused on war, monarchy and empire.[6] Here lies another reason for the comparative neglect. As Raphael Samuel observed, those on the political left, including many historians, have 'become accustomed to thinking of commemoration as a cheat, something which ruling elites impose on the subaltern classes'. According to this view, memory and the political use of the past are 'weapon[s] of social control, a means of generating consensus and legitimating the *status quo* with reference to a mythologized version of the past'.[7] This explains, at least in part, why much less has been written on dissident commemorations, though the newer field of critical heritage studies is beginning to redress this imbalance.[8] Critical heritage studies – or 'heritage from below' – rejects the conventional view that heritage is constituted by the inherent values of objects and practices; rather, it views heritage as the product of judgements made by not just elites but also the public about what is valuable from the past. As a result, it has tended to shift the focus of attention away from tangible forms of heritage – statues – to intangible heritage: the practice, rituals and representations, knowledge as well as the visual, material objects and spaces that collectively constitute cultural heritage.[9]

As the contributors to this volume attest, commemoration, the invention of tradition and political uses of the past have been much more central to British political culture than previously assumed. British politics, no less than communist, and post-communist regimes, has its mnemonic actors: 'political forces that are interested in a specific interpretation of the past' who 'treat history instrumentally in order to construct a vision of the past that they assume will generate the most effective legitimation for their efforts to gain and hold power'.[10] When individuals, groups and institutions from parliament to protesters go to the length of instituting discrete remembrance events, practices and rituals, it becomes clear just how important these things were, and British politics is no exception. The little scholarship that exists certainly suggests there is no shortage of material here: if some of the heroes are well known – Thomas Paine, the Tolpuddle Martyrs – and some of the historical episodes familiar – Magna Carta, the Glorious Revolution of 1688 – what function they were made to perform and how they have been imaginatively reconstructed and invoked remain unclear.[11] Focusing on social or collective memory, posthumous and heroic reputation, and on the contested and evolving creations of political traditions and canons can also shed new light on familiar historical figures and episodes. This book, which draws on a variety of perspectives and approaches from the history of political thought to cultural history, explores the evolving relationship between memory and politics from the 1790s to the present. It includes case studies of memorialization and 'statue-mania', iconography and material culture; paper pantheons and the invention of political 'canons'; anniversaries and on the wider invoking of 'dead generations'.

There is clearly a family resemblance when it comes to heritage, memory, the invention of tradition and the broader uses of the past, but these all constitute relatively discrete, if overlapping, endeavours. For example, the distinction drawn by the influential French historian of memory, Pierre Nora, between tradition and memory seems pertinent: 'Tradition is memory that has become historically aware of itself,' though like many such neat formulations this begs more questions than it, perhaps, answers.[12] While some of the chapters which follow range across all or several of these encounters with the past, some contributors focus more specifically on individual family members. The concept of memory rather than history has been chosen because the former seems a more appropriate portmanteau term that captures the variety, often more informal, and the presentist agenda of invoking the past than does the concept and practice of history. True, the relative status of history and memory, and the relationship between them, is a complex one and the boundaries can become blurred.[13] As Emily Robinson has shown, the wider mnemonic activities of contemporary British political parties can include professional historians, and some of those involved in party history groups, and commemorative projects have sometimes felt the need to consult professional historians or indeed train to become professional historians themselves. But in a sense these exceptions prove the rule: Robinson notes that 'great respect is accorded to professional historians' and that when objectivity is required, history groups and commemorative projects within parties feel the need to defer to academic history and its practitioners.[14] More perniciously, history has sometimes been viewed as a destroyer of memory, especially when written by 'colonial' victors and their post-colonial neophytes. As the Welsh historian Gwyn Alf Williams wrote of the Welsh people and their sense of the past in the late 1970s, '[o]ur history has been a history to induce schizophrenia and to enforce loss of memory ... We are a people with plenty of traditions but no historical memory'. The occasion for Williams's remarks was the overwhelming vote against Welsh devolution which he came to view as the product of the way in which much history in Wales had been told: 'We have no historical autonomy. We live in the interstices of other people's history'.[15]

These problematics and relationships – between history and memory, silencing and sanitizing – are addressed by several contributors. Marion Löffler looks at the sanitizing of the Welsh past in the nineteenth century. Colin Reid shows how canons of political thought are not just invented by scholars and philosophers in the present but are also the evolving product of accretions of memories as subsequent generations remember (and forget) thinkers, groups and episodes. In turn, the failure to recognize thinkers, groups and episodes as subjects of political thought by scholars in the present – because of the politics of memory and forgetting – shows how memory can shape the writing of history. But, broadly speaking, while memory – in both its individual, social and collective senses – is a more informal, group-specific and orally transmitted rendition of the past which presupposes a continuity of consciousness between past and present, history is a more formal, systematic and usually written record premised on a rupture between the past and present.[16] Seen from this perspective, any political group in the present invoking the past for whatever purpose is, arguably, constructing and perpetuating social or collective memory rather than engaging in history, if only because the past is being fundamentally subordinated to the needs of the present, which precludes the kind of critical engagement with the past that is the business of (professional) history.[17]

In the Western world, historians of modern France and the United States have led the way in illustrating the rich potential of approaching political culture from the perspectives of memory and the political uses of the past. For example, historians of the United States have long recognized that tracking the posthumous lives of 'founding fathers' can tell us a great deal about the goals, aspirations and identity of political movements.[18] Similarly, the influential work of several generations of French historians has demonstrated how cultures of remembrance are constructed and, above all, how they work in practice as 'realms of memory' and how they evolve. Inventing political traditions through commemoration or the broader political uses of the past was central to legitimating political goals, identities and strategies. But who invents these traditions, canons and collective memories? What form does pantheonism take, and how do the different forms work and with what consequences? Were these primarily top-down processes of political leaders invoking heroes or episodes in the past to legitimate their leadership? Was elevation to the pantheon immutable, or did the composition of it change: were figures demoted as well as promoted? Who was excluded from the pantheon, and why? As several of the chapters in this volume attest, forgetting and excluding can be just as revealing as remembering and including – an area in memory studies that is now receiving much attention.[19] Some of the remembrance practices and rituals were common to both elite and popular politics: portraiture, memorialization, dining and toasting. Those within the corridors of power, no less than those without, had their pantheons of heroes whether sculptured in marble and publicly displayed or printed on paper and folded away in political ephemera in the home. Other practices differed according to class, wealth and relative access to the public sphere. While elites had stone pantheons, the people had paper ones (a distinction explored in my own chapter on Chartist memory).

The structure of the volume is, broadly, chronological, though there is some inevitable overlap which is unavoidable when looking at memories, histories and legacies. Chapters 1–4 illustrate from different vantage points the seismic impact and legacy of the 1790s. Historians have long known that the French Revolution exerted a profound impact on British politics and society, but shifting the perspective to memory and the invention of political tradition reveals just how much the 1790s continued to cast a long shadow well into the nineteenth century and beyond. Chapters 5–8 consider various aspects of Victorian and Edwardian commemoration, while Chapters 9–11 focus mainly on the twentieth century, with the final chapter taking the narrative up to the present. While most of the chapters focus on British domestic politics, several chapters adopt either a 'four nations' approach and/or focus on Irish, Scottish and Welsh as well as English perspectives (Chapters 2, 3 and 5) or range even further by adopting lenses, by turns, Anglo-American (Chapter 10), European comparative (Chapter 8) or ex-British world (Chapter 11). The politicization of the past and its invocation can be a potent means of carving out political positions in the present in ways that underscore the connections, shared identity as well as the divisions and differences between the constituent nations of the UK, the commonwealth and even the English-speaking world. For example, the medieval Scots rebel William Wallace was more likely to be invoked in the nineteenth century to underline a distinctive Scottish contribution to an integrative British political tradition rather than to articulate a separatist Scottish nationalism.[20] By contrast, and much more recently, Plaid Cymru have laid claim to groups such as the Chartists as part of a narrative which views these episodes as forerunners of the independence movement.[21]

The first chapter of the volume begins not, as might be expected, with an examination of the impact of the French Revolution but with memories of Britain's own revolution a hundred years before: the Glorious Revolution of 1688. As Rémy Duthille reminds us, the response to the French Revolution was, at least initially, refracted through memories of 1688. Historians have argued that the beginnings of modern British political culture can be traced to the revolutionary settlement which ejected the Catholic Stuarts and imported the Dutch Protestant William of Orange and in the process transformed Britain into a parliamentary monarchy, a touchstone that even continues into contemporary British politics.[22] But Duthille's point of departure is not the history of political thought but Hayden White's notion of a 'practical past': the ways in which an historic episode is invoked as a way of providing ethical guidance in the world of politics.[23] While previous accounts have discussed the ways in which groups from across the political spectrum have invoked memories of 1688 to sketch out their rival, and largely immutable, versions of the mythical English constitution,[24] Duthille goes beyond this by showing how the 1790s constituted a major caesura as memories gave way to histories of 1688. Duthille problematizes that distinction by arguing that the transition from memory to history was protracted and uneven. In the process, he demonstrates that invocations of 1688 were much more complex, contested and contingent than previous accounts have suggested. Ranging across the period 1789 to 1848, Duthille's chapter examines moments when rival political groups vied for control of the memory and history of 1688. There was no single or immutable 'constitutional idiom' that was drawn on selectively by Tories, Whigs and Radicals: invocations of 1688 could also be used to contest the very meanings of tory, whig and radical. Beyond these party-political usages, Duthille detects a broader transformation of these invocations, from what had been rather rowdy, crowd-based memories in the eighteenth century, to more sedate and respectable histories by the early nineteenth century, though that shift was neither smooth nor complete as the Orange rendition of 1688–9 in Ireland demonstrates only too clearly. By focusing on the contested and fractured histories of 1688 – different groups even selected different days and types of events to commemorate 1688 – Duthille concludes that the Whig interpretation of the Glorious Revolution did not attain anything like the historiographical and cultural dominance in the first half of the nineteenth century that previous historians have often supposed.

If memories and histories of 1688 could look very different in England and Ireland, Marion Löffler explores in her chapter some of the factors specific to Wales which were responsible for silencing memories of the 1790s. Taking Kenneth Johnston's notion of a 'lost generation' as her point of departure, Loeffler explores why Victorian Welsh commentators forcibly forgot the Welsh Jacobins.[25] Remarkably, groups from across the political spectrum were concerned to erase any evidence of Welsh sedition as a way to demonstrate loyalty to Queen and Empire. As Loeffler shows, political silencing can assume various forms – some of which, paradoxically, can entail forms of remembering but which nevertheless serve to cleanse uncomfortable histories and memories. For example, humourizing radicals and presenting them as eccentrics were two notable ways of silencing their radical pasts. While this tendency was unsurprisingly at its strongest among conservatives, some radicals and reformers – notably Welsh Nonconformist Liberals – were also complicit in this silencing as it furnished them with a passport to respectability. Loeffler's chapter is also one of recovery: so successful were the Victorian Welsh in erasing their Jacobinism that some historians have followed suit and assumed that Wales was much more politically quiescent in the 1790s than was, in fact, the case. Part of the problem was and is that a good deal of Welsh radicalism hid beneath the protective shield of the Welsh language, which made it impenetrable to the English authorities and subsequently to those historians who do not read Welsh. As a reader of the Welsh language, Loeffler is able to penetrate this 'English' wall of silence and recover the lives of selected Welsh radicals and show how memory studies can shed new light not just on those who were remembering and forgetting but also on the period being remembered.

Colin Reid shifts the focus to the construction of a separatist tradition in Irish political thought from the 1790s to the 1920s and, in doing so, explores the blurred boundaries between history, memory and the invention of tradition. As Reid posits, the creation of a canon of Irish republicanism was a much more contested and evolving project than political usages at different stages since the 1790s have often suggested. Far too often, Irish republicanism has been reduced to demanding separation from Britain through violent means. Canons were made and unmade as subsequent generations of Irish politicians constructed traditions that legitimated their aims and methods. By focusing on the means through which this tradition was constructed – through newspapers, pamphlets and memoirs – rather than assuming that Irish republicans emerged ready-made, Reid demonstrates that there is much more depth to Irish political thought than historians of political thought have assumed, a depth and richness too often obscured by the dominance of the elastic concept of nationalism. Reid concludes that it is too simplistic to look for a single Irish republican tradition – even though many groups have made this assumption as a way of validating their own politics. Finally, Reid also reminds us that the invention of political tradition is also just as much about silencing and forgetting as it is about remembering.

My own chapter also takes as its starting point the issue of forgetting. This chapter explores the politics of remembrance through a case study of Chartism, the British mass movement for democratic and social rights in the 1830s and 1840s. It focuses on the 'paper pantheon' of radical greats constructed by the Chartists from the perspectives of Romanticism, the powerful cultural and literary effects of which were still being felt in the 1840s. The chapter highlights two linked aspects of romantic memory in Chartist heritage politics: first, the question, not of remembering, but forgetting and erasure; that is, which individuals and episodes in the radical tradition were either forgotten or consciously excluded by the Chartists. Second, particular attention is paid to recent scholarship in Romantic Studies which has explored the relationship between memory and reputation as a means of tracking the posthumous potential of John Thelwall, Thomas Paine and William Cobbett, three prominent radicals in the age of revolution. While the impact of Romanticism can be hardly denied and was part of the cultural inheritance of the Chartists, including the intense outpouring of feeling for heroes in the pantheon, it is important not to exaggerate its impact. Some Chartists rejected the unchecked appeals to the passions and introspection associated with Romanticism. Chartist aversion to this pull was a legacy, in part, of the enduring impact of radical Enlightenment and its associated affective politics. The final section explores some of the tensions between Romanticism and Enlightenment in Chartist heritage politics via a case study of the enduring legacy of the French revolutionary C. F. Volney and draws on recent work on the history of emotions to sketch out the affective politics of Chartist memory.

It was during the Reform Bill disturbances of the early 1830s that Volney made his reappearance in the world of British popular radicalism. As Gordon Pentland illustrates in his chapter, even before the Reform Act of 1832 was passed, a battle had begun to secure the memory of this momentous piece of legislation. The types of radicals – mainly future Chartists – who were invoking Volney were generally dissatisfied with the Reform Act as it left most workers without the vote. As Pentland shows, those elite Whig politicians who authored the Bill had a vested interest not only in enshrining their role but also in ways that underscored the finality of that settlement in ways that betrayed their distrust of radical politics and protest. Memorialization was central to this project, and as Pentland suggests, perhaps one of the reasons why the Reform Act of 1832 retains its status as 'Great' was because of the energies that they devoted to inscribing that greatness on to the civic landscape as well on canvass. And yet Whigs and their partisans were never the sole custodians of the memory of 1832; the political unions – the extra-parliamentary bodies who had whipped up popular support to put pressure on the governments for reform – also went to great lengths to memorialize their own contribution, sometimes in ways that were at odds with the whig project. One of the key reasons why it proved impossible to carve in stone a singular, consensual memorial to the Great Reform Act was because of the decentralized nature of the British state. Another reason was the persistence of a vibrant local political culture that enabled various groups and individuals from across the political and civic spectrum to shape the memory of 1832 as part of their respective attempts to mark the limits or to expand the boundaries of the political nation. When approached from this panoramic perspective, Pentland's chapter provides a virtual index of the many forms that political memory-making assumed: from the (semi-)permanent in the form of portraiture, monuments, naming practices, to the ephemeral of sights – illuminations, processions – and sounds – bell ringing, toasts, dinners and tea parties.

Kathryn Rix's chapter also begins with the Reform Act of 1832 and shifts the focus to a group of politicians who were the recipients of statues, a group we might think had little posthumous potential: MPs who were elected to the House of Commons between the Reform Acts of 1832 and 1867–8. While her sample (843 MPs from the North and Midlands) does include some of the familiar names who achieved celebrity status in this period – Peel, Gladstone, Cobden – many were backbench MPs who were also civic politicians, philanthropists and employer-paternalists, roles which in life and posthumously enabled some to transcend party divisions. Taking the midlands and the north as case studies (in part as a corrective to a historiography that has focused largely on London memorials), Rix locates this 'statuemania' in the context of the broader popular and cultural interest in Victorian politicians. As Henry Miller and Simon Morgan have recently shown, Victorian politicians could approximate to modern conceptions of celebrity (though in fairness that was usually reserved for national leaders, but not always).[26] Focusing on which MPs were memorialized enables Rix to explore a broader set of questions: the relationship between MPs and their constituents, the civic function of their statues, and how the meaning of statues evolved as subsequent generations invested them with new meaning. Of particular interest are the debates which often took place over how best to commemorate an MP. As Rix shows, there was often scepticism about the value of memorialization in statue form, with some arguing that there were more worthwhile ways of commemorating politicians, an important reminder that 'statuemania' was neither uniformly popular nor uncontested. In ranging over a broader period – from the 1830s to the present – and a much larger database of MPs who received statues – Rix also addresses the chronology of memorialization; that is, why there were periods when a lot more (or, conversely, a lot less) statues were erected.

The next chapter by Richard Gaunt explores the commemoration of a Victorian prime minister whose death, according to Rix, led to an upsurge in the memorialization of Victorian politicians: Sir Robert Peel. The outpouring of public grief following the death of Peel as the result of a riding accident in July 1850, and the myriad commemorative formats to which this gave rise, has formed a common reference point in recent considerations of the statesman's posthumous legacy. Yet Peel's death was first and foremost a family tragedy. Using a hitherto neglected group of family papers, comprising personal responses to Peel's death, this chapter considers the extent to which the Peel family initiated, shaped and encouraged the process of posthumous valorization of Peel which took place in the aftermath of the tragedy. While historians have traced the individual lineaments by which communities – especially across the industrial towns of the northern England – subscribed towards statues or named commemorative amenities (such as parks, towers and statues), the extent to which this ran side by side with – or counter to – more private, family-focused memorialization has not previously been considered. Given that Peel's death is seen as having a particularly transformative effect upon the way in which public figures were commemorated and remembered in Victorian England, this absence of the personal, family voice appears striking. By exploring the immediate consequences of Peel's death in its family setting, the chapter helps to restore a sense of context to the wider process of civic and community-based public commemoration to which it gave rise.

While Peel and even a Victorian backbench MP might have great posthumous potential, this was not the case with popular radical leaders. Antony Taylor's chapter asks why there have been so few memorials to British radicals, especially those from working-class backgrounds. He begins by comparing British memorialization with comparable European and North American projects. While the late nineteenth century witnessed a significant increase in memorialization on the continent – much of it devoted to legitimating nation-building, royal restorations, regime changes – Britain was comparatively untouched by a similar upsurge. In one sense, this was hardly surprising given the relative political stability of British politics, but Taylor detects important clues in this comparison as to why there would be few memorials raised to commemorate the British radical plebeian past: the lack of a tradition of commemorating moments of change, of freedoms gained or dangers to the nation averted, at least to the degree that was the case in parts of Europe. When workers were remembered it tended to be in their places of work or as part of their landscapes rather than as political actors. Another factor was a tradition of commemorating gentleman radicals rather than working-class leaders, as well as an aversion to cultures of remembrance by some of those on the political left – because of a puritan distrust of appealing to the senses along with irrational or negative feelings such as religious intolerance, dogmatism and militarism which they associated with elite forms of commemoration. There was also little space for plebeian leaders in the civic landscape of Victorian and Edwardian cities, as this challenged the bourgeois supremacy of civic leaders who were inventing their own traditions which validated their class, and the few working-class radicals who were co-opted into this consensus were divested of their radical lineages. Sometimes the reasons were much more prosaic: lack of access to the public sphere and lack of funds.

One group of plebeian radicals, however, has generated more remembrance activity than any other: the Tolpuddle Martyrs. As Marcus Morris shows in his chapter, the Dorchester labourers, as these agricultural labourers were originally termed, who were transported in 1834 for their trade unionism, have been accorded a prominent place in the trade union, labour and socialist movements. Much of this crystallized around the bicentenary in 1934 and was meant to serve as a rallying cry for a labour movement that was, by the mid-1930s, on the defensive. For the Labour party in particular, as a new political party, inventing a political tradition was part of its attempt to demonstrate that it had a lineage, and thus a venerable respectability, as well as serving to unite what was an increasingly disparate left. As Morris shows, memory and history could also highlight difference and division as well as unity, and, once again, absence and silencing could be just as revealing. While the martyrs have been accorded the status of a foundational myth from the 1930s to the present, in the years before the First World War, the story of the Dorchester labourers, while known, was not central to the history and memory of the political left. This was because they were not seen as relevant to a more modern and scientific socialist movement. This leads Morris to conclude that the invention of political tradition and pantheonization were not linear processes and that the relationship between the Labour party and the use of history has been complicated and even, at times, antagonistic.

The final pair of chapters moves beyond Britain and explores the uses of the British past in Anglo-American relations in the mid-twentieth century and Hong Kong protest since 1997. Sam Edwards in his chapter focuses on the commemoration of Magna Carta which was central to cultivating Anglo-American relations following the First World War, prompted by the 700th anniversary in 1915. From the establishment of a transatlantic 'Magna Charta Day Association', to the purposeful 'use' of the document during the Second World War, to the loan to the United States of an original copy during the United States Bicentennial (in 1976), Magna Carta found a new political life in the twentieth century. This was an era which witnessed the development of an increasingly close Anglo-American bond. Edwards argues that

Magna Carta had a unique resonance and utility, bound up as it was with notions of race, liberty, and justifications for resisting arbitrary rule. He detects a discernible shift in the ways in which Magna Carta was invoked. During the period from 1915 to 1940, it was mainly drawn on to assert racial notions of shared Anglo-Saxon ties, but after 1940 the emphasis shifted to a less exclusionary focus on the 'values of the English-speaking peoples' which assumed a new significance during the Cold War.

Historians have long known that colonial memories and the broader invoking of British history have played important parts in shaping new post-colonial regimes and cultures, but much of the focus has been on the former white dominions, though this imbalance is now being redressed. The chapter by Mark Hampton and Florence Mok examines the ways in which protest movements in the post-1997 Hong Kong Special Administrative Region have deployed memories of British rule. Against perceptions of growing political influence by Beijing, stagnating social mobility and increasing dependence on mainland Chinese migration and tourism, the last two decades of colonial rule have often been portrayed nostalgically, particularly among the young generation and anti-China activists – many of whom were too young to have first-hand memories of the colonial era. As Hampton and Mok suggest, it is, perhaps, no coincidence that political uses of memory have taken off as actual memories of colonial rule have faded. Thus, focusing on the role of memory can tell us much about the timing of protest and the ways in which that protest has been framed. These portrayals have often identified the rule of law as a British legacy and, notwithstanding the very limited extent of democratic development under British rule, have argued that the Sino-British Joint Declaration promises continued progress towards full democracy. Moreover, this discourse has often portrayed the 1980s and early 1990s as halcyon days of economic opportunity and a 'Hong Kong way of life' that has been undermined since 1997. Finally, memories of British rule have occasionally been invoked in order to articulate Britain's continued responsibility for its former colonial subjects.

While it would be fanciful to suggest that the invention of tradition, commemoration and the political uses of the past collectively constitute a new master-narrative of modern British political history, this cluster has and continues to operate in ways akin to the constitutional idiom, traced by historians influenced by the linguistic turn in the 1980s and 1990s.[27] Indeed, in the absence of a written constitution this cluster has, in some respects, served as a surrogate and thus assumed a greater significance. Taken together, what the following chapters show is just how embedded memory, tradition and history were and are in British political culture. This cluster was central to how political actors, leaders and members, imagined themselves, legitimated their goals and strategies. Again, like the constitutional idiom, precisely because of the contested, contingent, evolving and poly-vocal nature of commemoration, the invention of tradition, and the invoking of the past, it has been impossible to fix and secure a definitive narrative of the past. It is this ambiguity which has made memory, tradition and history such potent symbolic resources, not just in England or even Britain, but in the English-speaking world and beyond. The irony is that political invocations of the past invariably try to fix and secure definitive narratives of the past. Even the seemingly less overtly political acts of memorialization can function in these ways. As Pierre Nora has observed, there is a sense in which monuments inhibit memory because of the way the material form can supplant a community's memory work. In other words, once inscribed into the landscape, there is less need to actively (re)produce commemorative practices. And from a very different perspective, recent research has shown that the internet and social media can also lead to the 'offloading' of memory in contemporary societies (though, as the chapter by Hampton and Mok shows, social media can also operate in very different ways as a mnemonic practice).[28] To return to where this chapter began: the toppling of Colston's statue shows that memorials – even seemingly durable ones made out of stone and brass – are neither immovable nor inhibiting of memory work.

Notes

1   'Countering Colston – Campaign to Decolonise Bristol', https://counteringcolston.wordpress.com/ (accessed 9 September 2022).
2   Steven Fielding, 'The Defacing of Churchill's Statue', *OUPblog*, 5 September 2020, https://blog.oup.com/2020/09/the-defacing-of-churchills-statue/ (accessed 10 September 2022); Steve Poole, '"The Instinct for Hero Worship Works Blindly": English Radical Democrats and the Problem of Memorialization', *Patterns of Prejudice*, 54 (2020), 504.
3   Alan Rice, *Creating Memorials, Building Identities: The Politics of Memory in the Black Atlantic* (Liverpool: Liverpool University Press, 2010), 11, 13–16.
4   Madge Dresser, 'Obliteration, Contextualisation or "Guerrilla Memorialisation"? Edward Colston's Statue Reconsidered', *Open Democracy: Beyond Trafficking and Slavery*, 29 August 2016, https://www.opendemocracy.net/en/beyond-trafficking-and-slavery/obliteration-contextualisation-or-guerrilla-memorialisation-edward-colst/ (accessed 9 September 2022).
5   See, for example, Maurice Agulhon, *Marianne into Battle: Republican Imagery and Symbolism in France, 1780–1880* (Cambridge: Cambridge University Press, 1981); Sarah J. Purcell, *Sealed with Blood: War, Sacrifice, and Memory in Revolutionary America* (Philadelphia: University of Pennsylvania Press, 2002); Eveline G. Bouwers, *Public Pantheons in Revolutionary Europe: Comparing Cultures of Remembrance, c.1790–1840* (Basingstoke: Palgrave, 2012); *Twenty Years after Communism: The Politics of Memory and Commemoration*, ed. Michael Bernhard and Jan Kubik (Oxford: Oxford University Press, 2014); Robert Gerwarth and Lucy Riall, 'Fathers of the Nation? Bismarck, Garibaldi and the Cult of Memory in Germany and Italy', *European History Quarterly*, 39 (2009), 388–413; Robert Gerwarth, *The Bismarck Myth: Weimar Germany and the Legacy of the Iron Chancellor* (Oxford: Clarendon Press, 2005).
6   *The Invention of Tradition*, ed. Eric Hobsbawm and Terrance Ranger (Cambridge: Cambridge University Press, 1983); *Commemorations: The Politics of National Identity*, ed. John R. Gillis (Princeton: Princeton University Press, 1994); James Young, *The Texture of Memory: Holocaust Memorials and Meaning* (New Haven: Yale University Press, 1993); Avner Ben-Amos, *Funerals, Politics, and Memory in Modern France, 1789–1996* (Oxford: Oxford University Press, 2000); *Memory and Memorials: The Commemorative Century*, ed. William Kidd and Brian Murdoch (Aldershot: Ashgate, 2004); Jay Winter, *Sites of Memory, Sites of Mourning: The Great War in European Cultural History* (Cambridge: Cambridge University Press,

1995); Peter Mitchell, *Imperial Nostalgia: How the British Conquered Themselves* (Manchester: Manchester University Press, 2021); Sathnam Sanghera, *Empireland: How Imperialism Has Shaped Modern Britain* (London: Penguin, 2021).
7   Raphael Samuel, *Theatres of Memory, Volume 1: Past and Present in Contemporary Culture* (London: Verso, 1994), 17.
8   Iain Robertson, 'Heritage from Below: Class, Social Protest and Resistance', in *Ashgate Research Companion to Heritage and Identity* (Aldershot: Ashgate, 2003), 305–23; Gregory Ashworth and John Tunbridge, *Dissonant Heritage: The Management of the Past as a Resource in Conflict* (Oxford: Wiley, 1996); Steve Poole, 'The Politics of Protest Heritage, 1790–1850', in *Remembering Protest in Britain since 1500: Memory, Materiality and the Landscape*, ed. Carl J. Griffin and Briony McDonagh (Basingstoke: Palgrave, 2018), 187–213; Matthew Roberts, *Chartism, Commemoration and the Cult of the Radical Hero* (Abingdon: Routledge, 2020).
9   For a critical introduction to intangible heritage, see *Intangible Heritage*, ed. Laurajane Smith and Natsuko Akagawa (London: Routledge, 2009), introduction. On critical heritage studies, see Rodney Harrison, *Heritage: Critical Approaches* (Abingdon: Routledge, 2013).
10 Michael Bernhard and Jan Kubik, 'Introduction', in *Twenty Years after Communism*, 4.
11 Jon Lawrence, 'Labour – the Myths It Has Lived by', in *Labour's First Century*, ed. Duncan Tanner et al. (Cambridge: Cambridge University Press, 2000), 341–66; Emily Robinson, *History, Heritage and Tradition in Contemporary British Politics: Past Politics and Present Histories* (Manchester: Manchester University Press, 2012); Paul A. Readman, 'Commemorating the Past in Edwardian Hampshire: King Alfred, Pageantry and Empire', in *Southampton: Gateway to Empire*, ed. Miles Taylor (London: I. B. Tauris, 2007), 95–114; Richard Toye, 'The Churchill Syndrome: Reputational Entrepreneurship and the Rhetoric of Foreign Policy since 1945', *British Journal of Politics and International Relations*, 10, no. 3 (2008), 364–78; Philip Williamson, 'Baldwin's Reputation: Politics and History, 1937–1967', *Historical Journal*, 47, no. 1 (2004), 127–68.
12 Pierre Nora, 'Introduction to Realms of Memory Volume II', in *Realms of Memory: The Construction of the French Past Volume II: Traditions*, ed. Pierre Nora (New York: Columbia University Press, 1997), ix.
13 The best introduction is Geoffrey Cubitt, *History and Memory* (Manchester: Manchester University Press, 2007).
14 Robinson, *History, Heritage and Tradition*, 7.
15 Gwyn A. Williams, *The Welsh in Their History* (London: Croom Helm, 1982), 194.
16 This distinction owes a great deal to the French Durkheimian sociologist Maurice Halbwachs. For a summary, see Cubitt, *History and Memory*, 43–4.
17 The distinction between social and collective memory that some scholars have drawn also seems apposite here: while the former can be more diffuse, bottom-up, variegated in its construction and deployment, collective memory 'is the species of ideological fiction … which presents particular social entities as the possessors of a stable mnemonic capacity that is collectively exercised, and that presents particular views or representations of a supposedly collective past as the natural expressions of such a collective mnemonic capacity'. Cubitt, *History and Memory*, 18.
18 Gordon S. Wood, *The Americanization of Benjamin Franklin* (New York: Penguin, 2004); Harvey J. Kaye, *Thomas Paine and the Promise of America* (New York: Hill and Wang, 2005).

19 E.g. Guy Beiner, *Forgetful Remembrance: Social Forgetting and Vernacular Historiography of a Rebellion in Ulster* (Oxford: Oxford University Press, 2018); Carl J. Griffin, 'Memory and the Work of Forgetting: Telling Protest in the English Countryside', in *Remembering Protest*, 215–36.
20 Mark Nixon, Gordon Pentland and Matthew Roberts, 'The Material Culture of Scottish Reform Politics, c.1820–c.1884', *Journal of Scottish Historical Studies*, 32, no. 1 (2012), 37.
21 E.g. Liz Saville Roberts, 'Wales Has a Proud History of Protesting from Non-conformism to Chartism', *Plaid Cymru* Twitter account, 16 March 2021, https://twitter.com/Plaid_Cymru/status/1371792822106488834 (accessed 2 November 2022).
22 Robinson, *History, Heritage and Tradition*, 34–6.
23 Hayden White, 'The Practical Past', in *The Practical Past* (Evanston: Northwestern University Press, 2014).
24 James Vernon, *Politics and the People: A Study in English Political Culture, c.1815–1867* (Cambridge: Cambridge University Press, 1993), ch. 8.
25 Kenneth R. Johnston, *Unusual Suspects: Pitt's Reign of Alarm and the Lost Generation of the 1790s* (Oxford: Oxford University Press, 2013).
26 Henry Miller, *Politics Personified* (Manchester: Manchester University Press, 2015); Simon James Morgan, *Celebrities, Heroes and Champions: Popular Politicians in the Age of Reform, 1810–67* (Manchester: Manchester University Press, 2021).
27 *Re-reading the Constitution: New Narratives in the Political History of England's Long Nineteenth Century*, ed. James Vernon (Cambridge: Cambridge University Press, 1996).
28 *Memory Online: Remembering in the Age of the Internet and Social Media*, ed. Qi Wang, special issue of *Memory* 30 (2022).

2

A practical English past: Commemorating the Glorious Revolution in England from Tom Paine to T. B. Macaulay (1792–1848)

Rémy Duthille

Discussing the eighteenth century, Frank O'Gorman noted that '[t]he legacy of the Glorious Revolution may be taken to be the sacred core of British identity and British values'.[1] The Revolution was a topic of perpetual debate, both in political theory and in popular politics, as H. T. Dickinson and Kathleen Wilson have shown. Tories and radicals founded their claims on alternative interpretations of 1688 to challenge the dominant Whig order, which was itself buttressed by 'revolution principles'.[2] Whigs retained from the post-1689-9 'Revolution Settlement' the principle of parliamentary sovereignty; Tories saw Anglican hegemony as the main result of the revolution, and radicals, like Catherine Macaulay in her *History of England from the Accession of James I to That of the Brunswick Line* (1763–81), saw the Revolution as a missed opportunity for liberty, replacing royal despotism with ministerial corruption. While Anglicans usually celebrated the Revolution on 5 November, Dissenters tended to prefer the fourth: sermons preached on those days often proved controversial. Matters came to a head on 4 November 1789 when, on the day appointed for the celebration of the Glorious Revolution, the Dissenting clergyman Richard Price preached a sermon presenting the events in France as a Gallic version of Britain's revolution. In his view, the forced abdication of James II justified the people's religious liberty, their right to resist arbitrary power and 'right to chuse our own governors; to cashier them for misconduct; and to frame a government for ourselves'.[3] Price's sermon, boldly defending the right to popular resistance, nay revolution, set off the controversy around the French Revolution, Edmund Burke presenting the conservative case that the Glorious Revolution had been 'a small and temporary deviation' of the line of succession, confirming rather than undermining the rule of hereditary succession.[4] Price's notion of 1789 as a tardy version of 1688 quickly collapsed as the French Revolution took a more violent turn, and Thomas Paine's iconoclastic jibe at the 'Bill of Wrongs and Insult' in the second part of *Rights of Man* (1792)[5] seemed to seal an abandonment of 1688 by a new brand of republican radicals. Paine attacked the revolution of 1688 as an inglorious business, a palace revolution ushering in a century of political and financial corruption, following a long line of 'Patriot' and radical attack, but he also rejected the revolution and its constitutional outcome, the Bill of Rights, on the basis of abstract natural right, dismissing the binding value of *any* precedent.

Steve Pincus, rehearsing interpretations of the Glorious Revolution since the event, did not discuss historiography between Paine and T. B. Macaulay's multi-volume *History of England*, published from 1848, which established the triumph of Whig history. 'Thomas Paine, Pincus wrote, set the tone of future radical interpretations of 1688.'[6] Not all radicals, however, shared Paine's attitude. Many of them continued to stake claims on the Glorious Revolution. They did not leave the road free for a Whig, progressive but cautiously moderate, interpretation to dominate. On the contrary, this chapter contends that the meaning of the Glorious Revolution was still relevant, and disputed, in the first half of the nineteenth century. The point was not only the interpretations offered of the events of 1688–9 but even more the sociopolitical uses to which they were put.

The Glorious Revolution partook of the 'practical past', a category that Hayden White borrowed from Michael Oakeshott to denote the fantasies, dreams and experiences that provide guidance 'for information, ideas, models, formulas, and strategies for solving all the practical problems' of life.[7] In other words, the Glorious Revolution was not just a historiographical topic but also an example providing ethical guidance in the world of politics. This chapter explores the ideological uses which the Glorious Revolution was put to, as part of a 'practical past'.[8] But this begs a second question: whether it was still part of shared, communal memory or was becoming an object of history.[9]

The distinction drawn by the French sociologist Maurice Halbwachs between history and memory is useful here. 'Collective memory, Halbwachs argued, is a more informal, group-specific and orally transmitted rendition of the collective past which presupposes a continuity of consciousness between past and present, while history is a more formal, systematic and usually written record premised on a rupture between the past and the present.'[10] For Halbwachs, history starts where tradition dies out and writing becomes necessary because the group that bore the collective memory is no longer present.[11] The Glorious Revolution belonged to the realm of memory during the eighteenth century, fuelling many politico-theological disputes and encoding partisan and denominational identities. Did it pass into history during the first half of the nineteenth century, or did it remain a part of a living, experientially relevant memory? Of course, the Glorious Revolution and the Jacobite saga were a major source of inspiration for the Romantics. In the wake of Walter Scott, the British seventeenth century offered immense imaginative resources to historians, novelists and artists, well into the Victorian age.[12] Celebrations of seventeenth-century events moved away from sermons and dinners into other symbolic fields: literature, historiography, the arts. Some aspects of the Glorious Revolution and its aftermath were thus brought back to life in nostalgic form. This chapter does not touch on this well-researched area, concentrating rather on politics, especially the extra-parliamentary sphere of print, pamphleteering and sociability.

This chapter starts by sketching changes in the English system of theologico-political celebrations, showing that the French Revolution disrupted established patterns and ushered in a new, more unstable celebratory pattern not centred on the cult of 1688. The next two sections review Tory and Whig interpretations of the

Glorious Revolution, within this celebratory pattern and in wider culture. The last two sections discuss radical uses of the Glorious Revolution, and the 'trial by jury' dinners organized on the anniversary date of the revolution from 1794, which show that the memory of the event was displaced in the course of the early nineteenth century.

From Glorious Revolution to French Revolution: A new celebratory regime

The French Revolution provoked the fragmentation of the old Hanoverian celebratory calendar, which hinged on 13 January, appointed for the commemoration of Charles I's execution, and 5 November, celebrating the Glorious Revolution (specifically William of Orange's landing at Torbay). The Dissenters usually chose the date of 4 November to differentiate themselves from Anglicans. The French Revolution disrupted this calendar, and Richard Price's 4 November 1789 celebration of France in 1789 rather than England in 1688 was one of the last occasions 4 November proved controversial.

The new calendar that replaced the earlier Hanoverian cycle was characterized by its fragmentation. There was no single celebration, no day that brought everybody together. While Whigs and Tories stood apart and celebrated the birthdays of Fox on 24 January, and William Pitt the Younger on 28 May, respectively, even the camp of reform was split into constituencies celebrating various occasions, like Paine's birthday or the anniversary of Burdett's Middlesex election. Many of those dinners, whether Whig, Tory or radical, invoked the Glorious Revolution in ways sometimes unknown before 1789. However, in some areas and in some sociopolitical milieus, older patterns subsisted long into the nineteenth century: around the time of Peterloo in 1819, many clubs and communities in and around Manchester celebrated Royal Oak Day on 29 May (the anniversary of Charles II's accession at the Restoration).[13]

The traditional festival of 5 November stopped to be a significant focus of attention. By the end of the century, a radical interpretation had emerged among Rational Dissenters like Price and Priestley. Price's 1789 sermon 'on the love of our country' and Burke's *Reflections on the Revolution in France* centred the debate on the difference or similarity between 1688 and 1789, but Paine's *Rights of Man* promptly pushed the controversy forward, questioning the monarchy from a republican standpoint in 1791. Price had preached to the Revolution Society, a club that had been instituted to celebrate the Glorious Revolution. By 1791, that club celebrated the French Revolution instead; the last recorded meeting, in 1793, was Francophile in tone.[14] The Revolution Society apparently ceased its activities because its moderate members shrank away from it while the bolder ones flocked to the Society for Constitutional Information. The turning point was 1792, the year of Paine's second part of *Rights of Man* and of France's transformation into a republic. On 5 November of that year, as Britain was in the throes of loyalist, anti-Jacobin fear, William Winterbotham preached a sermon praising the French Revolution, for which he was sentenced to two years' imprisonment and a hefty fine.[15] Winterbotham had argued along Prician lines that the revolution gave the British people extensive rights and he criticized the Revolution Settlement.[16] While Price had escaped prosecution, Winterbotham was severely punished in the stringent context of 1792. This was the last of the long series of controversial 5 November sermons. The Winterbotham case showed that some radicals had not gone further than Price and suggested that Paine's demolition had made celebrations of 5 November almost irrelevant, Winterbotham being an isolated example. However, if this spelt the end of radical 5 November celebrations, the radicals still had their uses for the Glorious Revolution, as will be shown below.

The fifth of November, then, ceased to be a moment of celebration of the Glorious Revolution for radicals. The significance of that date and the political uses of the revolution must be analysed in conservative and Whig circles.

Conservative appropriations: From Jacobitism to the Williamite cult

The conservative appropriation of the Glorious Revolution is ironic, given that the Tories of 1689 found it difficult to accept the change of king, William's accession breaking up the rule of indefeasible succession. Their own principles of passive obedience sat uneasily with accommodation with the Williamite, and still worse, the Hanoverian regime. Yet, from the time of the French Revolution, the Tories grounded arguments for obedience and stability on the Glorious Revolution. That historical precedent was central to the loyalist movement which started in May 1792 and came to dominate public debate and stifle expressions of dissent. Loyalist pamphlets addressed to the masses taught reverence for the king and constitution founded on the 1689 settlement. This was true of England, Wales and Scotland: the Jacobite legacy there did not prevent loyalists from justifying their defence of the established order on reverence of the Bill of Rights, or its Scottish equivalent, the Claim of Right. A typical Scottish pamphlet, for instance, that was circulated around Dundee, claimed that the revolution of 1688 brought about 'a fair balance' that no one disputed the constitution since because it was settled.[17] The pamphlet was meant to dissuade farmers and artisans from joining the Scottish Friends of the People who were planning a reformist convention. The argument typically aligned with English loyalism and appealed to 'the British constitution'.

There were a few royalists who attacked the Glorious Revolution – not so much the proceedings, which were enshrined in statute book and were respectable, but the notion of 'Revolution principles' and celebrations of 1688. It was John Reeves who, in 1795, addressed the boldest challenge to the mainstream Whig culture of the times. Reeves iconoclastically wrote that 'most of the errors and misconceptions relative to the nature of our Government, have taken their rise from those two great events, *The Reformation* and what is called *The Revolution*'.[18] Reeves, however, praised the moderation of the English Reformation and the Glorious Revolution. What he found fault with was their admirers: 'Revolution principles', he wrote, was a meaningless phrase, and those who enthused for them at 'tavern meetings' were not excited by the events of 1688 but by 'the idea of a *Revolution* [...] a *Revolution in the abstract*',[19] like the horrid one raging in France of course. The Revolution Clubs should instead celebrate the King and the Hanoverian Succession. But Reeves's royalism was extreme, even by the standards of 1790s loyalism, and Richard Brinsley Sheridan attacked him in the Commons, reproaching him, inter alia, for maintaining in his pamphlet 'That the revolution in 1688 was a fraud and a farce; and that all the people got by it was a Protestant king.'[20] Reeves was prosecuted for libel but acquitted.

Not only did conservatives avoid such direct onslaughts on the Glorious Revolution, they appropriated parts of Whig history. J. C. D. Clark and James J. Sack have shown that the early nineteenth-century Tory party was refashioned partly by a rejection of some historical associations of Toryism because of the prestige of the Whig vision of the Glorious Revolution and the Protestant settlement it created: 'somehow the term "Tory" had to be grafted onto a vision of the past which encompassed a generally non-Tory view of certain events of the seventeenth and eighteenth centuries'.[21] In 1791, Edmund Burke, before he was elevated to the Tory pantheon, presented himself as an 'old Whig' in the cast of Lord Somers, as opposed to the revolutionary, Frenchified Foxite 'new Whigs'.[22] In the next generation, the notion was aired that present-day Tories had nothing to do with early-eighteenth-century Tories and were more like Williamite or Walpolean Whigs, who accepted the 1688 Revolution. References to 'Revolution Principles' fudged party labels. In 1824, an orator praised the Tory MP for the City of London Sir William Curtis at a dinner given in his honour: 'The friends of Sir W. Curtis were friends of the constitution. Their adversaries called them Tories; he denied that they were so. None of them advocated the divine right of kings, or doctrines of that nature. He said that they were the Whigs of 1688.'[23] The Tories rallying to the 'constitution as established at the Revolution' did not help to clarify party labels in an age in which they were in flux.

'Tories' (conservative, Pittite Whigs) laid claim to the Glorious Revolution as their banquet speeches and symbolism made clear. Though there was no standing toast to the Glorious Revolution, the Pitt dinners did appropriate some Whig symbolism and pay homage to the event in speeches or in songs. For instance, at the 1815 Pitt Dinner at the London Tavern, a glee included 1688 in the narrative of the unfolding of the ancient constitution:

> Our Henrys and our Edwards too
> > Fram'd once a constitution
> Which Orange William did renew
> > By the glorious Revolution.[24]

The Whig notion of an ancient constitution was balanced by an emphasis on kings rather than the people's agency. That same year, the Pitt Club of Nottingham raised their glasses to '[t]he House of Brunswick, and may they never forget the principles which placed their family on the Throne of these kingdoms',[25] a toast that is very close to some drunk at Whig clubs.

Pursuing J. J. Sack's line of thought, Katrina Navickas noted that 'the ideology of Orangeism invoked the established repertoire of Whig ideals'. The birthday of King William III on 4 November was publicly commemorated by Orange societies, for instance in Bolton parish church and Assembly Rooms in 1808. This reinforces the argument of J. J. Sack and Kathleen Wilson that Pittite Toryism appropriated the symbols of the Glorious Revolution in order to legitimize itself and drag its reputation away from its disgraced Jacobite past.[26] The Pittite Tories celebrated William III and the Battle of the Boyne, symbols that the Whigs never took to, William being an unpopular king and Whiggism being an aristocratic, rather than a royalist, party.

Among conservative circles, the anti-Protestant legislation enshrined in the Revolution Settlement buttressed a strong anti-Catholicism, throughout the 1820s, as Britain was agitated by the issue of the repeal of the Penal Laws.[27] In Ireland, Williamite themes inspired by the War of the Two Kings (1689–92), with episodes like the siege of Derry and especially the Battle of the Boyne, underpinned the identity and legitimacy of the Protestant loyalists.[28] Orange festivals and the Orange toast at official dinners, for instance in the city of Dublin and in Ulster, were obnoxious to Catholics.[29] In England and Scotland too, Orange Lodges and Brunswick Clubs appealed to working-class men, disseminating anti-Catholicism founded on the cult of William III and fidelity to the Protestant constitution as settled in 1689. The 12 July marches celebrating the victory of the Boyne in Ulster are now famous as occasions for violence and contention, but during the campaigns for Catholic emancipation, there were other marches, in Ireland and England, while 'indoor celebrations, respectable and convivial and involving roast beef dinners, poetry, song and memorials' took place 'in what were closed, private functions'.[30] The Glorious Revolution was invoked in parliament to oppose any measure of Catholic emancipation. Press organs in England reported on Orange Lodges in Ireland and argued for the finality of the constitutional settlement. For the *Antijacobin Review; True Churchman's Magazine; and Protestant Advocate*, the revolution was 'conclusive and final, from a knowledge of the permanent and unchangeable nature of the catholic system, religious and political', which was incompatible with the safety of Protestants.[31]

In a sense, the most fervent, and literal, adherents of the settlement of 1689 were those opponents of Catholic Emancipation. Here was a conservative, not to say reactionary, practical use of the revolution. It is wrong to ascribe it totally to the Tory/conservative party: though the majority of Tories in Parliament opposed emancipation, the issue transcended party boundaries and split the Tory party itself, the pro-emancipation Canning being accused of betraying Pitt's heritage.[32] Perhaps more prevalent in England, however, than this conservative exploitation of the Glorious Revolution, was the progressive Whig version, which however never became hegemonic in the period considered.

The Whig cult of the revolution: Sociability and the cultural sphere

Patrician Whigs pinned their legitimacy on the Glorious Revolution. They insisted that the British constitution was 'established on the consent and affection of the People', as the Declaration of the London Whig Club put it in 1795 in the middle of the French Revolution. The events of 1688 were glorious because they established the rights of the people, guaranteed by the benevolent Whig oligarchy.[33]

The Whig focused their attacks on George III, who excluded them from power and presented themselves as the guardians of popular rights and Revolution principles.

Whig discourse established a critical link between the corrupt present and the Glorious Revolution through constant comparison between Tory dominance and James II's tyranny through the theme of 'influence'. This was helped by the presence of the scions of the great Whig families that had engineered William of Orange's invasion in 1688 or had fallen as martyrs of Stuart absolutism. This was the case especially of the Russells, heirs of several martyrs of liberty (especially William Russell, who was executed after the Rye House plot in 1683 and had been ever since worshipped by Whigs and Commonwealthmen). The Russells, in L. G. Mitchell's words, 'laboured under the obligations imposed by history'.[34] The great families that had called William to the throne and supported him were still prominent and embodied the continuity and long-standing struggle for freedom that characterize the Whig interpretation of history.

The Fox anniversary dinners, in London and in the provinces, enabled the performance of rituals of remembrance through toasting, singing and speechifying.[35] The constitutional and partisan struggles of the seventeenth century, and especially of the time of the Glorious Revolution, were the prism through which the Whigs understood their own present situation. To give just an example, at an early Fox birthday dinner in 1796, Joseph Towers, Presbyterian minister and friend of Richard Price, declared that

> from the moment of passing these Bills [the two Acts known as the 'Gagging Acts' or 'Pitt and Grenville Acts'] there was not so much freedom in England as there was in the reign of James the Second. He was no flatterer of men of rank any more than other persons, but he was glad that the Russel of the present day was equal in patriotism to his ancestor.[36]

Publication in the press, especially in the *Morning Chronicle*, spread those principles and established party identity. The toasts, however, were often contentious; conservatives complained in 1822 that, at a Whig dinner, the toast to 'the constitution as established in 1688' preceded 'the King'.[37]

There were moderate reformers among the Whigs, who voiced some criticism of the post-1689 political order. Christopher Wyvill, at the head of the Association Movement in Yorkshire, was the most potent voice of this tendency in the 1790s. During the French Revolution, he continued to call for a return to the constitution as settled in 1689 but vitiated by corruption since. He did so in Yorkshire in 1795, in the thick of loyalist pressure against any reform.[38] His *Political Papers* contain several documents defending moderate reform on the basis on loyalty to the monarchy and the precedent of 1688. The 'Declaration of the Loyalty of the Town of Sheffield' passed in December 1792 grounded its claims on the constitution as settled in 1688, presented as revered yet perfectible.[39] In a period when counter-revolutionary associations had multiplied loyalty declarations, Wyvill and his allies had managed to express moderate dissent while professing loyalty to the constitution of 1689. The Glorious Revolution was also invoked in resolutions against the Treasonable and Seditious Practices, one of the 'Gagging Acts' (36 Geo. III, ch.7).[40] In this case, the Glorious Revolution remained a benchmark, offering the justification of a restoration of rights, rather than a forward-looking, disruptive conquest of new rights. This was reformism in the garb of constitutional conservation.

In 1801, Wyvill exhorted John Cartwright to agitate for limited, rather than universal, suffrage because such a parliamentary reform would 'complete what was perhaps unavoidably left unfinished by the Revolution in the year 1688'.[41] It is of course difficult to distinguish absolutely between Whig reformers like Wyvill and a 'radical' like John Cartwright, a landlord like Wyvill, who was Whig at heart but went further than him on the suffrage and electoral reform. Both Cartwright's and Wyvill's correspondents talked the language of the restoration of rights: on 14 February 1798, the Duke of Northumberland approved of Wyvill's meetings of freeholders, wishing as he did 'to preserve the Monarchy, and bring back the Constitution to that most enlightened and admirable system which was established at the Revolution'.[42]

However, in the late 1790s and early 1800s, at the high tide of loyalist hysteria, defending 1688, even as a moderate restoration of rights, smelt of sedition. Those who did so incurred the accusation of condoning 1789 or even 1793. As Francis Jeffrey, a major publicist of Whig values in the *Edinburgh Review*, retrospectively lamented in 1808:

> [T]he revolution of 1688 [...] could not be mentioned with praise without giving some indirect encouragement to the revolution of 1789; and it was thought as well to say nothing in favour of Hampden [...] or Sidney, for fear it might give spirits to Robespierre, Danton, or Marat. To this strict regimen the greater part of the nation submitted of their own accord: and it was forced upon the remainder by a pretty vigorous system of proceeding.[43]

Far from rehabilitating the Glorious Revolution or making it innocuous, the French Revolution provoked a moral panic that hampered most discussion and polarized its reception: for conservatives, and many more cautious Whigs, the Glorious Revolution became a dangerous precedent.

The problem was how to salvage the Glorious Revolution without condoning the horrors of 1793 or jettisoning reform altogether. The Foxite Whigs and their liberal successors, then, who donned the mantle of the Whigs of 1688–9, spent considerable time and energy in cultural work defending the Revolution. Both Charles James Fox and James Mackintosh penned bulky histories of the Revolution vindicating Whig ancestors.[44] Fox justified his own conduct by showing its congruence with that of the Whigs of 1688.[45] The connection between 1688 and 1789 had to be explained. As Jane Rendall noted, James Mackintosh, in his *History of the Revolution in England in 1688*, thought that 'the principles of 1688, which accelerated the spread of the enlightenment throughout Europe, indirectly led to the American Revolution – and from there to the revolution in France itself'.[46] This was in essence Price's position in his *Discourse on the Love of Our Country*. As for Macaulay, he did not simply popularize Burke's thesis. He examined all the alternative interpretations of William's demise at the time, including abdication, deposition and William's election. According to a recent interpretation, he recognized the 'fundamental principle of deposing a king that had failed his functions' and endorsed abdication, while also considering the radical thesis of deposition.⁴⁷ He was closer to Paine and Price than Burke on the notion of the popular choice legitimating a king's rule. The Whig historians of the early nineteenth century still adhered to earlier, classical, beliefs about the value of history as moral guidance. They were polemical, and Fox's posthumously published *History of the Early Part of the Reign of James II* (1808) was criticized for its party spirit.⁴⁸ The Whig historians did not produce a 'historical past' as later historians would but were still enmeshed in the debates of their times, taking sides and justifying particular men and policies.⁴⁹

Radical uses of the Glorious Revolution

For radicals, on the other hand, the proceedings of 1688 paled in comparison with the French Revolution. It is possible to document the instrumental uses of the Glorious Revolution, and especially the Bill of Rights, which provided a most 'usable past' to defend various rights and liberties. However, it is less certain whether the Glorious Revolution still belonged to Halbwachs's realm of 'memory'; it seems that the French Revolution precipitated it into the more abstract, colder realm of 'history'. In the 1790s, references to 1688 and William of Orange were still present in radical discourse. By 1848, they were virtually absent: a full-text search in a digitized copy of the *Northern Star* yields very few results about the Glorious Revolution, while the paper regularly published material about the French Revolution.⁵⁰ The phrase 'Glorious Revolution' became loosened from 1688 and was applied to recent events on the continent. When the Fraternal Democrats commemorated the French revolution of February 1848, they talked of 'Glorious Revolution' but they never mentioned the English precedent of 1688.⁵¹

However, though some radicals found it was a palace coup, an inglorious business or at best a missed opportunity for real change, others had their uses of the Glorious Revolution. It could justify a general right to revolution. As Edward Thompson noted, in 1817, 'Henry White, the editor of the moderate *Independent Whig*, was only one among many Radical journalists who reminded readers of the precedent of the Glorious Revolution of 1688': 'it is to a *Revolution*, White wrote, they will be ultimately compelled to resort, if all other legal means be denied of obtaining a Redress of Grievances'.⁵² But in general, the Bill of Rights was widely known to enshrine basic rights that the government must respect, especially the right to bear arms and the right to petition the king. The London Corresponding Society (LCS), for all its pacific stance, justified the possession of arms by the Bill of Rights.⁵³ In 1817, Jeremiah Brandreth also evoked the right to bear arms during his trial following the Pentrich rising.⁵⁴

The Hanoverian dynasty owed its position to the Revolution, which implied that loyalty to the reigning house and monarchs entailed not just the right but the *duty* of resistance to tyranny. The LCS expounded the right of resistance to oppression in a declaration of its principles printed in 1795:

> To resist oppression (when no other means are left) even with the same arms with which it is enforced, is, they are aware, not only a natural right, but a constitutional

duty; and if their ancestors had not so resisted, the *House of Brunswick* never would have swayed the British Sceptre, the exiled family of the *Stuart* would have been still upon the throne, and Britain never could have boasted her GLORIOUS REVOLUTION of 1688.[55]

Tellingly, 'constitutional duty' coincides here with 'natural right': the two main languages of 1790s radicalism, natural right and constitutionalism, converged. The idea of an abstract foundation, like a rational social contract, was usually coupled with justifications of English liberties in national history.

The Bill of Rights was felt to guarantee popular rights and liberties. Throughout the early nineteenth century, radicals, and later, Chartists, made use of the name, quotations and visual renditions of the Bill of Rights, often in conjunction with the Magna Carta.[56] When Henry Hunt made his triumphal entrance into London after his acquittal in September 1819, the procession comprised a 'horseman with a scroll inscribed on it, Magna Carta and Bill of Rights'.[57] The Chartists also displayed the Bill of Rights on banners, thus making use of a wide array of media in their repertoire of expression to lay claim to the 1688 Revolution and to define its meaning as one of emancipation justifying universal (male) suffrage. The words 'Magna Charta' and 'Bill of Rights' appeared on Chartist banners, for instance on that of the village of Middleton displayed at the mass meeting of Kersal Moor on 24 September 1838.[58]

If radicals and Chartists could lay claim to the Bill of Rights to justify popular rights, there were also many instances of doubt and even mocking distancing. Paine's challenge about the 'Bill of Wrongs' set many radicals thinking, sometimes for many years. John Cartwright exalted the Bill of Rights as the best approximation of a British written constitution in pamphlet after pamphlet, yet at the end of his life, he got closer to Paine's republicanism and, in *The Constitution Produced and Illustrated* (1823), he praised the Saxon constitution and criticized the Revolution Settlement as a failure to safeguard liberties. He pondered over Paine's phrase again and concluded that the Bill of Rights was worthless because the authorities ignored petitions and other expressions of the popular will that the document was supposed to enshrine.[59]

The Glorious Revolution and its precedent for the right of resistance also found humorous and satirical expressions in radical circles for a short-lived period in the mid-1790s, in response to loyalist campaigns. Publicists like Charles Pigott linked Burke's precious Glorious Revolution with regicide and the complete overhaul of the political régime, which were the most advanced, and controversial, positions possible after the execution of the French King in 1793. Pigott's *Political Dictionary* refers to the Glorious Revolution in two articles entitled 'Revolution' and 'Regifugium', which immediately follows 'Regicide'.[60] The Glorious Revolution also illustrates the meaning of revolution as 'the sudden overturning of an arbitrary government by the People'. 'The Revolution of 1688, no good and wise man can applaud. It was the despicable patch-work of a few addle-pated, Whig noblemen,'[61] which just replaced a tyrant with another. It fell short of the true revolution, defined as 'a total alteration of the forms of governments, and a re-assumption by the People of their long lost rights; a restoration of that equality which ought always to subsist among men'.[62] Pigott is typical of metropolitan radicals who scoffed at the Revolution as a Whig shibboleth and subscribed to the new, and

French, definition of revolution that includes 'equality' (socio-economic as well as legal). Such mocking appropriations of 1688, however, were typical of a very short moment of the French Revolution, immediately following Louis XVI's execution, in the context of loyalist exaltation of the Revolution Settlement. In later decades, such mockery disappeared because conservative uses of the Glorious Revolution were less extreme, and the radical London microcosm typical of the mid-1790s evolved.

Such instrumental, rhetorical treatment of the Glorious Revolution suggests that it was no longer (if it had ever been) an object of reverence. The French Revolution immediately questioned the relevance of celebrating the Glorious Revolution. The young Thomas Amyot, a Dissenter from Norwich who leant towards Godwinism at the time, raised the question explicitly in late 1794, a few months after Robespierre's Festival of Reason.[63] In the context of new revolutionary commemorative practices in France, as the French *fêtes révolutionnaires* and new republican calendar disrupted established forms, the question was whether 5 November was not an antiquated festival that encouraged anti-Catholic prejudice and celebrated an ultimately disappointing constitutional settlement. Amyot and his Godwinian friends found such celebrations wanting: they may not have been representative of many English people beyond a tiny, rarefied, sociocultural elite, but at least they discussed the matter frankly, suggesting the malaise that many more must have felt.

The trial by jury dinners: Displacing 1688 and other revolutions

The fourth of November, a classic date for Dissenting expression, therefore, lost its relevance shortly after 1789. Or did it? The London radicals appropriated 5 November for their own purposes, celebrating the acquittals of the twelve members of the LCS in the treason and sedition trials.[64] The date henceforth served to commemorate the radical fight for parliamentary reform. Press articles make it possible to document the 'trial by jury dinners' most years from 1795 to 1854.[65] The idea of popular resistance to an arbitrary king and his minions ran through the radical narratives of both the Glorious Revolution and the LCS's fight against Pitt. This, more than the fortuitous fact that Thomas Hardy was released from gaol on 4 November 1794, justified the takeover of the date in the service of a celebration of the English 'Jacobins'. The dinners clearly built up the political, and historical, memory of the London radicals. Central to this process was the presence of the men of 1794, like Hardy and John Thelwall, who attended until their deaths (in 1832 and 1834, respectively). The presence of veterans of earlier fights was important in keeping memory alive and sustaining group identity in nineteenth-century radicalism and Chartism, as historiography has established.[66]

In its early decades, the 'trial by jury' dinner served as a moment of conviviality for men whose political identities were defined by support for the French Revolution. Many former members of the LCS attended, as Francis Place recollected.[67] As the LCS veterans died off, chairmen increasingly refused to toast universal suffrage; the discontinuity of homages to Cartwright and other symbols signalled a centring of the discourse. The dinner applauded the 1832 Reform Bill as a final settlement, not a step to universal suffrage. The 5 November celebration, therefore, was not displaced once, in 1795, but twice, since the Whigs took it over in the course of the 1820s.[68] Steve Poole has rightly contended that this post-war Whig takeover of a full-blooded Jacobin celebration made the 'trial by jury' dinner a prime example of the 'fluidity of commemorative practices'.[69]

Another form of displacement, a memorial shift, happened during those decades, as well. Early in the history of the dinners, the French Revolution replaced the Glorious Revolution as memorial focus, but later, by the mid-nineteenth century, the French Revolution itself had receded into history. In 1852, the chairman said the trial was 'a passage of history' which 'a future Macaulay' could write.[70] In the same period, books like *Sketches of Reform and Reformers*, sometimes serialized in the press,[71] told the story of the 1794 trials as a page of history for the new generations. To take up Halbwachs's categories, the French Revolution and the radical fight against Pitt's Terror had moved from the realm of living, and oral-based, memory to that of history, with historians to consign to writing material that is past and cut off from the experiences of the present.

Over a period of sixty years, the 'trial by jury' dinner illustrated how the French Revolution had replaced the Glorious Revolution as focus of interest. The dinners changed political orientation, from radical to Whig, while building up continuities and tradition at the same time. The sixty-year time span makes clear the difference between the ebullience of the mid-1790s, with dinners steeped in radical culture and in contact with popular rituals and, at the end of the period, orderly, mid-Victorian dinners. Attendance slumped from 700 to 800 in 1796 to 'upwards of 100 gentlemen' in 1810 and leapt up in special years like 1837 until 'a few friends' decided in 1853 to terminate the dinner the next year.[72]

The memory of the 1794 trials erased the cult of the Glorious Revolution. In 1795, the French Revolution's impact on Britain, in the form of Pitt's 'Terror' and radical resistance, overshadowed the Glorious Revolution and the Gunpowder Plot. Those events, traditionally fêted on 5 November, were still present in the first years of the dinners, but they soon receded from view. In 1796, journalists wondered what the dinner exactly celebrated because the first toast about 'deliverance' could refer to William of Orange in 1688, yet the second one, 'The Rights of Man', denoted both the French Declaration of 1789 and Paine's book. One song discarded the seventeenth-century associations of 5 November as 'an old story':

> The landing of William is now an old story,
> Though it gave us great George, with a reign full of glory,
> Nor sing we of Jamie, and Gunpowder Treason;
> Our theme is far nobler – the triumph of reason,
> When Patriots encounter'd corruption's wild fury,
> By Virtue sustain'd, and the brave English Jury.[73]

John Thelwall declared that it was highly dubious whether the revolution of 1688 deserved praise because not long after, 'a daring, corrupt, and profligate Administration' was able to overthrow all constitutional safeguards and enslave Britons. He was rehearsing the radical Whig interpretation of the Revolution as a lost occasion. By 1811, the Glorious Revolution and the foiling of the Gunpowder Plot were historical examples, not a legacy to be cherished. In that year, the chairman noted that in 1794, a heroic jury rescued English liberties. In the same way, 'a foul conspiracy' had failed under James I, and 'under the yet more ignominious reign of a Second James, the people were rescued by the glorious Prince of Orange from the no less fatal conspiracy of their government'.[74] What mattered was the LCS's stand against Pitt. There was hardly any mention of the Glorious Revolution at later dinners – or if there was, the journalists did not mention them, possibly because the references would be thought to be uninteresting or matters of routine. A few mentions, in the early Victorian period, served to belittle the Glorious Revolution. In 1840, the chairman mentioned the Gunpowder Plot and the revolution of 1688, only to present 'the second centenary of the meeting of the Long Parliament', as a better cause for celebration.[75] The Long Parliament of 1640, he went on, was ancestor of Habeas Corpus, judiciary reform, and ministerial responsibility; it employed the luminaries of the day. The rehabilitation of Cromwell and the Puritans at the time[76] served to further marginalize the Glorious Revolution.

The year 1688 became decidedly old-fashioned. Seventeenth-century patriots, however, remained heroes for the 'trial by jury' organizers. A song from 1809, for instance, placed Hardy and the other acquitted men in a British tradition of opposition to arbitrary rule, comparing them to patriotic opponents to the Stuarts, like William Russell. Beheaded as he was following the Rye House plot, he became a Whig 'martyr', and this identification of the LCS with Russell by implication equated Pitt, 'the arch-fiend', with an evil Stuart king.[77] The main references, however, remained the acquitted men of 1794. From the 1820s, the dinners paid homage to contemporary revolutions that erupted in the Iberian world and, later, across Europe. In 1825, the dinner paid homage to Bolívar and the Greek cause and a toast to Washington, Paine and Franklin placed Paine within a pantheon of founding fathers of the American Republic.[78] From 1848, the Whig dinners discussed the Springtime of the Peoples, the 1850 dinner praising the German, Hungarian and Polish patriots.[79] There was therefore a certain cosmopolitan eclecticism in the pantheon of those Whig celebrants of the acquittals of 1794. By the 1850s, however, any tincture of Jacobinism was gone, and if the 'trial by jury' dinners still appealed to 'revolution', they applauded it abroad but consigned it to history and preferred piecemeal evolution when it came to Britain. Though the idea of 'revolution' was never absolutely disclaimed, it was progressively diluted into a glib narrative of the evolution, rather than revolution, of British liberties.

Conclusion

Whigs, radicals and Tories-turned-conservatives all developed rival interpretations of the Glorious Revolution long after the French Revolution seemingly made it irrelevant. The period shows that historical references and the canonical Bill of Rights adapted to various political uses. People of different political persuasions authored selective readings of the Glorious Revolution and its aftermath. The Tories appropriated the figure of William III, whom neither the Whigs nor the radicals liked, somewhat ironically given the Jacobite tincture of much of eighteenth-century

Toryism. This chapter has shown other displacements: the Tories insisted on the finality of the 1689 Revolution Settlement to safeguard Anglican hegemony, while the Whigs, while presenting themselves as guardians of Revolution Principles, wanted to reform the constitution. Probably the most equivocal were the radicals, who dismissed the Revolution as unfinished business, as inglorious fountain or corruption or mere palace coup, and brandished clauses from the Bill of Rights (no.5 and 7, on right to bear arms and to petition, essentially) to justify popular rights.

In the eighteenth century, celebrations of the Glorious Revolution had been central flashpoints of partisan and denominational confrontation because the actors felt they were still living out the conflicts of 1688–9. The decline of celebrations of the Glorious Revolution, and the demise of the date of 4–5 November, suggests a passage from memory to history. If this interpretation is correct, then the 'long eighteenth century' started to fade in the early 1790s. It is not easy, however, to infer the state of people's *mentalités* from such evidence, and it is certainly wrong to suggest a precise date as a tipping point from memory to history.

The success of Thomas Babington Macaulay's *History of England* could be explained by both the lingering relevance of 1688 and the need for a new form of narrative history adapted to post-Romantic times: celebration of the Revolution moved from the rowdy 5 November bonfires to the more sedate, yet far from passionless, domain of history. That Macaulay's popular success should come after the efforts of earlier Whigs, Fox and Mackintosh, to write the definitive history of the Revolution for the record of posterity, also suggests that the Whigs did not attain the historiographical and cultural hegemony from the 1800s to the 1840s. The influence of such efforts beyond the world of Whiggism, among radicals in particular, remained to be proved. For early-nineteenth-century radicals, 5 November meant Guy Fawkes and bonfires. John Belchem argued that, in 1839, the Chartists planned a rising in Monmouthshire on 5 November to take advantage of 'the traditional saturnalia'[80] (and not the revolution of 1688 then). However, the protracted references to William III, the Boyne and the Protestant Constitution among opponents of Catholic Emancipation would rather confirm J. C. D. Clark's influential interpretation, in which memories of the conflicts of the 1690s were not erased by the 1790s, and would endure until Catholic Emancipation and the First Reform Bill. This suggests that the transition from 'memory' to 'history', so appealing theoretically, is difficult to apply. There must have been different temporalities in the transition: the heritage of the Williamite, Protestant, aristocratic, settlement took different times to 'cool off' in different political constituencies.

Notes

1   Frank O'Gorman and Michael Schaich, 'Political Ritual in Eighteenth-Century Britain', in *Political Rituals in Great Britain 1700–2000*, ed. Jörg Neuheiser (Augsburg, Germany: Wissner-Verlag, 2006), 23.

2   H. T. Dickinson, 'The Eighteenth-Century Debate on the "Glorious Revolution"', *History*, 61, no. 201 (1976), 28–45; Kathleen Wilson, 'Inventing Revolution: 1688 and Eighteenth-Century Popular Politics', *Journal of British Studies*, 28, no. 4 (1989), 349–86.
3   Richard Price, 'A Discourse on the Love of Our Country', in *Political Writings*, ed. David Oswald Thomas, Cambridge Texts in the History of Political Thought (Cambridge and New York: Cambridge University Press, 1991), 190.
4   Edmund Burke, 'Reflections on the Revolution in France', in *The Writings and Speeches of Edmund Burke*, ed. Leslie George Mitchell, William Burton Todd and Paul Langford (Oxford: Oxford University Press, 1989), vol. 8, 68.
5   Thomas Paine, *Rights of Man* (Harmondsworth: Penguin, 1985), 193.
6   Steve Pincus, *1688: The First Modern Revolution*, The Lewis Walpole Series in Eighteenth-Century Culture and History (New Haven, CT, and London: Yale UP, 2009), 24.
7   Hayden White, 'The Practical Past', in *The Practical Past* (Evanston, IL: Northwestern University Press, 2014), 9.
8   Ibid., 3–24.
9   On the opposition between living memory and history as separation from the past and communal emotion: Maurice Halbwachs, *La Mémoire collective* (Paris: Presses universitaires de France, 1968).
10 Matthew Roberts, *Chartism, Commemoration and the Cult of the Radical Hero* (Abingdon, UK, and New York: Routledge, 2019), 63–4.
11 Halbwachs, *La Mémoire collective*, 67–8.
12 Anthony S. Jarrells, *Britain's Bloodless Revolutions: 1688 and the Romantic Reform of Literature* (Houndmills, Basingstoke and New York: Palgrave, 2005); Tony Gheeraert, Claire Gheeraert-Graffeuille, and Sylvain Ledda (eds.), *La Guerre civile anglaise des romantiques* (Mont-Saint-Aignan: Presses de l'Université de Rouen et du Havre, 2017); Roy Strong, *And When Did You Last See Your Father? The Victorian Painter and British History* (London: Thames and Hudson, 1978), 136–51, 163–8 on the English Civil War, the Glorious Revolution and Jacobitism.
13 Robert Poole, *Peterloo: The English Uprising* (Oxford and New York: Oxford University Press, 2019), 50, 53.
14 Rémy Duthille, '1688–1789: Au Carrefour des révolutions. Les célébrations de la Révolution anglaise de 1688 en Grande-Bretagne après 1789', in *Du Bon Usage des commémorations: histoire, mémoire et identité, XVIe–XXIe siècle*, ed. Lauric Henneton and Bernard Cottret (Rennes: Presses Universitaires de Rennes, 2010), 107–20.
15 William Winterbotham, *The Commemoration of National Deliverances: And the Dawning Day: Two Sermons, Preached November 5th and 18th, 1792, at How's-Lane Chapel, Plymouth, by W. Winterbotham* (London: printed for Wm. Winterbotham; Cambridge, 1794). See Susan J. Mills, Winterbotham, William (1763–1829), *ODNB*.
16 Emma Vincent Macleod, 'British Radical Attitudes towards the United States of America in the 1790s: The Case of William Winterbotham', in *Liberty, Property and Popular Politics: England and Scotland, 1688–1815: Essays in Honour of H.T. Dickinson*, ed. Gordon Pentland and Michael T. Davis (Edinburgh: Edinburgh UP, 2016), 150–1.
17 *Letter from a Farmer in Angus to His Friend, a Burgher of Dundee, and One of the Delegates to the Convention of the Friends of the People* ([Edinburgh?], 1793), 5.
18 John Reeves, *Thoughts on the English Government. Addressed to the Quiet Good Sense of the People of England. In a Series of Letters. Letter the First* (London, 1795), 25.

19 Ibid., 40.
20 William Cobbett (ed.), *Cobbett's Parliamentary History of England: From the Norman Conquest, in 1066, to the Year 1803* (London: Published by R. Bagshaw, 1806–1820), vol. 32, co.628–2, quotation 628.
21 James J. Sack, *From Jacobite to Conservative: Reaction and Orthodoxy in Britain, c.1760–1832* (Cambridge: Cambridge University Press, 1993), 70. See also J. C. D. Clark, *English Society: 1688–1832* (Cambridge: Cambridge University Press, 1985), 275–6.
22 *An Appeal from the New to the Old Whigs, in Consequence of Some Late Discussions in Parliament …* (London: J. Dodsley, 1791).
23 'Dinner to Sir Wm. Curtis', *Times*, 7 April 1820, 20.
24 *The Pitt Club: The Commemoration of the Anniversary of Mr. Pitt's Birth-Day, at the City of London Tavern, on Saturday the 27th of May, 1815. Sir Robert Peel, Bart. M.P. Vice-President, in the Chair* (London, 1815), 13.
25 'Miscellanies', *Anti-Jacobin Review and True Churchman's Magazine, or, Monthly, Political and Literary Censor*, 49, no. 209 (October 1815), 393.
26 Katrina Navickas, *Loyalism and Radicalism in Lancashire, 1798–1815* (Oxford and New York: Oxford University Press, 2009), 124.
27 George Ian Tom Machin, *The Catholic Question in English Politics, 1820 to 1830* (Oxford: Clarendon, 1964). The Roman Catholic Relief Act was passed in 1829.
28 James Kelly, '"The Glorious and Immortal Memory": Commemoration and Protestant Identity in Ireland 1660–1800', *Proceedings of the Royal Irish Academy. Section C, 1660–1800* (1994), 25–52.
29 Allan Blackstock, 'Loyal Clubs and Societies in Ulster, 1770–1800', in *Clubs and Societies in Eighteenth-Century Ireland*, ed. James Kelly and Martyn J. Powell (Dublin: Four Courts, 2010), 459–65; Shunsuke Katsuta, '"Aggregate Meetings" and Politics in Early Nineteenth-Century Dublin', *Leaves*, no. 12 (2021), https://climas.u-bordeaux-montaigne.fr/numeros-parus/71-leaves-n-12-textes/504-aggregate-meetings-and-politics-in-early-nineteenth-century-dublin-shunsuke-katsuta (accessed 21 July 2022).
30 Kyle Hughes and Donald M. MacRaild, 'Anti-Catholicism and Orange Loyalism in Nineteenth-Century Britain', in *Loyalism and the Formation of the British World, 1775–1914*, ed. Allan Blackstock and Frank O'Gorman (Woodbridge: Boydell, 2014), 61–80 quotation 70.
31 *The Antijacobin Review; True Churchman's Magazine; and Protestant Advocate*, 52 (March 1817), 64. On report of activities in Ireland, see e.g. 585–6: Meeting of the Grand Orange Lodge of the City and County of Londonderry, pledging their attachment to the constitution established at the Revolution.
32 Machin, *The Catholic Question in English Politics*, 2.
33 George Leslie Mitchell, *The Whig World: 1760–1837* (London: Hambledon, 2007), 140.
34 Ibid., 153.
35 T. E. Orme, 'Toasting Fox: The Fox Dinners in Edinburgh and Glasgow, 1801–1825', *History*, 99, no. 337 (2014), 588–606; Keisuke Masaki, 'Posthumous Cult and Memory of Charles James Fox: Whig Associations in the 1810s', *Leaves*, 12 (2021). On toasts related to the Revolution, see Peter Brett, 'Political Dinners in Early Nineteenth-Century Britain: Platform, Meeting Place and Battleground', *History*, 81, no. 264 (1996), 537; Orme, 'Toasting Fox', 597.
36 *Morning Chronicle*, 26 January 1796.
37 Brett, 'Political Dinners in Early Nineteenth-Century Britain', 535.

38 *The Freeholders of Yorkshire Who Are Friends to Their King and Constitution, as Settled at the Glorious Revolution, Are Hereby Informed, That an Address to His Majesty, and a Petition to the House of Commons for Securing to Us Our Present Constitution, and Restoring the Blessings of Peace, Lie for Signatures at the Guildhall, in York, for This Day Only* ([York], 1795).
39 Christopher Wyvill, *Political Papers, Chiefly Respecting the Attempt of the County of York, and Other Considerable Districts, Commenced in 1779 and Continued during Several Subsequent Years, to Effect a Reformation of the Parliament of Great-Britain*, 6 vols. (York, 1794), v, vii–viii.
40 Ibid., xliv.
41 Wyvill, *A Letter to John Cartwright, Esq.* (York, 1801), 8.
42 Wyvill, *Political Papers*, vol. 6, 4.
43 Francis Jeffrey, *Contributions to the Edinburgh Review*, 4 vols. (London: Longman, Brown, Green, 1844), vol. 2, 12. It Is Also quoted in Richard Gravil, 'Helen Maria Williams: Wordsworth's Revolutionary Anima', *Wordsworth Circle*, 40, no. 1 (2009), 57–8.
44 J. R. Dinwiddy, 'Charles James Fox as Historian', in *Radicalism and Reform in Britain, 1780-1850* (London and Rio Grande, OH, 1992), 19–30; James Mackintosh, *History of the Revolution in England in 1688. Comprising a View of the Reign of James II. From His Accession, to the Enterprise of the Prince of Orange, by Sir James Mackintosh; and Completed, to the Settlement of the Crown, by the Editor. To Which Is Prefixed, a Notice of the Life, Writings, and Speeches of Sir James Mackintosh* (London: Longman, Rees, Orme, Brown, Green, & Longman, 1834).
45 Dinwiddy, 'Charles James Fox as Historian', 20.
46 Jane Rendall, 'The Political Ideas and Activities of Sir James Mackintosh (1765–1832): A Study of Whiggism between 1789 and 1832' (PhD diss., University of London, 1972), 47.
47 Aude Attuel-Hallade, *T.B. Macaulay et la Révolution française: la pensée libérale whig en débat* (Paris: Michel Houdiard, 2018), chap. 2.1 quotation 176.
48 Dinwiddy, 'Charles James Fox as Historian', 27.
49 See Hayden White's definition of the 'historical past' as 'a theoretically motivated construction, existing only in the books and articles published by professional historians; it is constructed as an end in itself, possesses little or no value for understanding or explaining the present, and provides no guidelines for acting in the present or foreseeing the future' (White, 'The Practical Past', 9).
50 Jacob Dengate, 'Lighting the Torch of Liberty: The French Revolution and Chartist Political Culture, 1838–1852' (PhD diss., Aberystwyth University, 2017).
51 'The Fraternal Democrats of London to the True Republicans of Paris, Assembled to Commemorate the Glorious Revolution of February, 1848', *Northern Star*, 24 February 1849, 22.
52 E. P. Thompson, *The Making of the English Working Class* (1963; Harmondsworth: Penguin, 1980), 684. Thompson quotes from *Independent Whig*, 27 July 1817.
53 John Barrell, *Imagining the King's Death: Figurative Treason, Fantasies of Regicide, 1793–1796* (Oxford and New York: Oxford University Press, 2000), 225.
54 *Observer*, 26 October 1817.
55 London Corresponding Society, 'To the Parliament and People of Great Britain: An Explicit Declaration of the Principles and Views of the London Corresponding Society' (London, 1795), 4.

56 Josh Gibson, 'The Chartists and the Constitution: Revisiting British Popular Constitutionalism', *The Journal of British Studies*, 56, no. 1 (2017), 75. On earlier uses of the Magna Carta, see Harry Thomas Dickinson, 'Magna Carta in the Age of Revolution', *Enlightenment and Dissent*, 30 (2015), 1–67.
57 *Black Dwarf*, 15 September 1819, co.601.
58 'Chartist Banners in the Manchester Region, 1838–1843, compiled by Matthew Roberts', at https://www.matthewowenroberts.com/resources.
59 John Cartwright, *The English Constitution Produced and Illustrated* (London, 1823), 166, 13–14.
60 Charles Pigott, *A Political Dictionary: Explaining the True Meaning of Words …* (London, 1795), 113.
61 Ibid., 117.
62 Ibid., 118.
63 William Pattisson, Thomas Amyot, and Henry Crabb Robinson, *Youth and Revolution in the 1790s: Letters of William Pattisson, Thomas Amyot, and Henry Crabb Robinson*, ed. Penelope J. Corfield and Chris Evans (Far Thrupp, Stroud, Gloucestershire: Alan Sutton, 1996), 87–9.
64 Thomas Hardy, John Horne Tooke, John Thelwall, John Augustus Bonney, Stewart Kidd, Richard Hodgson, Thomas Holcroft, Jeremiah Joyce, Thomas Wardle, Matthew Moore, John Baxter, and John Richter. On the trials, see John Barrell and Jon Mee (eds.), *Trials for Treason and Sedition, 1792–1794*, 6 vols (London: Pickering & Chatto, 2006); Barrell, *Imagining the King's Death*.
65 The main newspapers covering those dinners are the *Morning Chronicle*, the *Telegraph*, the *Examiner*, the *London Dispatch*, the *Operative*, and the *Northern Star*.
66 Malcolm Chase, *Chartism: A New History* (Manchester: Manchester UP, 2007), 33. See also the figure of the 'Old Chartist' in late Victorian reform and socialist meetings: Antony Taylor, '"The Old Chartist": Radical Veterans on the Late Nineteenth – and Early Twentieth-Century Political Platform', *History*, 95, no. 320 (2010), 458–76.
67 Francis Place, *The Autobiography of Francis Place, 1771–1854*, ed. Mary Thale (Cambridge: Cambridge University Press, 1972), 199.
68 Interestingly, Marc Baer gives another example of an 'act of appropriation' in radical history: 'the London and Westminster Working Men's Constitutional Association held their annual dinner on 19 May 1868, the same calendrical moment at which Burdett's followers had met' a generation earlier: Marc Baer, 'Political Dinners in Whig, Radical and Tory Westminster, 1780–1880', *Parliamentary History*, 24 (2005), 189.
69 S. Poole, 'The Politics of "Protest Heritage", 1790–1850', in *Remembering Protest in Britain since 1500: Memory, Materiality and the Landscape*, ed. C. J. Griffin and B. McDonagh (Cham: Springer International Publishing, 2018), 197–200, quotation 200.
70 'Trial by jury. Anniversary celebration of the acquittal of Hardy, Tooke, and Thelwall', *Daily News*, 6 November 1852, 2.
71 Henry B. Stanton, *Sketches of Reforms and Reformers of Great Britain and Ireland* (New York and London: J. Wiley, 1849). See an extract on the trials in *Manchester Times*, 15 December 1849.
72 *Morning Post*, 7 November 1796; BL, Add Mss 27, 817, fo.97; *The London Dispatch and People's Political and Social Reformer*, 12 November 1837; *Manchester Times*, 12 November 1853.

73 *Morning Post*, 7 November 1796.
74 BL, Add Mss 27, 817, fo. 99.
75 'Trial by Jury', *Morning Chronicle*, 6 November 1840, 1.
76 Blair Worden, *Roundhead Reputations: The English Civil Wars and the Passions of Posterity* (London, 2002).
77 'Song, Written by one of the Stewards for the Fifteenth Anniversary of the Acquittal of Messrs. Hardy, Tooke, Thelwall, &c.' (1809). BL, Add Mss 27,817, fo. 95.
78 See also, in 1829: 'The Memory of Washington, Paine, and Franklin, the Founders of American Independence', *Morning Chronicle*, 6 November 1829.
79 'Trial by Jury', *Daily News*, 6 November 1850, 2.
80 John Belchem, *Popular Radicalism in Nineteenth-Century Britain*, Social History in Perspective (Basingstoke, Hampshire: Macmillan, 1996), 78.

3

'Generation 1789': Welsh Dissenters and radicals lost in translation

Marion Löffler

Silences enter the process of historical production at four crucial moments: the moment of fact creation (the making of sources*); the moment of fact assembly (the making of* archives*); the moment of fact retrieval (the making of* narratives*); and the moment of retrospective significance (the making of* history *in the final instance) ... Power does not enter the story once and for all, but at different times and from different angles. It precedes the narrative proper, contributes to its creation and to its interpretation.*[1]

Michael Trouillot's approach to 'losing' voices from the past explains the lack of public images, memorials and narratives on the Welsh religious Dissenters and political radicals of the 1790s, a generation excluded even from considerations of a 'lunatic fringe' of unusual suspects suffering during Pitt's 'reign of terror'. Subaltern during their life time, and forcibly 'forgotten' by the Welsh Victorians,[2] the sources available on them were later judged unreliable by mainstream historians or remain(ed) inaccessible to them. Similar to American scholarship, which 'still minimizes the vast areas of the continent west of the Appalachians and overlooks most early Americans',[3] British historians have tended to stay south of the Peak District, east of Offa's Dyke and within the bounds of standard English.[4] This has led to inaccurate statements, such as Gregory Claeys's comment that 'obscure' Wales only contributed one published text, and perhaps a disappeared manuscript translation of *Rights of Man* to the 'pamphlet wars' of the 1790s.[5] Assuming an indigenous Welsh publishing industry would have led to the inclusion of the numerous Welsh political publications first mentioned in a Welsh monograph in 1935.[6] Unlike northern English dialects, Irish and Scottish Gaelic, Welsh sported an established print culture which exponentially expanded in tandem with the democratization of the English radical discourse of the 1790s.[7] However, assumptions of its nonexistence and a focus on metropolitan culture have prevented their exploration as part of British history. Whether such assumptions and omissions may be categorized as the 'colonialist silencing of indigenous voices' enacted in imperial historiographies is arguable,[8] but they have certainly contributed to the eradication of Welsh agency, leaving what Gwyn Alf Williams called a narrative of 'surface deference and quietism in matters political' that masked 'a society riddled with tension, secret societies and the growing alienation of an increasingly Nonconformist people from all establishments'.[9] This process of public memory loss, kick-started after the Napoleonic Wars, was maintained for a century by the Welsh themselves. Nineteenth-century influencers were obsessed with demonstrating a respectable loyalty to Queen and Empire, underscoring an appropriately subaltern nationhood with ancient Celticism and proto-Christian bardism rather than political radicalism. The public memory of radical Welsh Enlightenment figures was cleansed accordingly, their political allegiances humourized, suppressed or forgotten.

Drawing on approaches to recovering England's 'lost generation', and on research into subaltern manifestations of Enlightenment and radicalism inclusive of Welsh-English cross-border connections,[10] this chapter also takes cues from indigenous American approaches to method and material that honour the subaltern and recent enquiries into the 'forced forgetting' that is part of historical narrative creation by those who are 'occupants of structural positions and actors in their own present'.[11] Its focus on three 'main suspects' of generation 1789 in their radical networks hopes to demonstrate how reading indigenous material and re-evaluating sources for a subaltern history may enable the recovery of non-canonical lives, voices and reputations.

Beyond England's 'lost generation'

Since the 1990s, historians of late eighteenth-century Britain have been reassessing Clive Emsley's judgement that the fewer than 200 prosecutions resulting from the punitive legislation of the 1790s did not justify the assumption of a 'reign of terror'.[12] Working on the West Country, Steve Poole argued persuasively that beyond Emsley's trials, prison sentences, deportations and executions, 'popular fears about prosecution, ... arrest, detention and judicial harassment may have served a better purpose than prosecution'.[13] Writing on Wales, Geraint H. Jenkins noted that for radicals fear of prosecution 'curtailed their liberties, invaded their private life, and perverted everything which made life worthwhile'.[14] In 2009, Kenneth R. Johnston first postulated a 'lost generation' of English radicals: 'usual suspects' who knew 'what they were letting themselves in for when they organized, met, published, spoke, and otherwise agitated for reform',[15] and 'unusual suspects', who suffered from an 'invasion of private space',[16] perpetrated by Pitt's 'interlocking system of spies, informers, packed juries, compliant magistrates, and "hegemonic" vigilante forces'.[17] The losses registered most obviously in the ruined careers, families and lives of Johnston's 'usual suspects' but also affected 'unusual suspects' – sympathetic fellow-travellers who did not expect to get into trouble for their sympathies situated on what he called the 'lunatic' fringes of the English reform movement and in a 'British' revolutionary underground.[18]

The Welsh 'suspects' who adapted the ideas of the French Revolution to the Welsh mindscape by reinventing a medieval Welsh institution as a democratic competition headed by an invented governing body of enlightened druids, and creating a public discourse via radical publications and new vocabularies, remain virtually unknown outside a small circle of scholars of Welsh Enlightenment and Romanticism.[19]

The focus has tended to be fixed on famous exports such as Richard Price and David Williams,[20] radical tourists like John Thelwall,[21] and the social history of moral-economy rioting.[22] This chapter contributes to retrieving the memory of and restoring agency to Welsh radicals by utilizing contemporary oral narratives, biographies and anecdotes, surely Johnston's 'fugitive evidence', or Poole's 'unofficial ... circumstantial documentation',[23] as well as closely reading their refit into a Victorian culture that celebrated loyalty to the British Crown without abandoning a national culture, and charting reinterpretations in the twentieth century. The interrupted lives, silenced voices and emasculated biographies of central figures Edward Williams (Iolo Morganwg), Thomas Evans (Tomos Glyn Cothi) and Morgan John Rhys (Morgan ab Ioan Rhys) will be complemented by evidence on fellow radicals Dafydd Dafis (of Castell Hywel), David Davies (of Holywell), John Jones (Jac Glan-y-Gors), William Jones (of Llangadfan) and William Richards (of Kings Lynn).[24]

Interrupted lives

Glamorgan stonemason, antiquary, forger and 'Bard of Liberty' Iolo Morganwg (1747–1826) is the best-remembered and best-researched of generation 1789. Travelling between his native south Wales and east England, deeply enmeshed in the radical Dissenting and Welsh circles of London, and there creating his democratic *Gorsedd Beirdd Ynys Prydain* (Assembly of the Bards of the Isle of Britain),[25] his burning radicalism was buried by a nineteenth-century public that wanted more respectable dissenting saints. The scarcity of published radical writing by him, a lack of official prosecution and the de-politicization of his *Gorsedd* after 1815 left numerous manuscripts and a substantial body of anecdotes as evidence. Between 1841, fifteen years after his death, and 1914, for instance, at least five versions of the following anecdote appeared:[26]

> In the year 1797 he opened a shop in Cowbridge, where he sold books, stationary and groceries ... He was aware that two persons named Rich and Curtis, then resident in Cowbridge, were employing themselves as spies upon his proceedings, anxious to implicate him in some political or theological misdemeanour, and he was inclined to tantalize their appetite for such discoveries. He therefore placed among his books in his window one labelled 'THE RIGHTS OF MAN', and the offensive title was speedily descried by these political hawks, one of whom instantly pounced upon the devoted volume, by entering the shop, asking for the book, and paying for it. On receiving it into his hands, he turned with an air of triumph to his companion who had followed him, when on opening the leaves, his eye caught the double columns, chapters, and verses – not of a proscribed political work, but of THE BIBLE! His countenance fell, and turning to the bookseller he upbraided him as a cheat, demanding the return of his money. 'No sir,' replied the Bard, 'I am no cheat – you will find in that book the best and dearest RIGHTS OF MAN – and I am glad of the opportunity which has put the Bible into your hands, for once in your life.' The brace of spies walked off in no very complacent mood, and everybody who learnt the story enjoyed their mortification.[27]

A good example of the new Welsh folklore, which fitted 'old Iolo' into the pantheon of Nonconformist bards and preachers invented by and for Victorian audiences, the narrative was denuded of serious political content by humour and reference to the Bible. Iolo was neither arrested nor did he suffer 'informal measures', such as the demolition of his house, like publisher John Campbell across the Severn estuary in Bath.[28] One may argue that there was no serious threat to Iolo or his livelihood. However, in the context of the 1790s and an extensive archive of similar narratives, the anecdote must be read as 'unusual' evidence of radical activity, indicative of the invisible persecution suffered by a Welsh radical underground at work on the colonial fringes of the English reform movement.

Iolo's shop was in Cowbridge, then an important market town close to the coast on the main route between London and Ireland. The failed Fishguard invasion of 1797 had created a hysteria which affected even English travellers who, in south Wales to enjoy the picturesque, were attacked as foreign spies.[29] We may not know what was in the shop window, but Iolo had, indeed, ordered seditious literature like the *Argus*, the *Watchman*, *Politics for the People* and *Rights of Man*.[30] Thelwall, then resident in neighbouring Breconshire, whose post was searched and every movement spied upon, was corresponding with the 'Dear Bard'.[31] Other anecdotes and Iolo's letters mention that his papers had been searched in London and that he had been summoned to Pitt twice.[32] There is no hard evidence of these incidents either, but Iolo's published writings, bardic on the surface, at second glance were Paineite. His introduction to a volume of Welsh *Heroic Elegies*, e.g. defined a leading bardic maxim as 'perfect equality':[33]

> EQUALITY. – A man cannot assume authority over another; for he may over one, by the same reason he may rule over a million, or over a world. All men are necessarily equal: ... their natural state, or every thing not manufactured by art, is the common property of all.[34]

His open-air *Gorsedd* assemblies of democratic druids, where subversive verses on mythical king slayers, satires on King George III and pacifist odes were recited, first on London's Primrose Hill and later in the Glamorgan hills, certainly attracted the attention of the authorities,[35] and were suppressed by south Wales magistrates for endangering 'the peace of the kingdom' with their 'democratic principles'.[36] It is, then, not far-fetched to assume an unnerving presence of spies in the vicinity of Iolo's shop in 1797. A trawl of anecdotes, biographies and letters of other Welsh suspects reveals a wider picture of harassment, intimidation and interrupted lives.

Arian schoolmaster Dafydd Dafis (1745–1827) of Castellhywel is a case in point. The oldest in a circle of the radical Dissenting ministers who built 'an enduring experiment in rural Enlightenment' in south-west Wales,[37] he published poetry in the radical *Cylch-grawn Cynmraeg* in 1793,[38] preached with John Estlin in Bridgend, met Letitia Barbauld in Llanelli and created Welsh versions of her and James Montgomery's hymns.[39] Dafis, a renowned 'excellent and successful teacher', attracted Dissenters and members of the Anglican church alike to his grammar school until Samuel Horsley, Bishop of St David's from 1788, decreed that none educated in a school kept by a Dissenting minister could join the Anglican clergy.[40] There is no hard evidence that this was a direct attack on Dafis, but it substantially reduced the number of his pupils, and thus income and reputation.[41] A biography published in 1828 alleges more pointed harassment:

> Since he was, like many men of renown, in favour of the *French Revolution*, he was marked by the authorities of the realm as one to be watched. The suspicions of the government concerning the unfaithfulness of Mr. Davis went so far as to appoint the *Surveyor of the Taxes*, a man called Johnson, to watch Mr. D. closely. The *Premier*, Mr. Pitt, authorized him to open every letter from or to Mr. D. Johnson.*[42]

The footnote to this paragraph points to the wider atmosphere of suspicion, but also the beginning process of mediating public memory, since Pitt's relationship with Iolo Morganwg appears in a different light:

> *Many of the most eminent men among the Dissenters were suspected of treason in the time of Pitt, but not entirely because of him. Iolo Morganwg was taken up, and all his writings with him, and he had to make his appearance before the assizes, but he was released honourably, and Mr. Pitt showed a measure of respect and invited him to his house, where he received the most gentlemanly treatment.[43]

One wonders if Dafis, had he not been thus intimidated, might have moved from Arianism to Unitarianism (illegal until 1813), thus avoiding the personally painful secession of many members of his congregation in 1801/2 and 1812.[44] However, as the father of nine children with a diminished income, he may have felt it advisable to refrain from taking this step.[45]

Of the other Welsh suspects, only Thomas Evans (Tomos Glyn Cothi, 1764–1833) – weaver, self-taught translator of radical literature and first Welsh Unitarian minister – would appear in an Emsley-type survey of successful prosecutions.[46] Attending the services of Dafis put him on a path that led to financial and intellectual patronage by leading Unitarians Joseph Priestley, Theophilus Lindsay and William Frend, whose literature he translated into Welsh, to establishing the first Unitarian chapel in Wales in 1796, to publishing a radical Welsh periodical and translating 'La Marseillaise'.[47] In 1801, he was tried for allegedly singing the 'Carmagnole' at a local bid-ale and, despite twenty-two affidavits in his favour, sentenced to two years in prison, to stand in the pillory twice and keep the peace for seven years. The charges appear trumped up, since few people, indeed, would have been able to sing an English song in rural west Wales (though his Welsh 'Marseillaise hymn' was performed). Judge George Hardinge's court speech and the harsh sentence were part of a campaign to cow Carmarthen's Unitarian hinterland into submission.[48] By comparison, in 1800 John Philips of Llangefni, north Wales, was sentenced to only one year in prison and bound over for two years for stating: 'I am a Jacobin and a Republican and know a Republican Government will be a much better one than the present … that the present King is a bad man and a sinner.'[49] The sentences reported from the West Country were even more lenient.[50] Tomos's appeal for a royal pardon was rejected,[51] and persecution continued during his time in prison. In 1802, Lord George Murray, Horsley's successor as Bishop of St David's, warned the Home Office that the stint in the pillory had been set up 'very advantageously' because Tomos's daughters were by his side 'in white dresses'. Learning of the Despard conspiracy to assassinate George III, Murray alleged that Tomos was[52]

> a very likely person to have papers in his possession which may lead to some discovery ... he was certainly formerly in correspondence with the societies in London ... he will ever be a dangerous member of Society, being of the most violent principles and having but too much influence amongst the people of this country from his abilities in writing in the Welch language.[53]

Despard was executed for High Treason in 1803.[54] If Murray himself had not died that June, further persecution may have lain in store for Tomos. As it was, his release from prison saw him 'at a loss to know what measures to take' and dreading 'returning to his old neighbourhood', where his accusers had turned even his wife against him.[55] In 1811, he accepted the call to be minister of the Unitarian chapel Hen Dŷ Cwrdd in industrial Aberdare and Merthyr Tydfil, where he died in 1833. He greatly furthered the Unitarian cause in this 'very populous town ... in the midst of the ironworks', according to 1816 visitor Richard Wright, though he was:

> under the necessity of employing in the loom. Could he be enabled to lay aside his business as a weaver entirely, I think his usefulness would be extended. I know of no man in Wales who seems so completely qualified to act a missionary as he is.[56]

To the end of his days, Tomos augmented his income further by working the vegetable plots of others, his diary entries indicating that poverty prevented him from paying rent for months on end.[57]

The experiences of fellow Unitarian David Jones (A Welsh Freeholder; 1765–1816) may not have been as harrowing, but his life trajectory also changed dramatically. A student and fellow lecturer of Richard Price at Hackney College, succeeding Joseph Priestley at the New Meeting House in Birmingham in 1792, and author of a series of radical Unitarian pamphlets,[58] he fell silent in 1795 when he was admitted to Lincoln's Inn. By 1800, he had graduated from Cambridge and been called to the bar.[59] His only known subsequent interaction with radical Dissent was the preparation of Tomos Glyn Cothi's unsuccessful plea for a royal pardon.[60] Nothing is known of the last fifteen years of his life. This fundamental break, necessitating a turn from Dissent and membership of the Anglican Church, remains unexplained but may well have been caused by his witnessing the Loyalist persecution of and violence against several of his teachers and their families.

The situation was not better in north Wales. To this day, little is known of David Davies (d. 1807), who had trained at the Dissenting academy at Swansea.[61] He ministered at Holywell Congregational chapel, in 1796, publishing *Y Geirgrawn* for 'y lliaws mochaidd' – his ironic translation of Burke's 'swinish multitude'.[62] Openly republican texts presented graphic descriptions of the cruelty of 'feudal tyranny' and celebrated the French Republic, which had 'secure[d] their rights as citizens and subjects of a free nation' (*diogelu ei breintiau fal dinasyddion a deiliaid gwlad rhydd*).[63] In 1800

Davies resigned his ministry at Holywell following 'unhappy misunderstandings' with the congregation.⁶⁴ Reappearing in Welshpool around 1800, he spent the last years of his life as the minister of Stoneway Independent chapel in Bridgnorth just over the border without any further participation in the public discourse.⁶⁵

Similar discontinuances, ruptures and migrations characterize the lives of other suspects. 'Rank Republican Leveller' William Jones of Llangadfan, whom the French Revolution jolted into composing odes on liberty and a Welsh national anthem, had his letters redirected to escape interception by the postmaster but was nevertheless sharply called to order by local magistrates in 1794.⁶⁶ In 1796, London-Welsh republican John Jones (Jac Glan-y-Gors; 1766–1821) was forced to abandon his Southwark tavern and make for his home village near Bala by the outraged reaction to his Paineite pamphlet *Seren tan Gwmmwl* (A Star under a Cloud).⁶⁷ According to local tradition, fellow-poet Rolant Huw provided a hiding place after Loyalist bard Dafydd Ionawr of Dolgellau had slammed the door in his face.⁶⁸ Equally interrupted were the lives of Dissenting ministers and adherents, printers and shopkeepers who appeared implicated in subversive activities through religion or profession. The radical periodical *Cylchgrawn Cyn-mraeg* was published by a succession of printers to keep ahead of persecution. Still, the Trefecca 'family' which brought out the first number feared that editor Morgan John Rhys's stance 'against secular and church government' (*yn erbyn llywodraeth y gwladaidd ac eglwysig*) would be their undoing. Titus Evans of Machynlleth, who printed part of the third number, lost his commission as Exciseman and moved to a port, ready to fly.⁶⁹ The all-permeating 'mist of suspicion' and ritual violence helps explain the remarkable joint meetings and desperate public declarations of loyalty to the Crown by Dissenting leaders of three counties in south-west Wales at the height of the Reeves campaign of 1792-3 and again in 1804.⁷⁰ Their repeated prostrations did not prevent the arrest and imprisonment of five Pembrokeshire Dissenters in the wake of the failed Fishguard invasion of 1797.⁷¹ Three men were released without trial after four weeks, but Baptist ministers Thomas John and Samuel Griffiths spent seven months in prison awaiting a trial for High Treason which collapsed when an anonymous Welsh 'treason trial' pamphlet composed by fellow Baptist and pacificist William Richards (1749–1818) laid open that the chief witness had been bribed by Anglican vigilantes.⁷² Nevertheless, on the first anniversary of the 1797 Fishguard invasion, the effigy of Dissenter Henry Dafydd, suspected of 'dealings with the French', was burnt publicly at market.⁷³

Emigration is a key category for inclusion in Johnston's 'lost generation', alongside illness, suicide, early death and a turning away from radicalism. Imagining America as the antidote to the oppressive 'old world' featured large in the writings of Welsh suspects, but some departed sooner than expected. In April 1794, Morgan John Rhys (1760–1805), a Millenarian Baptist minister from Glamorgan who had travelled to France in the wake of the Revolution, written anti-slavery pamphlets, founded Sunday schools and edited the first radical Welsh periodical in the Welsh language,⁷⁴ published a pamphlet urging emigration to America in which he cast Dissenters as the children of Israel fleeing from the tyranny of the Pharaos, who by remaining in Britain were 'supporting anti-Christ' (*gynnal anghrist*).⁷⁵ Exhorting artisans to emigrate to America was an offence in the 1790s⁷⁶ and may have occasioned his 'amazingly quick' (*hynod o sydyn*) departure from Carmarthen, forgotten until this anecdote of 1891:[77]

> In the year 1794 a Mr. Reed kept a hotel on the grounds where the Town Hall now stands. Morgan Rhys and his friends used to meet in a private room at this hotel. One night, about the close of July in the year stated, a stranger came suddenly in and asked for lodging there. After having had it, and been seated, he asked Mr. Reed if he knew a person in town by the name of Morgan Rhys. He received an affirmative answer, with the additional remark that Mr Rhys was a very good and a very respectable man. Then the stranger gave a hint that he had been sent from London, and that he had a warrant to arrest Morgan Rhys and to take him to the Capital (London). Mr. Reed promised to take the bailiff to the house of Mr. Rhys the next morning. Mr. Rhys happened to be in the hotel at that time, but in another room. Mr. Reed went to him and told him all, and also told him to flee at once without any delay. After Mr. Rhys had sent word to his friend, Mr. Watkins, and had given him some instructions, he fled, walking to Lampeter, and from thence to Newtown where he took a conveyance for Liverpool. After he had reached that place he made arrangements to sail for America, August 1st, but before he sailed Mr. Watkins reached Liverpool with clothes, etc., for Mr. R.[78]

In the 1930s, Rhys's first academic biographer devoted much effort to discrediting this oral tradition.[79] However, Rev. Joshua Watkins of Priory Church, Carmarthen, had himself related it to Carmarthen contemporaries E. Alcwyn Evans (to whose efforts as an antiquary we owe much fugitive radical material)[80] and Baptist author David Jones.[81] The earlier judgement of Thomas Shankland that it 'is not possible to get better historical testimony than from the lips of those who took part in the movements which are noted down' chimes better with current approaches than the disregard of the 1930s.[82] The timing of Rhys's departure was certainly not of his choosing;[83] he was pursuing publishing plans at the time, and his distress shines through on board the *Port Mary* on course for America.[84] Titus Evans, the printer of his *Cylchgrawn Cymraeg*, also considered emigrating 'in fear of being arrested or prosecuted by the Government' because of his connection with the 'Jacobin Rhys'.[85] Rhys himself chose to hide this aspect of his life in autobiographical notes written in America,[86] which may confirm Johnston's conclusion that 'writers often took great pains to keep hidden from prying eyes, of both the police and posterity' what had happened to them.[87] Rhys died early, aged only 44 in 1804, in the utopian Welsh settlement he had established and of which only the name Cambria County bears witness today.[88]

Political emigration and the idea of America left traces in other lives, too. William Jones distributed a seditious address at the Llanrwst eisteddfod meeting of 1791 which called on all 'indigenous Cambro-Britons' to sail for this 'promised land'.[89] Radical pamphleteer William Richards (1749–1818) lamented that his wish to emigrate to America was prevented by the refusal of his aged mother to accompany him.[90] Others left poetic traces. In March 1795, Sandemanian John Edwards composed 'A few Verses to persuade Christians to flee to America, out of the Way of the Dismal Outlook of this Country' (*Ychydig o Benillion er annogaeth i Broffeswyr fyned i America, oddiar yr olwg o Fyd Blin yn y Wlad hon*), which referred to Rhys as somebody who had already embarked on this journey to a better land, albeit 'at haste' (*ar frys*).⁹¹ Dafydd Glan Teifi (1769–1840) called on all to follow 'humanity' (*tiriondeb*) to 'dear Washington' (*at Washington anwyl*). His poem's fragmentation, ending as it does with 'to finish in the next' (*i'w orphen yn y nesaf*), sends a message, too.⁹² *Y Geirgrawn* ceased publication before the second part appeared.

Silenced voices

Having been accused of 'spreading riot and rebellion' (*lledu terfysg a gwrthryfel*),⁹³ its editor David Davies had adopted a more cautious approach and orders were multiplying 'however much some attempt to take a stand against it' (*er cymmaint mai rhai wedi ceisio ei wrthwynebu*).⁹⁴ *Y Geirgrawn*'s sudden disappearance with number nine is indicative of the interconnected taming and silencing of Welsh radical voices. The preface to Thomas Robert's 1798 anticolonial pamphlet *Cwyn yn erbyn Gorthrymder* (A Complaint against Oppression) explained that his intention had been to send it to Davies's *Geirgrawn*, 'but some *Knaves* (Scoundrels) took great care to frighten the man, and prevent him from going ahead with his work, and threatened to drive him out of the country (as I heard rumoured) for publishing beneficial things that struck at the root of oppression'.⁹⁵ The Welsh Freeholder's pamphlet war with Bishop Samuel Horsley in defence of Unitarianism came to pass only after his *Letter to the Right Reverend Samuel, Lord Bishop of St. David's* had been rejected by the *Gloucester Journal*, which attacked him to boot.⁹⁶ Iolo Morganwg may have been a procrastinating laudanum addict, but the harassment he experienced must have reinforced a self-censorship that prevented him from publishing radical poems like 'Breiniau Dyn' (The Rights of Man), perhaps written as early as 1789 and publicly performed at *Gorsedd* gatherings until their suppression in 1798. Anecdotes and biographical notes point to the taming of others. Poet Dafydd Glan Teifi resurfaced after the Napoleonic Wars to extol Sir Thomas Picton, bloody governor of Trinidad and Welsh 'hero of Waterloo' instead of 'dear Washington'.⁹⁷ The radical 'Welsh Shakespeare' Thomas Edwards (Twm o'r Nant; 1739–1810) was urged by fellow poet Robert Davies to respond to the violent suppression of the 1795 Denbigh corn and anti-militia riots, but the resulting poem was peculiarly non-committal, though Twm was prepared to vilify the elite in a private letter to Jac Glan-y-gors.⁹⁸ The latter's republican pamphlet *Seren tan Gwmmwl* (A Star under a Cloud) not only evoked a bitter political dispute in *Y Geirgrawn* but led to the intimidation of booksellers so that the author prefaced his equally republican sequel *Toriad y Dydd* (The Break of Dawn) with the plea 'that the people who call themselves Gentlemen in Wales will not be so oppressive as to threaten to ruin the livelihoods of booksellers because they desire to sell that which is true'.⁹⁹

At times, intimidation and silencing acknowledge the power of translation and indigenous political literature, which paradoxically furthered forgetting, since the majority of hegemonic researchers remain unable to access Welsh sources or imagine their existence. Tomos Glyn Cothi's continued persecution was justified by his 'influence amongst the people of this country from his abilities in writing in the Welch language',[100] a judgement born out by the contents of his *Trysorfa Gymmysgedig*.[101] William Richards, pioneer of radical self-translation and proud member of the American Society for the Abolition of Slavery, advertised an English version of his (anonymous) treason trial pamphlet *Cwyn y Cystuddiedig* as *The Triumph of Innocency*, but like Wordsworth, dissuaded by Joseph Johnson of publishing an epistle to Bishop Watson following the conviction of Gilbert Wakefield,[102] gave in to fear. Writing to American Baptist Samuel Jones on 19 March 1798, Richards noted that 'one of the most moderate of the clergy' had hinted that if he published an English version 'they would not answer for the consequence. I was therefore advised to defer it, and there the matter now rests'.[103] It rested until 2014, when an English translation appeared.[104] Richards turned away from political controversy around 1800 to write a celebrated *History of Lynn* and engage in increasingly obscure religious debates.[105] He remained attached to America, though, bequeathing his library to Rhode Island University.[106]

Perhaps the greatest loss resulted from the two-year incarceration, continued persecution and radical silencing of Tomos Glyn Cothi. The only surviving sizeable manuscript *Y Gell Gymysg* (The Mixed Cell) is testament to his bilingual, creative, radical mind,[107] while three heavily annotated almanacs from 1814, 1817 and 1818, and marginalia in contemporary pamphlets allow insights into his continued radicalism, but also his dire poverty.[108] Fear may have motivated Tomos's wife, mother of eleven children, to destroy most papers while he was in prison. After his release, Tomos had to tread carefully to avoid a fine of £100, a frightening prospect for the man of few financial means he remained to the end of his life. His first biographer judged that this accounted for his silence during the years 'in the desert' (*yn yr anialwch*).[109] The radicalism of his *Trysorfa Gymmysgedig*, of *Y Gell Gymysg* and of his Priestley, Lindsay and Belsham translations, had disappeared from the Welsh-English vocabulary he composed in prison and published in 1804,[110] or the hymnal that appeared in 1811.[111] Fugitive radical poetry by him survives in manuscript thanks mainly to the daring work of Alcwyn C. Evans, whose innocently entitled multi-volume *History of Carmarthen* contains a wealth of material by the likes of Iolo Morganwg and Tomos Glyn Cothi, their provenance and meaning hidden from unfriendly eyes through deleting titles and shortening bardic names to initials like 'T.G.C.', a code meaningful only for those intimately familiar with the Welsh language and culture of the time.[112] The English radical literature on which Welsh Dissenters drew also remained carefully hidden, some of it so well that even in the twenty-first century, two volumes of the *Hog's Wash* which, from a base at Lloyd Jack farm near Lampeter circulated in rural Wales into the 1810s, have not come to light.[113]

Johnston judged that to appreciate the long-term effects of the arctic 1790s on the development of British literature required recognizing the 'aggregate of individual consequences, and in particular in biographical terms'.[114] The biographies of all those mentioned above show ruptures and discontinuances resulting from persecution, harassment and intimidation, enacted locally, independently and under guidance from London. The resultant climate of fear, suspicion and self-censorship redirected, tamed, silenced or destroyed radical voices and texts. This silencing of radical life and literature was followed by a post-Napoleonic forgetting of those aspects of generation 1789 which did not fit the self image of the Welsh as respectable members of the

British Empire, an ancient Celtic proto-Christian tribe descended from Gomer, grandson of Noah.

Managing public memory

The processes set in train between the 1790s and 1815 were complemented by the reshaping of biographies, reputations and legacies until they fitted a scramble for respectability in the face of the Welsh working-class risings and community violence of the 1830s and 1840s which lead to the infamous governmental report of 1847 that blamed the Welsh language and religious nonconformity for Welsh backwardness, immorality and irrationality.[115] The religious census of 1851 may have revealed that the Welsh were, indeed, a 'Nonconformist nation' headed for political supremacy of the Liberal (and ultimately the Labour) party, but the nation's leaders firmly steered Welsh culture into a safe haven of ancient Christianity, and a public bardism controlled by rules which forbade political or religious controversy. Only the Europe-wide revolutionary activities of 1848 led to a public (re-)emergence of some radical works of generation 1789.

For Iolo Morganwg, the 'cleansing' encompassed sanctification of the man, a tight management of archives and the de-politicization of his public legacy, *Gorsedd Beirdd Ynys Prydain*. Quaker Elijah Waring, Iolo's friend and main biographer, and Iolo's son Taliesin ab Iolo ensured that radical evidence was hidden, while anecdotes recounting picaresque adventures, humourized encounters with state authority, and mythical biographical details were reworked to fit general folklore motifs. From 1826 until the early 1920s, three biographies, and numerous sketches, encyclopaedia entries and articles on Iolo highlighted his achievements as an antiquary; stressed his eccentricities as an early vegetarian; and elevated him to an almost superhuman latter-day saint. By the 1850s some stories resembled folk tales with interchangeable characters, in which Iolo or an unknown Welshman was pitched against Shakespeare, Pitt or the king. Others highlighted Iolo's disappointment with the French Revolution and his disapproval of Paine's alcohol consumption, or downplayed political credentials by humanizing state authority. Iolo's harassment during Pitt's 'Reign of Terror' had by 1851 been fully reworked into an encounter with a decidedly benevolent Prime Minister:

> Well, Mr Williams, said Mr Pitt, I'm glad that there was nothing dangerous for you in these papers; you can take them and go home, as you see fit. Sir, answered the poet you brought me and my papers here without my leave; so I'm confident that you'll be enough of a gentleman to carry them back. This is but reasonable, said Pitt, and then to the servant, Set some refreshments before Mr Williams, and after that, send him wherever he wishes to go in my carriage.[116]

Iolo's religious radicalism was equally forgotten. The first full Welsh-language biography, published by fellow Unitarian Thomas Stephens in 1852–3, contained a paragraph on Iolo's visit to the incarcerated Tomos Glyn Cothi but did not cite a single document or describe a single act devoted to Iolo's significant role in the formation of the South Wales Unitarian Society in 1802.[117] The tenor of these anecdotal writings on Iolo explains why the twenty-one lines dedicated to him in the 1908 biographical dictionary of *Eminent Welshmen* described him as 'an antiquary and poet ... [who] was esteemed by many illustrious men of his age, and [Robert] Southey'.[118]

Taliesin ab Iolo, respectable schoolmaster of industrial Merthyr Tydfil,[119] shaped his father's literary legacy. In 1829, he published *Cyfrinach Beirdd Ynys Prydain* (The Secret of the Bards of the Isle of Britain) on behalf of his father, while his 'information management' restricted use of the bardo-druidic material to himself, fuelling a prize-winning ode on Druidism and a lauded essay on the (invented) bardic runic script *Coelbren y Beirdd*. He ensured the survival of Iolo's archive by binding diverse notes on geography, apple growing, swallows, medicine and radicalism, into sixty neat volumes, but released fragments only to those who needed convincing of the antiquity of druidism or intent on engaging with 'innocent' legacies, such as folk song.[120] This changed little when the volumes were transferred to Llanofer Court, home of cultural patron Lady Augusta Hall, in 1851. A keen Celtophile, she continued Taliesin's policy so that the only major work based on the archive was *Barddas* by disciple John Williams, which in 1862 welded disparate material into a religious system utilized by neo-Druids to this day.[121]

By then, the *Gorsedd*, invented as a central pacifist assembly for a radical nation, had been attached to the revived medieval eisteddfod competitions. Combined, they developed into the annual Royal National Eisteddfod of Wales, a largely apolitical event that has survived into the twenty-first century. Depoliticization set in during the Napoleonic Wars,[122] when Bishop of St David's Thomas Burgess, patriotic Anglican priests and Welsh gentry started appropriating instead of suppressing Welsh culture. In 1814, Reverend Eliezer Williams, vicar of Lampeter and a friend of Burgess, had warned that 'there is a nest of sectarians and republicans in Glamorganshire, and even in this vicinity', advising to handle this by takeover:

> I send you, by this day's post, a Welsh paper called the 'Seren Gomer'. I differ from many of my brother clergymen, who are of the opinion that the publication should in no way be encouraged; for as we cannot prevent its being circulated, and as it is in sectarian and democratic hands, I think every friend of the establishment ought to watch it with a jealous eye, and contribute something occasionally towards occupying its columns with useful and edifying matter.[123]

Bishop Burgess applied this advice at the *Gorsedd* assembly of July 1819. Iolo Morganwg, the only Dissenter on the organizing committee, apparently seized the chance to legitimize his invention by binding it to the eisteddfod, which had enjoyed royal and aristocratic patronage since 1176.[124] While ensuring the survival of the *Gorsedd*, he buried any residual radicalism, since by publicizing admittance of Anglican Bishop Thomas Burgess to the druidic order, Welsh bardo-druidism declared itself apolitical. The contemporary press judged that the day

> revealed that religious prejudice had been left outside the audience by the mighty and the common. To see the *Bishop of St David's* thus honoured by an old *Dissenter*

was a sight a thousand times more beloved by the proponents of love and general goodwill, and opponents of prejudice and partisanship, than had the Arch-Bishop of Canterbury, with all his robes and his Archiepiscopal pomp been seen fulfilling the same task.[125]

On public display was a culture untrammelled by political or religious controversy, a politically inoffensive focus for a subaltern nation. From the 1820s, patriotic gentry were only too willing to finance eisteddfod prize competitions and preside over grand 'old rituals', and a 'royal' was added to all proceedings. In August 1834, Taliesin ab Iolo opened the aptly named 'Gwent and Dyfed Royal Eisteddfod and Musical Festival' in the presence of patrons like the Marquess of Bute and the Duchess of Kent; the equally grand and aristocracy-sponsored Abergavenny eisteddfodau held between 1832 and 1853 furthered Celtic scholarship but equally kept politics at arm's length and were patronized by European and British aristocracy.[126] The subjects of eisteddfod poem and essay competitions had long changed from 'Rights of Man' and 'Truth' to imperial war heroes, Queen Victoria's family, 'Jerusalem', the 'Antiquity of the Druids' and the 'Superior Morality of the Welsh Working Classes'. Instead of reciting radical poetry in the open air, participants of all classes now toasted the Royal family at grand dinners and sang 'God Save the Queen' at the close of mass choir competitions. Even former radicals in iron metropolis Merthyr Tydfil were by the 1860s proud to report that the subscription library they had established in 1842 'was never committed to any active expression of radicalism. The dignity of literature always remained about it'.[127]

Scholars, poets and translators

The taming of Iolo Morganwg and his public legacy was the most spectacular, but related nineteenth-century narratives on Tomos Glyn Cothi, Morgan John Rhys and other 'suspects' shed light on different ways public legacies were shaped by a generation keen to transform radicals into self-made poets, preachers, teachers and translators. One of the ways this process may be charted are the national biographies that in Wales, as elsewhere in Europe, began to assemble a canon of national worthies.[128] Tomos Glyn Cothi did not make it into the first effort, the 1852 *Enwogion Cymru. A Biographical Dictionary of Eminent Welshmen*.[129] A first essay on him did not appear until 1872, though the result of a competition at the 1853 Aberdare Carw Coch society eisteddfod. Casting him as a morally elevated 'apostle Paul',[130] his 1790s radicalism appears as outdated as witch hunts, which had

> completely disappeared ... There was also much upset and threats of punishment about the selling and owning of political authors, like Paine, Hobbes, Volney and others. But how useful where such things? And as Lord Brougham said about Carlisle's writings, the less secrecy one makes of them, the less the country will wish for them ... Are not things a million times more dangerous being sold on almost every bench at our markets these days, without any din or persecution because of them, and not one damage emanating from them?[131]

The remainder of the essay focused on illustrations of his patience, which allowed him to 'smoothly row though the bitterest arguments' (*rhwyfo yn esmwyth trwy y dadleuon chwerwaf*);[132] reproduced a poem on 'Knowledge' (*Gwybodaeth*) and Loyalist verses ascribed to him after the attempted French invasion of 1797; and closed with a list of translations. Very little of the promised material from *Y Gell Gymysg* was included. Only his 1833 memorial plaque in the Aberdare chapel where he ministered from 1813 notes a 'gratitude for his devotion to the cause of Civil and Religious Liberty'.[133] Short pieces in the Unitarian periodical *Yr Ymofynydd* in the 1890s link him to Iolo and cast him as a disappointed Samaritan whose last days were blighted by a thieving 'gwalch' (*knave*).[134] In a series on 'Aberdare celebrities', he only made fourth of five.[135] His entry in the 1908 *Eminent Welshmen* focused on his Unitarian hymns and the Welsh-English dictionary prepared 'while in prison', highlighting that 'his early education was very limited, but his desire for knowledge was intense'.[136]

Morgan John Rhys was not among the *Enwogion Cymru* of 1852 either. A first ten-page assessment of his life and work did not appear until 1891 when Thomas Lewis collected short notes into an essay centred on religion: from Rhys's 1792 journey to France, because the 'revolution had opened the way to the circulation of the gospel and the Bible in that country' (*wedi agor y ffordd i gylchrediad y Beibl a'r efengyl yn y wlad hono*), to his contribution to Raike's Sunday School movement, and his wish to evangelize the 'American Indians' (*Indiaid America*).[137] His emigration, associated with Tomos Glyn Cothi's incarceration, was condemned by adding the opinion of contemporary Christmas Evans (by then one of the icons of non-radical Welsh Nonconformity), who scolded 1790s emigrants for 'looking badly on their religious and civic privileges in Britain, and assuming that paradise was to be had in Ameria' (*i edrych yn wael ar eu breintiau crefyddol a gwladol ym Mhrydain, a thybiasant bod paradwys i'w cael yn America*).[138] The fact that Rhys and 'many families' suffered hardships and that he died young now appeared as God's judgement. Rhys's flight also meant that archives were harder to retrieve. The first short publication presenting written sources, published in 1899 in Pennsylvania, may have opened with the true statement that 'he was not properly known nor properly appreciated by the age in which he lived, nor the one that followed', but it was full of mistakes and inaccuracies.[139] Unsurprisingly, *Eminent Welshmen* muted his radicalism at the expense of a proud nod to colonial expansion by highlighting that Rhys 'bought a large tract of land in the Alleghany Mountains, which he called Cambria. This afterwards gave its name to Cambria County'.[140]

Of the remaining 'suspects' David Davies and Jac Glan-y-Gors are absent from the 1852 *Enwogion Cymru*, while others were emasculated by shaving away radicalism and highlighting cultural dependency. Perhaps the most telling entry was that of Dafydd Dafis:

> For many years, he kept a very celebrated school, which was attended, from time to time, by a vast number of youth from the surrounding districts, and other parts of the country, many of whom became eminent scholars, and filled distinguished situations in the Church and elsewhere. His poetical works were published under the title of 'Telyn Dewi'. This consists, in a great measure, of versions from

English authors; and, particularly, his translation of Gray's Elegy has always been deservedly admired.[141]

Very short entries on radicals like ballad singer and playwright Hugh Jones of Llangwm only mentioned his 'dramatic pieces, called Interludes, which were very popular among the Welsh peasantry during the last century'.[142] David Jones received a grudging acknowledgement of some pamphlets 'produced by him under the name of a "Welsh Freeholder"'.[143]

More members of generation 1789 made it into the 1908 *Eminent Welshmen*, their radicalism by now easier on the mind than Liberal ascendancy, trade unions, strikes and the new threat of the Independent Labour Party. All of whom had forgotten even the radical Iolo Morganwg.[144] When Liberal poet E. Ben Morus (Myfyr Teifi) called on the Labour party to include men like Iolo Morganwg 'on the roll call of its early soldiers' (*ar gofres ei milwyr cynnar*), he found no echo.[145] Generation 1789 had been transformed into self-taught teachers, preachers, scholars and translators, their early difficulties answering to ideals of the 'self-made man', which in Wales included mastering English. Dafis's entry still highlighted 'his imitative faculties' in poetry and as a 'translator into Welsh'.[146] William Jones's 'education was of the scantiest kind, but … he acquired a sufficient mastery of English to write in that language with ease and elegance'.[147] William Richards of Lynn

> had only one year at school, but his thirst of knowledge was insatiable and he soon became thoroughly acquainted with his Bible, and with the best English authors … He was the author of the 'History of Lynn', an elaborate work which is replete with information … He wrote his native language with great accuracy, and during his frequent visits to the Principality, he constantly preached in Welsh.[148]

Only Jac Glan-y-Gors, 'his poems … exceedingly rich in natural wit and humour', was acknowledged as the author of a 'little book called "Seren dan Gwmmwl", which favoured republicanism, and fiercely attacked monarchical government in general'. Even so, criticism and an insinuated lack of interest in the 'little book' dominate the last sentence that 'the author ably defended himself, to which no one seems to have replied'.[149] The Welsh had clearly never been interested in revolution and republics.

Revolutionary interruption

The narrative of Generation 1789 as apolitical self-made educators, poets, preachers and translators was rarely punctured. During the Merthyr Tydfil election campaign of 1835, the 'Ghost' of Tomos Glyn Cothi was apparently used to remind Dissenters of ironmaster and MP John Josiah Guest's earlier political convictions.[150] Iolo's radicalism surfaced in short-lived radical publications like *Y Gwladgarwr* (The Patriot) which in passing asserted that 'one of the governing principles in his career through the world was liberty'.[151] His 1798 poem 'Breiniau Dyn' (Rights of Man) did not enter the public sphere until 1841 as a supplement to the bilingual Chartist serial *Udgorn Cymru. The Trumpet of Wales*, which ran to only nine numbers. While the text is one of the few direct links between the Welsh radicalism of the 1790s and Welsh Chartism, it hardly disturbed the much-better known public image of eccentric saintly antiquary and bard.[152]

Only 1848 temporarily publicly reunited the 'single democratic tradition of the Jacobin 1790s [which had] splintered under the pulverizing hammer of class formation'.[153] The newly founded Unitarian periodical *Yr Ymofynnydd* (The Enquirer) augmented its regular column on 'France, its revolution and its effects' (*Ffrainc, ei chwyldroad a'i effaethau*) with recycled, amended and new poetry. The year 1848 was portrayed as an orderly change of the form of government but also as a warning to all monarchies:

> As of 24 February, there is no King above the French. On that day a *Republic* was set up in Paris, the capital. Soon, it was announced in every city and town, and it was received without any opposition in every corner of the country. With this change in the form of government, the exactly appropriate men were appointed to be a *Provisional Government* to administrate matters of the state until the National Assembly had set things in a satisfactory and steady state. Since then, these men – some of the most famous of their nation – have been fulfilling their various offices with quite considerable commendation; and so far, everything has proceeded as quietly as one can expect. It is difficult to assess – impossible so far – what the effects of the revolution in France on other countries will be. The present situation of the country, the liveliness, number and heroism of its inhabitants, as well as the memories of their achievements of the recent war are such that the revolution in France should not be disregarded … Woe to whoever will attempt to obstruct the work of establishing their liberty: and further, they will take the party of every weak nation which intends to struggle against their oppressors. This should be taken as a warning and as a threat. Thus European monarchies are judged by their *good behaviour*.[154]

In December 1847, a version of Dafydd Dafis's poem 'Chwyldroad Ffrainc' (The French Revolution) appeared, with the remark that many had been 'unhappy' about its exclusion from the anthology *Telyn Dewi* (Dewi's Harp) of 1824.[155] Editor Daniel Ddu (Daniel Evans, 1792–1846) had excised it because verses like the following threatened Dafis's image as apolitical schoolmaster:

> France turned an eminent, throned head – and His gold crown to the soil of the grave
> Where did the mighty Monarch go?
> He perished in huge disgrace!
> Now France will be on the throne and, – an amazing Queen of the countries
> Myriads will fly free from their bonds,
> Under her tender wings.[156]

April 1848 brought Iolo Morganwg's 'Gwawr Rhyddid' (The Dawn of Liberty), rather disappointingly religious considering the title,[157] but in June 1848 new stanzas by a poet who wisely chose to sign only 'E. T.' transported European events to Britain:

A new warning has now – been sounded / To those in highly elevated ranks,
Not to oppress, and smother / The masses with immense burdens …
Some thousands are for rising up – / Under this Crown here
Though they are keeping the peace, good will / for the lenient reign of Victoria …
We'll refuse Senate entry – from the County / To the dishonest member,
The arrogant are better far away to be honest / To lock them out if we can.[158]

Yet even in this most radical of nineteenth-century Welsh religious periodicals, the editor noted that revolution was not the British way, claiming that the author hinted at 'reform which could be made in the government of Great Britain, by removing the oppression and the hardship under which the greatest part of the subjects presently groan'.[159] The year of revolutions closed with an updated version of Tomos Glyn Cothi's 1796 radical translation of 'La Marseillaise' as 'Cân Rhyddid' (The Song of Liberty), clearly attributed to him for the first time:[160]

Oh Liberty! Who would reject you
Once having felt your heavenly fire?
Can more uncalled-for oppression
Prevent your complete victory?

Oh! Spread your banner across the whole world!
Bring complete and necessary riddance,
Standing steadfast forever for its cause,
To give success, peace and a joy.

(Chorus) The right of man – through the world,
May fairly and squarely win the day;
Fearlessly – with united will,
Shall we walk free from our bonds.[161]

The year 1848 remained the only notable radical intrusion into a public narrative of generation 1789 from which revolutionary radicalism and republicanism had been largely excised. By 1871, the gaze of the Welsh press was firmly on Prussia's military prowess and European nation building instead of the Paris Commune, and no attempt was made to reconnect with the French Revolution of 1789; by the onset of the new Welsh Labour movement in the 1890s, any Welsh radicalism of the 1790s had been forgotten.

Twentieth-century reassessments

Academic assessment and a modest assignment of 'retrospective' came with the easier availability of sources at the National Library of Wales from 1907, important anniversaries of Generation 1789 and the development of Welsh history as an academic discipline from the 1920s.[162] Given the importance of Iolo Morganwg's public legacy for Welsh nationhood and the enduring attraction of what must have been an extremely charismatic persona, it does not surprise that this process began with him. As his archive moved from Llanofer

Court to the National Library of Wales in 1916, academics jumped on the opportunity to scrutinize the material, albeit largely to prove long-held suspicions of forgery.[163] The hundredth anniversary of Iolo's death in 1926 was therefore marked by celebration but also condemnation. Local circles sponsored a plaque to the 'Stone Mason, Bard of Liberty, Antiquary and One of the Foremost Patrons of Welsh Literature and History' in Cowbridge High Street, where his shop had been,[164] and the Unitarian *Ymofynydd* dedicated a whole issue to him, albeit a year later and focusing on his religious radicalism.[165] On the other hand, the first scholarly monograph on his legacy *Iolo Morganwg a Chywyddau'r Ychwanegiad* (Iolo Morganwg and the Poems of the Appendix) by central cultural figure John Morris-Jones branded him an arch-corrupter, whose 'soiled hands' (*dwylo halogedig*) had tainted national traditions and sources.[166] The public repercussions entailed Iolo's wholesale denunciation as a 'forger', 'rogue' and 'disagreeable person' motivated by 'unbridled hate',[167] which lasted to the closing decades of the twentieth century and a research project on 'Iolo Morganwg and the Romantic Tradition in Wales'.[168] Only in 2009 was a plaque on 'the site of the first meeting of the Gorsedd of Bards of the Island of Britain' installed at Primrose Hill, Regents Park,[169] following campaigning and patronage by project leader and eminent historian Geraint H. Jenkins, whose monograph on *The Political Radicalism of Iolo Morganwg* appeared in 2012, a Welsh version published in 2018.[170]

Other members of generation 1789 did not fall from grace in the same way because public memory of them was faint, but significantly their modest rediscovery was framed in terms of religious radicalism. The hundredth anniversary of Tomos Glyn Cothi's death in 1933 led to a small exhibition of his publications and manuscripts at the National Library of Wales, among them two letters by Theophilus Lindsey and *Y Gell Gymmysg*.[171] A short bibliography of his works appeared yet belittled him as short of 'a great litterateur' because most of 'his publications, apart from the dictionary and a volume of hymns, were translations from English'.[172] *Yr Ymofynydd* dedicated twenty-three pages to a structured exploration of his life and work focused on him as 'Apostle of Liberty' (*Apostol Rhyddid*).[173] Even in the 1930s, the ideas of generation 1789, including Thomas Paine, were fitted into a Christian tradition:

> One influence on their works one observes clearly is that of the Puritan tradition ... the right of man to think for himself was the Puritan credo; therefore it was the enemy of the dictator king and the state church alike ... One should reject the authority of the past, the governance of the living by the dead, and replace old 'historical movements' with democratic ones. And that is Tom Paine's big argument later on, and the same ideas exactly are found in the Welsh reformers, like Morgan John Rhys, Iolo Morganwg, Jac Glan y Gors, Thomas Roberts Llwynrhudol, Dr William Richards and Thomas Glyn Cothi.[174]

As part of the 'Centenary Celebrations', a memorial plaque to this 'Great Soul' was attached to Capel Sant Silyn cottage in the isolated hamlet of Gwernogle where Tomos was born, remembering him as 'Preacher, Reformer, Hymnist, Author' (*Pregethwr, Diwygiwr, Emynydd, Llenor*), and his 'Liberty Song' was performed.[175] A fuller attempt to assess his radical legacy did not emerge until 1963, when Geraint Dyfnallt Owen published a slim, but closely researched Welsh-language volume which charted the patronage extended to Tomos by English Unitarians, paid homage to the political character of his periodical and unearthed some of the results of bardic competitions.[176] A whole chapter was dedicated to the radical politics he pursued in the hinterland of 'riotous' market town Carmarthen. Though the volume has become a springboard for this author's interest in Tomos Glyn Cothi, it has to date only been followed by one substantial article on the 'horrid affair' of his incarceration.[177] The cottage where he was born and first established Unitarianism in Wales has been demolished.

As a distinct school of professional Welsh history writing developed after the Great War three authors – David Davies, John James Evans and R. T. Jenkins – began to explore eighteenth-century politics and personalities as part of their wider research. In 1926, Davies published *The Influence of the French Revolution on Welsh Life and Literature* (the only English-language volume on Generation 1789 until long after the Second World War), followed in 1928 by Evans's *Dylanwad y Chwyldro Ffrengig ar Lenyddiaeth Cymru* (The Influence of the French Revolution on Welsh Literature).[178] R. T. Jenkins, most renowned of the three and first editor of the *Dictionary of Welsh Biography*, provided two overview volumes on Welsh history in the eighteenth and early nineteenth centuries for the newly established University of Wales Press in 1928 and 1933, tellingly, in its *Cyfres y Brifysgol a'r Werin*, i.e. 'University and Common People Series'.[179] The first full-length monograph on *Morgan John Rhys a'i Amserau* (Morgan John Rhys and His Times) by John James Evans was part of this rediscovery. Evans's raw research is still valuable, though like Emsley, his reliance on official printed sources rejected a possible membership of Rhys in the 'Friends of the People' and suggestions of Welsh branches.[180] Rhys's 1794 departure was interpreted as a planned migration, referencing contemporary comments that he had 'gone to America', Rhys's warning that he may have to leave soon and (counterintuitively) a diary entry on journey that he had escaped the 'political storm' (*tymhestl boliticaidd*) of his fatherland.[181] Like his Victorian predecessors, Evans framed the movement of dozens of leading Dissenters to America negatively as an 'emigration sickness' or 'fever' (*clefyd ymfudo; twymyn ymfudo*).[182] Overall, much of the study was taken up with the British educational, anti-slavery and missionary movements into which Rhys fitted. The chapter on 'The Movements for Political and Religious Liberty' (*Y Symudiadau o Blaid Rhyddid Gwleidyddol a Chrefyddol*) may have been the most substantial, yet it persisted in placing generation 1789 in the 'Puritan tradition' (*y traddodiad Piwritanaidd*),[183] only dedicating some ten pages to Rhys's stance for political liberty in Wales and America.

Conclusion

In 1933, R. T. Jenkins had described generation 1789 as 'wan candles' (*canhwyllau gwelw*), unable to exert much influence on 'unthinking commoners' (*y werin ddifeddwl*).[184] In 1962, Gwyn Alf Williams kick-started a reassignment of significance with an article on 'Morgan John Rhys and Volney's *Ruins of Empires*',[185] followed by a series of publications that moved Generation 1789 firmly from puritanism to political radicalism,[186] and concomitant Welsh-nation building efforts into an international context of subaltern responses to the French Revolution of 1789:

In the 1790s, a handful of intellectuals in Wales, in common with men like them from other 'non-historic' peoples in Europe, those antiquarians, historians, poets, of the Czechs, the Catalans, Serbs, Croats, who were stamping nations out of the ground and weaving tricolours out of old legends, summoned the Welsh to the re-creation of a Nation they had rediscovered. ... This Welsh Nation of the intellectuals was born of an alternative society which had been slowly forming in Wales under the carapace of the gentry-parson squirearchy and which, no less that that *ancien régime*, was a product of Great Britain with its Atlantic dimension.[187]

Williams's work substantially influenced Geraint H. Jenkins, whose publications prepared the ground for the 'Iolo Morgannwg and the Romantic Tradition in Wales' project, and the wider research conducted by scholars like Hywel M. Davies, John Barrell, Jon Mee and Damian Walford Davies.

Yet, despite the rediscovery of the radical lives, transnational connections, reputations and voices of Generation 1789, which has contributed some academic acknowledgement, public awareness and commemoration of this senior radical Welsh tradition, it remains very much in the shadow of nineteenth-century Liberal heroes like 'apostle of peace' Henry Richard, and twentieth-century Welsh Labour greats, such as Aneurin Bevan. Marginalized by poverty, a rurality and the use of a subaltern language, the silencing of a Welsh 1790s radicalism that failed to generate mass appeal was almost pre-programmed 'at the moment of fact creation'.[188] Political Welsh-language publishing, then perhaps at its zenith, was drowned in a flood of religious material during the subsequent 'golden age' of Welsh-language publishing.[189] The few Welsh publications of the new radicalism of the 1830s and 1840s made only sparing use of Jacobin material, partly because it had been destroyed or was hidden in inaccessible archives but also because theirs was a new, working-class tradition. By the time trade unionism and Labour politics dominated the Welsh public sphere, the texts were inaccessible to a by then mainly English-speaking working class, while their artisan creators – remodelled into apolitical preachers and teachers by the Welsh Victorians – appeared irrelevant. Even though eisteddfod and *Gorsedd* may be interpreted as nineteenth-century 'people's universities', their apolitical loyalism and visual medievalism have made it difficult for twentieth-century historians to fit them into a tradition of Welsh history writing that had highlighted party politics, radicalism and Welsh Labour movements. Unsurprisingly, Generation 1789 thus lost most of its 'retrospective significance' for a narrative that constructed the nation as characterized by its working-class traditions so that the evidence of their radical work remained hidden to the wider world until almost the end of the twentieth century.

Notes

1   Michel-Rolph Trouillot, *Silencing the Past: Power and the Production of History. With a New Foreword by Hazel V. Carby* (Boston: Beacon Press, 2015), 27–8.
2   Kenneth R. Johnston, 'Whose History? My Place or Yours? Republican Assumptions and Romantic Traditions', in *Romanticism, History, Historicism Essays on an*

Orthodoxy, ed. Damien Walford Davies (New York and London: Routledge, 2009), 81 (79–102).

3 Alyssa Mt. Pleasant, Caroline Wigginton and Kelly Wisecup, 'Materials and Methods in Native American and Indigenous Studies: Completing the Turn', *The William and Mary Quarterly*, 75, no. 2 (2018), 225 [207–36]. I am grateful to my colleague Rachel Herrmann for drawing my attention to readings on Native American and indigenous history.

4 For exceptions, see Katrina Navickas, *Loyalism and Radicalism in Lancashire, 1798-1815* (Oxford: Oxford University Press, 2009); John Barrell, *Edward Pugh of Ruthin 1763-1813. 'A Native Artist'* (Cardiff: University of Wales Press, 2013).

5 Gregory Claeys, 'General Introduction', in *Political Writings of the 1790s. Volume 1: Radicalism and Reform: Responses to Burke 1790-1791*, ed. Idem (London: William Pickering, 1995), lv.

6 John James Evans, *Morgan John Rhys a'i Amserau* (Caerdydd: UWP, 1935), 120–2; Marion Löffler (with Bethan Jenkins), *Political Pamphlets and Sermons from Wales, 1790-1805* (Cardiff: University of Wales Press, 2014), xi–xii, 4–11.

7 Eiluned Rees, *Libri Walliae. A Catalogue of Welsh Books and Books Printed in Wales 1546-1820* (Aberystwyth: National Library of Wales, 1987); Geraint H. Jenkins, 'The Cultural Uses of the Welsh Language', in *The Welsh Language before the Industrial Revolution*, ed. Idem (Cardiff: University of Wales Press, 1997), 369–406.

8 David A. Change, 'The Good Written Word of Life: The Native Hawaiian Appropriation of Textuality', *The William and Mary Quarterly*, 75, no. 2 (2018), 255 (237–58); Ever since Michael Hechter, *Internal Colonialism. The Celtic Fringe in British National Development* (1979; new edition, New Brunswick, 1999), Welsh historians have explored Wales's (colonial) status. See Martin Johnes, *Wales: England's Colony?* (Cardigan: Parthian, 2019).

9 Gwyn Alf Williams, 'Druids and Democrats: Organic Intellectuals and the First Welsh Nation', in idem, *The Welsh in Their History* (London and Canberra: Croom Helm, 1982), 46.

10 See Damian Walford Davies, *Presences that Disturb. Models of Romantic Identity in the Literature and Culture of the 1790s* (Cardiff: University of Wales Press, 2000); idem and Linda Pratt (eds.), *Wales and the Romantic Imagination* (Cardiff: University of Wales Press, 2007); Hywel M. Davies, 'Morgan John Rhys and James Bicheno: Anti-Christ and the French Revolution in England and Wales', *Bulletin of the Board of Celtic Studies*, XXIX, no. 1 (1980), 111–27.

11 Trouillot, *Silencing the Past*, 23–5.

12 Clive Emsley, 'An Aspect of Pitt's Terror: Prosecution for Sedition during the 1790s', *Social History*, 6, no. 2 (1981), 155–84.

13 Steve Poole, 'Pitt's Terror Reconsidered: Jacobinism and the Law in Two South-Western Counties, 1791–1803', *Southern History. A Review of the History of Southern England*, 17 (1995), 65, 69 [65–87].

14 Geraint H. Jenkins, 'The Bard of Liberty during William Pitt's Reign of Terror', in *Heroic Poets and Poetic Heroes in Celtic Tradition: A Festschrift for Patrick K. Ford*, eds. Joseph Falaky Nagy and Leslie Ellen Jones (Dublin: Four Courts Press, 2005), 186.

15 Johnston, 'Whose History?', 81.

16 John Barrell, *The Spirit of Despotism: Invasions of Privacy in the 1790s* (Oxford: Oxford University Press, 2006), 4.

17 Johnston, 'Whose History?', 81; see also Kenneth R. Johnston, *Unusual Suspects. Pitt's Reign of Alarm and the Lost Generation* (Oxford: Oxford University Press, 2013), xiv–xv.

18 Johnston, 'Whose History?', 87–9.
19 The same applies to the Welsh Loyalist movement, despite the efforts of Hywel M. Davies.
20 The latest in a long line of publications on Price is Paul Frame, *Liberty's Apostle, Richard Price, His Life and Times* (Cardiff: Cambridge University Press, 2015); Whitney R. D. Jones, *David Williams: The Anvil and the Hammer* (Cardiff: University of Wales Press, 1986).
21 Kenneth R. Johnston, 'Before and After Lives: John Thelwall and William Godwin' & '"Whispering Tongues Can Poison Truth": Coleridge and Thelwall, 1796-1798', in idem *Unusual Suspects*, 23–46 & 235–49.
22 The classic account is David J. V. Jones, *Before Rebecca. Popular Protest in Wales 1793-1835* (London: Allan Lane, 1973).
23 Johnston, 'Whose History? My Place or Yours?', 98; Poole, 'Pitt's Terror Reconsidered', 71.
24 The names in brackets are the regular bardic pseudonyms used by the radicals or the place with which they are usually associated. These pseudonyms are used throughout to reflect indigenous Welsh tradition. Occasional pseudonyms were used in addition to these in order to hide identities in the public discourse.
25 Geraint H. Jenkins, *Bard of Liberty. The Political Radicalism of Iolo Morganwg* (Cardiff: University of Wales Press, 2012). For 'Iolo Morganwg and the Romantic Tradition in Wales, 1740-1914' project publications, see https://www.wales.ac.uk/en/CentreforAdvancedWelshCelticStudies/Publications/Project6/SeriesProject6.aspx (accessed 7 September 2022).
26 This chapter uses the first English version, but in chronological order they are: Daniel Ddu, 'Bywgraffyddiaeth. Cofiant Edward Williams, (Iolo Morganwg)', *Y Gwladgarwr*, 9, no. 100 (Ebrill, 1841), 97–100 & ibid., no. 101 (Mai, 1841), 129–32; William Williams, 'Iolo Morganwg', *Y Traethodydd*, XI (1855), 42–57; W. Rowland Jones, 'Dyngarwch a'r Beirdd Cymreig', *Y Geninen*, 29, no. 2 (1911), 133–7; 'Cymeriad Iolo Morganwg', *Yr Ymofynydd*, 14, no. 9 (Ebrill, 1914), 90–1.
27 Elijah Waring, *Recollections and Anecdotes of Edward Williams* (London: Charles Gilpin, 1850), 108–9.
28 Poole, 'Pitt's Terror Reconsidered', 71, 85 fn. 38.
29 Richard Warner, *A Second Walk through Wales by the Revd. Richard Warner in August and September 1798* (Bath: R. Crutwell, 1800), 77, 334.
30 *The Correspondence of Iolo Morganwg. Volume I 1770-1796*, eds. Geraint H. Jenkins, Ffion Mair Jones and David Ceri Jones (Cardiff: University of Wales Press, 2007), 787–90 and 810–11: 'Anonymous to Iolo Morganwg, 11 November 1795' & 'John Reed, 30 March 1796 to Iolo Morganwg' contain lists of seditious items sent to his shop.
31 Penelope J. Corfield, 'Rhetoric, Radical Politics and Rainfall: John Thelwall in Breconshire, 1797-1800', *Brycheiniog*, XL (2009), 24–5, 33.
32 Geraint H. Jenkins, *Iolo Morganwg y Gweriniaethwr* (Aberystwyth: Canolfan Uwchefrydiau Cymraeg a Cheltaidd, 2010), 20–2; Waring, *Recollections and Anecdotes*, 85–6 interpreted Iolo's meeting with Pitt very differently.
33 *Heroic Elegies and Other Pieces of Llywarç Hen, Prince of the Cumbrian Britons*, ed. William Owen. (London: J. Owen and E. Williams, 1792), xviii.
34 Ibid., liv–lv.
35 Cathryn A. Charnell-White, *Welsh Poetry of the French Revolution* (Cardiff: University of Wales Press, 2012), 20, 27–8, 148–52, 144–99, 322–33.

36 David Williams, 'Remarks on the History of Monmouthshire', *Cambrian Register*, I (1796), 465.
37 Martin Fitzpatrick, 'Enlightenment', in *An Oxford Companion to the Romantic Age: British Culture, 1776-1832*, ed. Iain Mccalman (Oxford: Oxford University Press, 1999), 302-3 [299-311].
38 George Eyre Evans (ed.), *Lloyd Letters (1754-1796) Being the Extant Letters of David Lloyd, Minister of Llwynrhydowen* (Aberystwyth: William Jones, 1908), lvii; Geraint Dyfnallt Owen, *Thomas Evans (Tomos Glyn Cothi)* (Abertawe: no imprint, 1963), 8-9; for the poem and its translation, see Charnell-White, *Welsh Poetry of the French Revolution*, 132-4.
39 Thomas Griffiths, *Cofiant am y Parch. David Davies, gynt o Gastell-Hywel, Ceredigion* (Caerfyrddin: J. Evans, 1828), 44-50; Telyn Dewi; *Sef Gwaith Prydyddawl y Parch. David Davis o Gastell-Hywel, Ceredigion; Yn Cynnwys Amryw Gyfansoddiadau o ei eiddo ei hun, a chyfieithiadau allan o waith rhai o'r prydyddion enwocaf yn y Iaith Saesonaeg; Addison, Young, Gray, Barbauld, Pope, &c. Ar Destunau Crefyddol, Hyfforddus, A Difyr* (Llundain: Longman, 1824), 138; Marion Löffler, 'Pedwar Cyfieithiad o Emyn Saesneg i'r Gymraeg', *Llên Cymru*, 39 (2016), 94-8; Kenneth R. Johnston. The Radical Moravian: James Montgomery (1771-1854)', in idem, *Unusual Suspects*, 64-78.
40 Eyre Evans, *Lloyd Letters*, lviii.
41 Griffiths, *Cofiant am y Parch. David Davies*, 28-9; Eyre Evans, *Lloyd Letters*, lviii.
42 Griffiths, *Cofiant am y Parch. David Davies*, 27-8: 'Gan ei fod, gyda llawer o'r dynion mwyaf eu cymmeradwyaeth, yn ffafriol i'r chwyldroad, neu yn hytrach y cyfnewidiad Ffrengig (French Revolution), nodwyd ef allan gan uchelwyr y deyrnas, fel un i wylied arno. Aeth drwg-dybiau y llywodraeth wladol mor bell am anffyddlondeb Mr. Dafis, fel ag y gosodwyd Goruwchwyliwr y Trethi (Surveyor of the Taxes), o'r enw Johnson, i graffu'n wyliadwrus ar Mr. D. Cenadodd, neu awdurdododd y *Premier*, Mr. Pitt, ef i agor pob llythyr oddiwrth neu at Mr. D. Dywedodd Johnson wrth y Parch. Mr. Griffiths, Llwyndyrus, am hyn; tystiodd yr Offeiriad parchus hwnnw nad oedd ganddynt un achos yn y byd i ofni ei fod fel ag y tybient, pa beth bynnag oedd ei syniadau, ac yma y terfynodd y peth disail hwn'.
43 Ibid.: 'Cafodd llawer o ddynion enwog yn mhlith yr Ymneillduwyr eu drwg-dybio o fradwriaeth, yn amser Pitt, ond nid o'i herwydd ef yn gyfangwbl. Iolo Morgannwg a gymerwyd i fyny, a'i holl ysgrifeniadau gydag ef, a gorfu arno wneyd ei ymddangosiad gerbron y frawdle, ond rhyddhawyd ef yn glodfawr, a dangosodd Mr. Pitt barch nid bychan iddo, ac a'i gwahoddodd ef i'w dŷ, lle y cafodd y driniaeth fwyaf foneddigaidd.'
44 Griffiths, *Cofiant am y Parch. David Davies*, 28-9.
45 Eyre Evans, *Lloyd Letters*, xvi.
46 For a short biography, see Owen, *Tomos Glyn Cothi*; Marion Löffler, 'The "Marseillaise" in Wales', in *Footsteps of Liberty and Revolt': Essays on Wales and the French Revolution*, ed. Mary-Ann Constantine and Dafydd Johnston (Cardiff: University of Wales Press, 2013), 93-114.
47 Eyre Evans, *Lloyd Letters*, lvii; Owen, *Thomas Evans*, 8-9; Marion Löffler, *Welsh Responses to the French Revolution: Press and Public Discourse 1789-1802* (Cardiff: University of Wales Press, 2012), 28-9.
48 Geraint H. Jenkins, '"A Very Horrid Affair": Sedition and Unitarianism in the Age of Revolutions', in *From Medieval to Modern Wales: Historical Essays in Honour of Kenneth O. Morgan and Ralph A. Griffiths*, ed. R. R. Davies and Geraint H. Jenkins (Cardiff: University of Wales Press, 2004), 175-96. For the depositions and judge's

speech, see National Library of Wales Manuscript [NLW MS] 2137D; G. J. Williams, 'Carchariad Tomos Glyn Cothi', *Llên Cymru*, 3 (1954), 120–2.
49 NLW, Courts of Great Sessions 4/256/4: Document 32. 23 June 1800.
50 Poole, 'Pitt's Terror Reconsidered', 80–3.
51 Jenkins, 'A Very Horrid Affair', 191.
52 Owen, *Tomos Glyn Cothi*, 63; PRO H.O. 42/44, 23 November 1802.
53 Ibid., 42.
54 Mike Jay, *The Unfortunate Colonel Despard and the British Revolution That Never Happened* (Revised and updated edition; London: Robinson, 2019).
55 Thomas Evans to Iolo Morganwg, 25 October 1803, in *The Correspondence of Iolo Morganwg. Volume II 1797–1809*, 557.
56 Cited from the *Monthly Repository* (1816), in Owen, *Tomos Glyn Cothi*, 51–2.
57 NLW Minor Deposit 312A, May, August 1814; NLW Minor Deposit 313A, April 1814; NLW MS 21970A, 8, 10, 20.
58 Löffler, *Political Pamphlets*, 19–24: 'Samuel Horsley versus the Welsh Freeholder'.
59 T. R. Roberts, *Eminent Welshmen: A Short Biographical Dictionary of Welshmen Who Have Attained Distinction from the Earliest Times to the Present* (Cardiff & Merthyr Tydfil: The Educational Publishing Company, 1908), 222; Hywel Meilyr Davies, 'Jones, David [pseud. the Welsh Freeholder] (1765–1816)', in ODNB, https://doi.org/10.1093/ref:odnb/14993.
60 Jenkins, 'A Very Horrid Affair', 191.
61 John James Evans, *Cymry Enwog y Ddeunawfed Ganrif* (Aberystwyth: Gwasg Aberystwyth, 1937), 182–4; R. T. Jenkins, Davies, David (died 1807), in *Dictionary of Welsh Biography*, https://biography.wales/article/s-DAVI-DAV-1807 (accessed 22 September 2022); Löffler, *Welsh Responses*, 29–35.
62 Löffler, *Welsh Responses*, 36–7, 152–4.
63 'Crynodeb o'r Achosion o'r Cyfnewidiad yn Ffrainc', *Y Geirgrawn*, 1, no. 3 (1796), 87. He was probably the author of the English series published in the *Chester Chronicle* between 13 November 1795 and 29 January 1796, and the Welsh series published in *Y Geirgrawn*, nos. 1 to 3 at the beginning of 1796.
64 *Hanes Eglwysi Annibynol Cymru*, ed. Thomas Rees and John Thomas (Liverpool: Tyst Cymreig, 1871–5), vol. I, 373.
65 Evans, *Cymry Enwog y Ddeunawfed Ganrif*, 184; E. Gwynn Matthews, 'Holywell and the Marseillaise', *Flintshire Historical Society Journal*, 38 (2010), 121–2.
66 Geraint H. Jenkins, '"A Rank Republican [and] a Leveller": William Jones, Llangadfan', *Welsh History Review*, 17, no. 3 (1995), 374, 383, 385.
67 See Löffler, *Political Pamphlets and Sermons*, 55–60, 111–58 for Welsh and English texts of the pamphlet.
68 Middleton Pennant Jones, 'John Jones of Glan-y-Gors', *Transactions of the Honourable Society of Cymmrodorion* (1911), 74–6; Evans, *Cymry Enwog y Ddeunawfed Ganrif*, 163.
69 Evans, *Morgan John Rhys*, 26, 27–8.
70 David Davies, *The Influence of the French Revolution on Welsh Life and Literature* (Carmarthen: W. Morgan Evans & Son, 1926), 116–18, 233–5; see also Hywel M. Davies, 'Loyalism in Wales, 1792–1793', *Welsh History Review*, 20, no. 4 (2001), 687–716.
71 Hywel M. Davies, 'Terror, Treason and Tourism: The French in Pembrokeshire in 1797', *Footsteps of Liberty and Revolt' Essays on Wales and the French Revolution*, ed. Mary-Ann Constantine and Dafydd Johnston (Cardiff: University of Wales Press, 2013), 247–70.

72 For the pamphlet and its translation, see Löffler (with Jenkins), *Political Pamphlets*, 63–5; 235–92.
73 John James Evans, *Dylanwad y Chwyldro Ffrengig ar Lenyddiaeth Cymru* (Lerpwl: Hugh Evans, 1928), 178.
74 Löffler, *Welsh Responses*, 28–9.
75 Morgan ab Ioan Rhus, *Y Drefn o Gynnal Crefydd yn Unol-Daleithiau America: Ynghyd â Darluniad Byr o Kentucky. A Rhesymau digonol i gyfiawnhau'r cyfryw sy'n myned o'r Wlad hon i AMERICA, a Chyngor i'r CYMRY* (Caerfyrddin: John Ross, 1794), 10–11; See also Hywel M. Davies, '"Very Different Springs of Uneasiness": Emigration from Wales to the United States of America during the 1790s', *Welsh History Review*, 15, no. 3 (1991), 368–98.
76 5 Geo I, c. 27; 23 Geo III, c. 14; S. C. Johnson, *A History of Emigration from the United Kingdom to North America* (London: Routledge, 1913), 57.
77 Thomas Lewis, 'Morgan John Rhys', *Seren Gomer*, 12, no. 53 (May 1891), 103, 107–8.
78 John T. Griffith, *Rev. Morgan John Rhys: 'The Welsh Baptist Hero of Civil and Religious Liberty of the Eighteenth Century'* (Lansford, Pennsylvania: private, 1899), 12. This is a translation of the 1891 Welsh version in Lewis, 'Morgan John Rhys', 107–8.
79 Evans, *Morgan John Rhys*, 33–4; Hywel M. Davies, *Transatlantic Brethren. Rev. Samuel Jones (1735–1814) and His Friends. Baptists in Wales, Pennsylvania and beyond* (Bethlehem: Leigh University Press; London: Associated Press, 1995), 186.
80 B. G. Charles and M. N. Jones, 'EVANS, ALCWYN CARYNI (1828–1902)', in *Dictionary of Welsh Biography*, https://biography.wales/article/s-EVAN-CAR-1828 (accessed 22 September 2022).
81 R. T. Jenkins, 'JONES, DAVID (1789?–1841', in *Dictionary of Welsh Biography*, https://biography.wales/article/s-JONE-DAV-1789 (accessed 22 September 2022).
82 T. Shankland, 'Ai Ffoi i America wnaeth Morgan John Rhys?', *Seren Cymru*, 23 (Rhagfyr 1898), 11: 'Nid yw'n bosibl cael tystiolaeth hanesyddol uwch nag o enau y rhai a gymmerasant rhan yn y symudiadau a gofnodir.'
83 Griffith, *Rev. Morgan John Rhys*, 20–6.
84 Hywel M. Davies, '"Transatlantic brethren": a study of English, Welsh and American Baptists with particular reference to Morgan John Rhys (1760–1804) and his friends'. Thesis presented for the degree of Ph.D. at University College, Cardiff in 1984, 480; See Davies, *Influence*, 169.
85 James Ifano Jones, *A History of Printing and Printers in Wales to 1810, and of Successive and Related Printers to 1923: Also, a History of Printing and Printers in Monmouthshire to 1923* (Cardiff: University of Wales Press, 1925), 136–7.
86 Davies, 'Transatlantic Brethren', 479, 508.
87 Johnston, 'Whose History? My Place or Yours?', 95.
88 Gwyn A. Williams, *The Search for Beulah Land. The Welsh and the Atlantic Revolution* (London: Croom Helm, 1980), 174.
89 Jenkins, 'A Rank Republican [and] a Leveller', 374, 383, 385.
90 Davies, 'Transatlantic Brethren', 527.
91 Davies, 'Very Different Springs of Uneasiness', 368.
92 For text and translation of the poem, see Löffler, *Welsh Responses*, 293–7; D. Stansfield, 'Agweddau ar Fywyd a Gwaith Dafydd Saunders', *Trafodion Cymdeithas Hanes y Bedyddwyr* (2008), 35–51.
93 [David Davies], 'At ein Gohebwyr, a'r Cyffredin', *Y Geirgrawn*, 1, nos. 3 and 5 (1796), inside cover.
94 Idem, 'At ein Gohebwyr a'r Cyffredin', *Y Geirgrawn*, 1, no. 5 (1796), inside cover.

95   Thomas Roberts o Lwynrhudol, *Cwyn yn Erbyn Gorthrymder* (Llundain: John Jones, 1798), in Löffler (with Jenkins), *Political Pamphlets*, 192, 213: 'Fy mwriad i yn y dechreuad oedd gyru y sylwiadau canlynol i *Dafydd Davies* o Dreffynnon i'w rhoddi yn ei *Eirgrawn Cymraeg*, ond fe gymmerodd rhyw *Gnafiaid*, (Dihirwyr) fawr ofal i ddychrynu y dyn, a'i rwystro i fyned ymlaen yn ei orchwyl, a bygwth ei yrru i ffwrdd o'r wlâd (mal y clywais sôn) am iddo gyhoeddi pethau buddiol, fel yr hyn ag oedd yn taro at wreiddyn Gorthrymder'.
96   Löffler, *Political Pamphlets*, 10, 19–25.
97   B. G. Owens, 'SAUNDERS, DAVID II (Dafydd Glan Teifi; 1769–1840)', *Dictionary of Welsh Biography*, https://biography.wales/article/s-SAUN-DAV-1769 (accessed 22 September 2022).
98   Glyn Ashton, *Hunangofiant a Llythyrau Twm o'r Nant* (Cardiff: University of Wales Press, 1962), 18–19. A more radical poem by Twm o'r Nant on bitter militia experiences remained unpublished. 'Rhyddhad o'r Milisia', in *Canu Twm o'r Nant*, ed. Dafydd Glyn Jones (Bangor, 2010), 182–4, 307.
99   See Löffler (with Jenkins), *Political Pamphlets*, 160, 175: 'na bydd y bobl ag y sydd yn eu galw eu hunain yn Fonheddigion yn Nghymru, ddim mor orthrymus, a bygwth torri bywoliaeth llyfrwerthwyr, o herwydd eu bod yn chwenych gwerthu yr hyn a fo wir'.
100 Owen, *Tomos Glyn Cothi*, 42.
101 Marion Löffler, 'Challenging the State: Subversive Welsh Translators in Britain in the 1790s', in *Translation and Global Spaces of Power*, ed. Stefan Baumgarten and Jurgi Cornella-Detrell (Bristol: Multilingual Matters, 2018), 75–88.
102 Johnston, 'Whose History? My Place or Yours?', 84.
103 Davies, 'Transatlantic Brethren', 404.
104 Löffler (with Jenkins), *Political Pamphlets*, 160–90.
105 Richards, *The History of Lynne, Civil, Ecclesiastical, Political, Commercial, Biographical, Municipal and Military* (Lynn: W. G. Wittingham, 1812).
106 John Oddy, *The Writings of the Radical Welsh Baptist Minister William Richards (1749–1818) Selected, Edited, and Annotated with an Introduction* (Lewiston – Queenston – Lampeter: The Edwin Mellon Press, 2008), 381–2.
107 NLW MSS 6238A. (Lleufer Thomas 41) 'Y Gell Gymmysg'.
108 NLW Minor Deposit 312A. Almanac for the year 1814; NLW Minor Deposit 313A. Almanac for the year 1814; NLW MSS 21970 A. 'Diary of (1817–19)'; NLW MSS 7893A. Milton's *Treatise of Civil Power* 'which belonged to Thomas Evans and bears manuscript notes by him and others'; NLW MS 6868B. '*Rhyddid, Traethawd a ennillodd Ariandlws Cymdeithas y Gwyneddigion … gan Walter Davies*'.
109 Owen, *Tomos Glyn Cothi*, 45.
110 Thomas Evans, *An English and Welch Vocabulary: Or, an Easy Guide to the Ancient British Language. To Which Is Prefixed, a Grammar of the Welch Language. By Thomas Richards* (Merthyr: W. Williams, 1804) and subsequent editions.
111 Thomas Evans, *Cyfansoddiad o hymnau, wedi cael eu hamcanu at addoliad cyhoeddus; ag yn enwedig at wasanaeth Undodiaid Cristianogol* (Caerfyrddin: Jonathan Harris, 1811).
112 NLW MSS 12364-12365D. (Alcwyn C. Evans 9–10.)
113 Löffler, *Welsh Responses*, 1.
114 Johnston, 'Whose History? My Place or Yours?', 89.
115 Prys Morgan, 'From Long Knives to Blue Books', in *Welsh Society and Nationhood. Historical Essays Presented to Glanmor Williams*, ed. R. R. Davies et al. (Cardiff,

1984), 199–215; Gwyneth Tyson Roberts, *The Language of the Blue Books. The Perfect Instrument of Empire* (Cardiff: University of Wales Press, 1998; another edition 2011).
116 Dafydd Rhys Stephen, 'Iolo Morganwg Rhif II', *Seren Gomer*, 34, no. 426 (1851), 98: "'Wel, Mr. Williams", ebai Mr. Pitt, "yn mae'n dda genyf nad oes dim yn beryglus i chwi yn y papyrau hyn; gellwch eu cymeryd, a myned adref fel y gweloch yn dda". "Syr", atebai y Bardd, "daethoch chi â fi a'm ysgrifau yma heb fy nghenad; hyderwyf y byddwch yn ddigon o ŵr boneddig i'n cario yn ôl". "Nid yw hyny ond y sydd yn rhesymol", ebai Pitt; ac yna wrth y gwas, "Dodwch luniaeth o flaen Mr. Williams, ac wedi hyny, danfonwch ef i'r lle y myno fyned yn fy ngherbyd I.'"
117 Thomas Stephens, *Yr Ymofynnydd*, V, no. 56 (1852), 77–82 to VI, no. 66 (1853), 29–35; idem, 'Iolo Morganwg: Ei Nodweddion', ibid., VI, no. 65 (1853), 12–13. See also Geraint H. Jenkins, "'A Very Horrid Affair'".
118 Roberts, *Eminent Welshmen*, 557. He was, however, honoured with a quarter-page illustration on 560.
119 Brynley Roberts, "'The Age of Restitution": Taliesin ab Iolo and the Reception of Iolo Morganwg', in '*A Rattleskull Genius*': *The Many Faces of Iolo Morganwg*, ed. Geraint H. Jenkins (Cardiff, 2005), 461–79.
120 Löffler, *The Literary and Historical Legacy of Iolo Morganwg 1826–1926* (Cardiff: University of Wales Press, 2007), 81.
121 John Williams (ab Ithel) (ed.), *Barddas*, 2 vols. (Llandovery: Rees, 1862, 1874); latest edition *The Barddas of Iolo Morganwg: A Collection of Original Documents, Illustrative of the Theology, Wisdom, and Usages of the Bardo-Druidic System of the Isle of Britain* (Boston, MA: Weiser Books, 2004).
122 Williams, 'Reviews: Recollections and Anecdotes', 102; Griffiths, *Hanes Emynwyr Cymru*, 255.
123 Eliezer Williams to Burgess, 21 February 1914, in St. George Armstrong Williams, *English Works of the late Rev. Eliezer Williams, M.A. Vicar of Lampeter, and Caio cum Llansawel, Prebendary of St. Davids etc. with a Memoir of his Life* (London: Cradock and Co., 1840), xciv.
124 For the religious background, see Geraint H. Jenkins, 'The Unitarian Firebrand, the Cambrian Society and the Eisteddfod' in Jenkins, *Rattleskull Genius*, 267–92.
125 Löffler, *The Literary and Historical Legacy*, 44.
126 Mair Elfet Thomas, *The Welsh Spirit of Gwent* (Cardiff: University of Wales Press, 1988).
127 Charles Wilkins, 'Men Whom I Have Known. Thomas Stephens: Author of *The Literature of the Cymry*', *Cymru Fu*, 9 November 1889, 72.
128 Dafydd Johnston, 'Writing the Nation in Two Languages: The Dictionary of Welsh Biography', in '*True Biographies of Nations?*': *The Cultural Journeys of Dictionaries of National Biography*, ed. Karen Fox (Canberra: ANU Press, 2019), 159–75.
129 Robert Williams, *Enwogion Cymru. A Biographical Dictionary of Eminent Welshmen* (Llandovery and London: William Rees & Longman & Co., 1852).
130 John Rees, 'Traethawd o Hanes Bywyd y diweddar Barch. Thomas Evans (Tomos Glyn Cothi)', in *Gardd Aberdar, yn cynnwys Cyfansoddiadau Buddugol yn dal Cysylltiad a Phlwyf Aberdar a'r Cylchoedd*, ed. W. Lloyd (Aberdâr: W. Lloyd, 1872), 65.
131 Ibid., 68–9: 'Ond erbyn heddyw, braidd nad yw swyddogion yr un deyrnas a gweinyddwyr yr un gyfraith yn gwenu o dan eu penwigau llwydion am y fath ynfydrwydd; ac er mawr syndod, mae rheibiaeth a dewiniaeth wedi cilio yn hollol o'r tir, er nad oes neb yn erlid na chospi o'u herwydd. Bu hefyd lawer o gynhwrf a bygwth cospi am werthu a meddiannu ysgrifeniadau awduron politicaidd, megys Paine, Hobbes, Volney, ac eraill. Ond o ba leshad oedd pethau fel hyn? Onid

peri i'r byd awyddu mwy am danynt? Ac fel y dywedai Arglwydd Brougham am ysgrifeniadau Carlisle, mai pa leiaf y dirgelwch a wnaed o honynt, lleiaf oll a fyddai awch y wlad am danynt … onid oes pethau mwy eu perygl filiwn o weithiau yn cael eu gwerthu ar bob mainc braidd yn ein marchnadoedd y dyddiau hyn, heb un twrf na hela o'u plegid, ac heb un niwed yn eilliaw oddi-wrthynt?'

132 Ibid., 70-1.
133 Ibid., 77. See Royal Commission of Historic and Ancient Monuments of Wales, Coflein #6434104: Detail of memorial to Rev. Thomas Evans in vestibule (accessed 5 January 2022).
134 Quis, 'Iolo Morganwg a Thomas Glyn Cothi', *Yr Ymofynydd*, XX, no. 101 (1896), 127-30; 'Thomas Evans (Tomos Glyn Cothi)', ibid., XXII, no. 119 (1897), 534-5; P. P., 'Pennod 10 – Tori Tŷ'r Pregethwr', ibid., XVIII, no. 78 (1894), 133-4.
135 'Enwogion Aberdâr IV', *Cymru* XXV (1903), 209-10.
136 Roberts, *Eminent Welshmen*, 118.
137 Thomas Lewis, 'Morgan John Rhys', *Seren Gomer*, XII, no. 53 (May 1891), 104, 108.
138 Ibid., 104-5, 108.
139 Griffith, *Morgan John Rhys*, 7.
140 Roberts, *Eminent Welshmen*, 453.
141 Williams, *Enwogion Cymru*, 113.
142 Ibid., 256.
143 Ibid., 252-3.
144 Martin Wright, *Wales and Socialism. Political Culture and National Identity before the Great War* (Cardiff: University of Wales Press, 2016), 203-6.
145 Ben Morus, 'William Williams (Carw Coch)', *Cymru*, XL, no. 234 (1911), 59; see also idem, *Enwogion Aber Dâr: Sef Byrr-nodion am rai o Gewri Ymadawedig Y Dref a'r Cylch* (Llanbedr Pont Stephan, 1910), 39.
146 Roberts, *Eminent Welshmen*, 35.
147 Ibid., 286.
148 Ibid., 459.
149 Ibid., 245.
150 Gwyn A. Williams, 'The Merthyr Election of 1835', *Welsh History Review*, 10, no. 4 (1981), 390. However, no source is indicated for this information.
151 Daniel Ddu, 'Bywgraffyddiaeth. Cofiant Edward Williams (Iolo Morganwg)', *Y Gwladgarwr*, 9, no. 101 (Mai, 1841), 130.
152 Cardiff University Salisbury Collection, T. J. 3664, 'Breiniau dyn: Can newydd Iolo Morganwg a'i cant, 1789, yng ngorfedd yr Alban Eilir. Ac a'i ysgrifenodd a llaw flinderus iawn, y chwechfed fore o'r ail Leuad gwedi'r Alban Eilir, cyn codi haul', [handwritten note] 'Published as a Supplement to "Udgorn Cymru", 1 October 1841'. On this poem in the 1790s, Mary-Ann Constantine and Elizabeth Edwards, 'Bard of Liberty: Iolo Morganwg, Wales and Radical Song', in *United Islands? The Languages of Resistance. Political Poetry and Song in the Age of Revolution Volume 1*, ed. John Kirk, Andrew Noble and Michael Brown (London: Pickering and Chatto, 2012), 63-76.
153 Williams, 'The Merthyr Election of 1835', 363.
154 *Yr Ymofynydd*, I, no. 8 (April 1848), 188-92: 'Nid oes Frenin ar y Ffrancod oddi ar y 24ain o Chwefror, Ar y dydd hwnw gosodwyd i fyny werin-lywodraeth (Republic), yn Paris, y brif-ddinas. Yn fuan cafodd ei chyhoeddi yn mhob dinas a thref, a chafodd ei derbyn yn ddiwrthwynebiad trwy bob cwrr o'r wlad. Gyda'r cyfnewidiad yn ffurf y llywodraeth, apwyntiwyd yn union wyr cymmeradwy i fod yn Llywodraeth Ddarparawl (Provisional Government) i weinyddu dros amser fatterol y wladwriaeth, hyd nes bydd i Gyfarfod Cenedlaethol (National Assembly) i osod pethau mewn

trefn boddhaol a sefydlog. Oddiar hyny y mae y gwyr hyn – rhai o'r enwoccaf o'u cenedl – yn cyflawni eu gwahanol swyddi gyda chryn gymmeradwyaeth; ac hyd yma y mae pob peth wedi myned ymlaen more dawel ag y gallesid ei ddisgwyl. Y mae yn anhawdd – y mae yn amhosibl ar hyn o bryd – ddirnad maint effeithiau y chwildroad hwn ar Ffraingc ac ar wledydd eraill. Y fath yw sefyllfa berthynasol y wlad, bywiogrwydd, amlder a gwroldeb ei thrigolion, ynghyd a'r cof am eu gorchestion mewn rhyfel nid llawer iawn o flynyddau yn ôl … fel nad peth i'w diystyrru yw chwildroad yn Ffraingc … gwae fydd i'r neb a geisia eu rhwstro neu eu hattal yn eu gwaith yn sefydlu eu rhyddid: ac, yn mhellach, y bydd iddi gymeryd plaid pob cenedl wan a fyddo yn ymdrechu yn erbyn eu gormeswyr. Cymmerer hyn fel rhybudd ac fel bygythiad. Fel hyn y mae brenhiniaethau Ewrop yn cael eu dodi ar eu *good behaviour*.'

155 *Yr Ymofynydd*, I, no. 4 (December 1847), 96.
156 Ibid.: 'Troes Ffrainc orseddfaingcwr swyddfawr – ac aur Ei goron i'r priddlawr / Ble'r aeth y Monarch mawr? / Darfu mewn amharch dirfawr! / Bellach Ffraingc ar faingc a fydd, – yn hynod / Frenhines y gwledydd / Hed myrddiynau'u rhwymau'n rhydd / O dan ei mwyn adenydd.'
157 *Yr Ymofynnydd*, 1, no. 6 (April 1848), 192.
158 E. T. (Horeb, Ceredigion), 'Englynion', *Yr Ymofynnydd*, I, no. 10 (June 1848): 240: 'Rhybudd o newydd yn awr – a roddwyd / I'r graddau uchelfawr, / Rhag gwasgu, llethu i lawr / Dorfoedd a'u beichiau dirfawr … Rhyw filoedd am wrthryfela – a geir / Dan y goron yma; – / Er cadw hedd o duedd da, / Tirion fo braich Victoria … Gommodd i'r Senedd o'r Sir – a wnelom / Un aelod anghywir, Y balch o bell gwell mewn gwir / Ei gau allan os gellir.'
159 Ibid.: 'bod yr Awdur yn awgrymu at y diwygiad a ellid ei wneuthur yn llywodraeth Brydain Fawr, trwy symmud ymaeth y gormes a'r caledi dan y rhai y mae rhan fawr o'r deiliaid yn gruddfan yn bresennol'.
160 For a detailed analysis of the 1796 translation, see Marion Löffler, 'The "Marseillaise" in Wales', in *Footsteps of Liberty and Revolt*, 93–114.
161 *Yr Ymofynydd*, I, no. 16 (December 1848), 380: 'Cân Rhyddid, gan y diweddar Barch T. E., Glyn Cothi. A gyfansoddwyd tua diwedd y cannrif [sic] diweddaf. Ar y don Marseillaise': 'O Rhyddid! Pwy mor ffol a'th wrthod / 'Nol unwaith deimlo'th nefol dan? / A gaiff creulonder mwy di-orfod / Rhwystro'r fuddugoliaeth lan? / O! lleda'th faner dros yr hollfyd! / Llwyr warediaeth dwg wrth raid, / Yn gadarn aros byth o'u plaid, / Er rhoddi llwyddiant, hedd, a gwynfyd. // (Cydgor,) Hawl dyn – trwy'r byd, / Llwyr deg ennillo'r dydd; / Heb fraw – drwy unol fryd, / O'n rhwymau awn yn rhydd.'
162 See Peter Lambert, 'The Institutionalisation of History in the University Colleges of Wales, 1880–1939: Aberystwyth and Bangor', in *Writing a Small Nation's Past: Wales in Comparative Perspective, 1850–1950*, ed. Neil Evans and Huw Pryce (Farnham: Routledge, 2013), 177–94.
163 Löffler, 'The Case against Iolo Morganwg', in eadem, *Literary and Historical Legacy*, 130–150.
164 'Saer Maen, Bardd Rhyddid, Hynafiaethydd ac Un o Gymwynaswyr Mwyaf Llên a Hanes Cymru'. The plaque is in situ at 14 Cowbridge High Street. See also Hywel Gethin Rhys, '*A Wayward Cymric Genius*'. *Celebrating the Centenary of the Death of Iolo Morganwg* (Aberystwyth: CAWCS, 2008).
165 *Yr Ymofynydd*, 27, no. 3 (March 1927).
166 Löffler, *Literary and Historical Legacy*, 145–6.
167 *Western Mail*, 11 January 1927.

168 See note 25 above.
169 https://www.royalparks.org.uk/parks/the-regents-park/things-to-see-and-do/memorials,-fountains-and-statues/iolo-morganwg-memorial-plaque (accessed 12 January 2022).
170 Jenkins, *Bard of Liberty*, above; Geraint H. Jenkins, *Y Digymar Iolo Morganwg* (Talybont: Y Lolfa, 2018).
171 Irene George, 'Tomos Glyn Cothi', *The Journal of the Welsh Bibliographical Society*, 4, no. 3 (1933), 111–12.
172 George, 'Tomos Glyn Cothi': 106; see also Daniel Lleufer Thomas, *Cyfieithiadau Dienw Tomos Glyn Clothi (Y Parch. Thomas Evans, 1764–1833)* (Caerfyrddin: Spurrell, 1931).
173 *Yr Ymofynydd*, XXXIII, no 7 (1933), 97–120.
174 J. J. Evans, 'Apostol Rhydd', in ibid., 105: 'Un dylanwad a welir yn eglur ar eu gweithiau yw eiddo'r traddodiad Piwritanaidd … Hawl dyn i feddwl trosto'i hun oedd sylfaen credo'r Piwritan; am hynny yr oedd yn elyn i frenin unbenaethol ac i eglwys sefydledig fel ei gilydd. … Dylid ymwrthod ag awdurdod y gorffennol, llywodraeth y byw gan y meirw, a disodli'r hen "symudiadau hanes" gan rai democrataidd. A dyma ddadl fawr Tom Pain[e] yn nes ymlaen, a cheir yr un syniadau yn gymwys gan y diwygwyr Cymreig, megis Morgan John Rhys, Iolo Morganwg, Jac Glan y Gors, Thomas Roberts Llwynrhudol, Dr. William Richards a Thomas Glyn Cothi.'
175 'Tomos Glyn Cothi. The Centenary Celebrations', *Western Mail*, 9 June 1933, 8.
176 Owen, *Tomos Glyn Cothi*, 12–20; For an overview, texts and translations, see Löffler, *Welsh Responses*.
177 Jenkins, '"A Very Horrid Affair"'.
178 Davies, *The Influence of the French Revolution*; Evans, *Dylanwad y Chwyldro*.
179 R. T. Jenkins, *Hanes Cymru yn y Ddeunawfed Ganrif* (Cardiff: University of Wales Press, 1928); idem, *Hanes Cymru yn y Bedwaredd ganrif ar Bymtheg Cyfrol I (1789–1843)* (Cardiff: University of Wales Press, 1933).
180 Evans, *Morgan John Rhys*, 32–4. Albert Goodwin, *The Friends of Liberty: The English Democratic Movement in the Age of the French Revolution* (London: Routledge, 1979), 513, mentions LCS correspondence with a 'provincial radical society' in Cardiff and in Chester (then a centre of radical Welsh printing). Bishop Murray certainly suspected political links with west Wales.
181 Evans, *Morgan John Rhys*, 36.
182 Ibid., 37, 39. For a reinterpretation, see Hywel M. Davies, '"Very Different Springs of Uneasiness"'.
183 Evans, *Morgan John Rhys*, 117.
184 Jenkins, *Hanes Cymru yn y Bedwaredd Ganrif ar Bymtheg*, 27.
185 Gwyn A. Williams, 'Morgan John Rhys and Volney's *Ruins of Empires*', *Bulletin of the Board of Celtic Studies*, XX, no. 1 (1962), 58–73.
186 Gwyn A. Williams, 'Morgan John Rhys and His Beulah', *Welsh History Review*, 3, no. 4 (1967), 441–72; idem, 'Welsh Indians: The Madoc Legend and the First Welsh Radicalism', *History Workshop Journal*, 1 (1976), 136–54; idem, 'John Evans's Mission to the Madogwys, 1792–1799', *Bulletin of the Board of Celtic Studies*, XXVII, no. 4 (1978), 569–601; idem, *The Search for Beulah Land: The Welsh and the Atlantic Revolution* (New York: Holms and Meyer, 1980); idem, *Madoc: The Making of a Myth* (Oxford: Oxford University Press, 1987); idem, *When Was Wales? A History of the Welsh* (Cardiff: University of Wales Press, 1985, 1991).

187 Gwyn A. Williams, 'Druids and Democrats', 32, 48.
188 Trouillot, *Silencing the Past*, 27.
189 Philip Henry Jones, 'Printing and Publishing in the Welsh Language', in *The Welsh Language and Its Social Domains*, ed. Geraint H. Jenkins (Cardiff: University of Wales Press, 2000), 317–47.

4

The canon of Irish republicanism: Constructing a separatist 'tradition'

Colin W. Reid

What is distinctively Irish and republican about Irish republicanism?[1] While Irish republican movements and personalities continue to attract many historians, the ideas underpinning Irish republicanism remain elusive. The ground breaking work of Quentin Skinner, J. G. A Pocock and Philip Pettit has elevated republicanism more broadly as a scholarly area of inquiry within the history of political thought and intellectual history, but Ireland is largely absent from their best-known work.[2] Subsequent scholarship on republicanism as a body of European political ideas also tends to follow the exclusion of the Irish variety.[3] There are several structural reasons for this. Irish republicanism has not produced thinkers of the global stature of James Harrington or Alexander Hamilton, nor texts with the universalist appeal of Sieyes's *Qu'est-ce Que le Tiers-état?* or Rousseau's *Social Contract*. To be a republican in Ireland is often reduced to solely championing separation from Britain through violent means, obscuring the more nuanced dynamics of Irish republicanism at any given time.[4] In one of the rare engagements with Irish republicanism as an intellectual enterprise, Iseult Honohan has emphasized that beyond the essential doctrine of national independence, republicanism in Ireland contained a range of social perspectives, resulting in radically different interpretations of the ideal structures of government, education and the economy.[5] In the same volume, Margaret O'Callaghan makes the point that Irish republicanism's historical association with violence since the 1790s drove ideas of the 'Republic' underground. To be a republican in Ireland was seditious, and the lack of open political debate about the concept was a consequence of the secretive, militant nature of its adherents.[6] This partially accounts for the paucity of accounts of republicanism as an *idea* in Irish political thought, which in turn serves to hinder Irish republicanism gaining a place within European or more global political thought.

That said, there are great possibilities to engage with the ideas underpinning Irish republicanism. As Stephen Small, one of the few historians of Irish political thought, has noted, the turn to revolutionary tactics 'required a theory justifying armed resistance'.[7] Despite their clandestine status, Irish republicans did not shy away from penning newspapers, pamphlets and memoirs with this aim in mind. A common theme that emerges in many Irish republican texts is historical continuity, creating a genealogy of struggle for political independence. Often, this is intimately bound up with the idea of the national; republicans have struggled to develop a political vocabulary 'not already corrupted by nationalism'.[8] With several honourable exceptions, there is little theoretical engagement with the concept of republicanism in textual sources. Historical consciousness – meaning not only how history is understood but how it shaped political ideas about the present and future – trumped appeals to political philosophy within the Irish republican canon.[9] Indeed, within the revolutionary tradition in Ireland, history *was* philosophy. In the preface to a new edition of Mitchel's *Jail Journal*, which was published in 1913, Arthur Griffith explicitly rejected political theories concerning natural rights as the basis for Irish independence in favour of championing the nation's historic claims. Griffith took a certain glee in reminding his audience that Mitchel cared nothing for 'republicanism in the abstract'.[10] Seventy years later, in expressing its opposition to partition, the Provisional Irish Republican Army proclaimed itself as the authentic bearer of the popular will of the Irish people, which expressed its right to self-determination at the General Election of 1918.[11] Democratic legitimacy thus was understood as a historicized phenomenon which British imperialism had suppressed, resulting in a just armed campaign by the PIRA to end the 'occupation'.[12]

In a controversial article published in 1972, Father Francis Shaw condemned the fostering of a 'canon of history' which suggested that Irish independence was the glittering prize won solely by armed rebels. 'This canon moulds the broad course of Irish history to a narrow pre-conceived pattern,' bemoaned Shaw. 'In effect it teaches that only the Fenians and the separatists had the good of their country at heart.'[13] The bulk of the article was written in reaction to the Irish state-led golden jubilee commemoration of the Easter Rising of 1916, which Shaw believed whitewashed the contribution of non-militants, such as the Home Rulers, in the delivery of independence. Shaw's 'canon' was one of historical deviants, who egotistically and unethically waged war in the name of the 'People' without any popular consent. His argument became subsumed into the 'revisionist' debates within Irish historiography in the 1980s and 1990s.[14] Space has been found, however, in the post-revisionist age to more critically interrogate the meanings of political languages deployed in Ireland, especially the vocabulary of legitimation.[15] Shaw was – understandably – concerned about the fostering of a canon of history that simplified history and legitimized violence. But historians can learn much from the self-fashioned canons and traditions exalted by Irish republicans, as the identification with historical figures, movements and ideas sheds light onto the evolution of separatist political thought over the centuries. The personalities, texts and events included – and excluded – in the canon of republicanism reveal much about the world view of later generations of revolutionaries. Canons were made and unmade; the need to construct a 'tradition' turned separatism into a literary practice as much as a political programme.

Constructing a 'tradition'

The organizational lineage of Irish republicanism can be said to begin with the Society of the United Irishmen in the 1790s. Following the rebellions of 1798 and 1803, republican ideas were seemingly suppressed in Ireland, before coming to the fore once again with the Young Irelanders in the 1840s, who embarked on a failed rising at the height of the Great Famine. In 1858, the secretive Irish Republican Brotherhood (IRB) was established, with a sister transatlantic organization, the Fenian Brotherhood, emerging concurrently in the United States of America. The Irish Republican Army flowered from the seed of the Irish Volunteers, the latter of which was a paramilitary organization founded during the Home Rule crisis in 1913. The more radical wing of the Volunteers rejected the rationale that Irishmen should fight for the British on the outbreak of war in 1914; two years later, a faction seized buildings around Dublin, commencing the Easter Rising. The Volunteers – now christened the Irish Republican Army (IRA) – launched a guerrilla campaign in the aftermath of the First World War, with the aim of creating an Irish republic. Following the compromise of the Anglo-Irish Treaty of December 1921 and the creation of the Irish Free State, the IRA split, resulting in a civil war. This was the first of many schisms in republicanism during the twentieth and twenty-first centuries. A bewildering number of different organizations have laid claim to the letters 'IRA' in the years since 1922, the most significant of which was the Provisional IRA, the largest violent republican grouping in Northern Ireland's thirty-year 'Troubles'.

Despite all being classed as 'republican', there were sizeable differences between these organizations. The United Irish movement and Young Ireland were originally open societies who were influenced by the major radical (yet constitutional) reform impulses of their day. Only after governmental repression and the example of continental revolutionary impulses did these movements adopt out-and-out separatist language and a willingness to use force. The clandestine Irish Republican Brotherhood (or Irish Revolutionary Brotherhood, in some early accounts),[16] established in 1858, was the first separatist society in Ireland dedicated to revolutionary overthrow of the British state from the off. It was a central player in the Easter Rising of 1916. The IRA continued in this vein, albeit on a larger scale during the War of Independence (1919–21), deploying irregular tactics such as guerrilla warfare as a tool to achieve the Republic. The Provisional IRA combined the secretive element of the IRB and the tactical approach of the IRA.

While acknowledging the existence of an enduring political platform called 'republicanism' in Ireland across time, Tom Garvin has dismissed the notion of intellectual or cultural continuity linking personalities and organizations.[17] What it meant to 'be' republican radically altered from generation to generation. The supposed 'fathers' of Irish republicanism, such as Theobald Wolfe Tone and Thomas Davis, were not initially doctrinal separatists, nor necessarily advocates of violence. Both reflected the values of their times. Tone had little time for concepts such as national literature or indigenous language, the raison d'être of Davis's activism. Influential historiographical takes on Tone by Marianne Elliott and Tom Dunne have also emphasized his social conservatism and lingering disdain for the poor, despite his latter embrace of radical politics.[18] Davis, who died three years before the Young Ireland rebellion of 1848, was not a separatist in a straightforward sense, being a member of O'Connell's Repeal Association. He has been positioned by one biographer as a 'constitutional reformer', hardly a ringing endorsement of a revolutionary soldier.[19] Nevertheless, Davis had become firmly ensconced in the republican pantheon by the early twentieth century, largely because of the prominent place he occupied in Patrick Pearse's writings. Some latter-day republicans, not entirely sympathetic to the concept of nationalism, are, however, dismissive of a man who penned ballads instead of encouraging the arming of Ireland.[20]

So the application of the label 'republicanism' in Ireland is not without its problems when constructing ideas of a 'tradition'. Only from the birth of the IRB in 1858 was a more or less consistent argument made by republicans that political freedom equated separation from Britain, and that violence was a necessary tool to achieve liberty. In contrast, the Society of the United Irishmen was drawn to contemporary American and French-style republicanism, which fused classical and modern radical ideas to secure civic liberty, including patriotic citizen militias, an anti-aristocratic impulse and an ambition to overthrow religious sectarianism. Young Ireland, which followed some forty years later, was partly a literary expression of a rising expectation that Ireland was on the cusp of regaining self-government with the Repeal of the Act of Union. Daniel Rodgers' assessment of republicanism in the United States – that its historiographical manifestations are often too diverse and diffuse to render it a useful conceptual tool – is clearly applicable to Ireland.[21] The republicanism of, for example, Young Ireland and the Provisional IRA is so obviously different that any comparison can quickly become a pointless exercise. Rodgers argued that studies of American republicanism need to abandon fixed definitions: there is no republican 'tradition', as key terms and ideas were continually contested.[22] Each generation finds in republicanism what it wants to find.

Yet the idea of 'tradition' within Irish republicanism is worth exploring, not least the historicized self-fashioning of modern adherents. Republicans were rarely born but often were created in moments of profound crisis, such as Anglo-French tension during the 1850s, in reaction to the brutality of the Crown forces in 1920 or loyalist attacks on Catholic areas of Belfast in 1969. One former member of the PIRA, who completed a doctoral degree in prison, has asserted that the re-emergence of physical force republicanism in 1969 was not a rekindling of the unfinished business of 1921; rather, republican violence was a manifestation of the failure of the British state to enshrine equal rights in Northern Ireland.[23] Such an interpretation does much to explain why violence broke out in 1969 – as a response to structural inequalities, discrimination and a heavy-handed police response to civil rights campaigners – but ignores the impulses within separatist movements to link itself to the struggles of the past. In 1971, Provisional Sinn Féin, the political wing of the PIRA, declared itself 'the same organization as was founded in 1905 and has the same objectives as it set itself in 1918', laying claim to an unbroken lineage to the party of the same name that Arthur Griffith established in 1905 and the democratic mandate of the General Election of 1918.[24] The PIRA was thus the 'same' IRA who fought for Ireland's independence some fifty years before. This might have been factually incorrect, but it served to legitimize and clarify the purpose of the PIRA once the cycle of brutal violence in Northern Ireland became seemingly endless.

Historical consciousness rather than political theory tended to inform the separatist mindset in Ireland. An imagined past with clear connections to the present animated republicans, much more so than abstract notions of virtue and liberty, especially as the nineteenth and twentieth centuries rumbled on.[25] Figures associated with republicanism in Ireland – John Mitchel, Patrick Pearse, or Éamon de Valera, for instance – rooted their political ideas in a historicized analysis of Irish politics, often drawing on the words and examples of previous revolutionaries. Alice Stopford Green noted in 1912 the 'very condition of thought' in Ireland, in which 'the far past and the far future are part of the eternal present', capturing something of a belief in a historically rooted manifest destiny.[26] In 1907, the neo-Fenian Dungannon Clubs – itself a historical name with associations with the Irish Volunteers of the eighteenth century – issued a pamphlet that bemoaned that 'Irish ignorance of the history of Ireland has so sapped our interest in ourselves and our faith in ourselves that some of us have been even brought to believe that we alone among civilized peoples are unfit for the ordinary duties of self-government'.[27] In this context, the production of historical writing, and wider engagement with themes and figures from the past, should be seen as part of wider political argument. Sustaining a republican 'tradition' was one manifestation of a wider embrace of a historical idiom that permeated Irish society in the age of Pearse and Green. But was it always this way?

Republicanism in Ireland is typically dated by historians and its adherents to the 1790s. Radicalized by the tumult of the French Revolution and the British suppression of reformist-minded societies, the United Irish movement shifted from open, peaceful agitation for political equality between Catholics and Protestants in Ireland to full-blown insurrection in 1798, in pursuit of national independence from Britain. The rebellion was suppressed, and the United Irish movement was fatally damaged. Another rebellion, this time led by Robert Emmet, broke out in 1803 but was swiftly crushed. The United Irish movement came to an end with Emmet's execution. The nominal leader of the United Irishmen, Theobald Wolfe Tone, became Ireland's first republican visionary and martyr, the founding father of a radical, revolutionary tradition that profoundly shaped the Irish political experience to the present day.[28] It became a rite of passage for every Irish republican writer who followed in Tone's wake to draw on his life and writings for inspiration, guidance and legitimation. Writing in 1937, Seán Ó Faoláin, a member of the IRA during the War of Independence and Civil War, conceded that while Tone did not 'achieve greatly' during his lifetime, 'he started much. Without him, republicanism in Ireland would virtually have no tradition'.[29] Ó Faoláin, however, was also aware of Tone's limitations as a political guide. What 'Tone would have done had he been first President of an Irish Republic nobody knows, because he has not told us'.[30] Tone provided the basic elements which later republicans adopted to construct a political philosophy – national independence, the sovereign people, a non-sectarian definition of the Irish nation – but not a blueprint. Yet Ó Faoláin was accurate in positing Tone as 'the beau-ideal of Irish rebels, the alpha and the omega on which all later would-be revolutionaries instinctively modelled themselves'.[31]

Tone's writings do indeed belie a man who was not a diligent reader of deep political tracts of political philosophers such as John Locke. He was certainly not a republican theorist in a Kantian mould.[32] Indeed, such was Tone's political ambiguity that Thomas Bartlett has mischievously asked 'was Wolfe Tone a republican?'[33] It depends, as always, on definitions. Tone did not shy away from the republican tag, but it came to mean different things after his time. For Tone, republicanism was a civic humanist concept which celebrated the sovereignty of the people. He was not an original political thinker, but, like his famous contemporary, Thomas Paine, possessed an adroit ability to capture the radical zeitgeist in his pamphlets.[34] His most famous pamphlet, *An Argument on*

Behalf of the Catholics of Ireland (1791), was an appeal for equal political rights through Catholic enfranchisement. *An Argument* contended that political liberty could not exist in a country that denied political rights to the majority of its population. The problem, Tone surmised, lay in the semi-colonial structure of government in Ireland, with an Irish parliament proclaiming its independence, when in reality was subordinate to Britain. This paradox underpinned one of Tone's best-known rhetorical flourishes: 'We are free in theory, we are slaves in fact.'[35] Tone's solution was the breaking of 'the English influence', a term he used to describe the government of Ireland, through a more popular franchise. Only then would Ireland have an Irish government, free from the undignified corruption of foreign domination.[36]

An Argument was a product of radical reformist ideas that cascaded widely across Britain and Ireland in the aftermath of the French Revolution.[37] Fundamentally, the pamphlet raged against the remnants of the penal laws, which denied Catholics key political and social rights. But several of the underlying assumptions of *An Argument* – the evils of English dominance over Ireland, the need to overcome religious sectarianism and recognize the sovereignty of the people – became universal themes within later Irish republican thought, long after full Catholic Emancipation was achieved in 1829. Tone's writings after *An Argument* became more explicitly radical after the United Irishmen was suppressed in 1794, mirroring the wider radicalization of the Society after being banished to the shadows. In a pamphlet written in France in 1796, Tone emphatically embraced French-style republicanism, a doctrine that overthrew the 'absurdity of hereditary monarchs' and aspired to 'equal rights, liberties and laws'. Despite his enthusiasm for the French project and strengthening anti-monarchism, Tone refused to publicly advocate a particular form of government for Ireland, stressing that an independent Ireland had a right to choose its own constitution.[38] Separation first, thinking about the form of government later; whether this principle was implicitly learned from Tone or not, it became a stable of Irish republican thought during the nineteenth century.

Tone committed suicide to evade the British hangman following the collapse of the Irish rebellion in 1798. His political reputation languished after his death. The two-volume *Life of Theobald Wolfe Tone*, based on Tone's unpublished papers, was published in Washington in 1826, but failed to trigger an immediate political interest in the United Irishmen.[39] Tone and the United Irishmen were rarely cited in the extensive pamphlet debates surrounding the nascent idea of Repealing the Act of Union in the 1830s, suggesting that the personalities, writings and activities of the generation of the 1790s had little political purchase in the age of reform.[40] Despite serious structural flaws of the operation of the Union during the thirty or so years since Emmet's rebellion in 1803, the republican ideas associated with the United Irishmen rarely received an airing. The United Irishmen's emphasis on a non-sectarian definition of nationality jarred uneasily with the contemporary reality of the mobilization of Catholic Ireland behind Daniel O'Connell's Repeal Association, with Protestant Ireland largely remaining aloof. The brutal violence of 1798 also had little appeal for many in the wake of a successful parliamentary struggle for Catholic Emancipation 1829. Indeed, when Tone and the United Irishmen were sympathetically 'rediscovered' in the nineteenth-century turn to historicism, it was the idealism of the 1790s that was emphasized, not the realities of rebellion.

Framing Separatist Traditions: Young Ireland and the Irish Republican Brotherhood

Tone became a figure of fascination for the Young Ireland wing of the Repeal Association. In 1842, a number of youthful writers, including Thomas Davis, Charles Gavan Duffy and James Blake Dillon, all of whom were affiliated to the O'Connellite movement, founded the *Nation* newspaper. 'Young Ireland', as this faction was dubbed, was drawn to expressions of Irish national identity, such as ballads, the language and folklore, and worked tirelessly to promote them in the *Nation* and other publications.[41] Like his Italian contemporary, Giuseppe Mazzini, Davis, the leading Young Ireland figure, pushed the idea of 'culture' as a unifying force in a divided society. Tone was a pivotal figure in this ambition. He was an appealing character because of an unwavering commitment to overcome religious sectarianism and his promotion of inclusive vision of nationality. As a number of the Young Irelanders were Protestant – Davis was Anglican, while John Mitchel, the most influential writer after Davis, was Presbyterian – the example of Tone was particularly alluring. While the aspiration of a nationality that overcame denominational division was laudable, the vision rubbed uneasily with the contemporary realities. This tension occasionally spilled over into the *Nation*, such as its enthusiastic reprinting of the analysis of the British journal, *Tait's Magazine*, in 1844:

> The *Nation* is not a mere O'Connellite, nor a mere Catholic organ. It has a life of its own. Its writers treat Catholicism with all due respect, as the religion of their country; but they do not write at all like Popish devotees: they venerate and love O'Connell, but do not seem to subscribe implicitly to certain items of his political creed. There is as much of Theobald Wolfe Tone in these men as Daniel O'Connell.[42]

Given O'Connell's well-known animosity to the United Irish movement's embrace of revolutionary violence, the positive interpretation of Tone presented in the *Nation* was a striking counterbalance to O'Connellite orthodoxy. Indeed, Davis's friend and fellow editor of the *Nation*, Charles Gavan Duffy, depicted Davis as the second coming of Tone, the man who 'aimed to unite the whole force of the nation in honourable union'.[43]

Davis was so enraptured by Tone that he aimed to publish a biography in the 'Library of Ireland' history series, established by the Young Irelanders. Unfortunately, Davis's untimely death in 1845, at the age of thirty, meant that the book remained unfinished.[44] Despite this, Davis, in his short career, did much to popularize Tone and present him as the iconic figure of Irish nationality. Davis's poem, 'Tone's Grave', foreshadowed the pilgrimages to Bodenstown cemetery in Kildare, which became an annual tradition for Irish nationalists from the 1870s.[45] Young Ireland should not, however, be viewed simply as the Society of United Irishmen 2.0. The adulation of Tone masked a fundamental difference of opinion about the political legitimacy of the nation that reflected the temporal shift from the 1790s to 1840s. The United Irishmen appealed to French Revolution-inspired natural rights in making the case for Ireland's political freedom; Young Ireland were suspicious of such universalism and embraced

Ireland's historical rights to nationhood.[46] The Young Ireland pen thus separated the biblical Tone from the historical Tone, emphasizing his Irishness over his transnational republicanism. This became an influential revision: for later generations Tone was more of a nationalist than an internationalist revolutionary.

Given Davis's immersion in the life of Tone at the moment of his death, it is surprising, perhaps, that the other literary and historically informed figures in Young Ireland did not take on the biography. Indeed, references to Tone are fleeting in the work of John Mitchel, one of the most significant Young Irelanders after the death of Davis. Where Davis's political thought was framed by a historicized image of Ireland as a nation, Mitchel preached the righteousness of hatred as a legitimate political expression and the chief motivating force behind radical agitation. After a split in the Young Ireland, Mitchel set up a short-lived newspaper called the *United Irishman* in 1848, which carried an obvious appeal to the legacy of the 1790s. But beyond the title and a reference to the 'Holy War' of 1798 in the first edition, there was little on Tone or the United Irishmen.[47] Tone is mentioned only in passing in Mitchel's two best-known works, *Jail Journal* (1854) and *The Last Conquest of Ireland (Perhaps)* (1861). Mitchel's *History of Ireland* (1869) covered the 1790s, but there was little serious reflection on Tone's personality or political philosophy. If later generations of separatists proclaimed Tone as the founding father of Irish republicanism, Mitchel is the ideological *enfant terrible*. Mitchel was arrested and tried for sedition in 1848 (before the rebellion) on account of his violent journalism, which did not shy away from stoking insurrection at the height of the Famine.[48] The works that he penned in captivity and after his subsequent escape and settlement in the United States bristle with bitterness at the wretched state of Ireland during the 1840s. In 1861, Mitchel popularized the still prevalent idea that the British committed a deliberate act of genocide in Ireland during the Famine.[49] He argued that the experiences of the 1840s legitimized violent insurrection: the horrors of war 'were by no means so terrible as the horrors of peace which their own eyes had seen', and that the survivors of the trauma were 'ashamed to see their kinsmen patiently submitting to be starved to death, and longed to see blood flow, if it were only to show that blood still flowed in Irish veins'.[50] Hate and vengeance had emerged as empowering political principles.

The essence of Mitchel's thesis – that British rule of Ireland was an abomination and should be despised and resisted – gained much traction in the decades after the Famine. The foundation of the Irish Republican Brotherhood (or Irish Revolutionary Brotherhood) by James Stephens in 1858, and its rapid growth throughout Ireland, unquestionably benefited from the popularization of the Mitchelite analysis of British-Irish relations. Coupled with the parallel founding of the Fenian Brotherhood in the United States by two Irish exiles, John O'Mahony and Michael Doheny, 'Fenianism' (as ideology of the IRB became known) introduced a transnational dynamic into separatist politics.[51] Stephens, O'Mahony and Doheny had taken part in the 1848 rising in Ireland, and the swift failure of the venture left an indelible mark on the three men: the grim but necessary lesson was that for a rebellion to be successful and become the vital stepping stone to a national revolution, organization, discipline and, above all, secrecy, were necessary. Fenianism thus adopted the organizational structure of a secret revolutionary society in Ireland, supported by an open and semi-constitutional body in the United States.

That said, the boundaries of what a secret society could do were remarkably fluid. In 1863, the clandestine IRB founded a newspaper called the *Irish People*, which was published out of an office located only a brief walk away from Dublin Castle, the seat of British rule in Ireland.[52] This was the most notable example during the nineteenth century of an Irish revolutionary vanguard attempting to radicalize public opinion not through the propaganda of the deed but through words, interpretation and polemic argument. Publishing a newspaper was a marker of seriousness and intent, especially for a movement or cause that might otherwise be considered 'fringe'. In the Irish context, the success of the *Nation* during the 1840s unquestionably altered the boundaries of political expression and popularized the ideas of Young Ireland. It was no coincidence that the primary figures behind much of the editorial content of the *Irish People* – John O'Leary, Thomas Luby and Charles Kickham – were all diligent readers of the *Nation* during its heyday.

In publishing the *People*, the IRB pioneered a form of literary separatism that later republican organizations, such as the PIRA, also deployed. But while, say, *An Phoblacht*, the newspaper associated with the PIRA, took great efforts to connect the contemporary campaign to historical uprisings in Ireland, the *People* was more content to plough its own furrow. There were occasional references to republicanism during the 1790s, but no sustained attempt to create a lineage to suggest that the IRB was the present day manifestation of a timeless struggle. The United Irishmen were rarely discussed in editorials, and the Young Ireland legacy was often viewed solely through the prism of the disastrous rebellion of 1848, which the *People* dismissed as an 'abortion' that 'disheartened the people and damaged our reputation for bravery at home and abroad'.[53] The attempt at revolt was 'a failure and a disgrace' because of the failure of the Young Ireland leadership to 'prepare' the people for insurrection.[54] A later issue took aim at 'the quantity of bluster and bunkum vented by the prominent men of that period', which can be interpreted as a critique of the firebrand, Famine-era editorials of the *Nation* and Mitchel's paper, the *United Irishman*. Young Ireland was ignored entirely in the *People's* assertion that 'for the first time since '98 we have an organization worthy of the name'.[55]

The *People* also did not hold back in its analysis of the earlier years of the *Nation*, when the paper was edited by Thomas Davis. Davis was the great driving force behind the rise of a literary nationalism during the 1840s; the *Nation* nurtured the idea that Ireland needed to recover its cultural identity as a precondition of meaningful political independence. While Davis was lauded for his role in challenging sectarianism through verse and personal example, the *People's* hard-headed perspective at times rubbed against the grain of Davisian literary nationalism.[56] One editorial in the *People* can be read as a rebuff to the school of thought preached by the *Nation*:

> We might be content with mere sentimental patriotism; dreamily loving our green island, gloating over her unrivalled scenery, studying her language, sobbing with sorrow and love while we listened to her entrancing music; pondering over

her ancient glories, and haply making ballads or essays upon them; bewailing her slavery, and the web of discord, which a wayward fate wove for her – and, anon, smashing the Saxon foe to atoms in rhyme or prose. But the stern necessities of the hour forbid this puny self-delusion.[57]

The true patriot, according to the *People*, was not a poet but an Irish republican soldier. As the paper declared, 'patriotism, not militarily organised, is worth nothing'.[58]

This openness about the IRB's revolutionary intent made the organization a very different creature to the United Irishmen and Young Ireland, both of which were radicalized by external events and largely driven by desperation into acts of rebellion. Indeed, the IRB styled itself as the founding moment of modern Irish republicanism. Its frame of reference was contemporary in outlook: editorials looked to developments abroad, such as the Civil War in the United States and the plight of the Māori in New Zealand, the need to drive priests out of the Irish political sphere, and the poverty of constitutional approaches to achieve meaningful change in Ireland. There was no attempt to situate the IRB within a republican past in Ireland because that history was associated with painful and demoralizing defeat. The *People* was written by young men who bitterly experienced a failed rebellion in 1848. It is notable, then, that John O'Leary, one of the chief architects of the *People's* editorial line, praised the idealism of Young Ireland in his memoirs published in the 1890s.[59] The suppression of the *People* in 1865, the IRB's own (failed) attempt at rebellion two years later and subsequent decades of revolutionary inertia perhaps prompted a revision of the achievements of Young Ireland.

Claiming the past

The painful memories of sectarian violence and ignoble defeat soured readings of the recent separatist past within Young Ireland and the mid-Victorian generation of Irish Fenians. It is striking that the separatist canon was popularized not by militant republicans, but constitutional nationalists eager to appropriate virtuous elements associated with past rebellions such as patriotism, idealism and self-sacrifice. A key publication that did much to popularize a republican canon was *Speeches from the Dock*, which first appeared in 1867. *Speeches from the Dock* was an anthology of separatist oratory delivered in the courtroom, compiled by the Sullivan brothers, who were associated with the constitutional wing of Irish nationalism. It was one of the most successful publication enterprises in Irish political history, going through numerous editions throughout the nineteenth and twentieth centuries, with the final version appearing as late as 1968. The book introduced Irish readers to some of the boldest separatist rhetoric of the past, while doing much to create an accessible canon of revolutionary figures, movements and ideas. The mass appeal of *Speeches from the Dock* served to sanitize rebellions against the Crown, stripping away the violence and bloodshed – and failure – while affirming the courage of the rebels and the attractive idealism of their politics. It was less a manifesto of republicanism than a celebration of patriotism, a distinction which bestowed respectability on erstwhile rebels. Writing only a few years after the first edition, Isaac Butt recorded that *Speeches from the Dock* had already become 'a portion of the national literature of Ireland'.[60] This was an insightful observation: like Davis's sculpting of the biblical Tone during the 1840s, *Speeches from the Dock* did much to construct a literary separatism that centred on defiant oratory rather than the actuality of rebellion.[61]

The enterprise also did much to perpetuate the idea of a singular separatist political culture in Ireland that linked rebels across time. The courtroom speeches of Tone and other United Irishmen sat beside those of Young Irelanders such as Mitchel and John Martin, and Fenians such as Charles Kickham and Thomas Luby. Distinctions between the natural rights-inspired republicanism of the United Irishmen, the historicized nationalism of the Young Irelanders and the clandestine separatism of IRB were dissolved by the book. In their introduction, the Sullivans justified beginning with the trials following the 1798 rebellion because 'there is consequently in the speeches which follow such a unity of purpose and sentiment as render them especially suitable for presentation in a single volume'.[62] A 'tradition' was taking form, but it had more to do with constitutional nationalists seeking to harness the patriotic idealism of past rebels than the promotion of republicanism as a motivating political idea. Writing in 1877, when he was a Home Rule MP, A. M. Sullivan posited that 'Constitutional Nationalists' and 'Revolutionary Nationalists' were 'two sections of the national party', implying that republicanism was, in all essence, simply a form of nationalism.[63] From this perspective, Tone, Emmet and Mitchel 'belonged' to constitutional nationalists as much as militant separatists. Indeed, the ebullience of the Parnellite campaign during the late 1870s and 1880s significantly blurred these boundaries: Charles Stewart Parnell had few qualms about cooperating with the IRB and, indeed, may have taken their secretive oath himself.[64] For Parnell, the association with militant republicanism was mostly a rhetorical and symbolic one but did much to boost a projection of a muscular Irish nationalism at Westminster. Indeed, versions of a political canon can be found within the pages of constitutional nationalists newspapers, connecting Parnell to Tone, Davis, Mitchel, and Stephens.[65]

The constitutional nationalist claim to the separatist canon was an underlying theme of the centenary of the 1798 rebellion. While the old separatist, John O'Leary, re-emerged to chair the Wolfe Tone Memorial Association, which attracted neo-Fenians such as W. B. Yeats and Maud Gonne, constitutional nationalists also publicly seized the legacy of the United Irishmen. The iconography of the Wolfe Tone Memorial Association connected the French affinity of the United Irishmen to the IRB: lavish membership cards were adorned by the tricolour of France and the green and yellow sunburst flag embraced by the Fenians.[66] The radical secularism of the United Irishmen was praised in the *Shan Van Vocht*, the influential periodical founded in Belfast in 1896 by Alice Milligan and Anna Johnston. Milligan's biography of Tone, published in 1898, called for 'defiant, unswerving patriotism' in the face of continuing 'English misrule'.[67] Constitutional nationalists, however, played down the revolutionary intent of the United Irishmen, positioning them as proto–Home Rulers rebelling against a corrupt parliament that discriminated against Catholics.[68] It was the leaders of the (then divided) constitutional nationalist movement, John Redmond and John Dillon, who took the most prominent public-facing roles in the unveiling of the foundation stone of the Wolfe Tone memorial in Dublin in 1898. Redmond penned a periodical article praising the patriotism of the United Irishmen but condemning their turn to violence.[69] Images of Tone were used on membership cards issued by the United Irish League, a grassroots organization founded in 1898, which quickly became an affiliated body of the Home Rule movement.[70] The legacy of the United Irishmen, especially their anti-sectarianism and fraternal idealism, was claimed by all wings of Irish nationalism, from constitutional Home Rulers to militant radicals, highlighting the malleability of historical memory in a fragmented political culture. Republicans and constitutional nationalists fished from the same historical pond but displayed their catches in radically different ways. Constitutional nationalists were largely responsible for the popularity of a separatist canon, but the pantheon of Irish republicans was reclaimed by militants during the First World War.

Constructing canons

Patrick Pearse was nineteen years old at the time of the centenary of the 1798 rebellion and was already an enthusiastic activist in the Gaelic League, an Irish language revivalist movement established five years before.[71] He founded a remarkable school in Dublin called St Enda's, which promoted the Irish language, sports and literature. In 1916, the school master was executed for his part in the Easter Rising, a rebellion organized by the IRB and the socialist Irish Citizens' Army. The Proclamation of the Irish Republic, which was partly drafted and read aloud by Pearse at the commencement of the Rising, was an assertion of separatist tradition. Armed insurrection was justified by appealing to 'the dead generations from which [Ireland] receives her old tradition of nationhood'.[72] Pearse was greatly animated by a Davisian interpretation of Irish history, the primary purpose of which was to arouse the passions of the living. As Davis argued, with echoes of his Scottish contemporary, Thomas Carlyle, history should 'set up in our souls the memory of great men, who shall then be as models and judges of our actions'.[73] This rang especially true for Pearse. The reference to the 'dead generations' in the Proclamation drew explicitly on one of his final essays, 'Ghosts', written over Christmas in 1915. Here, Pearse grouped together four separatist figures – Theobald Wolfe Tone, Thomas Davis, James Fintan Lalor and John Mitchel – as the 'ghosts' haunting modern Ireland, 'dead men who have bequeathed a trust to us living men'. In keeping with the constitutional nationalist/republican hybridity of the canon, Charles Stewart Parnell was included as an honorary separatist.[74] As a political philosophy, Pearse's embrace of the revolutionary past ironically chimed more with Edmund Burke's interpretation of the social contract – society as 'a partnership not only between those who are living, but between those who are living, those who are dead, and those who are to be born'[75] – than the natural rights agenda of the United Irishmen. Just as Burke believed that nations had no right to dismantle its constitution at will, Pearse asserted that the Irish nation had no right to dismantle its separatist history.[76] 'Separatism', he argued, 'is the national position'.[77]

Pearse's writings provide vivid insights into a historically minded conception of Irish nationality and the intellectual rationale for an independent Ireland. While political manifestations of Irish republicanism since the 1790s had hardly been sustained continuously, Pearse was drawn to a form of history that emphasized the theme of eternal struggle. 'The chain of the Separatist tradition has never once snapped during the centuries', he proposed, before depicting various displays of martial virtue – from the battle of Kinsale in 1601 to the Irish Volunteers of his own day – as a cyclical pattern that demonstrated Ireland's sustained resistance to British attempts at dominance.[78] 'A nation's fundamental idea of freedom', Pearse proclaimed,

> is not affected by the accidents of time and circumstance. It does not vary with the centuries, or with the comings and goings of men or of empires. The substance of truth does not change, nor does the substance of freedom. Yesterday's definition of both the one and the other is today's definition and will be tomorrow's.[79]

Whereas the early IRB largely positioned themselves as the originators of a subversive and militant republicanism, Pearse, a prominent figure in the Brotherhood, dramatically extended the historical pedigree of Irish separatism.

Pearse interpreted the contemporary political world through the prism of history, deploying a historicized idiom to articulate his political ideas. The 'ghosts' of Irish history were used by Pearse to advocate a radical programme of political independence, representative government and universal suffrage, with each canonical figure representing distinctive national virtues. Pearse cited Tone's mantras on the need 'to break the connection with England' and 'unit[ing] the whole people of Ireland' as Irish nationalism in its purest form.[80] In Pearse's reading, Tone was the father of Irish democracy, the champion of the 'men of no property', who asserted the right of the people of Ireland to choose their own form of government, free from English domination. Davis was, in Pearse's words, the 'first of modern Irishmen to make explicit the truth that a nationality is a spirituality'. If Tone's most important 'truth' was that 'Ireland must be free', then Davis extended this logic by affirming that Ireland should be not merely a 'self-governing state', but 'authentically the Irish nation, bearing all the majestic marks of her nationhood'. Pearse thus connected the Gaelic League, one of the most influential cultural bodies of his own day, to Davis's teaching.[81] Lalor – hitherto, an obscure figure associated with the radical fringes of Young Ireland – was the 'fiery spirit' who developed Tone's democratic thought, preaching the 'gospel of the Sovereign People' in an effort to undo the 'conquest' of Ireland.[82] Pearse praised Mitchel's weaponization of hatred to combat 'English' government, commercialism and militarism in Ireland. When confronted by a political programme designed to erase Irish nationality, Pearse asserted that hate 'is not only a good thing, but is a duty'.[83]

Pearse thus chose and deployed four figures with very different personalities and politics, who, taken together, for him, represented the essence of Irish nationality. This was the first major attempt by an Irish separatist to create a literary-minded canon that went beyond Tone. The word 'gospel' was used liberally to describe the thought of each man; the four deliberately were sculpted as apostles or prophets. Pearse claimed that 'God spoke to Ireland through Tone', setting Irish separatism apart as a divine mission.[84] Three years after Pearse's execution, Desmond Ryan, a graduate of Pearse's school, published an insightful character profile of his former teacher. Following Pearse's lead, Ryan described Tone, Davis, Mitchel and Lalor as the 'Fathers of the One True Church of the Irish Nation'.[85] The catholicity of Irish separatism was one of the most notable aspects that followed the execution of the leaders of the Easter Rising and one of the rebellion's lasting legacies. The 'martyrs' took on an overtly Catholic complex as the Church increasingly provided a vehicle for sympathy for the rebels.[86] Despite the deliberate conflation of past Irish separatists and the divine, each of the 'ghosts' allowed Pearse to advocate certain political concepts. He embraced a democratic idiom, but one expressed through the works of Tone and Lalor. His belief that political self-government was insufficient for the realization of nationality, and must be combined with a distinctive cultural identity, was articulated through Davis. The right and, indeed, duty of the Irish to resist the British state was affirmed through Mitchel's words.

The separatist canon constructed by Pearse was thus the medium to develop republican political argument. As such, Pearse's 'ghosts' are notable for who was *not* included among the undead haunting the nation. Robert Emmet is conspicuous by his absence, especially given Pearse's hero worship of the leader of the 1803 rebellion.[87] In a lecture in 1914, Pearse conceded that while the rebellion was disastrous, the manner of Emmet's death – with his astonishing speech from the dock before being publicly beheaded – left a 'sacrifice Christ-like in its perfection'.[88] Emmet was *the* example of the Irish separatist par excellence, but as Pearse conceded, he did not leave a 'body of teaching' – books, essays, poems – for succeeding generations to study.[89] Nevertheless, the power of his speech from the dock secured a form of literary immortality. Such was the allure of Emmet's performance in court that the Chartists staged historical re-enactments of the oratory and frequently toasted his name.[90] Yet, for all his sense of theatre (drama was, it should be remembered, an important part of the education offered by St Enda's),[91] Pearse was drawn to political texts in his pursuit of literary separatism, an impulse which his own final works self-consciously attempted to replicate.

The absence of the mid-Victorian originators of Fenianism in Pearse's canon is also noteworthy, given his membership of the IRB. There was no room for James Stephens, the founder of the Brotherhood; John O'Leary, Thomas Luby and Charles Kickham, the editors of the *Irish People*; nor senior Irish-American Fenians such as John O'Mahony and Michael Doheny. O'Leary had, of course, been immortalized by W. B. Yeats in 'September 1913' – 'Romantic Ireland's dead and gone / It's with O'Leary in the grave' – but for Pearse, the intellectual rationale for separatism had been laid down in place before the IRB was founded. At his oration at the graveside of the old dynamiter, Jeremiah O'Donovan Rossa in 1915, Pearse professed that there is 'only one definition of freedom' and that 'it is Tone's definition' and 'it is Mitchel's definition'. Despite the hardships that Rossa and his generation endured in British prisons, they were not originators but followers of a creed already consecrated by the patriotic dead.[92]

The canon and the 'Troubles'

In many ways, Pearse succeeded in emulating his separatist heroes. His name was, and remains, intimately bound up in the public mind as *the* key personality of the Rising of 1916. During the jubilee of the Rising in 1966, however, it was James Connolly who emerged as the most alluring of the 1916 leaders.[93] Connolly was the leader of the socialist Irish Citizens' Army and co-author of the Proclamation of the Irish Republic of 1916. His historical analysis was radically different from Pearse's. Viewed through the prism of class struggle, Connolly condemned the Young Irelanders and the mid-Victorian Fenians as expressions not of genuine revolutionary intent but as bourgeois nationalism. While Pearse folded separatist figures such as Tone and Mitchel together, proclaiming their common allegiance to the one never-shifting national question, Connolly stressed the radical democratic and internationalist impulses of the United Irishmen, which set them apart from each separatist movement that followed.[94] Connolly's mixture of socialism, republicanism and anti-colonialism set him apart in turn from the other leading figures of 1916, and these characteristics made him adaptable to the radical political climate of the 1960s. While the Provisional IRA drew extensively from the canon laid out by Pearse in 1916, Connolly also featured prominently in 'Troubles'-era republican literature. In the eyes of many leaders of the PIRA, radical socialism was an essential component of the Irish republican tradition. From the late 1970s, the Provisional movement frequently affirmed their commitment to a 'democratic, socialist republic'.[95] Quotes from Connolly, including his famous line, 'the cause of Ireland is the cause of labour', are peppered throughout the written works of Gerry Adams, who became president of Sinn Féin, the PIRA's political wing, in 1983.[96] Like many self-proclaimed socialist movements, however, the Provisionals found the 1990s an ideologically challenging period, and references to socialism were largely dropped.[97]

The early months of the 'Troubles' in Northern Ireland politicized and radicalized large swathes of people. Brendan Hughes, who became a prominent PIRA commander, recalled that during the late 1960s, many young men and women 'did not have a great deal of political ideology'. The PIRA was created from a split within the IRA during the winter of 1969, with Northern Ireland engulfed in bitter communal violence. In Hughes's recollection, the radicals who flocked to the Provisionals were the same people who were defending their predominant areas and the Catholic Church from attacks by loyalists. For Hughes, the politics of the gun was initially about survival and defence; in his words, 'it wasn't until later that we really began to learn what Republicanism meant'.[98] But this republicanism, for some, was tainted by the stain of sectarianism. For Des O'Hagan, a prominent figure in the 'Official' wing of the IRA following the split, the Provisionals represented a gross betrayal of the Irish republican ideal. In his reading, the 'vicious sectarian murders' perpetrated by the PIRA were 'counter-revolutionary': each attack widened the gulf between Protestant and Catholic in Northern Ireland, with the unintended consequence of strengthening the grip of the British state.[99] O'Hagan's judgement on the PIRA's actions drew heavily from the well of republican tradition, especially Tone's anti-sectarianism. While representatives of the Provisional IRA travelled to Bodenstown for the annual pilgrimage to Tone's grave, O'Hagan suggested that 'republican authenticity and legitimacy must be judged on the contribution actions either make to securing Tone's "means" or to frustrating them'.[100] For O'Hagan, the overwhelming presence of Protestants among the victims of the PIRA told its own story. If Tone represented an anti-sectarian ethos, then the PIRA, in the eyes of many in the 'Officials', fell far short.

The Provisionals, nonetheless, emerged as the most significant (and lethal) Irish republican group during the Troubles. Their political wing, Sinn Féin, was, however, almost an invisible presence until the late 1970s, when a new leadership, centring on the northern duo of Gerry Adams and Martin McGuinness, assumed command. Prior to this, Sinn Féin was merely the mouthpiece of the PIRA; political activity was discouraged as a potential distraction from the military campaign and the inevitable path to unsavoury compromise.[101] The Adams-McGuinness leadership openly advocated a more active political agitation to accompany the violence of the PIRA since at least the mid-1970s, as a means of widening the means of republican resistance to the British state.[102] It also became imperative to legitimize the PIRA's violence in the face of British denunciation of 'terrorism' in Northern Ireland, with one eye on a domestic audience and the other on international opinion. It was to the Irish republican canon that the leadership of the Provisional movement turned. Gerry Adams recorded that he was largely ignorant of politics during his teens, but the jubilee of the Easter Rising in 1966 alerted him to the writings of the executed leaders. A major aspect of this political awakening, according to Adams, was 'the popularisation of the writings of the leaders of the 1916 Rising', especially those of James Connolly.[103] Early Sinn Féin pamphlets expanded this interest. The 'Sinn Féin Education Department' issued a number of publications during the late 1970s and 1980s, many of which stressed the PIRA's place in the historical lineage of Irish republicanism. A two-part *History of Republicanism* provided an overview of the tradition since the days of Tone, affirming the 'present-day struggle' as part of the historical-sanctioned struggle against British domination over Ireland.[104] The historical legitimacy of violence was affirmed throughout Provisional pamphlets. Another publication suggested that the 'most consistent element of the Irish republican tradition is armed struggle', casting the PIRA as the prodigal children of the Proclamation of the Irish Republic of 1916.[105]

The PIRA was at pains to style themselves as the same organization that contested the War of Independence, emphasizing a shared political ambition, tactical malleability and an awareness of the importance of an 'intelligence war'.[106] In 1985, the newly established Sinn Féin Publicity Department issued a notorious pamphlet that listed the atrocities carried out by the IRA during the 'Tan War', implying that dreadful actions were required to achieve a radical political objective. The point of the publication was to 'confront those hypocritical revisionists who winsomely refer to the "Old IRA" whilst deriding their more effective and, arguably, less bloody successors'.[107] Still, the guerrilla campaign of the 'Old IRA' was regarded with great esteem within the PIRA. The Provisionals' newspaper, *An Phoblacht*, commenced a series on 'Famous Guerrilla Leaders' in 1974, with Tom Barry, the Cork IRA veteran as their opening choice.[108] The director of the IRA campaign during the War of Independence, Michael Collins, was beyond the pale for the Provisionals, given his role in brokering the compromise

Anglo-Irish Treaty in December 1921. Collins thus never entered the PIRA's canon; Adams dubbed Collins, along with Arthur Griffith and Éamon de Valera, as 'non-republicans' who assumed the leadership of Sinn Féin after the 1918 election.[109] When David Trimble, the leader of the Ulster Unionist Party, raised the possibility in 1998 that Adams 'could be a Michael Collins', the man to broker a settlement, this was a double-edged judgment.[110] To compromise is to defy the separatist canon; Adams was well aware of Collins's fate.

Conclusion

In 1796, Wolfe Tone visited the Panthéon in Paris. Travelling through the Catacombs, Tone passed the cenotaphs of Voltaire, Jean-Jacques Rousseau and the revolutionary Marquis de Dampierre. It was a cathartic experience. Tone recorded in his notebooks that 'nothing can be imagined more likely to create a great spirit of a nation than a repository of this kind'. That 'great spirit' should be at the heart of all nations who desired freedom. 'If we have a republic in Ireland', Tone surmised, 'we must build a Pantheon'. He suggested a few names to start this proposed temple of Irish freedom, including the Anglo-Irish writers William Molyneux and Jonathan Swift, and the radical MP, Charles Lucas. Tone's physical pantheon would have included the individuals who were certainly not republican or separatists; they were, in Tone's words, simply 'good Irishmen'.[111] That such names would not feature in the metaphysical pantheon of Irish republicanism as it emerged during the nineteenth and twentieth centuries is testament to the political innovations of the separatist platform, and the desire to view historical figures in the light of the present. Tone partly styled himself as part of a radical Anglo-Irish constitutional tradition, but this was not the biblical Tone for later generations, who emphasized his separatism and militancy to legitimize violence in the pursuit of national independence. There have been republicans in Ireland since the 1790s, but the idea of a singular republican 'tradition' is far from straightforward.

While the United Irish movement can be said to be the first modern Irish republicans, they were internationalists inspired by the revolutionary and egalitarian possibilities of the Rights of Man and, as the case of Tone's Pantheon reveals, decidedly non-republican Irish ideas. Irish independence during the 1790s was viewed predominately through these lenses.[112] The bulk of Young Ireland were formally separatists rather than republicans; indeed, this distinction might also be applied to various prominent figures in the 'republican' pantheon, such as John Mitchel and Patrick Pearse, who did not develop a blueprint for the 'Republic'. The IRB was formed in the wake of the botched rebellion of 1848, and the Brotherhood's newspaper, the *Irish People*, was often disparaging when reviewing the Young Irelanders' revolutionary potential, displaying little interest in a sentimental connection to the past. Indeed, while a statue of William Smith O'Brien, the leader of the attempted rising, was unveiled in Dublin in 1870 (at the height of the Fenian amnesty campaign), he is rarely mentioned in later republican texts. Thomas Davis's identity-centred cultural activism, Lalor's social radicalism and Mitchel's intense Anglophobia were, instead, the concepts taken from the Young Ireland project after the 1840s, not least by Patrick Pearse, whose writings did much to provide the intellectual basis for Irish separatism. Yet Pearse, like his hero, Mitchel, was not interested in developing a *republican* language that was distinctive from nationalism; rather, he asserted that separatism was the singular path to realize nationality. If separatism took the form of republicanism, so be it, but this was not necessarily a given.[113]

The legacy of Theobald Wolfe Tone sits uneasily in the creation of the separatist tradition in Ireland. The cult of Wolfe Tone took full shape by the 1890s, one hundred years after his death, and even then his legacy was claimed by all shades of Irish nationalism.[114] There were numerous Wolfe Tone clubs, flute bands and memorial committees formed in and after 1898, pressing the name of the United Irishman into common currency. Tone's internationalism, however, was often folded into nationalism, and his oft-quoted phrase about uniting the Irish people rang hollow with the convergence of separatism and Catholicism during the nineteenth and twentieth centuries. Indeed, Tone, like other Protestant separatists, was often cited to counter claims that Irish republicanism was inherently sectarian.[115] A cynic might infer that this became the chief purpose of Tone within elements of militant republicanism. Tone was, of course, ever present in republican literature during the twentieth century, standing as the alpha and omega of separatism in Ireland. His writings were widely and regularly published, especially during the twentieth century. Bulmer Hobson's edition of Tone's *Letters* appeared in the middle of the War of Independence period: Hobson opined that along with Mitchel's *Jail Journal*, the *Letters* were the 'two best books produced under the influence of the national idea in modern Ireland'.[116] Once again, Tone became the beacon of Irish nationality rather than civic republicanism. The highest praise that Kevin O'Shiel, the Ulster-born separatist, bestowed on the circle of men surrounding Michael Collins who directed the War of Independence was that they were 'all men full of the Wolfe Tone and Fenian traditions'.[117] This fusion was revealing: the biblical Tone was a fully fledged Fenian militant, an image of a man divorced from his political and intellectual contexts.

Hobson's edition of Tone's writings reminds us of the importance of a literary separatist culture in Ireland, particularly centring on life writing.[118] In 1913, Pearse wrote excitedly about receiving Arthur Griffith's new edition of *Jail Journal*, the 'last gospel of the New Testament of Irish Nationality, as Wolfe Tone's Autobiography is the first'.[119] Desmond Ryan recalled that Pearse often carried a well-thumbed copy of Tone's writings.[120] Ernie O'Malley, a prominent IRA leader during the War of Independence period, recorded the prevalence of texts such as *Jail Journal* and *Speeches from the Dock* in rural Ireland. 'I have listened to old men,' O'Malley recalled, 'who could recite parts of these books, especially the speeches made by men who were expecting death or life imprisonment'.[121] Mossie Harnett, another IRA veteran from the early 1920s, recorded in his memoir that he devoured books on the 1798 rebellion and the 'exploits of the Fenians' as a teen, weeping over 'our sad history, the fate of our martyrs and the unending tale of blighted hopes'.[122] The neo-Romanticism of this form of literary separatism – and the emotional impact it had on some of its readers – left a lasting legacy. Figures such as Tone, Emmet, and Davis were still powerfully relevant during the upheavals of the Irish revolutionary period of 1912 to 1923. The Pearsian canon was first and foremost a literary one: the four 'ghosts' haunting Irish nationality were writers in some form or other. While these figures were found in PIRA literature, the idea of a republican 'tradition' within the Provisionals was primarily a political one; the emotive excesses of a Mitchel or Pearse, or the cultural emphasis of a Davis, simply were not as relevant to a conflict framed by the global rise of civil rights, armed protests against oppressive regimes and terrible violence inflict by paramilitary groupings. James Connolly, however, spoke to the radicalism of the post–Second World War generation; the largely working-class Provisional IRA turned to iconic socialist for intellectual inspiration after 1969.

The publishing world thus played a significant part in the fostering of a separatist mentality. Like other radical traditions, such as Chartism in Britain, the stables of Irish republicanism were popularized in newspapers, books and pamphlets.[123] Newly published collected writings and reissues of older texts enabled later generations to access past ideas. While Pearse was not explicit about how he 'discovered' Lalor, it is highly likely that John O'Leary's collection of Lalor's writings, which was published in 1895, was the gateway. Without such collected works, such figures may have remained obscure. It is striking that during the period 1891 to 1922, encompassing the death of Charles Stewart Parnell to the foundation of the independent Irish state, a large number of collected works by historical separatist figures was published. Like Lalor, Thomas Davis's reputation benefited from the publication of a volume of prose writing in 1890.[124] Given Davis's literary themes, the writings provided a further intellectual rationale for the 'Irish-Ireland' cultural project spearheaded by the Gaelic League, breathing new life – sometimes critically – into the Young Ireland legacy.[125] Tone and Mitchel, as mentioned above, enjoyed frequent new editions and a continuing influence over nationalist, republican and separatist political thought in Ireland throughout the twentieth century. Indeed, the potential political impact of historical material was something that concerned the British state, which saw such publications as incendiary propaganda. In 1918, for instance, a new edition of Lalor's writings was briefly suppressed under the Defence of the Realm Act. While the publisher affirmed that 'matter written 70 years ago could not have any detrimental effect at the present day', the authorities, no doubt with an awareness of the weight placed on historical content in separatist literature, begged to differ.[126]

Irish separatism has been historically malleable in its ideological outlook, formally encompassing internationalists such as Tone, socialists such as Connolly, Anglophobes such as Mitchel, and nationalists such as Pearse. The figures associated with rebellion and violence were not, however, the intellectual property of militants; constitutional nationalists played a key role in popularizing notions of a canon of resistance to British rule in Ireland. The need to demonstrate 'ownership' over the radical tradition was a vital legitimizing drive within nationalist and republican politics, especially from the late 1870s to the foundation of the Irish Free State in 1922 and beyond.

While nationalists and separatists competed for the likes of Tone and Davis, militant republicanism has ensured countless splits, with each newly created faction claiming to be the 'true' representative of an unbroken separatist tradition. Again, a connection with past struggles was vital for the legitimacy of present-day action. In 1938, seven members elected to the Second Dáil, the last all-Ireland parliament convened by Sinn Féin in 1921, conferred the authority of that iconic assembly to the Army Council of the IRA. From that point on, the IRA leadership declared itself to be the legitimate government of the Irish Republic. When the last surviving member of the Second Dáil, Tom Maguire, 'transferred' this authority to the Provisional Army Council following the split in 1969, it was a major public relations coup for the fledging PIRA. When the Provisionals themselves split in 1986 over the decision to take seats in the southern Irish parliament, Maguire again emerged to bestow the authority of a government on the newly created Continuity IRA.[127] The socialist activist, Eamon McCann, has explained 'that this idea of the IRA leadership as the sole source of political legitimacy in Ireland will seem fantastical to many ... [but] it provides the moral basis of all its actions'.[128] Indeed, in this sense, republican political thought was more historicized than theorized. In 1998, when Sinn Féin were participants in the negotiations that led to the Belfast (or Good Friday) Agreement, the Continuity faction published a book containing key separatist texts, including the Proclamation of the Irish Republic from 1867, a selection from Pearse's pamphlets and Maguire's statement, reminding sympathetic readers that the Provisionals lacked republican authenticity. 'Though these documents are from history', the preface declared, 'they cannot be safely locked away in an historical archive to be forgotten about'.[129] The Continuity IRA opposed the PIRA's ceasefire and the premise of the peace process in Northern Ireland, which it believed ran contrary to republican tradition. More recently, a glut of splinter groups declaring themselves as 'the' IRA has sprung up, at times with deadly effect. The question of separatist authenticity has sustained republican politics for over one hundred years in Ireland and shows little sign of disappearing. Yet, given the political and cultural diversity within Irish republicanism stretching back to the days of Tone, and the widespread desire of a myriad of nationalists to appropriate elements of the separatist canon, it is difficult to substantiate the existence of a singular 'tradition'. Like their American counterparts, the Irish find in republicanism what they want to find.

Notes

1 My thanks to Ultán Gillen, Matthew Kelly and Caoimhe Nic Dháibhéid for their insightful reading of previous drafts of this chapter.
2 Quentin Skinner, *The Foundations of Modern Political Thought*, 2 vols. (Cambridge: Cambridge University Press, 1978); J. G. A. Pocock, *The Machiavellian Moment: Florentine Political Thought and the Atlantic Republican Tradition* (Princeton, NJ: Princeton University Press, 2003; first published 1975); Philip Pettit, *Republicanism: A Theory of Freedom and Government* (Oxford: Oxford University Press, 1997). Pettit has, however, provided the context for the growth of republicanism in Ireland during the 1790s in 'The Tree of Liberty: Republicanism: American, French and Irish', *Field Day Review*, 11, no. 1 (2005), 29–42.
3 Martin Van Gelderen and Quentin Skinner (eds.), *Republicanism: A Shared European Heritage*, 2 vols. (Cambridge: Cambridge University Press, 2002). Also see the special issue on republicanism in the *History of European Ideas*, 38, no. 3 (2012).
4 Nancy J. Curtin, *The United Irishmen: Popular Politics in Ulster and Dublin, 1791–1798* (Oxford: Oxford University Press, 1994), 5.
5 Iseult Honohan, 'Introduction', in *Republicanism in Ireland*, ed. idem (Manchester: Manchester University Press, 2008), 13.

6   Margaret O'Callaghan, 'Reconsidering the Republican Tradition in Nineteenth-Century Ireland', in ibid., 34.
7   Stephen Small, *Political Thought in Ireland, 1776–1798: Republicanism, Patriotism, and Radicalism* (Oxford: Oxford University Press, 2002), 256.
8   Norman Porter, 'Introduction', in *The Republican Ideal: Current Perspectives*, ed. idem. (Belfast: Blackstaff, 1998), 13.
9   For the concept of historical consciousness in politics, see Theodor Schieder, 'The Role of Historical Consciousness in Political Action', *History and Theory*, 17, no. 4 (1978), 1–18.
10 Arthur Griffith, 'Preface', in *Jail Journal*, ed. John Mitchel (Dublin: M. H. Gill & Son, Ltd., 1913), xiv–xv.
11 Richard Bourke, 'Languages of Conflict and the Northern Ireland Troubles', *Journal of Modern History*, 83, no. 3 (2011), 575.
12 For a fuller treatment of this theme within PIRA thought, see Richard Bourke, *Peace in Ireland: The War of Ideas* (London: Pimlico, 2003).
13 Francis Shaw, 'The Canon of Irish History: A Challenge', *Studies*, 61, no. 242 (1972), 118.
14 Patrick Maume, Father Francis Shaw and the Historiography of Easter 1916', *Studies*, 103, no. 412 (2014/15), 530.
15 Bourke, 'Languages of Conflict'; Andrew Phemister, 'Introduction: Religion and Political Thought in Irish History', *History of European Ideas*, 46, no. 7 (2020), 9367; Colin W. Reid, 'Democracy, Sovereignty and Unionist Political Thought during the Revolutionary Period in Ireland, *c.*1912–1922', *Transactions of the Royal Historical Society*, 27 (2017), 212.
16 See, for example, the autobiographical accounts in Jeremiah O' Donovan Rossa, *Rossa's Recollections, 1838 to 1898* (New York: Mariners Harbor, 1898) and Joseph Denieffe, *A Personal Narrative of the Irish Revolutionary Brotherhood* (New York: Gael Publishing Co., 1906), both of which refer to the 'Irish Revolutionary Brotherhood'.
17 Tom Garvin, 'An Irish Republican Tradition?' in *Republicanism in Ireland*, ed. Holohan, ed. Holohan, 23.
18 Marianne Elliott, *Wolfe Tone: Prophet of Irish Independence* (New Haven, CT: Yale University Press, 1989), 3; Tom Dunne, *Theobald Wolfe Tone, Colonial Outsider: An Analysis of His Political Philosophy* (Cork: Tower Books, 1982), 36–9.
19 Helen F. Mulvey, *Thomas Davis & Ireland: A Biographical Study* (Washington, DC: Catholic University of America Press, 2003), 241.
20 I owe this point to Dr Ultán Gillen.
21 Daniel T. Rodgers, 'Republicanism: The Career of a Concept', *Journal of American History*, 79, no. 1 (1992), 32.
22 Ibid., 37.
23 Anthony McIntyre, 'Modern Irish Republicanism: The Product of British State Strategies', *Irish Political Studies*, 10, no. 1 (1995), 97–122.
24 Sinn Féin, *Yesterday and Today* (Belfast: Sinn Féin, 1971).
25 For the concept of historical consciousness in politics, see Theodor Schieder, 'The Role of Historical Consciousness in Political Action', *History and Theory*, 17, no. 4 (1978), 1–18; J. G. A. Pocock, 'Working on Ideas in Time', in *Political Thought and History: Essays on Theory and Method* (Cambridge: Cambridge University Press, 2009), 24.

26 Alice Stopford Green, *The Old Irish World* (Dublin: M. H. Gill and Son, Ltd., 1912), 1–2.
27 Riobard Ua Fhloinn, *The Orangemen and the Nation* (Belfast: Republican Press, 1907), 28.
28 Elliott, *Wolfe Tone*, 1.
29 Seán Ó Faoláin, *Autobiography of Theobald Wolfe Tone* (London: Thomas Nelson & Sons, Ltd., 1937), xvii.
30 Seán Ó Faoláin, *The Irish* (London: Penguin Books, 1947), 101.
31 Ibid., 99.
32 See, for example, the detailed discussion of republicanism in Kant's *Perpetual Peace* (1795), in H. S. Reiss (ed.), *Kant: Political Writings*, second edition (Cambridge: Cambridge University Press, 1991), 99–102.
33 Thomas Bartlett, 'The Burden of the Present: Theobald Wolfe Tone, Republican and Separatist', in *The United Irishmen: Republicanism, Radicalism and Rebellion*, ed. David Dickson, Dáire Keogh and Kevin Whelan (Dublin: Lilliput Press, 1993), 1.
34 Thomas Bartlett, *Life of Theobald Wolfe Tone* (Dublin: Lilliput Press, 1998), xviii.
35 T. W. Moody, R. B. McDowell, and C. J. Woods (eds.), *The Writings of Theobald Wolfe Tone, 1763–1798*, 3 vols. (Oxford: Oxford university Press, 1998), i, 110, 115, 125.
36 Ibid., 126–7.
37 There is an extensive literature on this. For an excellent introduction, see Gregory Claeys, *The French Revolution Debate in Britain: The Origins of Modern Politics* (Basingstoke: Palgrave Macmillan, 2007).
38 Moody, McDowell and Woods (eds.), *Writings of Tone*, ii, 377–9.
39 Guy Beiner, *Forgetful Remembrance: Social Forgetting and Vernacular Historiography of a Rebellion in Ulster* (Oxford: Oxford University Press, 2018), 202; James Quinn, 'Theobald Wolfe Tone and the Historians', *Irish Historical Studies*, 32, no. 125 (2000), 114.
40 O'Connell's hostility to revolutionary violence may have played a part in this. See C. J. Woods, 'Historical Revision: Was O'Connell an United Irishman?', *Irish Historical Studies*, 35, no. 138 (2006), 173–83, for wider context.
41 For an overview of the *Nation*, see Ann Andrews, *Newspapers and Newsmakers: the Dublin Nationalist Press in the Mid-Nineteenth Century* (Liverpool: Liverpool University Press, 2014), 18–74.
42 *Nation*, 6 July 1844.
43 Charles Gavan Duffy, *Short Life of Thomas Davis* (London: T. Fisher Unwin, 1895), 56.
44 Thomas Davis, *The Prose Writings of Thomas Davis*, ed. T. W. Rolleston (London: Walter Scott, n.d. [1890]), xii.
45 Thomas Davis, *The Poems of Thomas Davis* (New York: P. M. Haverty, 1860), 177–8; C. J. Woods, *Bodenstown Revisited: The Grave of Theobald Wolfe Tone, Its Monuments and Its Pilgrimages* (Dublin: Four Courts Press, 2018).
46 David Dwan, *The Great Community: Culture and Nationalism in Ireland* (Dublin: Field Day, 2008), 30–1.
47 *United Irishman*, 12 February 1848.
48 Bryan P. McGovern, *John Mitchel: Irish Nationalist, Southern Secessionist* (Knoxville, TN: University of Tennessee Press), 80.

49 John Mitchel, *The Last Conquest of Ireland (Perhaps)* (Glasgow: Cameron & Ferguson, 1861), 219.
50 Ibid., 154.
51 Much has been written about this aspect of Fenianism, but particularly insightful is Niall Whelehan, *The Dynamiters: Irish Nationalism and Political Violence in the Wider World, 1867-1900* (Cambridge: Cambridge University Press, 2012).
52 For an overview of the *Irish People*, see Andrews, *Newspapers and Newsmakers*, 188-91; Matthew Kelly, 'The Irish People and the Disciplining of Dissent', in *The Black Hand of Republicanism: Fenianism in Modern Ireland*, ed. Fearghal McGarry and James McConnel (Dublin: Irish Academic Press, 2009), 34-54; Marta Ramón, *A Provisional Dictator: James Stephens and the Fenian Movement* (Dublin: UCD Press, 2007), 135-59.
53 *Irish People*, 26 December 1863.
54 *Irish People*, 9 January 1864.
55 *Irish People*, 19 November 1864.
56 *Irish People*, 16 April 1864.
57 *Irish People*, 23 January 1864.
58 *Irish People*, 6 February 1864.
59 John O'Leary, *Recollections of Fenians and Fenianism*, 2 vols. (London: Downey & Co., Ltd., 1896), i, 1-6.
60 Isaac Butt, *Ireland's Appeal for Amnesty: A Letter to the Right Hon. W. E. Gladstone, MP* (Glasgow: Cameron and Ferguson, 1870), 14.
61 Colin W. Reid, 'Constitutional Rhetoric as Legal Defence: Irish Lawyers and the Languages of Political Dissent in 1848', in *Crime, Violence and the Irish in the Nineteenth Century*, ed. Kyle Hughes and Donald M. MacRaild (Liverpool: Liverpool University Press, 2017), 116-17.
62 A. M. Sullivan, D. B. Sullivan and T. D. Sullivan, *'Guilty or Not Guilty?' Speeches from the Dock, or Protests of Irish Patriotism* (Dublin: no stated publisher, 1867), 9.
63 A. M. Sullivan, *New Ireland*, 3rd edition (New York: Peter F. Collier, 1878; first published 1877), 260.
64 Patrick Maume, 'Parnell and the IRB Oath', *Irish Historical Studies*, 29, no. 115 (1995), 363-70.
65 Matthew Kelly, *The Fenian Ideal and Irish Nationalism, 1882-1916* (Woodbridge: Boydell Press, 2006), 61.
66 See a digitized example held at the National Library of Ireland: http://catalogue.nli.ie/Record/vtls000040218 (accessed 29 June 2021). For an analysis of the 'French affinity' within Irish nationalist political culture during the nineteenth century, see Matthew Kelly, 'Languages of Radicalism, Race, and Religion in Irish Nationalism: The French Affinity, 1848-1871', *Journal of British Studies*, 49, no. 4 (2010), 801-25.
67 Alice L. Milligan, *Life of Theobald Wolfe Tone* (Belfast: J. W. Boyd, 1898), 6. Also see Virginia Crossman, 'The *Shan Van Vocht*: Women, Republicanism, and the Commemoration of the 1798 Rebellion', *Eighteenth-Century Life*, 22, no. 3 (1998), 128-39.
68 Senia Pašeta, '1798 in 1898: The Politics of Commemoration', *Irish Review*, 22 (1998), 46-53.
69 J. E. Redmond, 'The Centenary of '98', *Nineteenth Century*, 43, no. 254 (1898), 612-24.

70 See a digitized example held at the National Library of Ireland: http://catalogue.nli.ie/Record/vtls000101773 (accessed 29 June 2021).
71 Joost August, *Patrick Pearse: The Making of a Revolutionary* (Basingstoke: Palgrave Macmillan, 2010), 80.
72 'Poblacht Na hÉireann: The Provisional Government of the Irish Republic to the People of Ireland' (1916). The full text can be found at http://cain.ulst.ac.uk/issues/politics/docs/pir24416.htm (accessed 25 August 2021).
73 Quoted from the *Nation*, 30 November 1844, in James Quinn, *Young Ireland and the Writing of Irish History* (Dublin: UCD Press, 2016), 4.
74 Pádraic Pearse, *Collected Works of Pádraic H. Pearse: Political Writings and Speeches* (Dublin: Maunsel and Co., Ltd., 1917), 221.
75 Edmund Burke, *Reflections on the Revolution in France*, ed. Conor Cruise O'Brien (London: Penguin, 1986; first published 1790), 194–5.
76 Richard Bourke, *Revolution and Empire: The Political Life of Edmund Burke* (Princeton, NJ: Princeton University Press, 2015), 773.
77 Pearse, *Collected Works*, 238.
78 Ibid., 238–9.
79 Ibid., 226.
80 Ibid., 270–1.
81 Ibid., 303–4.
82 Ibid., 345–6.
83 Ibid., 366.
84 Ibid., 293.
85 Desmond Ryan, *The Man Called Pearse* (Dublin: Maunsel and Co., Ltd., 1919), 96.
86 Feargal McGarry, *The Rising: Ireland, 1916* (Oxford: Oxford University Press, 2010), 282; Caoimhe Nic Dháibhéid, 'The Irish National Aid Association and the Radicalization of Public Opinion in Ireland, 1916–1918', *Historical Journal*, 55, no. 3 (2012), 722.
87 Marianne Elliott, *Robert Emmet: The Making of a Legend* (London: Profile Books, 2003), 153.
88 Pearse, *Collected Works*, 69.
89 Ibid., 245.
90 Matthew Roberts, *Chartism, Commemoration and the Cult of the Radical Hero* (London: Routledge, 2020), 11, 66.
91 Elaine Sisson, *Pearse's Patriots: St Enda's and the Cult of Boyhood* (Cork: Cork University Press, 2004).
92 Pearse, *Collected Works*, 134–5.
93 Roisín Higgins, 'Remembering and Forgetting P. H. Pearse', in *The Life and After-Life of P. H. Pearse*, ed. Roisín Higgins and Regina uí Chollatáin (Dublin: Irish Academic Press, 2009), 124, 135.
94 James Connolly, *Labour in Irish History* (New York: Donnelly Press, 1919), 17, 57–68.
95 Gerry Adams, *The Politics of Irish Freedom* (Dingle: Brandon, 1986), 8.
96 Ibid., 128.
97 Timothy Shanahan, *The Provisional Irish Republican Army and the Morality of Terrorism* (Edinburgh: Edinburgh University Press, 2009), 229.
98 Ed Moloney, *Voices from the Grave: Two Men's War in Ireland* (London: Faber, 2010), 47.

99 Des O'Hagan, *The Republican Tradition* (Dublin: Republican Education Department, 1975), 6, 9.
100 Des O'Hagan, 'The Concept of Republicanism', in *Republican Ideal*, ed. Porter, 91.
101 Ed Moloney, *A Secret History of the IRA* (London: Allen Lane, 2002), 203–4.
102 M. L. R. Smith, *Fighting for Ireland? The Military Strategy of the Irish Republican Movement* (London: Routledge, 1995), 147.
103 Adams, *Politics of Irish Freedom*, 6.
104 Sinn Féin, *History of Republicanism, Part 1* (Dublin: Sinn Féin Education Department, 1981), 1.
105 Sinn Féin, *What Is a Republican?* (Dublin: Sinn Féin Education Department, [1979?]), 6.
106 Seán Ó Riain, *Provos: Patriots or Terrorists?* (Dublin: Irish Book Bureau, 1974), 21.
107 Danny Morrison, *The Good Old IRA: Tan War Operations* (Dublin: Sinn Féin Publicity Department, 1985), 3.
108 *An Phoblacht*, 22 March 1974, 6. Barry was an early supporter of the PIRA campaign but grew disillusioned with the high civilian death toll. See *Irish Times*, 6 December 2020.
109 Adams, *Politics of Irish Freedom*, 39.
110 *Irish Times*, 29 August 1998.
111 Moody, McDowell and Woods (eds.), *Writings of Tone*, ii, 102.
112 For a recent interpretation of Tone's radicalism in the context of his time, see Ultán Gillen, 'Democracy, Religion, and the Political Thought of Theobald Wolfe Tone', *History of European Ideas*, 46, no. 7 (2020), 951–63.
113 Arthur Griffith's dual monarchy idea, which became the policy of the first incarnation of Sinn Féin, comes to mind here. See Owen McGee, *Arthur Griffith* (Dublin: Merrion Press, 2015), 73–95.
114 Elliott, *Wolfe Tone*, 415–16.
115 Marianne Elliott, *When God Took Sides: Religion and Identity in Ireland – Unfinished History* (Oxford: Oxford University Press, 2009), 258.
116 Bulmer Hobson (ed.), *The Letters of Wolfe Tone* (Dublin: Martin Lester, Ltd., 1920), 3.
117 Kevin O'Shiel, Witness Statement no. 1770, Bureau of Military History, Military Archives of Ireland.
118 Matthew Kelly, 'Irish Political Autobiography from Wolfe Tone to Ernie O' Malley', in *A History of Irish Autobiography,* ed. Liam Harte (Cambridge: Cambridge University Press, 2018), 100–16.
119 Pearse, *Collected Works*, 168.
120 Ryan, *Man Called Pearse*, 5.
121 Ernie O'Malley, *Rising Out: Seán Connolly of Longford* (Dublin: UCD Press, 2007), 15.
122 Mossie Harnett, *Victory and Woe: The West Limerick Brigade in the War of Independence* (Dublin: UCD Press, 2002), 6.
123 Roberts, *Chartism, Commemoration and the Cult of the Radical Hero*, 4.
124 Davis, *Prose Writings*.
125 R. F. Foster, *Words Alone: Yeats & His Inheritances* (Oxford: Oxford University Press, 2011), 140–3; Kelly, *Fenian Ideal*, 96–129.
126 W. G. Lyon to the Press Censor, 28 March 1918, Colonial Office Papers, National Archives (London), CO904/162/3/499.

127 Andrew Sanders, *Inside the IRA: Dissident Republicans and the War for Legitimacy* (Edinburgh: Edinburgh University Press, 2011), 6.
128 Eamon McCann, *War and an Irish Town* (Chicago, IL: Haymarket Books, 2018; first published 1974), 22.
129 Máirtín Ó Catháin, *Beir Bua: The Thread of the Irish Republican Movement from the United Irishmen Through to Today: Republicanism in History and Today* (Dublin: Republican Sinn Féin, 1998), 6.

5

Romantic memory? Forgetting, remembering and feeling in the Chartist pantheon of heroes, c.1790–1840

Matthew Roberts

Chartism, the British mass movement for democratic and social rights in the 1830s and 1840s, was profoundly shaped by the radical tradition from which it emerged. While the constituent parts of that tradition were inherited – the French Revolution, Thomas Paine, William Cobbett, for example – the processes by which these were transformed into a radical tradition were at the hands of the Chartists themselves. They eagerly appropriated and subverted many of the ritualized forms of commemoration used by elites, including the construction of a pantheon of heroes, though for reasons of cost and access to the public sphere the Chartist heritage project tended to be a paper pantheon rather than one set in stone. Makeshift memorialization was often resorted to, such as when Welsh Chartists marked the conviction of the Newport rebels, leaders of the ill-fated uprising in November 1839, by inscribing pennies then in circulation with messages of support and defiance.[1] Makeshift memorialization and this broader heritage project were constituted and reconstituted through 'mnemonic practices' and the performance of cultural remembrance: commemorative dinners and soirees which revolved around a rollcall of toasts to the memory of radical greats; portraiture; publishing and reading practices; the naming of Chartist children after radical greats; the regular quoting of words from the radical canon in speeches, extracts in the Chartist press and on banners – indeed the reuse of banners from earlier radical campaigns.[2] Far from being a nostalgic culture of consolation, radical groups such as Chartists drew strength, legitimacy and tenacity from the traditions and heritage politics that they practised. The amount of time and resources that Chartists devoted to their heritage is testament to the importance of memory in political and social movements.

This chapter focuses on two linked aspects of the Chartist heritage project from the perspectives of Romanticism, the literary and cultural force of which was still being felt at mid-century, with popular politics no exception.[3] First, it shows how the form and composition of the Chartist pantheon were shaped by a romantic aesthetic by exploring the question, not of remembering, but forgetting and erasure; that is, which individuals and episodes in the radical tradition were either forgotten or consciously excluded. As Guy Beiner has recently observed, '[w]hile it is commonly acknowledged that memory involves both remembering and forgetting, studies of social and cultural memory have mostly focused on remembering and overlooked forgetting'.[4] This theme of forgetting – or what might be more accurately described as excluding – is explored here through a case study of the 'radical Romantic' John Thelwall (1764–1834), a hugely popular radical associated with the London Corresponding Society (LCS) in the 1790s.[5] A number of scholars have attributed to Thelwall an enduring legacy bequeathed to subsequent radical movements, including Chartism.[6] And yet the fact remains that he was not a prominent figure in the Chartist pantheon. It may seem slightly strange to devote part of an essay to a radical who hardly featured in Chartist heritage, but forgetting and excluding can be just as revealing as remembering and including. This case study of Thelwall is used to explore what might be termed 'posthumous potential' in cultures of remembrance.[7] In the 1790s Thelwall was seen by the government as one of the most dangerous radicals in the country. In the last decade or so, his historical and literary reputation has been transformed: from being a relatively obscure radical and poet known only to specialists, he has been restored to his rightful place as a major radical and literary figure, complete with blue plaque on a house in Bloomsbury where he lived.[8] An exploration of why Thelwall was largely forgotten by the Chartists sheds new light on the broader question of why he was a neglected figure for so long, and, broader still, why fame does not always outlast the life of the famous.

Building on the theme of Thelwall's radical Romanticism, the second area of focus is the contested legacy and memory of Romanticism. By making use of a range of neglected manuscript material and Chartist newspapers/periodicals, this section draws on recent scholarship in Romantic Studies which has explored the problematic relationship between memory and posthumous reputation by showing how coteries, conviviality, publishing circles and print culture made authors and radical greats serve the radical cause of the people beyond their own lifetimes.[9] While the impact of Romanticism can be hardly denied and was part of the cultural inheritance of the Chartists, it is important not to exaggerate its impact: not all Chartists were keen to dress their heroes in romantic clothing. Some of them rejected the unchecked appeals to the passions and introversion associated with Romanticism. Romantic literature, it has been argued, was 'the most powerful register of the period's gravitational pull toward feeling'.[10] Chartist aversion to this pull was a legacy, in part, of the enduring impact of the radical Enlightenment, which suggests that the 'emotional culture of Enlightenment Britain' did not totally collapse in the 1790s but endured.[11] The cluster of ideas, attitudes and assumptions associated with the radical wing of the Enlightenment was also part of Chartism's intellectual and cultural heritage: some of the individuals in the Chartist pantheon were prominent figures of the Enlightenment.[12] The final section explores some of the tensions between Romanticism and Enlightenment in Chartist heritage politics, taking as a case study the French philosopher and revolutionary Constantin François Volney (1757–1820), who featured regularly in the Chartist pantheon. It draws on recent work on the history of emotions – in particular, the recasting of the Enlightenment as an affective construction – to sketch out the politics of feeling in Chartist memory.

Forgetting John Thelwall

One of the most important aspects of any form of commemoration is inclusion and exclusion. Who is remembered, who is forgotten, who is absent, and who is excluded are questions not only generative of the pantheon but also key dynamics in the politics of commemoration. While absence, forgetting and excluding appear to be similar in some respects; in others they are quite different. It is not always clear to the historian whether absences denote forgetting or a conscious attempt to exclude which, by definition, entails a form of remembering, at least for those policing inclusion and exclusion in the pantheon. As Carl Griffin puts it, '[t]o forget required – requires – developing devices and strategies, an act of placing out of mind but in sight'.[13] In a related way, and a further problem for the historian, 'silences usually become visible in historical records only when they are broken'.[14] How, then, do we account for Thelwall's absence from the Chartist pantheon? Had Chartists simply forgotten him? This seems unlikely given that as late as October 1832, he had delivered a eulogy at the graveside of his LCS colleague, Thomas Hardy, at which a number of future Chartists were present.[15] Clearly, his absence did not reflect a wider lack of interest by Chartists in the 1790s and in some of the radical leaders associated with that decade, the foremost of whom was Paine. But for preliminary purposes, it may be instructive to note some of the other absences or those who seldom made it into the pantheon from the 1790s. Neither Mary Wollstonecraft, William Godwin, Richard Price nor Joseph Priestley was accorded anything more than a marginal place in the pantheon, though extracts from Wollstonecraft and Godwin did appear occasionally in the Chartist press. This appears less surprising when we recall that none of these influential radicals participated in any significant way in popular, grassroots politics, whether for reasons prudential or elitist.[16] Thelwall put this very clearly when he complained of Godwin's aversion to popular politics; the public mind, Thelwall sardonically retorted, was not going to be transformed 'by writing quarto volumes and conversing with a few speculative philosophers by the fire side'.[17]

Ironically, there may be a clue here why Thelwall himself was not raised to the Chartist pantheon. True, he certainly *was* a figure of grassroots popular radicalism, culminating in his impassioned speeches on the public platform at Copenhagen Fields in 1795, famously immortalized in Gillray's print. But the clamp-down on radicalism in the mid-1790s, which resulted in Thelwall's arrest and trial for treason (acquitted though he was), and then the 'Gagging Acts' forced him to abandon overt Jacobinism, the name given to the advocates of ultra-radicalism in imitation of the French Jacobins. Even lecturing under the guise of an historian of classical antiquity to camouflage his radicalism did not save Citizen Thelwall from the vigilante anti-radical mob. Although his radicalism was little dented, there can be no doubt that Thelwall's abandonment of platform politics and his reinvention, following his peripatetic tour of the West country, first as a recluse farmer-poet in rural Wales and then as a well-to-do elocution lecturer, did little to ensure his posthumous potential.[18] None of the main radical newspapers or periodicals marked his death in 1834, much less contained lengthy obituaries. More revealing, though, several fashionable titles *did* note Thelwall's passing.[19]

Ultimately, Thelwall reinvented himself too many times and too successfully to ensure posthumous fame. Although his personal commitment to radicalism endured – hence his re-emergence as a radical journalist in the 1810s and 1820s – he did not re-establish himself as a leader of popular radicalism in the post-war years. Rather, he was a literary radical, akin to Hazlitt and the brothers Hunt of the *Examiner*, but his literary and radical output paled in comparison. And just at the very moment when he appeared to be reconnecting with metropolitan popular radicalism in the aftermath of Peterloo and the Cato Street Conspiracy, a threatened charge of conspiracy in 1822, allied to the commercial failure of his newspaper, the *Champion*, saw Thelwall distance himself once again.[20] Too radical for his middle-class readers and too removed from any potential working-class radical constituency, he fell between these two stools. This was evident when he reappeared on the public platform at the time of the Reform Bill demonstrations. Associated with Francis Place's moderate, middle-class National Political Union, Thelwall awkwardly counselled support for the Whig Reform Bill in 1831 but acknowledged that it did not go far enough.[21] This temporizing would have done little to endear him to future Chartists who rejected anything less than manhood suffrage. Thelwall ended his career as he had begun it: a figure in the world of letters with the episode as the foremost orator of the LCS appearing precisely as such – an episode, and an atypical one at that. In contrast to Thelwall, neither Paine nor Cobbett appeared to have abandoned radicalism, despite imprisonment, while persecution, banishment and exile – Paine in 1792, Cobbett in 1817 – did wonders for their posthumous careers as radical heroes.[22]

Ironically, what also helped with Paine and Cobbett's posthumous potential was the sustained vitriol of their enemies, during their lives and even after they had died. It was the loyalists on both sides of the Atlantic who did more than most to keep memories of Paine alive in the decade following his death (1809).[23] Thelwall lacked Paine and Cobbett's notoriety, at least by the time he died: the 'acquitted felon' label of the 1790s had long been buried beneath his reclusiveness and reinventions. What also aided Paine's posthumous life was the persecution and thousands of symbolic deaths that he had suffered in the 1790s: Paine died not once but many times when effigies of him were fired in the spate of loyalist burnings which spread across England.[24] In the years after Paine's death, a number of his devotees mounted defences of him – most notably Cobbett, who went from being one of Paine's arch-enemies to his greatest defender – which again did wonders for Paine's posthumous reputation.[25] A further, and linked, dampener on Thelwall's posthumous potential may be that he ceased to be what Kenneth Johnston has termed a 'usual suspect' – high-profile radicals who overtly took on the establishment and often suffered the judicial consequences – and became an 'unusual suspect': sympathetic fellow travellers, who were much less prominent radicals who shied away from overt confrontation but who nevertheless were often the victims of less official harassment often with devastating long-term consequences. While Thelwall briefly occupied the former status in the mid-1790s, he spent the remainder of his career as an unusual suspect (unlike Cobbett or Paine to a lesser extent). Thelwall found himself the victim of vigilante harassment during his provincial lecture tour, and it seems likely that the experience stuck with him – understandably.[26]

A further factor in Thelwall's absence from the Chartist pantheon was that, unlike Paine or Cobbett, he was not a great writer, at least when it came to radical pamphleteering and journalism. His pungent and highly effective style on the radical platform (he was known colloquially as John 'Tellwell'), which, by definition, was more transient, did not translate effectively onto the printed page, though it is true that the published versions of these lectures in his short-lived periodical, the *Tribune*, achieved some immediate success in the aftermath of his acquittal.[27] But as Hazlitt observed, possibly with Thelwall in mind, '[t]he most dashing orator I ever heard is the flattest writer I ever read'.[28] Here we begin to see the relative importance of print over the spoken word in securing posthumous fame: Paine and to a much lesser extent Cobbett were not great orators like Thelwall, but that mattered little for their posthumous careers as they achieved political immortality through their pens in a way that Thelwall was unable.[29] Unfortunately for the latter, the depths of his radicalism as expressed in his poetry, and the heights of his literary ability, did not match that of Byron and Shelley, both of whom were firm favourites with many Chartists. It may be telling that the closest Thelwall came to having a group of followers was in rural Wales where, if hostile reports and legend are to be believed, during his time there he kept the radical embers burning by participating in secret readings of Paine and other radical writers in the mountains of South Wales. Reports from spies and informers allege that Thelwall had been present at Merthyr in September 1800, and at Hereford where he was a member of a Jacobin group who used to meet at the Crown and Sceptre.[30] Thus, it was oral tradition and the memories of these secret mountain gatherings, which were retold in the nineteenth century and gained with the telling, that may have kept memories of Thelwall alive among Welsh radicals.[31]

It is revealing that those who were commemorated the most by Chartists tended to be gentlemen, broadly defined.[32] The only notable exceptions appear to have been Paine and Cobbett. Chartists sometimes emphasized the humble origins of this pair, but this was rare – perhaps because the enemies of the two men had often drawn attention to their plebeian backgrounds as a way of discrediting them.[33] Even the prickly artisan William Lovett, who worked tirelessly to keep Chartism in the hands of his fellow working men, in a eulogistic article on Cobbett only mentioned his humble origins in passing.[34] This is not that surprising as neither Paine nor Cobbett could, in truth, be described as working class by the time of their deaths. The working-class identity of those in the pantheon was also further obscured by the tendency to label luminaries as 'nobles of nature'.[35] The visual culture of Chartism also reflects this obscuring. Portraits of Paine and Cobbett issued by Chartists invariably depicted their subjects as gentlemanly, in part to underline the movement's respectability via its patrimony.[36] In short, there was nothing explicitly comparable to the American posthumous cult of Benjamin Franklin as the 'working man's symbol', traced by Gordon S. Wood, in which artisans and middling sorts read into his humble birth and self-made status a validation of productive labour and upward social mobility.[37] Franklin himself, we might note, was invoked by Chartists much less often than George Washington, whose life lent itself much more readily to Romantic brushstrokes than did Franklin's. Indeed, it was painted in these terms by and for the Chartists: 'that illustrious soldier of freedom, and emancipator of America' began a series of biographical articles on

Washington, commenced in the first issue, no less, of the *English Chartist Circular*.[38] Paine, and to a lesser extent Cobbett, had died as scourges of the establishment, and their careers illustrated not so much the triumph of the working-class man but the frustrated, talented man who, despite having risen to the status of gentleman, was still persecuted. By the time that Thelwall died, he was no such scourge. Ironically, it was only after his career as a radical leader was over that he truly achieved gentlemanly status as an elocution lecturer.

The rarity of Chartist celebration of Paine and Cobbett's working-class origins is also consistent with the composition and emphases within the wider pantheon. In this respect, Chartist heritage politics was hardly congruent with the Romantic pastoral rediscovery of the people. On the other hand, it *was* congruent in the sense that gentleman radicals, in the present as well as the past, like lyric poets spoke for the people and drew attention to their plight. This was most evident with Cobbett whose sympathy for the poor was grounded in his knowledge and politicization of popular culture, and in *Rural Rides* which was addressed to readers who were not of the people.[39] Even those Chartists like Thomas Cooper and Ernest Jones, who went to great lengths to sketch out a 'people's history' for the Chartists, which certainly included working-class groups such as medieval peasants, still tended to place most emphasis on gentleman radicals and reformers. In an amended version of Charles Cole's poem *The Spirit of Wat Tyler*, the Carmarthen Chartist leader Hugh Williams situated Tyler (a blacksmith by trade) mainly in the tradition of gentleman leaders: Thomas Muir and the 'Scotch Martyrs' of the 1790s, the United Irishmen Lord Edward Fitzgerald and Robert Emmet, while the lowly origins of Tyler, John Archamber (one of the leaders of an insurrection against Henry VII), Jack Cade and Robert Kett (eponymous leaders of rebellions in, respectively, 1450 and 1549) are mentioned either in passing or not at all.[40] To take another example, in his periodical *The Midland Counties Illuminator*, Thomas Cooper serialized the 'Lives of the Commonwealthsmen', John Hampden, Sir John Elliot and John Pym.[41] Chartists rarely explicitly invoked the Levellers, though no doubt this had less to do with their social composition (the most prominent leaders were, in any case, gentlemen) and rather more with the dangerous levelling connotations that the name could still excite among the upper classes, reactivated during the 1790s when Jacobin and leveller were synonymized.[42]

There were few toasts to the plebeian radicals of the LCS; indeed, the LCS itself does not feature as prominently as one might expect for this obvious progenitor of Chartism, but then its closest descendant, the London Working Men's Association (LWMA), for reasons which will become clearer later on, were reluctant commemorators. Thelwall, along with Thomas Hardy and the other radicals who were acquitted of treason in the 1790s, *were* commemorated each year by a group of gentleman radicals into the 1850s (the 'friends of trial by jury' and 'friends of parliamentary reform', led by the ex-Unitarian radical W. J. Fox), for upholding the principle of trial by jury, the reports of which duly appeared in the Chartist *Northern Star*. But these were commemorative events organized by groups largely extraneous to Chartism, and this did not escape the attention of some Chartists such as Harney.[43] The trial of the Newport rebels – the leaders of the South Wales Chartist rising in November 1839 – for treason and the return of a guilty verdict in January 1840 led some Chartists to make comparisons with the treason trials in the 1790s, but no biographical details of Thelwall or a rediscovery of his writings ensued.[44] In death, Thelwall was the property of bourgeois radicalism, a direction in which he had been moving since the 1790s as demonstrated by his connections with the anti-war networks in the first decade of the nineteenth century.[45] Thelwall was never the subject of a Chartist toast; Hardy only once; and no extracts from his writings appeared in the Chartist press.[46] Far more attention was paid to the 'Martyrs of Liberty' – the victims of the Scottish sedition trials of 1793 and 1794 – perhaps because they were found guilty and transported rather than acquitted. But once again none of the Scottish Martyrs – Muir, Gerald, Skirving, Palmer, Margarot or Watt – could be described as working class.[47]

The most popular figure from this period was the Irish nationalist Robert Emmet who, in the words of Chartism's first historian, R. G. Gammage, 'was a young gentleman with good promise of success in life', until, that is, his failed rebellion of 1803 led to his execution at the young age of twenty-five.[48] The portrait of Emmet issued by the *Northern Star* was by far the most sought-after of all its portraits.[49] Chartists seem to have been no less fascinated by gentlemen leaders in the past than they were in the present; few working-class heroes were raised to the pantheon. Emmet was a Romantic radical par excellence: young, idealistic, foolhardy (some Chartists were fully alive to the flaws in his Romantic character) and a tragic death at the hands of the English state and, as we shall see in the next section, an exemplar of posthumous life writing.[50] As the Scottish Chartist weaver William Farish recalled of Emmet in his autobiography: 'the fervour of his youthful patriotism and the poetic passion of his sweetheart Miss Curran ... throw a halo around a memory which is always attractive to sentimental and sympathetic natures'. Farish framed his copy of the *Northern Star* engraving of Emmet and hung it in his bedroom.[51]

Romancing the pantheon

The absence of Thelwall from the Chartist pantheon was certainly not symptomatic of a wider rejection of Romanticism, at least not for some Chartists. Three key aspects of Chartist pantheonism clearly registered its enduring cultural impact. First, building a paper pantheon around a set of flawed radical individual leaders who were accorded heroic status, among whom numbered some of history's most Romantic heroes, and were commemorated as such by the Chartists, was quintessentially, if rather stereotypically, Romantic. For example, in addition to Emmet, also in the pantheon were the United Irishman Lord Edward Fitzgerald who died during the 1798 Irish rebellion, Wat Tyler, William Tell and Andreas Hofer, 'The Tell of the Tyrol'. A second vector of Romanticism was the invoking, publishing and reading of Romantic authors, notably Byron and Shelley. The short-lived Chartist *Sheffield Working Man's Advocate* published extracts from Shelley's *Queen Mab*, interestingly opening with the stanza from book III: 'Nature rejects the monarch, not the man', which may have reflected the less-than-subtle republicanism of the periodical. But it was not just Byron and Shelley who were invoked but also occasionally William Wordsworth, Robert Southey and Robert Burns. Some Chartists even partook of the 'literary tourism' and pilgrimages by visiting the birthplaces or the former residences of romantic writers that was such a marked feature of literary commemoration in the Victorian period.⁵² The neo-Jacobin, ultra-Chartist London Democratic Association placed at the head of its constitution and rules not a quotation from Paine or a French revolutionary, but an extract from Robert Southey's dramatic play *Wat Tyler*.⁵³ When Thomas Cooper tried to encourage the Leicester Chartist William Jones to compose a long poem, he entreated him to 'Read – think', and he asked: 'What books have you? – a Shakespeare, a Milton, a Byron, a Keats, a Shelley? Do you get Scott's novels from any of the circulating libraries?'⁵⁴

The third register of Romanticism was the literary formation and cultural productions of a number of Chartist imaginative writers, notably Ernest Jones, Thomas Cooper and G. W. M. Reynolds.⁵⁵ The cultural stylistics of several Chartist leaders, such as Feargus O'Connor, Drs John Taylor and Peter Murray McDouall along with the young George Julian Harney, also hinted strongly at the influence of Romanticism with their flare for the melodramatic, exotic appearances and eccentricities of dress and style.⁵⁶ The Romantic facets of these national leaders are well known to historians and literary scholars, less well known are the ways in which Romanticism was registered by local figures in the movement through poetry and song, figures such as Hugh Williams or William Jones – cited above, the framework knitter-cum-poet and hymn writer whose outputs, which included pastoral and lyrical poems, were frequently published in Cooper's Chartist periodicals. One of Jones's 'Ode's' was printed alongside Shelley's defence of poetry in an issue of the *Chartist Pilot*, which, inter alia, emphasized the important role played by poetry in activating feelings – key to successful political mobilization in Shelley's view.⁵⁷ Cooper, unsurprisingly, took the view that poetry and song were crucial to the movement. As he informed William Jones in 1845: 'You may guess that I am bent on resurrecting Chartism in earnest, in London, – and, therefore, intend to introduce singing.'⁵⁸ In an earlier letter, Cooper elaborated a little more fully that he valued songs, and in particular the radical verses that Jones had composed and sent him 'as a means of restoring, if possible, the spirit that seems nearly too extinct' among Chartism's followers.⁵⁹ But it was not just among the 'labour laureates' that the influence of Romanticism was registered. Even the down-to-earth Salford Chartist R. J. Richardson composed a monody to the memory of his infant son, Harry, who tragically died aged seven months in July 1844.⁶⁰ The monody, a poem which laments another's death, had classical origins but had been revived by the Romantics, notably in Coleridge's monody on the death of Thomas Chatterton.⁶¹

The invention of tradition and myths of (re)creation 'were central to the Romantic imagination'.⁶² Legitimating appeals to the glorious democratic past of the English Constitution, of benevolent monarchs like Alfred the Great, and the recovery of Saxon liberties from the foul imposition of the Norman Yoke were each incarnations of the Romantic creation of historical myths by the Chartists.⁶³ It would be inaccurate, however, to assume that Chartist heritage productions necessarily viewed the past through rose-tinted spectacles. Remembering traumatic episodes, often reactivated by events in the present, such as the Peterloo Massacre or the exile, execution and tragic death of radical martyrs, could be just as Romantic.⁶⁴ When news arrived that the Sheffield Chartist Samuel Holberry had died – one of the few working men to be admitted to the Chartist pantheon – as a result of the deplorable conditions he had suffered in prison, the affective response of Chartists was similar to that which a previous generation of radicals had experienced in the aftermath of Peterloo: shock, anger, betrayal and grief. Writing to his friend Thomas Cooper, the Chartist lecturer Jonathan Bairstow conveyed his affective state on learning of Holberry's death (during the middle of a lecture at Sheffield): 'I was struck dumb, I staggered, my head reeled to and fro like a drunken man's – I felt mad.'[65] A funeral hymn for Holberry composed by the Leicester Chartist J. H. Bramwich, while expressing the movement's sadness, struck a more defiant note: 'Tho' Freedom mourns her murder'd son, / And weeping friends surround his bier; / Tho' tears like mountain torrents run, / Our cause is water'd by each tear.'[66] One Chartist broadside implicitly linked Holberry's death with Peterloo by exclaiming 'Murder demands Justice', a refrain that was repeatedly heard in the aftermath of the Manchester massacre. The genre of the broadside is distinctly melodramatic.[67] Another broadside – addressed to 'Working Men of Barnsley!' – warned Chartists not to attend a mass meeting lest the authorities repeat the 'Drama of Peterloo'.[68]

Like all Romantic heroes, the members of the pantheon were flawed characters and Chartists occasionally dwelt on this as seen previously with Emmet, invariably excusing the less-savoury aspects of their characters as products of the vilification and persecution they endured or the exceptional circumstances in which they found themselves.[69] The idealism – a key Romantic characteristic – that Chartists read into their heroes had less to do with the personalities of individual figures and rather more with a transcendent timelessness that they were part of an ongoing struggle for liberty that would never die. William Jones, whom we have already encountered, captured this in his hymn 'Immortality', which is a paean to the radical patriots of bygone days, not one of whom is named; all are subsumed under the identity of patriot, 'spirits of the dead'. Jones also captured how the heritage politics of Chartism was no mere exercise in consolation, of turning inwards and backwards; akin to what some have read into Romanticism's 'transmutation of radical political idealism into purely imaginative revolution and redemption'.[70] Even in death, and by extension in defeat, Jones sounds the note of eventual, inexorable triumph: 'Oh how gloriously they fought, how triumphantly they fell!' The reward of the fallen patriots was 'immortality of fame'.[71] Thus, the radical tradition invented by the Chartists was empowering: they stood on the shoulders of giants and were part of a movement that was bigger than its participants and which had history on its side. Speaking at a joint meeting of Chartists and Irish Repealers at Manchester in 1848, O'Connor relayed to the crowd how his uncle, the United Irishman Arthur O'Connor, had told him as a young boy not to mourn the deaths of Lord Edward Fitzgerald and Robert Emmet for 'every drop of blood spilled of theirs, ten thousands patriots would arise'.[72] Far from being individualizing, the radical tradition invented by the Chartists was a collaborative and social practice: there were commemorative dinners, communal readings of radical greats, and there were reading and debating classes in which Chartists engaged in critical dialogue over the composition of the pantheon and with the ideas of those in it. While the pantheon may have been populated with individual radical greats, they were symbolically made the communal property of the people.[73]

The round of dinners, teas and soirees complete with rollcalls of toasts to departed heroes, which punctuated the Chartist calendar, could be intensely sentimental and melodramatic occasions, as could the poems and songs composed for these occasions.[74] R. Beith's song 'Spirits of the Mighty Dead' (a variation on an American song of that name from the war of 1812) invoked radical greats as protectors and tonics: 'Shield my devoted head / From the ills that wound me, / Milton, Shelley, Byron, Burns, / The weary heart-delighting … Franklin, Washington and Paine banish woe from every land! Ye set all hearts in motion.'[75] Expressions of sorrow and mourning at the passing of heroes, whose 'like will never be seen again', could form part of Chartist commemorative rituals and were accompanied by songs and poems such as the 'Death of Henry Hunt', often tellingly called laments. A dinner held at Ashton-under-Lyne in November 1838 to commemorate the birthday of the regency radical Henry Hunt concluded with a line from Thomas More's poem about Robert Emmet, recited by the local Chartist leader William Aitken: 'The tear that we shed, tho' in secret it rolls, / Shall long keep his memory dear in our souls'. Other Romantic notes on these occasions could also include enduring feelings of anger and outrage over the loss of life at Peterloo and the unrepentant authorities who inflicted death and injury on the defenceless crowd, feelings that were heighted by the presence of Peterloo veterans and paintings of the Massacre. Some of the toasts were 'drunk to in solemn silence', while the toasts themselves could be melodramatic.[76] When the juvenile members of the Ashton-under-Lyne National Charter Association performed Robert Emmet's trial, the report in the *Northern Star* observed that 'everyone concerned acquitted himself so well, that the hearers could not but be struck with the reflections of reality – indeed, while the character of Emmet was being performed, tears were seen trickling down many cheeks'.[77]

The ritualized commemoration of radical heroes, the mourning at their passing and the repeated invoking of their names by Chartists hints at the collaborative relationship between the dead and the living that has been the subject of recent work in Romantic Studies on posthumous life writing. Several Romantic authors were extremely anxious about their posthumous reputations. As Mark Sandy has shown, this is a theme that some Romantic authors explored in their own writing.[78] It is hardly surprising that radical greats who were most anxious in their own lifetimes about immortality were often more likely to gain admission to the future Chartist pantheon. Few radical leaders were more concerned with their legacy than Paine and Cobbett, a facet, it could be argued, of their more general and widely acknowledged egotism. In fairness to both Paine and Cobbett it was the power of their prose and the way in which they directly addressed posterity that began their posthumous careers, as we saw in the comparison with Thelwall. 'Tis not the concern of a day, a year, or an age; posterity are virtually involved in the contest,' Paine wrote in *Common Sense*.[79] Even though Paine spent the last decade of his life living in obscurity, so well had he laid the groundwork for his posthumous life, in part by trumpeting his self-importance, that this did little to dent his immortality. Cobbett was even more concerned in his last years with his legacy, even calling some of his final works *Legacies*. As he explained in the dedication (to Sir Robert Peel) appended to his *Legacies to Labourers*, which was an attack on the New Poor Law:

I call it a LEGACY, because I am sure, that, not only long after I shall be laid under the turf; but after you shall be laid there also, this little book shall be an inmate of the cottages of England, and will remind the working people, whenever they shall read it, or see it, or hear it, that they once had a friend, whom neither the love of gain on the one hand, nor the fear of loss on the other, could seduce from his duty towards God, towards his country, and towards them.[80]

The archetypal posthumous radical was, of course, Robert Emmet. We have already seen something of the affective intensity with which Chartists remembered him. This intensity was heightened not just by the tragic circumstances of Emmet's death but also by the way he directly engaged posterity in his defiant courtroom speech:

Let no man write my epitaph ... let no man dare to calumniate me. Let my character and my motives repose in obscurity and peace, till other times and other men can do them justice. Then shall my character be vindicated. Then may my epitaph be written.[81]

As Emmet's huge popularity with the Chartists implies, this injunction was not just taken up by subsequent generations of Irish nationalists but also by British radicals. By contrast, those radicals who were less preoccupied with their own immortality – John Thelwall, at least in political terms – were less assured of a place in the pantheon. Thelwall clearly wrote poetry with posterity in mind.[82] But this was clearly not the case when it came to his role as a radical leader. When it comes to pantheons, there is no room for modesty.[83]

Posthumous life writing often takes on a collaborative relationship between the dead author and those in the present who perpetuate that life through a 'web of reception' in the form of biographies, especially the genre of lives and letters, elegies, epitaphs, tombstones, monuments and sculptures.[84] Tim Chiou has persuasively shown in a study of Romantic posthumous life writing that 'the posthumous endurance of the artist is contingent not on his works alone, but also on a large community of friends, family, colleagues and readers committed to the ethics of remembrance'.[85] There is an obvious parallel here with Chartist commemorative practices. A recurring refrain, and one that goes all the way back to the Roman poet Horace, is the notion that a writer's oeuvre represents a monument in itself, and one far more lasting, interactive and dynamic than a flat, inert monument. Chartists made this very point when recommending the works of radical greats.[86] The advertisement columns by radical booksellers in the Chartist press are littered with editions, old and new, of works by radical greats (often interspersed with Romantic prose and poetry). Paine and Cobbett were fortunate that they had devoted followers, some of whom became Chartists, who went to great lengths to keep their names before the public, not least by ensuring that their works continued to be published well into the nineteenth century.[87] Cobbett left behind a veritable mini-family publishing business dedicated to editing, publishing and selling his works. Thelwall was poorly served in respect of this 'assisted authorship'; his second wife managed to publish the first volume of his biography, but the second volume detailing his life from 1795 never appeared.[88]

Feeling for Volney

Chartism clearly registered the long reach of Romanticism, but it did so critically. For example, as Jen Morgan has shown, some of those Chartists who used Shelley's poetry were discriminating. Casie LeGette reaches similar conclusions by showing how radical publishers and editors in the early nineteenth century used extracts from Romantic era texts for their own political ends, effectively remaking those texts in the process.[89] There were also some Chartists who were deeply uneasy, if not resistant, to what we would now recognize as some of the key characteristics of Romanticism: the unchecked expression of feeling (or passions in the language of the period); nostalgia and a romantic attachment to the past; cultural nationalism; and last, but by no means least, the cult of the individual hero.[90] This aversion is hardly surprising given the close association between certain strands within Romanticism and conservatism, reaction and counter-revolution.[91] The linking thread in much of this anti-Romantic current concerned the destructive potential of inflaming the passions. Those Chartists who were exercised by this followed those Enlightenment thinkers who posited a fundamental separation between reason and feeling, which led them to create and practise what might be termed an 'ascetic radicalism'. This ascetic radicalism owed a great debt to luminaries of the radical Enlightenment, in particular Godwin and Wollstonecraft, notwithstanding their relative absence from the pantheon.[92]

Godwin and Wollstonecraft had been particularly anxious about the passions and their destructive potential in the public sphere, in part because both were acutely aware of how dangerous passions could be from their own private lives.[93] Reacting against the sentimentalism of the late eighteenth century, they had rejected the deterministic view that humans were entirely or largely helpless victims of their passions; such a view, they held, was dangerous as it reinforced passivity. The rejection of obfuscating, effeminate and enervating sentimentalism had formed the basis of Wollstonecraft's rebuttal of Edmund Burke's *Reflections* in her *Vindication of the Rights of Men*. In Wollstonecraft's view, Burke had elevated passions to a nauseating and saccharine level in his attack on the rationalism of Richard Price's effusive support of the French Revolution. For Wollstonecraft and other 'rational' radicals, this base appeal to feelings was dangerous as it threatened to undermine the radical cause. Humans needed to control their passions through the exercise of individual rational will, which would lead to the acquisition of disciplined habits (like temperance). For Wollstonecraft in particular, men and women had the same basic capacity for thinking and feeling, even if there was a tension in her gender politics between denying and satisfying female appetites and desires.[94] There is some evidence that Chartists were aware of these aspects of Wollstonecraft's thinking. The Chartist *Midland Counties Illuminator* printed an extract from the *Vindication of the Rights of Woman* in which Wollstonecraft emphasized the political evils and social miseries which flowed from baser passions: 'The desire of dazzling by riches, the pleasure of commanding sycophants, and many other complicated low calculations of self-love, have all contributed to overwhelm the mass of mankind.'[95] Such evils, Wollstonecraft inveighed, were an affront to reason. In another extract from the *Vindication*, reprinted in the Scottish *Chartist Circular*, Wollstonecraft complained of how 'mere Gothic grandeur' exhibited by aristocracy with 'stupid pomp before a gaping crowd' had dulled reason.[96]

All this was grist to the mill for self-improving, respectable moral-force Chartists, such as William Lovett, who dismissed in Wollstonecraftian tones the irrationality of 'gothic ignorance' (in Lovett's words), with its romantic preoccupation with historical precedents, baubles, pageants and 'military spirit' which 'tends to Gothicize a nation ... the bane of all happiness'.[97] In place of this gothic irrationality, moral-force Chartists sought to re-establish an age of reason: 'We felt anxious to redeem by reason what had been lost by madness and folly', in the words of the National Association, set up by Lovett as a successor body to the LWMA.[98] This ascetic radicalism was increasingly accented within Chartism following the early setbacks it suffered in 1838–9 and was conceived as an antidote to the unchecked passions of the masses, whipped up by demagogues such as Feargus O'Connor who made 'furious appeals to their passions' and 'spurn[ed] with Gothic ferocity all knowledge, truth of justice'.[99] In January 1839, the LWMA moved a resolution declaring that 'all appeals to the passions of the multitude tending to excite to violence and disorder can only be productive of evil'.[100] The moderate voices in the first Chartist Convention similarly rebuked neo-Jacobins such as Harney and Dr Taylor who were, in glorying in the names of Marat and Robespierre, dangerously inflaming the passions of the people.[101] In fairness to these neo-Jacobins, the organization with which they were associated, the (East) London Democratic Association, had declared in its founding address in the words of Robespierre that '[w]e desire an order of things, in which all the mean and cruel passions shall be chained down; all the beneficent and generous passions awakened by the laws'.[102] In many respects this proved to be an affective manifesto for radicalism for at least the next fifty years, but for those Chartists who were preoccupied with rescuing radicalism from the emotional legacy of the French Revolution, invoking Robespierre was damaging. The *National Association Gazette* implied what their model of the ideal leader was in a biographical article on George Washington: 'if he had strong passions, he had learned to subdue them, and to be moderate and mild'.[103] This also explains why temperance, self-improvement and respectability were central to this ascetic radicalism. One of the guiding principles of moral-force Chartism was of the need for the working classes to exercise restraint and master their passions to demonstrate their fitness for the franchise.

In whipping up the masses into frenzied advocates of physical force, demagogues like the Reverend Joseph Rayner Stephens, Richard Oastler and O'Connor were no friends of the working class, at least in the view of the LWMA. The latter body was averse to the movement's reliance on gentleman leaders like O'Connor, which they denigrated as irrational and immature 'man-worship'.[104] This charge could also extend to the pantheon. Bronterre O'Brien, Chartism's greatest theoretician, believed that man-worship of Paine was a barrier to critically engaging with his ideas, which, in his view, were outdated by the 1830s.[105] But even the LWMA struggled to rid itself entirely of man-worship, though their ideal type of radical leader was somewhat different. On occasion, Lovett delivered, recited and possibly composed poetry which commemorated radical greats.[106] In his autobiography, Lovett recalled how he 'cherished' the memory of both Hunt and Cobbett 'for, without seeking to extenuate the failings of either, I regard them as two noble champions of the rights of the millions who ... stamped the necessity *for reform* so deeply into the heart and mind of England'.[107] O'Brien, in effect, had his own pantheon, though in his case it was populated largely by one radical great: Robespierre. To O'Brien at least, he was not engaged in a romanticized worship of the French Revolutionaries; rather he was trying to rescue their reputations from lies told by their enemies, past and present. 'The day will come', O'Brien told the readers of his newspaper, the *Operative*, 'when the injured shades of Marat and Robespierre will be avenged of the outrages inflicted on their memories by lying romances, dubbed historians'.[108] Yet there is a sense in which the LWMA and O'Brien, in denigrating man-worship, were not giving Chartists their due. Sentimental they may have been when the occasion demanded, but this did not necessarily act as a barrier to critical engagement with the ideas of those in the pantheon. Many Chartist admirers of Paine were quick to distance themselves from the latter's views on religion, to take one example. There were also many Chartists who followed Paine in dismissing the irrationality of Romantic attachments to the past.[109]

There was, then, an anti-Romantic current within Chartist heritage politics. True, it was hardly dominant, but it does suggest that the tension, highlighted in Romantic Studies, between Enlightenment and Romanticism, was still being played out in the 1840s at the level of popular politics. As revisionist work has underlined, these two cultural movements were never fixed, stable and antithetical; rather, they were heterogeneous and to some extent interlocking and chronologically overlapping. The Enlightenment was not about unbridled reason and cold rationality at the expense of feeling, just as Romanticism was not an expression of unbridled feeling. As historians of emotion have reminded us, the 'age of reason' was itself an affective construction: Paine, the apostle of the 'age of reason' appealed to sentiments repeatedly in his works, and he 'denied that there was any conflict between the rational and the emotional'.[110] The notion of a fundamental separation between reason and feeling was also a construction that concealed the passions and was, in some respects, a retrospective construction invented by those like Godwin and Wollstonecraft who were anxious about the sentimentalism of their era (including their own).[111] Romanticism was, it has been argued, born from *within* the Enlightenment and can more accurately be seen as a reaction to a particular kind of Enlightenment – one that was associated with an over-refined Neo-classicalism. Several Romantics fused Enlightenment thinking with what we have come to identify as Romantic currents.[112]

The inability of those 'rational' Chartists like Lovett to fully liberate themselves from the romantic memory which played such an important generative role in Chartist heritage politics can be interpreted as evidence of the complexities, interactions and tensions between Enlightenment and Romanticism. The pursuit of reason itself could be an affective experience: after all, a fundamental component of asceticism is suffering and pain as hundreds of incarcerated Chartists, including Lovett, knew only too well. As Rob Boddice observes, 'restraint is a form of expression, but also inescapably a form of action to change how a feeling feels',[113] hence the coining of the concept of affective asceticism by historians of emotion.[114] We should also be wary of the binary posited between reason and passion in the ascetic radicalism of those like Lovett when much that was passed off as reason could, in fact, be seen as disgust – at the adulation of the masses for Feargus O'Connor, for example. This hybridity was also reflected, and in part created, by working-class reading practices, which were far from uniform: 'as a group and as individuals they consumed the racy and the religious, the lyrical and the sensational'.[115]

We can observe some of these tensions and hybrids in the popularity of the French revolutionary, Volney, a second-tier figure in the Chartist pantheon, another figure of the radical Enlightenment. Reading Volney's *Ruins; or a Survey of Revolutions of Empire* (1791) was a formative experience for many future Chartists, especially those who had trodden the path of freethought into the movement. Volney had been 'no agitator among the sans culottes',[116] but his memory and *Ruins*, unlike Thelwall, had been kept alive since the 1790s by ultra-radical freethinkers, an inheritance claimed subsequently by Chartists who occasionally displayed Volney's portrait at commemorative events.[117] The ubiquity of references to Volney's *Ruins* in metropolitan radicalism in the early 1830s, along with the freethinking lectures and discussions surrounding it, suggests that historians have seriously underestimated the centrality of an infidel current in popular radicalism at this time – even at the height of the Reform bill agitations.[118] The government were certainly alive to this current and saw it as one of the manifestations of declining morals, hence the recourse to royal proclamation for the encouragement of piety and virtue in 1830 which included the issuing of a table of penalties for profanes, Sabbath-breaking and immorality.[119]

In the early 1830s, the French socialist Pierre Baume, then residing in London, printed an extract from the *Ruins* (chapter 15, on which more below), as part of a tract advertising his 'French Optimist Chapel' in Windmill Street, Finsbury, a radical school of free discussion, which found its way into the Home Office files as a seditious publication. Baume also appended an English translation of the French *La Marseillaise* hoping no doubt to capitalize on the French revolution of 1830.[120] Thomas Cooper later recalled how, as a young man, 'he fell in love' with Volney's *Ruins*.[121] The radical infidel Richard Carlile and the mercurial defrocked Robert Taylor began their Sunday lectures at the Rotunda, the premier venue of London radicalism in the early 1830s, by reciting chapters from Volney's *Ruins* much as a religious service began with readings from scripture.[122] The future leaders of the LWMA were regular attenders and speakers at the Rotunda and Optimist Chapel, as the secret service files attest. Volney's *Ruins* gained renewed notoriety in the mid-1830s as it was a formative influence on Alibaud, the Frenchman who had tried to assassinate Louis Philippe in 1836, whose actions won plaudits from some Chartists.[123] Volney's *Ruins*, along with his *Lectures on History*, and *Law of Nature* were frequently advertised in the Chartist press. The metropolitan Chartist trio of John Cleave, James Watson and Henry Hetherington, along with Abel Heywood of Manchester, were selling Volney's *Ruins* in cheap instalments for as little as 2*d*.[124] Watson also included several extracts from Volney in his encyclopaedic periodical *The National: A Library for the People*.[125]

Based on Volney's tour of Ottoman Egypt and Greater Syria between 1782 and 1785, *Ruins* was, in part, a study in comparative religion, which highlighted irreconcilable contradictions between belief systems. To Volney this was evidence that all religions were man-made, the product of history and culture, and could be traced back to 'human needs or natural experiences ... objectified in deities, thence abstracted from their original impulse, and exploited as serviceable mysteries by priestcraft and by privileged orders'.[126] Revealed religion was bogus and divisive and served no other purpose than to enslave mankind. *Ruins* is essentially a plea for deism and freethought, and an attack on priestcraft, political exclusion, unproductive labour, and personal greed, all familiar to historians of freethought. Less familiar, *Ruins* can also be read as an extended essay on the destructive potential of the passions. Volney singles out 'unbridled desires', 'the perpetual play of passions', 'the inordinate desire of accumulation' as evils responsible for the decline of empires. More specifically, 'under the name of *aristocracy* the state has been tormented by the passions of the wealthy and the great'. Monarchy and aristocracy survive by appealing to the 'egotism that divide[s] mankind ... he flattered the vanity of one, excited the jealously of another, favoured the avarice of a third, inflamed the resentment of a fourth, irritated the passions of all'. So important were the passions in Volney's estimation that they furnish the motor of history: the rise and fall of empires 'have sprung from an eternal circle of passions'.[127]

The popularity of *Ruins* with Chartists has been attributed to the persistence of, inter alia, 'enlightenment moral philosophy'.[128] While this was clearly a factor, another was that *Ruins* was 'drenched in the new Romanticism'.[129] Some of this drenching may have derived from the exuberance and embellishment brought to the original text by the early English translations. When Volney discovered how garbled these translations were, he provided a new translation. It is possible that the original translation was the one read by some Chartists.[130] Either way, there is no denying that there are Romantic themes. The protagonist is a lonely and depressed wanderer among the ruins of former eastern empires whose 'heart was oppressed with sorrow and indignation' not just at the decay he witnesses but by the prospect of his own civilization withering which 'brought tears into my eyes'. He wishes the ruins could speak and tell of why former glorious empires decayed. And so it proves: the protagonist is confronted by an apparition who enables him to transcend his earth-bound form, by literally transporting him into outer space where, ranging backwards and forwards in time, he is versed in the eternal, transcendent natural laws of the creator-God. If the content of Volney's *Ruins* was Romantic, so, too, was the form with its ruins motif, lyrical mode and hybrid genre – part philosophical treatise, part poem and part novel. This stylistic ambivalence is characteristic of the Romantic aesthetic.[131] As with other exponents of radical Enlightenment, Volney's deployment of reason as an antidote to political corruption, religious authority and societal atrophy was not constructed in opposition to feeling. As Alexander Cook has argued, Volney transcends the dichotomy of reason and sentiment by showing how the pursuit of 'reason could teach people that the path to virtue was also the path to happiness'.[132]

The Chartists themselves contributed to this splicing of Enlightenment with Romanticism by including readings of Volney's *Ruins* at commemorative events, which as we have seen could be very sentimental affairs. A dinner at Ashton-under-Lyne to commemorative Henry Hunt's birthday concluded with a reading of the infamous chapter 15 of *Ruins*, the 'New Age', the most radical chapter of the book in which the people confront the privileged.[133] Extracts were reprinted in the Chartist press. Henry Vincent's *Western Vindicator* even included a Welsh translation of chapter 15 for its

Welsh readers, a practice continued by the Welsh-medium Chartist periodical *Udgorn Cymru*, most likely using the Welsh translation undertaken in the 1790s.[134] Vincent had already, implicitly at least, signalled the importance of Volney by including an extract from chapter 15 as early as the second issue of the *Western Vindicator*. Printed on the front page, this extract was clearly no 'filler' of spare column inches, appearing next to a letter from the Welsh Chartist leader John Frost, in which the central message was an attack on unproductive labour. Chapter 15 not only reinforces this critique but recasts Volney's work as a politically radical text, rather than a freethinking religious text. By only republishing or reciting chapter 15, the Chartists conveniently erased the geographical and temporal specificities of Volney's *Ruins*, including what some have regarded as its orientalism. In addition, focusing on the *Ruins* rather than the life of Volney also conveniently preserves the latter's radical credentials, dented somewhat by his subsequent association with Napoleon and French imperialism.[135]

The popularity of chapter 15 is further evidence of how Chartist heritage politics was not merely backwards looking but also directly concerned with linking the past, present and future in symbolically empowering ways. Having thoroughly depressed the protagonist with visions of why and how previous empires ended in ruins, he is then transported to the future in chapter 15 where the apparition shows him the beginnings of the people rising up against the privileged, casting them out and creating a new society based on productive labour. Chapter 15 is distinctly millenarian in tone, as is the thrust of the whole book which 'carries the reader forward on a wave of enthusiasm, not to a politic wisdom of the world, but to the vision of a "New Age" in which men will shed their warring religions and attain brotherhood in clear-eyed self-knowledge'.[136]

The London radical freethinker and pornographer William Dugdale published a complete edition of Volney's works, complete with portrait, and advertised it in the Chartist *Northern Star* alongside some of the most popular romances and gothic fiction of the day which he stocked in his bookshop on Holywell Street. Few other radicals personified to the extent Dugdale did of the contested legacies and blurring of Enlightenment, Romanticism, philosophy and pornography.[137] It is unfortunate that the Chartists were silent on Volney's wider *oeuvre*, particularly his *Law of Nature*, included in Dugdale's complete edition, as Volney outlined a moral code of personal conduct that touched on the need to discipline the passions and appetites which would have resonated with moral-force Chartists. The Chartist freethinker James Watson also conjoined Enlightenment and Romanticism in his bookshop and in the advertisements he placed in the Chartist press, in which the works of Volney appeared next to Shelley's *Queen Mab*. This was fitting given that Shelley reproduced Volney's account of his visits to Syria and Egypt in *Queen Mab*.[138] It is conceivable that it was formative encounters with Shelley's *Queen Mab* that led Chartists to Volney, or possibly via Mary Shelley's *Frankenstein* as Volney's *Ruins* was one of the texts read by the creature: Chartists were certainly familiar with *Frankenstein* as it is referenced in numerous speeches and the press.[139] Volney's popularity with the Chartists, then, was a manifestation of that heady brew of rationalism, millenarianism and religious enthusiasm that was such a marked feature of the 'age of revolution'.[140]

Conclusion

Addressing the Hull Working Men's Association in September 1837, and reaching his peroration, the charismatic Chartist lecturer Henry Vincent asked his audience: 'For whom lived Volney, Voltaire, Mirabaud, Rousseau, Paine, Bentham, Cartwright, Byron, Shelley, Godwin, Cobbett?' '[T]hey loved, struggled, and died for universal man,' Vincent responded. Vincent's cast and his style are further evidence of the blending of Enlightenment and Romanticism. At the same time, we have seen how the boundaries between Enlightenment and Romanticism were mapped onto an affective politics which pitted reason against feeling, illustrating the importance of feeling in popular politics and the illuminating potential of the history of emotions. Vincent's concluding injunction to his audience was just as revealing: 'we will build up upon their ruins the great temple of democratic freedom, beneath whose capacious arch shall be promoted and protected the universal happiness of the great family of man'.[141]

Vincent's pantheon, like that of the wider Chartist movement, was clearly a paper one, which had certain advantages such as portability and greater curatorial ownership and freedom for individuals to populate as they saw fit. Vincent even took part of his paper pantheon into prison in the form of Cobbett's works which he read in the early hours of each morning.[142] As Tony Taylor shows elsewhere in this volume, the statues and monuments that were such a marked feature of elite culture in Britain and elsewhere were conspicuous by their absence in Chartism and in British radicalism more generally. In addition to the significant barriers of cost and access to the public sphere, this absence may also have reflected, and indeed reinforced, the shifting and heterogeneous nature of the Chartist paper pantheon. There was no equivalent of an 'authorized heritage discourse' operating in Chartism, with the movement's leaders and organizations trying to determine the form and content of its heritage politics.[143] As befits a democratic movement, the heritage politics emerged just as much from below as it did from above. Inclusions and exclusions in the paper pantheon there certainly were, but as the case study of Thelwall suggests, a whole raft of factors – some of them contemporary to the lives of the radical greats, some contemporary to those remembering and forgetting – account for presence and absence in the pantheon of political and social movements. By drawing on recent work in Romantic Studies on posthumous life writing, we have seen how posthumous potential was dependent on the extent to which historical figures initiated a dialogue with posterity but also on a dedicated group of followers who work collaboratively to further posthumous careers. Paine and Cobbett – and even Volney to some extent – had great posthumous potential; Thelwall did not. To return to Vincent one last time. His metaphorical allusion to a future temple of democratic freedom is a reminder that commemoration, the invention of tradition and heritage politics are often just as forward looking as they are backwards. In this, and in so much else, the Chartists were heirs, custodians, creators and, on occasion, prisoners of Romantic memory.

Notes

1. Noel Cox, 'Newport and the Chartist Rising of 1839', *Token Corresponding Society Bulletin*, 9 (2009), 304–9. The Chartists did, however, issue specially commissioned medals on some occasions, notably when Feargus O'Connor was liberated from York Castle in 1840.
2. Gordon Pentland coined the concept of 'paper pantheon' in 'The Posthumous Lives of Thomas Muir', in *Liberty, Property and Popular Politics: England and Scotland, 1688–1815*, ed. Gordon Pentland and Michael T. Davis (Edinburgh: Edinburgh University Press, 2016), 211. For loyalist, tory and whig cults, see J. J. Sack, 'The Memory of Burke and the Memory of Pitt: English Conservatism Confronts its Past, 1806–1829', *Historical Journal*, 30, no. 3 (1987), 623–40; Alison Yarrington, *The Commemoration of the Hero 1800–1864: Monuments to the British Victors of the Napoleonic Wars* (New York: Garland, 1988); J. E. Cookson, 'The Edinburgh and Glasgow Duke of Wellington Statues: Early Nineteenth-Century Unionist Nationalism as a Tory Project', *Scottish Historical Review*, 83, no. 215 (2004), 23–40; Belinda Beaton, 'Materializing the Duke', *Journal of Victorian Culture*, 10, no. 1 (2005), 100–7; T. E. Orme, 'Toasting Fox: The Fox Dinners in Edinburgh and Glasgow, 1801–25', *History*, 99, no. 4 (2014), 588–606; Emily Jones, *Edmund Burke and the Invention of Modern Conservatism, 1830–1914* (Oxford: Oxford University Press, 2017). On the shift away from static sites of memory to the performance of a more dynamic concept of memory, see Ann Rigney, 'The Dynamics of Remembrance: Texts between Monumentality and Morphing', in *Cultural Memory Studies: An International and Interdisciplinary Handbook*, ed. Astrid Erll and Ansgar Nünning (Berlin: De Gruyter, 2008), 345–53.
3. Miles Taylor, *Ernest Jones, Chartism and the Romance of Politics, 1819–1869* (Oxford: Oxford University Press, 2003), 10. See also G. S. R. Kitson Clark, 'The Romantic Element – 1830 to 1850', in *Studies in Social History: A Tribute to G. M. Trevelyan*, ed. J. H. Plumb (London: Longmans, 1955), 209–39; Rohan McWilliam, 'Sweeney Todd and the Chartist Gothic: Politics and Print Culture in Early Victorian Britain', in *Edward Lloyd and His World: Popular Fiction, Politics and the Press in Victorian Britain*, ed. Sarah Susan Lill and Rohan McWilliam (Abingdon: Routledge, 2019), 198–215. On the difficulties of defining romanticism, especially in a British context, see Iain McCalman, 'Introduction: A Romantic Age *Companion*', in *An Oxford Companion to the Romantic Age: British Culture, 1776–1832* ed. Iain McCalman (Oxford: Oxford University Press, 1999), 1–11.
4. Guy Beiner, *Forgetful Remembrance: Social Forgetting and Vernacular Historiography of a Rebellion in Ulster* (Oxford: Oxford University Press, 2018), 17.
5. A number of recent works have positioned Thelwall as a Romantic radical, e.g. Judith Thompson, 'Citizen Juan Thelwall: In the Footsteps of a Free-Range Radical', *Studies in Romanticism*, 48 (2009), 67–100; *Romantic Radical and Acquitted Felon*, ed. Steve Poole (London: Pickering & Chatto, 2009); *John Thelwall: Critical Reassessments*, ed. Yasmin Solomonescu (Romantic-Circles, 2011); 'John Thelwall Special Issue', *Romanticism*, 16, no. 2 (2010).
6. Gwyn A. Williams, *Artisans and Sans-Culottes: Popular Movements in France and Britain* (London: Libris, 1989), 66; Judith Thompson, 'Introduction', in *The Peripatetic*, ed. Judith Thompson (Detroit, MI: Wayne State University Press, 2001), 15, 18.

7. In a recent essay Steve Poole has taken me to task for providing an insufficient explanation for Thelwall's absence in the Chartist pantheon, which I largely attributed to Chartist preference for gentleman leaders in the past as well as the present, and Thelwall's ambiguous social status did not qualify him for admission to the pantheon. While I maintain that the Chartist pantheon was mostly populated by gentleman radicals, I accept Poole's criticism that there was more to Thelwall's absence than his class status. Steve Poole, 'The Politics of "Protest Heritage", 1790–1850', in *Remembering Protest in Britain since 1500*, ed. Carl J. Griffin and Briony McDonagh (Basingstoke: Palgrave, 2018), 187–213.
8. On the rediscovery of Thelwall, see Nicholas Roe, 'The Lives of John Thelwall: Another View of the "Jacobin Fox"', in *John Thelwall: Romantic Radical*, 13–24; 'Thelwall, John (1764–1834)', *Blue Plaques*, English Heritage, https://www.english-heritage.org.uk/visit/blue-plaques/john-thelwall/ (accessed 13 November 2022).
9. For this characterization of the evolution of Romantic Studies, see Joseph Rezek, 'Romanticism in the Atlantic World', *Studies in Romanticism*, 55 (2016), 313.
10. See Joel Faflak and Richard C. Sha, 'Feeling Romanticism', in *Romanticism and the Emotions*, ed. Joel Faflak and Richard C. Sha (Cambridge: Cambridge University Press, 2016), 2. The relationship between Romanticism and emotion was, of course, much more complex than this. As well as the above collection, see the special issue 'Romanticism and Affect Studies', *Romantic Circles Praxis Volume* (2018).
11. For the argument that the 1790s saw the collapse of 'the emotional culture of Enlightenment Britain' and was 'replaced by a new approach to feeling and desire', see Rachel Hewitt, *A Revolution of Feeling: The Decade That Forged the Modern Mind* (London: Granta, 2017), 2.
12. It is worth noting that Jonathan Israel has argued that the radical Enlightenment – that wing which was committed to universal rights such as manhood suffrage – endured down to the 1848, at which point it was displaced by socialism: *The Enlightenment That Failed: Ideas, Revolution, and Democratic Defeat, 1748–1830* (Oxford: Oxford University Press, 2019), 28.
13. Carl J. Griffin, 'Memory and the Work of Forgetting: Telling Protest in the English Countryside', in *Remembering Protest in Britain since 1500: Memory, Materiality and the Landscape*, ed. Carl J. Griffin and Briony McDonagh (Basingstoke: Palgrave, 2018), 230.
14. Matthijs M. Lok, '"Un oubli total du passé"? The Political and Social Construction of Silence in Restoration Europe (1813–1830)', *History and Memory*, 26 (2014), 43. On the complex relationship between remembering and forgetting, see Beiner, *Forgetful Remembrance*, 17–30.
15. The National Archives (TNA), Home Office (HO) 64/12, Secret service reports, 19 October 1832, f. 157v.
16. Roberts, *Chartism, Commemoration and the Cult of the Radical Hero* (Abingdon: Routledge, 2020), 21–2. Godwin enjoyed greater posthumous fame with the Owenite socialists on account, no doubt, that he had been a mentor of Owen while his philosophical anarchism and necessitarianism lent itself much more readily to the communitarian ethos of Owenism. This was also consistent with the anti-political thrust of Owenism as Godwin, like Owen, was dismissive of the potential of democratic politics to redress popular grievances. See Gregory Claeys, *Citizens and Saints: Politics and Anti-politics in Early British Socialism* (Cambridge: Cambridge University Press, 1989), 33–5.
17. E. P. Thompson, *The Romantics: England in a Revolutionary Age* (Rendlesham: Merlin, 1997), 99.

18 Penelope J. Corfield, 'Rhetoric, Radical Politics and Rainfall: John Thelwall in Breconshire', typescript of an essay published in *Brycheiniog*, 40 (2008), http://www.penelopejcorfield.co.uk/PDF%27s/CorfieldPdf14_Thelwall.pdf (accessed 16 August 2019).
19 *York Herald*, 8 February 1834; *London Courier*, 19 February 1834; *Morning Chronicle*, 19 February 1834.
20 Michael Scrivener, 'John Thelwall's Political Ambivalence: Reform and Revolution', in *Radicalism and Revolution in Britain, 1775–1848*, ed. Michael T. Davis (Basingstoke: Macmillan, 2000), 70.
21 *Sun*, 11 November 1831.
22 At the time of his fleeing to the United States in 1817, Cobbett was accused of cowardice by some radicals though this charge was either conveniently airbrushed out of Cobbett's posthumous career or else it was justified as Cobbett did at the time: had he remained in Britain he would almost certainly have been imprisoned (if not for sedition then possibly insolvency), a fate he had already endured in 1811 for sedition. George Spater, *William Cobbett: The Poor Man's Friend Volume 2* (Cambridge: Cambridge University Press, 1982), 357–58. For an example of a Chartist homage to Cobbett which excused his failings, see William Lovett's appreciation in *Advocate & Merthyr Free Press*, 1 April 1841.
23 Matthew Roberts, 'Posthumous Paine in the United Kingdom, 1809–1832: Jacobin or Loyalist Cult?', in *The Legacy of Thomas Paine in the Transatlantic World*, ed. Sam Edwards and Marcus Morris (Abingdon: Routledge, 2018), 107–32.
24 Frank O'Gorman, 'The Paine Burnings of 1792–93', *Past and Present*, 193 (2006), 111–55.
25 Corinna Wagner, 'Loyalist Propaganda and the Scandalous Life of Tom Paine: "Hypocritical Monster!"', *British Journal for Eighteenth-Century Studies*, 28, no. 1 (2005), 97–115.
26 Kenneth R. Johnston, *Unusual Suspects: Pitt's Reign of Alarm and the Lost Generation of the 1790s* (Oxford: Oxford University Press, 2013), 25–33.
27 Ibid., 25.
28 Thompson, *Romantics*, 158. For Thelwall's lecturing and the democratic culture he sought to create through it, see Jon Mee, *Print, Publicity, and Popular Radicalism in the 1790s* (Cambridge: Cambridge University Press, 2016), ch. 6.
29 Hazlitt, for one, judged that 'Mr Cobbett Speaks Almost as Well as He Writes'. William Hazlitt, *The Character of William Cobbett* (London, 1835), 12.
30 TNA, HO 42/51, Home Office papers, disturbance correspondence, Samuel Homfrey to Home Office, 23 September 1800; HO 42/43, Edward Edwards to Home Office, 30 April 1798.
31 Williams, *Artisans and Sans Culottes*, 66.
32 Roberts, *Chartism*, 19, 75, 171. Manon Nouvian has recently challenged this argument, but the fact remains that most of those in the pantheon were gentlemen, the only notable exception being Samuel Holberry who, despite the understandable anger and grief which greeted his death, never came close to rivalling the place of the longer-established gentlemen figures in the pantheon. The other working-class figures that Manon cites as member of the Chartist pantheon were only admitted after the movement had largely ceased to exist as a mass movement. Manon Nouvian, 'Defiant Mourning: Public Funerals as Funeral Demonstrations in the Chartist Movement', *Journal of Victorian Culture*, 24, no. 2 (2019), 208–26.
33 See, for example, the satirical *Life of William Cobbett* by James Gillray (1809) which lampooned Cobbett's humble background and his upstart pretensions. The way in

which the loyalist press and satirists parodied Paine's occupation as a stay-maker is well known.
34 *English Chartist Circular*, No. 8, 1841.
35 E.g. *Northern Star*, 5 February 1842 (Paine birthday commemoration at Merthyr Tydfil), 7 February 1846 (Paine commemoration at Ashton-under-Lyne), 4 January 1845 (Cartwright, Hunt and Cobbett described as 'nobles of nature' at Rotherham).
36 Malcolm Chase, 'Building Identity, Building Circulation: Engraved Portraiture and the Northern Star', in *Papers for the People: A Study of the Chartist Press*, ed. Joan Allen and Owen R. Ashton (London: Merlin, 2005), 26.
37 Gordon S. Wood, *The Americanization of Benjamin Franklin* (New York: Penguin, 2004).
38 *English Chartist Circular*, No. 1 & 2. The main articles on Washington were by Charles Phillips, and extracts from Guizot's life, translated by Paul Parnell. A little under a year later, this newspaper began a much fuller, serialized life of Washington, which commenced in issue 48.
39 Ian Dyck, *William Cobbett and Rural Popular Culture* (Cambridge: Cambridge University Press, 1992). For these sorts of tensions in Romanticism's relationship to the people and popular culture, see Philip Connell and Nigel Leask, 'What Is the People?', in *Romanticism and Popular Culture in Britain and Ireland*, ed. Philip Connell and Nigel Leask (Cambridge: Cambridge University Press, 2009), 3–48.
40 Hugh Williams, *National Songs and Poetical Pieces* (London: Henry Hetherington, 1839), 13–21.
41 *Midland Counties Illuminator*, 20 March, 3 and 17 April 1841.
42 As Fred Donnelly has argued, when radicals – including Thelwall – did invoke the Levellers they locked them 'carefully within a Whiggish view of the seventeenth century conflict'. F. K. Donnelly, 'Levellism in Eighteenth and Early Nineteenth-Century Britain', *Albion*, 20 (1988), 268.
43 *Operative*, 11 November 1838; *Northern Star*, 12 November 1842, 11 November 1843, 8 November 1851; Poole, 'The Politics of "Protest Heritage"', 200.
44 *Northern Liberator*, 23 November 1839 ('Insurrection in Wales'), 18 January 1840 ('Mr Frost').
45 E. P. Thompson, 'Hunting the Jacobin Fox', *Past & Present*, 142 (1994), 114–15.
46 *Northern Star*, 16 November 1839 (toast to Hardy at Ashton).
47 The memoirs of Thomas Hardy were, however, serialized in the *English Chartist Circular*. For Chartist commemoration of the Scottish Martyrs, see Roberts, *Chartism*, 12–13; Pentland, 'The Posthumous Lives of Thomas Muir'.
48 *Robert Gammage: Reminiscences of a Chartist*, ed. W. H. Maehl (Manchester: Society for the Study of Labour History, 1983), 38.
49 Chase, 'Building Identity', 38.
50 For Emmet's life retold as a cautionary tale against physical force Chartism, see *Chartist Circular* (Scotland), 10 July 1841.
51 William Farish, *The Autobiography of William Farish: The Struggles of a Handloom Weaver* (London: Caliban, 1996 [1889]), 50. On the use and display of radical objects in homes as a way of demonstrating emotional attachment to radicalism, see Ruth Mather, 'The Home-Making of the English Working Class: Radical Politics and Domestic Life in Late-Georgian England, c.1790–1820' (Queen Mary University of London PhD, 2016), 176.
52 For literary tourism, see *Commemorating Writers in Nineteenth-Century Europe: Nation-Building and Centenary Fever*, ed. Ann Rigney and Joep Leerssen

(Basingstoke: Palgrave, 2014). *Sheffield Working Man's Advocate*, 3 April 1841; *Advocate and Merthyr Free Press*, August 1840; R. J. Richardson, *Political Almanac* (London, 1840), copy in TNA, HO 45/55; Taylor, *Ernest Jones*, 79; Mike Sanders, *The Poetry of Chartism: Aesthetics, Politics, History* (Cambridge: Cambridge University Press, 2009), 8–9, 47; *Robert Lowery: Radical and Chartist*, ed. Brian Harrison and Patricia Hollis (London: Europa, 1979), 116. For the contested legacies and invoking of Burns by Chartists, see Christopher A. Whatley, '"It Is Said That Burns Was a Radical": Contest, Concession and the Political Legacy of Robert Burns, ca. 1795–1859', *Journal of British Studies*, 50, no. 3 (2011), 653–54; Ann Rigney, 'Embodied Communities: Commemorating Robert Burn, 1859', *Representations*, 115 (2011), 71–101.

53 *The Constitution of the London Democratic Association* (London: B.D. Cousins, 1838), copy in TNA, HO 44/52, f. 221.

54 Leicestershire Record Office (LRO), DE 2964/22, Papers of William Jones, Thomas Cooper to William Jones, 30 September 1845. See also Ian Haywood, 'The Literature of Chartism', in *The Oxford Handbook of Victorian Literary Culture*, ed. Juliet John (Oxford: Oxford University Press, 2016), 87–8.

55 Anne Janowitz, *Lyric and Labour in the Romantic Tradition* (Cambridge: Cambridge University Press, 1998), chs 5–6; *G. W. M. Reynolds: Nineteenth-Century Fiction, Politics and the Press*, ed. Anne Humpherys (Aldershot: Ashgate, 2008); Taylor, *Ernest Jones*; Simon Rennie, *The Poetry of Ernest Jones: Myth, Song and the 'Mighty Mind'* (Oxford: Legenda, 2016).

56 *McDouall's Chartist Journal and Trades Advocate*, 7 August and 4 September 1841 (Byron), 28 August 1841 (Shelley), 18 September 1841 (Southey); P. Pickering and S. Roberts, 'Pills, Pamphlets and Politics: The Career of Peter Murray McDouall (1814–54)', *Manchester Region History Review*, 11 (1997), 35. I explore the Romantic and Gothic facets of O'Connor (and the 'Tory-Radical' Richard Oastler) in my book, *Democratic Passions: The Politics of Feeling in British Radicalism, 1809–1848* (Manchester: Manchester University Press, 2022). For Taylor, see W. Hamish Fraser, *Dr John Taylor, Chartist: Ayrshire Revolutionary* (Trowbridge: Ayrshire Archaeological & Natural History Society, 2006), 16, 25.

57 *Chartist Pilot*, 22 December 1843. Jones's poetry deserves more extended treatment. For a selection of his poems, see *The Anthology of Leicester Chartist Song, Poetry & Verse*, ed. Ned Newitt (Leicester: Leicester Pioneer Press, 2006).

58 LRO, DE 2964/20, Papers of William Jones, Thomas Cooper to Jones, 30 June 1845.

59 LRO, DE 2964/17, Cooper to Jones, 4 March 1845.

60 Archives+, Manchester Central Library, R. J. Richardson Papers, 'Monody on the Death of Harry Richardson', July 1844, f. 195.

61 The generic shift from satire to melodrama in popular radical imaginative literature, traced by Sally Ledger and Mike Sanders in the transition from regency radicalism to Chartism, was also, arguably, indicative of the aesthetic purchase of Romanticism: Mike Sanders, 'No Laughing Matter: Chartism and the Limits of Satire', in *Nineteenth-Century Radical Traditions*, ed. J. Bristow and J. McDonagh (Basingstoke: Palgrave, 2016), 21–35. On Chartism and song, see David Kennerley, 'Strikes and singing classes: Chartist culture, "rational recreation" and the politics of music after 1842', *English Historical Review*, 135, no. 576 (2020), 1165–94.

62 Roy Porter and Mikuláš Teich, 'Introduction', in *Romanticism in National Context*, ed. Roy Porter and Mikuláš Teich (Cambridge: Cambridge University Press, 1988), 3.

63 *Charter*, 17 March 1839. See Also Christopher Hill, 'The Norman Yoke', in *Puritanism and Revolution* (London: Secker & Warburg, 1969), 119–25; James Epstein, *Radical*

Expression: Political Language, Ritual and Symbol in England, 1790–1840 (New York: Oxford University Press, 1994), ch. 1; Peter Spence, *The Birth of Romantic Radicalism: War, Popular Politics and English Radical Reformism, 1800–1815* (Aldershot: Scolar Press, 1996).

64 TNA, TS 11/602, Treasury Solicitor's Papers, confiscated letters of Thomas Cooper, Jonathan Bairstow to Thomas Cooper, 22 June 1842.
65 Sheffield Local Studies Library, MP 1216 S, J. H. Bramwich, 'Funeral Hymn, Samuel Holberry', June 1842. For the choreographing of Holberry's funeral, see Novian, 'Defiant Mourning'.
66 TNA, MFQ1/265, 'Murder Demands Justice', broadside, n.d. [1842].
67 TNA, HO 40/51, 'Working Men of Barnsley!', 6 August 1839, f. 361.
68 W. J. Linton, *The Life of Thomas Paine* (London: James Watson, 1842), 43.
69 Aidan Day, *Romanticism* (London: Routledge, 1996), 90.
70 LRO, DE 2964/7, Papers of William Jones, 'Immortality', by William Jones, n.d.
71 *Northern Star*, 25 March 1848.
72 I develop these points at a greater length in Roberts, *Chartism*, 68–71, 207–8.
73 On the relationship between melodrama and popular politics, see Patrick Joyce, *Democratic Subjects: The Self and the Social in Nineteenth-Century England* (Cambridge: Cambridge University Press, 1994), ch. 14; Rohan McWilliam, 'Melodrama and the Historians', *Radical History Review*, 78 (2000), 57–84.
74 *Chartist Circular* (Scotland), 13 March 1841. For the original American rendition, see Jennifer Clark, *The American Idea of England, 1776–1840: Transatlantic Writing* (Abingdon: Routledge, 2013), 107.
75 *Northern Star*, 17 November 1838.
76 *Northern Star*, 31 October 1840.
77 Mark Sandy, *Romanticism, Memory and Mourning* (Aldershot: Ashgate, 2013). See Also H. J. Jackson, *Those Who Write for Immortality: Romantic Reputations and the Dream of Lasting Fame* (New Haven and London: Yale University Press, 2015).
78 *The Thomas Paine Reader*, ed. Michael Foot and Isaac Kramnick (London: Penguin), 80.
79 *Cobbett's Legacy to Labourers* (London: Charles Griffin, 1870 [1835]), 31. See also *Cobbett's Legacy to Parsons* (London: Charles Griffin 1870 [1835]).
80 On the making of the 'Emmet Legend' see *Reinterpreting Emmet: Essays on the Life and Legacy of Robert Emmet*, ed. Anne Dolan, Patrick M. Geoghegan and Darryl Jones (Dublin: UCD Press, 2007).
81 Jon Mee, 'The Dungeon and the Cell: The Prison Verse of Coleridge and Thelwall', in *John Thelwall: Romantic Radical*, 107.
82 This explains why Major John Cartwright was not as prominent in the paper pantheon as Paine and Cobbett. Cartwright was certainly a notable presence in the pantheon, with some Chartists bestowing the accolade of 'father' of Chartism on him, but despite his very long political career in campaigning for radical reform, he did not quite equal the status of Paine and Cobbett, perhaps because, like Thelwall, his contribution was mainly on the platform and as radical organizer rather than as a writer, and he was also a rather modest character combined to Paine and Cobbett. In the words of Cartwright's best biographer, Rachel Eckersley, he was a 'poor self-publicist'. Unlike Thelwall, Cartwright was not a great oratory. Also like Thelwall, posthumous Cartwright was appropriated by more moderate radicals and reformers, a project that was enshrined in the memorial to him in Cartwright Gardens,

Bloomsbury. For Chartists and Cartwright, see Matthew Roberts, 'Chartism, Commemoration, and the Cult of the Radical Hero, c.1770–1840', *Labour History Review*, 78, no. 1 (2013), 1–32. For Cartwright, see Rachel Eckersley, 'The Drum Major of Sedition: The Political Life and Career of John Cartwright (1740–1824)' (University of Manchester PhD, 1999) (quote at 248). Thanks to Pippa Catterall for helping and clarifying Cartwright's status in the Chartist pantheon.

83 For 'webs of receptions', see Tom Mole, *What the Victorians Made of Romanticism: Material Artefacts, Cultural Practices, and Reception History* (Princeton: Princeton University Press, 2017).

84 Tim Yi-Chang Chiou, 'Romantic Posthumous Life Writing: Inter-stitching Genres and Forms of Mourning and Commemoration' (PhD thesis, University of Oxford, 2012), 14. Chiou defines posthumous life writing as 'anticipatory death writings, works of mourning, commemorative life writings, memorial aids, and belated defences', 20.

85 *The Political Works of Thomas Paine* (London: T. M. Wheeler, 1846), n.p., copy held by the Working Class Movement's Library, Salford.

86 Malcolm Chase, 'Cobbett, His Children and Chartism', in *William Cobbett, Romanticism and the Enlightenment*, ed. James Grande and John Stevenson (London: Pickering & Chatto, 2015), 123–36.

87 Corfield, 'John Thelwall in Breconshire', 17. For 'assisted authorship', see Jackson, *Those Who Write for Immortality*, 23.

88 Jen Morgan, 'The Transmission and Reception of P.B. Shelley in Owenite and Chartist Newspapers and Periodicals' (PhD thesis, University of Salford, 2014); Casie LeGette, *Remaking Romanticism: The Radical Politics of the Excerpt* (Basingstoke: Palgrave, 2017), 1.

89 For Chartist resistance to cultural nationalism, see Matthew Roberts, 'Daniel O'Connell, Repeal and Chartism in the Age of Atlantic Revolutions', *Journal of Modern History*, 90, no. 1 (2018), 9–10.

90 Marilyn Butler, *Romantics, Rebels and Reactionaries: English Literature and Its Background, 1760–1830* (Oxford: Oxford University Press, 1981), 180–1.

91 Brian Harrison, 'Teetotal Chartism', in *The People's Charter: Democratic Agitation in Early Victorian Britain*, ed. Stephen Roberts (London: Merlin, 2003), 45.

92 Rob Boddice, *A History of Feelings* (London: Reaktion, 2019), 118; Corinna Wagner, *Pathological Bodies: Medicine and Political Culture* (Berkeley: University of California Press, 2013), 71–2. Godwin would later reject the excessive rationalism of his puritan inheritance and assert the primacy of feeling over reason as the most useful and proper determinant of human behaviour, a cruel irony given that it was Godwin's accusation that mob-orators like Thelwall were dangerously inflaming the passions which had led to the falling out of the two men in 1795. Rowland Weston, 'Politics, Passion and the "Puritan Temper": Godwin's Critique of Enlightened Modernity', *Studies in Romanticism*, 41 (2002), 448; Johnston, *Unusual Suspects*, 27.

93 G. J. Barker-Benfield, *The Culture of Sensibility: Sex and Society in the Eighteenth Century* (Chicago: University of Chicago Press, 1992), 1–3 and ch. 7; Wagner, *Pathological Bodies*, 114–21. See Also Hewitt, *A Revolution of Feeling*, 41–2, 54, 63–9.

94 *Midland Counties Illuminator*, 13 February 1841.

95 *Chartist Circular* (Scotland), 2 January 1841.

96 *London Dispatch*, 1 October 1837; *Chartist Circular*, 3 October 1840. For Wollstonecraft's attack on 'gothic beauty' – in which she depicts the French

aristocracy as insidious ivy, see Mary Wollstonecraft, *A Vindication of the Rights of Woman and A Vindication of the Rights of Men*, ed. Janet Todd (Oxford: Oxford University Press, 1994), 8.
97 William Lovett, *The Life and Struggles of William Lovett in His Pursuit of Bread, Knowledge and Freedom* (1876; London: Kegan Paul, 1976), 209.
98 *London Dispatch*, 25 February 1838; *Northern Star*, 25 September 1841.
99 British Library, Add MS 37,773, Working Men's Association Minutes, 2 January 1839, f. 135.
100 *Northern Star*, 27 April 1839.
101 *Constitution of London Democratic Association*, TNA, HO 44/52, f. 223.
102 *National Association Gazette*, 16 July 1842. For a similar appreciation of Washington, see the poem in the *Scottish Patriot*, 19 October 1839.
103 On the problems of 'man worship', see the series of articles under that name which appeared in the *Northern Star*, the first of which was published on 7 January 1843. Tellingly, even the author of this article reached for great men – Washington and Tell – when warning against the dangers of 'man worship'. These leaders were acceptable because they 'check[ed] every disposition of the people to God [them]'. *Northern Star*, 21 January 1843.
104 *Poor Man's Guardian*, 8 and 15 December 1832; *Northern Star*, 27 March 1841.
105 'Liberty of the Press', n.d. [1836], Library of Birmingham, Wolfson Centre for Archival research, William Lovett Collection, LF 76.13, vol. 1, f. 12.
106 Lovett, *Life and Struggles*, 44–5.
107 *Operative*, 21 April 1839.
108 Roberts, *Chartism*, 112–16.
109 Boddice, *History of Feelings*, 112–13; Nicola Eustace, *Passion Is the Gale: Emotion, Power and the Coming of the American Revolution* (Chapel Hill: University of North Carolina Press, 2008), 445.
110 William Reddy, *The Navigation of Feeling: A Framework for the History of Emotions* (Cambridge: Cambridge University Press, 2001), 142; Hewitt, *Revolution of Feeling*, 188.
111 Day, Romanticism, ch. 3; Alexander Regier, *Fracture and Fragmentation in British Romanticism* (Cambridge: Cambridge University Press, 2010); idem, *Exorbitant Enlightenment: Blake, Hamann and Anglo-German Constellations* (Oxford: Oxford University Press, 2018).
112 Rob Boddice, *The History of Emotions* (Manchester: Manchester University Press, 2018), 62.
113 Barbara H. Rosenwein and Riccardo Cristiani, *What Is the History of Emotions?* (Cambridge: Polity, 2018), 76.
114 Rob Breton, 'Genre in the Chartist Periodical', in *The Working-Class Intellectual in Eighteenth and Nineteenth Century Britain*, ed. Aruna Krishnamurphy (Farnham: Ashgate, 2009), 112.
115 Ibid., 197.
116 Epstein, *Radical Expression*, 195; E. P. Thompson, *The Making of the English Working Class* (New York: Vintage Books, 1963), 98–9; *Sheffield Iris*, 22 October 1839.
117 The best treatment of metropolitan working-class radicalism in the early 1830s is Iorwerth Prothero, *Artisans and Politics in Early Nineteenth-Century London: John Gast and His Times* (Folkestone: Dawson, 1979), ch. 14.

118 For a copy of the proclamation and the table of penalties, and evidence of its circulation, see Nottingham Archives, CT 12/55/20, *A Proclamation by the King*, 28 June 1830, and accompanying *A Table of Penalties*.
119 TNA, HO 64/17, Seditious publications, 1830–31, 'A Revolution in England', f. 77. Extracts from Volney were also serialized in the radical press, e.g. *Cosmopolite*, 21 April 1832.
120 *Address to the Jury by Thomas Cooper* (Leicester: T. Warwick, 1842), 13. Henry Vincent also listed Volney as a formative influence: *Nottingham Review*, 9 April 1841, as did Linton: W. J. Linton, *Memories* (London: Lawrence and Bullen, 1895), 26.
121 TNA, HO 64/11, Secret Service reports of seditious meetings, 1830, fos 147, 170.
122 *London Dispatch*, 25 December 1836; *Champion*, 1 January 1837.
123 *Cleave's London Satirist and Gazette of Variety*, 9 December 1837.
124 *The National: A Library for the People*, ed. W. J. Linton (London: James Watson 1839), 95, 142, 157, 187, 245.
125 E. P. Thompson, *Witness against the Beast: William Blake and the Moral Law* (Cambridge: Cambridge University Press, 1993), 199–200.
126 Francois Constantin Volney, *The Ruins, or a Survey of the Revolutions of Empire* (Otley: Woodstock Books, 1791 [2000]), 25, 29, 34, 36–7.
127 Tom Scriven, *Popular Virtue: Continuity and Change in Radical Moral Politics, 1820–70* (Manchester: Manchester University Press, 2017), 15–18.
128 Gwyn A. Williams, 'Romanticism in Wales', in *Romanticism in National Context*, 15.
129 For a comparison of the various translations, see Richard Carlile's *Lion*, 25 July 1828.
130 For Volney, the *Ruins*, and its pre-Chartist reception in Britain, see: Alexander Cook, 'Reading Revolution: Towards a History of the Volney Vogue in England', in *Anglo-French Attitudes: Comparisons and Transfers between English and French since the Eighteenth Century*, ed. Christophe Charl, Julien Vincent and Jay Winter (Manchester: Manchester University Press, 2007), 125–46; Sanja Perovik, 'Lyrist in Britain; Empiricist in France: Volney's Divided Legacy', in *Historical Writing in Britain, 1688–1830*, ed. Ben Dew and Fiona Price (Basingstoke: Palgrave, 2014), 127–44.
131 Cook, 'Reading Revolution', 128, 130.
132 *Northern Star*, 17 November 1838. For other recitals of Volney's *Ruins*, see *Northern Star*, 16 October 1841 (City of London), 1 June 1844 (Bethnal Green), 17 October 1846 (Camberwell).
133 *Chartist Circular* (Scotland), 28 December 1839; *Western Vindicator*, 20 April 1839; *Udgorn Cymru*, 1 April 1841, copy in TNA, HO 45/54, f. 47; *London Democrat*, 13 April 1839; *Chartist Pilot*, 7 December 1844. The Chartist freethinker James Watson appended chapter 15 to *A Brief Sketch of the Life of C.F. Volney* (London: James Watson, 1840). For the Welsh translation in the 1790s, see Gwyn A. Williams, 'Morgan John Rhys and Volney's *Ruins of Empire*', *Bulletin of the Board of Celtic Studies*, 20 (1964), 58–65.
134 *Western Vindicator*, 2 March 1839. For this approach to reprinting excerpts, see LeGette, *Remaking Romanticism*, 1–12; Matthew Roberts, 'Labouring in the Digital Archive', *Labour History Review*, 78, no. 1 (2013), 113–26. For a useful overview and critique of Volney's orientalism, see Urs App, *The Birth of Orientalism* (Philadelphia: Pennsylvania Press, 2010), ch. 8.
135 Thompson, *Witness against the Beast*, 200.
136 *Northern Star*, 6 April 1844. For Dugdale, see Iain McCalman, *Radical Underworld: Prophets, Revolutionaries and Pornographers in London, 1795–1840* (Oxford: Oxford University Press, 1993), ch. 10.

137 *Cleave's Penny Gazette*, 7 July 1838; *Northern Star*, 9 September 1843.
138 'Proceedings of the Birmingham Deputation in Scotland', n.d. [August 1838], Lovett Collection, LF 76.13, vol. 2, f. 185; *Charter*, 27 January 1839; *London Dispatch*, 13 January 1839; *Northern Star*, 2 June 1838, 17 July 1841; Feargus O'Connor, *A Series of Letters from Feargus O'Connor, Esq., Barrister at Law, to Daniel O'Connell, Esq., M.P. Containing a Review of Mr. O'Connell's Conduct during the Agitation of the Question of Catholic Emancipation, together with an Analysis of His Motives and Actions, since He Became a Member of Parliament* (London: Henry Hetherington, 1836), 29, 33, 43.
139 McCalman, *Radical Underworld*, viii; Jon Mee, *Dangerous Enthusiasm: William Blake and the Culture of Radicalism in the 1790s* (Oxford: Oxford University Press, 1992), 3–8, 14; Philip Lockley, *Visionary Religion and Radicalism in Early Industrial England: From Southcott to Socialism* (Oxford: Oxford University Press, 2013), 166–8.
140 *London Dispatch*, 17 September 1837.
141 People's History Museum, Manchester, Henry Vincent Papers, VIN 1/1/16, Henry Vincent to John Minikin, 1 June 1839.
142 Roberts, *Chartism*, ch. 4.

6

'A new political baptism': Memorializing the Reform Acts in 1832

Gordon Pentland

On Sunday 24 June 1832, Edmund Harden, curate of All Saints in Upper Norwood in the parish of Croydon, baptized a foundling girl of unknown parentage. The great drama of the passage of parliamentary reform was reaching its end stages as the English bill limped through a chastened House of Lords. In the context of this compelling national drama, which had engrossed the attention of communities across Great Britain and Ireland since the fall of Wellington's ministry in November 1830, the curate had a ready name for the foundling: Mary Reform.[1] It was one of the many ways in which individuals, groups and communities sought to memorialize the passage of reform in 1832 and which form the focus for this chapter.

The Reform Acts of 1832 have long been the keystone in the foundation myth of modern British politics. As a shibboleth of Whig historiography and a pivotal moment within the development of the modern polity, the question of what the legislation actually changed has been a central concern of those interested in the history of parties and institutions; political ideas and languages; and, most prominently, electoral structures, behaviours and cultures.[2] While decades of creative scholarship have questioned their actual significance, the Reform Acts remain stubbornly embedded in popular and official accounts of the UK's political past. Theresa May's efforts, at her first party conference as prime minister, to badge the EU Withdrawal Bill as the 'Great Repeal Bill' is only one recent (thwarted) effort to tap into the popular memory and heritage surrounding the Reform Acts.[3]

Thus far, the Reform Acts of 1832 have largely evaded scholarship on memorialization and commemoration. This chapter aims to survey the different ways in which reformers and others sought to memorialize and commemorate an event which they saw as formative (for better or worse) in 1832. It proceeds from the premise that 'reform', especially when used both in its primary association with parliamentary and constitutional, but also in its secondary association with moral and social reform, was a major preoccupation in the public life of Victorian and Edwardian Britain and Ireland.[4] Contributing to its near hegemonic status in the 1830s and beyond was the volume and variety of memory-making activities undertaken to mark the passing of the Reform Acts as a turning point. It is a truism, of course, that any effort to 'fix' the memory of an event, group or individual is liable to contestation. Similarly, some efforts to establish a memory of 1832 appeared to be failures at the time. Nonetheless, examining how contemporaries sought to memorialize reform in 1832 is both a superb vantage point from which to explore the sheer range of activities that constituted 'political memory' in nineteenth-century Britain and a new way of rehabilitating the Reform Acts and of demonstrating their centrality to Victorian political culture.

Elite memorialization

Elite politicians who devised, passed or contested the reform legislation had very clear reasons to wish to memorialize it. The consciousness of the gravity of what they were trying to achieve prompted them to consider how future generations would view their struggle. Macaulay was only the most famous to advert to this sense of historic drama in the peroration to his widely reported and much anthologized speech on the introduction of the first bill, when he pleaded with MPs: 'Pronounce in a manner worthy of the expectation with which this great Debate has been anticipated, and of the long remembrance which it will leave behind.'[5]

Efforts to shape and curate this 'long remembrance' necessarily involved contests and disagreements over the precise ways in which reform was to be remembered. Any memorial, monument or painting entailed a series of interpretational choices about how reform had been achieved and what it represented. Was it the triumph of ministers, monarch or the people at large? If it was all three, how was the delicate balance between these constituent parts of the British constitution to be represented? If 'the people' were to be central, should they feature allegorically, or could Political Unions (as they themselves claimed) stand proxy for reformers as a whole?

Such dilemmas shaped the efforts of one artist who embarked on a series of projects that sought to commemorate reform. Benjamin Haydon was a thorn in the side of a number of ministers in the early nineteenth century. He pestered relentlessly for government to support history painting, regarded since the seventeenth century as the most elevated branch of the art. He was particularly inspired by the support afforded to the art form by the July Monarchy in France and made a habit of citing Guizot to English ministers, provocatively asking Wellington in 1830 'if he would suffer England to be inferior to France'.[6] While the illustration of great moral truths from antique and biblical episodes remained his key artistic concern, he found the reform crisis all-encompassing and a fertile source of inspiration. He was thus willing to bend his talents to increasingly popular forms of genre painting and 'bastard "High Art Works"' that deployed the techniques of history painting to immortalize contemporary events.[7] He was driven in part by the example across the channel of Guizot's commissioning of a series of grand paintings of contemporary political events to decorate the Salle de Séances of the Chamber of Deputies.[8]

Three of Haydon's works or projected works dealt directly with the reform crisis. The best – the genre painting 'Waiting for the Times; the Morning after the Debate on Reform, 8 October 1831' – captures a keen sense of anticipation, as one man in a coffee house impatiently waits for another reader to finish the report in the

Times.⁹ It was a sense of anxious anticipation Haydon shared: 'I lay awake from one till four in the morning, my heart beating violently about this Reform Bill.'¹⁰ On the resolution of the reform crisis, with the restoration of Grey's ministry in May 1832, Haydon was in commemorative mode and approached the Birmingham Political Union and Thomas Attwood. Attwood at this point was on a triumphal tour of London and in high demand: 'Mr Turner, Mr Stothard and other painters plague me to death.'¹¹ Haydon pushed the notion of launching a subscription for a painting of one of the great meetings of the Unions on Newhall Hill. His selected theme – the Rev. Hugh Hutton leading a thanksgiving prayer for the recall of the Grey Ministry at the meeting on 16 May – would have unequivocally commemorated the Political Unions as the great engine that secured reform. Haydon travelled to Birmingham in June, made sixteen individual portraits and an oil sketch for the painting, and launched the subscription.¹² It was not a success and, indeed, there were very few pictorial representations of Political Unions as a body.¹³ Political Unionists instead sought to remember reform in the different ways discussed below. In addition, individual unionists, Attwood in particular, featured in portraits, prints and medals.

The most notable refusal to subscribe to the Birmingham picture came from Earl Grey. He remained unswayed by Haydon's arguments that the painting was of 'the finest moral nature', demonstrating the power of religion over men's passions, and the lasting spectacle of 'the industrious classes obeying the men of property'.¹⁴ Grey and the reform ministers had an uneasy relationship with the popular movement that sustained them. A week before Haydon's visit, Grey had received a deputation from the Birmingham Political Union who were to present a memorial. He confided to Ellenborough 'how annoyed he was to see them come with their ribbons and badges, knowing the misrepresentation that would be made of his reception of them in that character'. A fortnight later he was adamant that ministers should find some means of dissolving the Political Unions.¹⁵ The notion of valorizing these bodies through subscription to a grand painting was clearly out of the question.

Grey did, however, suggest an alternative which Haydon took up with alacrity and which consumed his artistic efforts for two years. 11 July had been fixed as the day for a 'civic festival' at London Guildhall, not the first or last, but certainly the grandest 'public entertainment to commemorate a national event'.¹⁶ Grey and Althorp were admitted as freemen of the city (notably this was eight weeks after Attwood had received the same honour), before eight hundred reformers sat to dinner in the hall, with a gas-lit crown surmounted by the word 'Reform' covering the entirety of the great eastern window. Haydon was commissioned by Grey to capture 'this immortal commemoration' and spent the next two years painting portraits and recording his lively conversations with his subjects in his diary.¹⁷ When the picture was exhibited, at the Great Room, St James's Street, in August 1834, it was both a commercial and a critical flop. Haydon lost £230 in the enterprise and endured some savage reviews, especially (and predictably) from the Tory press.¹⁸ A similar fate – though the critics were kinder – met another epic effort to commemorate reform in the shape of George Hayter's massive canvas 'The House of Commons, 1833'. This effort to represent the renewed 'balanced constitution' in the siting of the first reformed parliament took

Hayter ten years to complete. While he considered it a great 'national document' it took him a further fifteen years to secure it a permanent home.[19]

These paintings were efforts to commemorate elites by elites. As Carlisle has pointed out, the most interest in Hayter's painting came not from a wider public attracted to its representation of the achievements of reform, but from the MPs who flocked to scrutinize it at the private view.[20] This self-referential approach to viewing and writing histories of reform was evident too in publications across the nineteenth century, penned by the elite protagonists of reform themselves or by their relatives.[21] Perhaps most notable among other elite commemorations is Francis Chantrey's relief 'The Signing of the Magna Carta' at Holkham Hall, the seat of Chantrey's good friend Thomas Coke. Conceived of before the accession of Grey's ministry, Coke, in consultation with Chantrey, the Duke of Sussex and others, developed the relief into a direct, and unblushingly partisan, memorialization of reform. The assembled barons bear the faces of the Whig reform ministers and their supporters, whose names were added beneath. No name was recorded beneath the figure of King John, though it took no great leap to identify it as William IV.[22]

Public memorialization

In addition to these limited or private efforts by elites to commemorate themselves, there was initially some wider appetite for *public* monuments to those elites. There were, for example, fitful calls for 'one great national subscription' to erect statues to Earl Grey in London, Edinburgh and Dublin (and potentially in Manchester, Birmingham and Liverpool as well). In common with other commemorative reform projects, the model proposed was for a large number of limited (one shilling) subscriptions, rather than reliance on the substantial aristocratic donations that characterized 'pre-reform' monument-funding.[23] In Edinburgh, grateful reformers initially established a committee to build such a statue. Other individual efforts resulted in memorials to Grey, such as the 'Earl Grey Tower' built in Stanton Lees by the young liberal William Pole Thornhill or the standing stone monument at West Craigs farm in Dumfriesshire: 'To Grey and Reform/ 1832/ Honesty is the best Policy'.[24] Earl Grey would, of course, receive his monument in Newcastle upon Tyne (completed 1838) after his death, expressly conceived to commemorate the reform acts 'after an arduous and protracted struggle safely and triumphantly achieved'.[25]

Overall, however, there was reticence about building permanent memorials to individuals, particularly ministers, as part of reform commemorations. The same was not true for smaller commemorative objects. Market-minded publishers and patriotic publicans advertised subscriptions for commemorative prints of ministers 'as a token of national gratitude' or for gold cups to be presented to Grey and Brougham.[26] Ministers and other celebrated individuals featured prominently on medals and banners worn or carried at the reform celebrations discussed below. Similarly, ministers and local reform leaders had their roles commemorated during the dizzying round of dinners that followed the passage of the act.[27] The Edinburgh proposal for a Grey statue was transformed into one for a great *national* monument for reform at the west end of

Princes Street (which remained unbuilt) and Edinburgh's reformers instead turned their resources and attention to a national festival in honour of Grey in September 1834.[28]

There are perhaps comparatively few discrete standalone monuments to reform, given the conjunction of intense national interest in the question and the 'monument mania' which characterized nineteenth-century Britain.[29] Part of this was down to divisions over the appropriate subjects and forms for such monumental commemorations. The 'reform movement' was a diverse collection of groups, individuals and agendas, and so any kind of consensus on the individuals or episodes most fit for a national memorial was bound to be elusive. For example, the call for statues to Grey was a clear prompt to some to consider 'martyrs' from the 1790s and the 1810s: 'When the Reform Bill shall have brought about a new era, may we not hope to see some noble national monument erected to the memory of those patriotic pioneers in the cause of civil and religious freedom.'[30] As will be seen below, public meetings convened to discuss commemorating reform frequently disagreed on the *forms* of commemoration appropriate to the passage of reform.

Smaller, more localized efforts at permanent reform memorials along the lines of the monuments to Grey mentioned above were more frequent. Examples include the Reform bridge in Forest-of-Dean, or the two monuments completed at Peterhead, one a renovated town cross, the other a tower on Meethill, reputed locally as an ancient gathering place.[31] Other reformers did indeed take the opportunity to memorialize previous 'martyrs', either by the construction of a new monument or the renewal of an existing one. In Glasgow, a coalition of radicals, Whigs and the pre-eminent radical journalist Peter Mackenzie planned a permanent memorial (erected in November 1832) on James Turner's land at Thrushgrove, with the dual aim of commemorating the first mass meeting in Glasgow in 1816 to petition for parliamentary reform and those who had been executed in 1820, sacrificed 'for the cause of Reform now triumphant'.[32] About twenty miles to the south, in Strathaven, when the monument to two Covenanter martyrs, shot in 1685, was renewed, an inscription was added: 'Renewed by the Reformers of Avondale at the passing of the Reform Bill – ANNO DOMINI 1832'.[33]

Naming and renaming practices were even more widespread as a means of memorializing reform and the individuals associated with it in 1832. In Edinburgh, the feuars of Wellington Street pointedly renamed it Earl Grey Street during the 'days of May' and it would shortly be joined by Brougham Street.[34] There were Reform Streets (Arbroath, Crowland, Dundee, Dunfermline, Montrose, Kingston-upon-Hull, Islington), Reform Places (Durham, Maybole, Perth, Sleaford) and Reform Squares (Campbelton and Bethnal Green). Ships and steamships were christened 'Reform' and 'Earl Grey' in 1832.[35] Even these more modest commemorations were sometimes marked by contests. Members of Dundee's town council, for example, were pressing to rename Reform Street the following year because of the 'very general offence' they claimed the name had caused.[36]

Drawing on Protestant traditions, naming practices for infants had long acted to commemorate notable events, individuals and the virtues these embodied. Such political naming has been examined within radical political culture – around, for example, Peterloo – and it would be hard to ascribe the baptism of Thomas Liberty Broad in July 1830 to any other stimulus than a radical endorsement of the French Revolution.[37] In England at least twenty-one boys and girls were christened with the middle name 'Reform' in 1831–2, many of them in the summer of 1832 as the legislation made its way into law and local communities discussed commemoration. That scratches the surface of such naming practices: these years also witnessed a proliferation of Charles Greys, Henry Broughams, a Liberty Hunt and a Samuel Magna Charter (baptized 29 July 1832, though there was a family tradition at play as his father was also a Samuel Magna).[38] Though we can only guess at the rationale behind most of these naming practices one parent, at least, did go into greater detail. In welcoming Earl Grey ahead of his visit to Scotland, the radical editor of the *Reformers' Gazette*, Peter Mackenzie, reminded Grey of his own commemorative efforts:

> [W]hen your Lordship resigned office at the now memorable period of the rejection of the Reform Bill by the House of Lords, May 1832, I brought out and distributed amongst the Reformers of Scotland (*gratis*) upwards of 20,000 copies of a small Portrait of your Lordship to mark my sense of your noble conduct on that occasion; and on the day I sent your Lordship a copy of that Portrait, I had my only boy Christened Charles Grey after the illustrious name of your Lordship; and now he is probably one of the youngest Reformers in Scotland, that lisps the words 'Earl Grey, the Father of Reform'![39]

National celebrations

While these practices of naming, renaming, commissioning monuments and producing commemorative objects were certainly widespread, none was universal. An experience that was genuinely pan-British in 1832 was the staging of communal festivities to mark, celebrate and commemorate the passage of reform. These events were initiated and conducted without central direction from parliament. In February 1831, Hunt had attempted to torpedo one of Spencer Perceval's intermittent calls for a national fast and thanksgiving with an alternative proposal: 'when Reform in Parliament should have been granted, and a reduction in taxation made, the Houses would concur in an humble address to his Majesty, praying him to appoint a general feast and jubilee.'[40] Hunt's suggestion was tongue-in-cheek, but feasting and jubilee were taken up widely in the summer of 1832 as the reform measures became law and quickly became a national experience.

These events followed on from more immediate celebrations which had greeted the restoration of the Grey ministry and the safety of the reform legislation. Attwood and members of the Birmingham Political Union delegation were fêted on their return to the city and the Manchester scene described by Absalom Watkin was repeated in many other places: 'Flags were hoisted, huzzas uttered, and the bells set a-ringing, and firearms and cannon were discharged in all parts of the town.'[41] The arrangements for a more settled and staged nationwide celebration of reform were made by that coalition of forces that had coalesced into the reform movement over the previous eighteen months: the press, Political Unions and local reformers. From the start their efforts were certainly conceived of as celebratory, but discussions also broached the wider commemorative, didactic and political functions involved in marking the passage of reform. One correspondent of the *Times* summed up these lofty aspirations: 'The reform sentiment which a public celebration would diffuse through the empire, would operate as a new political baptism, and would be transmitted from father to son as the legacy of their liberties until the end of time.'[42]

There was far more scope for discussion and disagreement about how to achieve such goals. One immediate issue was timing. Press and reform leaders initially underlined the desirability of a single national celebration. A simultaneous 'loud, unanimous, national burst of joy' encompassing England, Scotland and Ireland would do justice to the measures of reform as an episode of national regeneration.[43] Parliamentary reform, however, had to be piloted through the Commons and the Lords as three separate measures. The bill for England and Wales became law first (on 7 June) leaving the Scottish and Irish bills to limp on in its wake (receiving royal assent on 17 July and 7 August, respectively). While the Political Unions and many other voices called for all celebrations to wait until all three bills had passed – mindful of the pitfalls that might wait for the Scottish and Irish legislation and with heightened suspicion of their opponents – in practice this was impossible to reconcile with local demands that their 'burst' of celebration be marked more immediately.[44]

Early discussions in the press identified a range of notable dates suitable for a simultaneous celebration. The anniversary of Magna Carta in June was a popular choice given the multiple parallels drawn between the reform legislation and the medieval charter.[45] Despite the injunctions to delay celebrations, it was marked in a number of places, including in Scotland. In the Lanarkshire village of Carnwath, for example, 5,000 assembled and marched on 'the anniversary of Runnymede', despite the fact that what would widely be referred to as Scotland's Magna Carta was not made law for another month.[46] Another possible date – and a similarly useful means of underlining the popular, patriotic and national dimensions of the celebration – was the anniversary of the accession of William IV. This would additionally allow the reform commemorations to piggyback on the institution which could most readily command national jubilee celebrations.[47] In the event, the decentralized nature of the events and the parliamentary timetable meant that the notion of a single pan-British event got lost and there was instead a rolling series of jubilees, and commemorations between June and August of 1832.

There was also considerable scope for discussion as to the forms that celebrations ought to take. Initial newspaper coverage tended to highlight the standard forms of national celebration, familiar from the commemorative calendar and from the ways in which military victories and royal events had been marked.[48] This meant, of course, illuminations, which had already been a highly contested aspect of the reform struggle: 'Then may beacons blaze on every height; bells ring out from every steeple; every town, city, and village, be one vast blaze of light.'[49] It was inevitable that illuminations, which acted both to express and to enforce the communal expression of joy at an event, in part gave vent to the desire to exult over fallen enemies. This, after all, had been part of their function in marking great military triumphs and the broken windows of those who elected not to illuminate litter the political high points of Georgian Britain.

When alternatives to illumination were proposed, in part to spare the properties of those who would not illuminate, correspondents mounted a defence of 'a British manifestation, in its full force and energies', denounced proposals for other celebrations as the misguided ruses of 'lukewarm' reformers (or worse still of anti-reformers), and explicitly contrasted their own illumination with the 'patriotic' military demonstrations of the recent past: 'If bloody and equivocally desirable victories have been celebrated with three nights' rejoicings, is not reform worthy a week's.'[50] A 'British manifestation' meant, of course, the breaking of unilluminated windows and targeting of the property of anti-reformers, in a jubilant re-enactment of the scenes during the illumination that had followed the King's dramatic dissolution of parliament in 1831.[51]

The Tory press was naturally opposed to general illumination 'in which individuals will be *compelled* to give up their feelings as Englishmen, and their rights as citizens – and to put on a shew of rejoicing for a measure which they deprecate'.[52] Such opposition was partly based on distrust of such popular events, which had seen crowds wreak vengeance on anti-reformers' windows in 1831. The memory of the Bristol riots was fresh to hand for these condemnations:

> The *second city of England* was sacked and in part burnt but six months ago upon a lighter occasion […] And is this the time at which the discontented Republicans and but half-satisfied rabble Reformers, and their allies […] are to be invited to a drunken midnight triumph in the metropolis?[53]

In general, however, both the press and prominent reformers also turned quickly against the idea of a general illumination. In common with their claims to leadership across the duration of the reform crisis, they sought to discipline reform celebrations, to check excesses and to encourage the kind of 'good temper, sobriety, and moderation' which had been such an important rhetorical trope of the reform movement, and a key means of demonstrating the middling classes' fitness for the franchise.[54] The 'frivolous custom' of a general illumination was problematic in that context and, though it might be 'the national predilection', the corresponding danger to the persons and property of those who 'do not happen to chime in with national feeling' was too great. In contrast, public processions and dinners – more voluntaristic, but similarly marking the sense of the community and providing a suitable spectacle to mark the event – were preferred as 'a much more rational mode of evincing the national feeling'.[55]

In a similar vein, there was considerable discussion around identifying more 'moral', 'rational' or 'educational' means of commemorating the reform legislation. The most widely taken up was the use of subscriptions not to fund illuminations but to provide a ticketed dinner for all the inhabitants of a community and, in many cases, to fund fireworks as a less confrontational source of illumination. In Edinburgh, there was a campaign to divert the subscriptions for a national monument away from 'mere ornament' and towards educational and moral instruction as a more effective permanent memorial of reform, while in York the magistrates tried to set an example by applying the expenses they would have incurred in illuminating to the funds of the new cholera hospital.[56] In London, a sustained campaign for reform almshouses opposed the 'cruel and senseless' waste of an illumination to indulge 'the momentary and crazy applause of a gin – drinking and senseless rabble' in favour of a memorial of enduring benevolence.[57] Indeed, London politics witnessed a long-running dispute pitching the popular advocates of illumination against the promoters of more 'rational' means of marking the legislation.[58] Nonetheless, in many places, general illuminations were held, and in some special constables were sworn in to maintain the peace.[59] As this should make clear, even in the planning of this unanimous celebration of the triumph of reform, unanimity was in short supply.

Festivals and jubilees

The scale and coverage of commemorative events was spectacular. Even if reformers did not manage to achieve the goal of a single and synchronous 'burst of national joy' they did match their aspiration of seeing a genuinely pan-British demonstration. *The Scotsman* – Scotland's leading reform newspaper – listed and covered well over one hundred discrete events marking the passage of reform in Scotland between late July and mid-August.[60] These ranged from large jubilees and processions in the principal cities to dinners and processions in small communities across Scotland. For example, both the villages of Balmerino in Fife and Monymusk in Aberdeenshire held celebrations.[61] Even accounting for the perhaps inflated Scottish enthusiasm for parliamentary reform, which did not come attended with the disfranchisements that featured in the English and Irish acts, the scale of celebrations is notable and was replicated elsewhere.

In examining the content of these decentralized efforts to celebrate reform, we should not expect to encounter uniformity. Events were filtered through local traditions and rituals and shaped by the politics of particular communities. In communities likely to witness fierce contests in the upcoming election, the celebration of reform was an early opportunity for candidates to pin their colours to the reform mast. In Leeds, for example, the reform celebration became a conduit for discussions around the factory reform movement.[62] In Whitby, the 'Pinks' (conservatives) and 'Blues' (liberals) launched rival subscriptions and the Pinks held a large procession and dinner a week after the Blues, reorienting it as a celebration of the enfranchisement of Whitby, rather than of reform per se.[63]

Celebrations across Great Britain did, however, share a considerable family resemblance, not least in their mnemonic functions. Processions, dinners, dances and games were nearly everywhere the preferred public mode of marking reform in the summer of 1832. Organized by local reformers, magistrates, the trades and the newer arrival of the Political Unions, they constituted an aural, visual and gastronomic assault on the senses, calculated to produce in what was a common refrain 'a day which will long be remembered by all the inhabitants'.[64] In recent suggestive contributions, Mark Philp has highlighted the ways in which, during the French Wars (1793–1815), a loyalist near-monopoly on these immersive activities acted as an important buttress to the status quo. Operating 'relatively unconsciously', music and dancing (and by extension other related activities) forged both 'a common sense of place and identity' and powerful collective memories of the recent past but did so mainly in one political direction before 1815: 'most musical occasions largely confirmed the status quo, and it is difficult to identify areas of common experience that would have reinforced more reformist aspirations and identities'.[65] The widespread celebration of the passage of reform provided just such a common experience in many places across Britain. In doing so, the events did a great deal to contribute to a Victorian political culture for which the memory of the Reform Acts was a constant reference point.

The multi-sensory celebrations were frequently initiated by the pealing of bells, reported in the press as one key marker of the 'spontaneous, authentic response of the whole community'.[66] Barnstaple was typical: 'at an early hour, the ringing of our parish bells and the repeated firing of cannon ushered in the festive day'.[67] By and large newspaper accounts focused on the consensual dimensions of the celebrations. They dwelt, often at considerable length, on the decorations made to the town or village (triumphal arches, liberal use of evergreens and flowers, illuminated transparencies) and on the preparations and arrangements for processions and dinners.

The spectacle of the procession itself was a centrepiece, with banners in particular described in detail. In some cases, the press invited the trades and societies to send in the inscriptions and designs for the banners in advance, in case reporters missed or misrepresented them in the throng.[68] And while dinners and fireworks were more evanescent markers of reform, banners were part of the rich material culture of the reform celebrations that helped to underline their function as memory-making events. Though there are relatively small numbers of surviving banners now (largest proportion of those surviving from the Edinburgh jubilee), accounts of later reform demonstrations in 1886–7 and 1884 and of jubilee celebrations in 1882 make it clear that in many cases these banners were used and reused across the nineteenth century.[69] At Irvine in 1882, for example, the jubilee demonstration (with new mementoes in the form of admission tickets printed on wood hewn by Gladstone at Hawarden) embodied elements of re-enactment with over one hundred surviving reformers invited: 'a platform had been erected, opposite Irvine Academy, as near as possible to the exact spot occupied by the hustings of 1832. Two of the banners which figured in the procession of that year floated over the platform.'[70]

The same is true for the reform medals, many of them produced either for members of the Political Unions or for the reform jubilees, or both. They were designed to be worn and many of the accounts have them worn in processions, frequently on a patriotic ribbon. Entrepreneurial sorts, such as Mr Bradney in Sheffield 'Wholesale and Retail Dealer in MEDALS, and Manufacturer of the UNION JACKS', advertised a range of medals suitable for both the public and Political Unionists.[71] In Edinburgh, a run on union jack ribbon was reported, and in Aberdeen, medals on blue ribbons were on display in many shop windows on the day of the jubilee, while medals made from sweetmeats were on sale at a halfpenny for the children.[72] These medals from 1832 survive in large numbers, many of them holed, which is a good indication of their having been worn and then kept.

Banners and medals were joined by other mementoes on jubilee days. In many trades' processions working models were deployed, both as a means of advertising the products of a particular craft and to demonstrate that craft's attachment to reform. Pre-eminent in many places was the printing press, widely identified as a key auxiliary. These produced a range of commemorative sheets. At Sheffield multiple presses under their flag heralding them as the 'dispeller of darkness' threw off sheets including a new song, 'The Triumph of Reform' by Ebenezer Elliott, the 'corn law rhymer', which was set to the tune of 'Rule Britannia'.[73] At Lanark, two boys in pink dresses handed out extracts from Junius, while in Bungay, a commemorative printed sheet from the town's first printing press reminded electors of their solemn new duties.[74]

In line with suggestions that subscriptions should be directed towards a feast for inhabitants, there were frequently multiple dinners on the day of the celebration. Especially where these were put on for the poorer inhabitants by subscription, the menu was well calculated to chime with and enhance the grand patriotism of the display. Roast beef, plum pudding and ale were the order of the day, or as the *Sheffield Independent* boasted of the Rotherham dinner, 'substantial dishes of old English fare'.[75] The preparations for dinner could become central to the festivities and at Barnstaple in Devon, where a subscription yielded £60 to feed around three thousand indigent individuals, the two bullocks purchased 'were driven round the town on Saturday night, preceded by a placard – "A sacrifice for the poor on the triumph of Reform"'.[76] The jubilee events aimed to engage entire communities with a heady mixture of spectacle, consumption and entertainment. In many communities they took on the aspect of fairs. So, for example, at Reading and Watford, dinner was followed by a range of sporting and leisure activities: donkey and sack races, competitive eating of treacle rolls, and 'maidens' racing to win a gown.[77]

All of this range of activities – processions, dinners and displays – was minutely and painstakingly planned by reformers.[78] Celebrations served to discipline and place boundaries around communities at the same time as they claimed to represent the entirety of those communities and the nation at large. Dinners, for example, were strictly ticketed affairs, with elaborate arrangements for the dinners for the poor inhabitants indicating a lingering unease about untamed popular activity. They were also clearly gendered events, with men processing, dining, and toasting and women reformers attending their own events (commonly tea parties) or else fulfilling auxiliary roles waving handkerchiefs, preparing plum puddings, and as the subjects of toasts.[79]

A final and important common aspect to this attempt to make *enduring* memories of reform involved the mobilization of children to ensure that 'such a happy day will never be forgotten by the *youngest* and has never been observed by the *oldest* inhabitant'.[80] If the celebrations were indeed to constitute a 'new political baptism' then children were both symbolically and practically important.[81] Children played prominent roles in processions. At Bristol, for example, the procession was headed by 'Sons of Reformers'.[82] At Stonehaven the description of the procession indicated 'GIRLS – Dressed in white, each wearing a Reform Medal, suspended by a blue ribbon. A very interesting and beautiful part of the procession'. The girls were followed by 'SCHOOL-BOYS' – to the number of about two hundred, headed by several of their teachers, each wearing a Reform Medal. Banners with mottoes 'Young, but staunch' – 'Magna Charta 1215; Bill of Rights 1688; Reform Bill 1832. These were received by our fathers, and these will be transmitted to our posterity'.[83] At other celebrations, the role of children was centre stage. For example, at Melbourne:

> At ten o'clock, the children under ten years of age proceeded from their respective districts, each district headed by a banner, to the open space in the centre of the town, and there forming a circle, the parents or friends stood behind holding in their arms those children who were too young to walk in the procession, the bands all the while playing in the centre, when a substantial piece of plum pudding was presented to every child present. The number of children amounted to nearly six hundred, many of whom carried banners bearing inscriptions of political and moral character, suitable to the occasion, and calculated to make a lasting impression on the juvenile mind.[84]

Divisions and conclusions

These events were not always successful. On a mundane level the widespread use of firearms, fireworks and cannon led to sometimes fatal accidents.[85] Others detected ill omens in mishaps, such as the dinner at Farringdon where the illuminated crown burst into flames and had to be extinguished, leaving only the names of reforming ministers.[86] More seriously and despite the language of unanimity and union which was pervasive in the reform press, efforts to memorialize reform often papered over real conflicts and divisions. Correspondents questioned reports of attendance at jubilees, claiming instead that these were attended by boys and the less-respectable parts of the community only.[87] Claims to a singular and unified community response were aspirational. In a number of places, for example, reports of the 'spontaneous' pealing of church bells concealed contests over access to and use of church bells, which reactivated older disputes and revealed fundamental political and religious tensions.[88] The Home Office correspondence contains a number of accounts showing these fissures in local communities. In Devizes, for example, a correspondent accused the mayor – 'a violent anti' – of permitting a firework display in the marketplace only so that he could blame reformers should this result in disaster for the town's many thatched roofs.[89]

As should be clear, many criticisms came from other reformers, especially from radicals who baulked at either the subject or the means of memorialization, or both. At the National Political Union's grand reform festival in London, for example, the majority of diners refused to join in the toast to the king, who they regarded by this point as having betrayed reform.[90] In many respects, radicals had developed their own pantheon and their own myth history, which was, in important respects, at odds with the versions which dominated in the summer of 1832.[91] In his critique of the content of the Whigs' reform bills, for example, Henry Hunt underlined his ongoing memorialization of Peterloo as highlighting the different and altogether more radical reform that was required.[92] The radical *Poor Man's Guardian* contested efforts by supporters of the Reform Acts and their limited vision of citizenship to establish ownership of key figures in the history of reform, such as Major Cartwright.[93]

Divisions were very obvious and very serious in one community profoundly scarred by the conflicts of the reform crisis. In Bristol, reformers followed other Political Unions in eschewing a general illumination, perhaps with more reason given the all-too-recent memory of the Bristol riots.[94] The suggestion for a dinner for the inhabitants offered a chance to heal and to arrest the 'destruction of the social compact'.[95] In the context of a city where the mayor was anxiously writing to the Home Office about the increased sale of firearms in the city in the summer of 1832 (and whose purchasers claimed they wanted them 'to use upon the celebration of the passing of the Reform Bill') the memorializing of reform was tense.[96] On the day of the celebration, the tightly ticketed affair on Brandon Hill was disrupted by the urban poor, who contested their exclusion from this 'unanimous' celebration and made off with food and barrels of beer.[97] Conservative papers could draw their own conclusions: this unrestrained mob power, abetted by the Grey ministry, was the real first fruits of reform.[98]

Efforts to memorialize reform in 1832 were clearly not uncontested. The single nation that reformers conjured up first to press for and then to celebrate reform only ever existed in their rhetoric and their imaginations. The exceptionally broad range of activities expressly aimed at marking the Reform Acts as a 'new political baptism' are, nevertheless, significant. The widespread reform jubilees, in particular, represented the apotheosis of the reform movement and its albeit temporary capture of public space.[99] All of the rituals, sights and sounds which had supported a broadly based patriotic loyalism during the French Wars – the ringing of bells, militarized display, large public dinners – could be mobilized in support of reform in the summer of 1832. This could be done in ways well calculated to create enduring memories for both communities and individuals. None of this is to suggest that understandings of or aspirations for reform were monolithic in that year, let alone in succeeding decades. Nonetheless, the sheer volume and range of memory-making activities involved certainly help to explain the underexplored shift in people's perceptions that made the Reform Acts such a turning point in British political culture and ensured that '[s]oon, the world before 1832 was pictured as a lost world, to which (for good or ill) there could be no return'.[100]

Notes

1   www.ancestry.co.uk (accessed 12 February 2021).
2   The literature is too large to summarize here; see Gordon Pentland, 'Parliamentary Reform', in *The Oxford Handbook of Modern British Political History, 1800–2000*, ed. David Brown, Robert Crowcroft and Gordon Pentland (Oxford: Oxford University Press, 2018), 383–99.
3   Cm 9446, Department for Exiting the European Union, 'Legislating for the United Kingdom's Withdrawal from the European Union' (March 2017), 5.
4   Joanna Innes, '"Reform in English Public Life: The Fortunes of a Word', in *Rethinking the Age of Reform: Britain 1780–1850*, ed. Arthur Burns and Joanna Innes (Cambridge: Cambridge University Press, 2003), 71–97; Derek Beales, 'The Idea of Reform in British Politics, 1829–1850', in *Reform in Great Britain and Germany, 1750–1850*, ed. T. C. W. Blanning and Peter Wende (Oxford: Oxford University Press, 1999), 159–74.

5   *Parliamentary Debates*, 3rd ser., vol. 2, col. 1204, Commons, 2 March 1831.
6   Tom Taylor (ed.), *Life of Haydon, Historical Painter, from His Autobiography and Journals*, 2nd edition, 3 vols. (London, 1853), ii. 287.
7   Cited in Janice Carlisle, *Picturing Reform in Victorian Britain* (Cambridge: Cambridge University Press, 2012), 72.
8   Taylor (ed.), *Life of Haydon*, ii. 287–8, 403–4; Michael Marrinan, 'Resistance, Revolution and the July Monarchy: Images to Inspire the Chamber of Deputies', *Oxford Art Journal*, 3, no. 2 (1980), 26–37.
9   Two versions of the painting were made; one now hangs at *The Times*, news international plc.
10 Taylor (ed.), *Life of Haydon*, ii. 338.
11 C. M. Wakefield, *Life of Thomas Attwood* (London, 1885), 228.
12 Taylor, *Life of Haydon*, ii. 340–4. The portraits and sketch are all held at Birmingham Museum and Art Gallery.
13 Wakefield, *Life of Attwood*, 243–4 mentions only one representation of the Newhall Hill meetings in addition to Haydon's sketch, a lithograph by Henry Harris, 'The Gathering of the Unions', British Museum, 1871,0812.5331.
14 Taylor, *Life of Haydon*, ii. 344–5.
15 Arthur Aspinall (ed.), *Three Early Nineteenth Century Diaries* (London: Williams & Norgate, 1952), 266, 271–2.
16 *The Times*, 12 July 1832.
17 Benjamin Robert Haydon, *Description of Haydon's Picture of the Reform Banquet* (London, 1834); Taylor (ed.), *Life of Haydon*, ii, 345–97.
18 Taylor (ed.), *Life of Haydon*, ii. 396–7; Carlisle, *Picturing Reform*, 71–7.
19 Carlisle, *Picturing Reform*, 64–70, 74–84.
20 Ibid., 78.
21 See, for example, the 'Preface' to Henry, Earl Grey (ed.), *The Reform Act, 1832. The Correspondence of the Late Earl Grey with His Majesty King William IV and with Sir Herbert Taylor from November 1830 to June 1832*, 2 vols. (London, 1867), i. v–xviii; J. A. Roebuck, John Arthur Roebuck et al., *History of the Whig Ministry of 1830, to the Passing of the Reform Bill*, 2 vols. (London, 1852).
22 A. M. W. Stirling, *Coke of Norfolk and Friends*, 2nd edition (London, 1912), 547; W. O. Hassall and N. B. Penny, 'Political Sculpture at Holkham', *The Conoisseur*, 195 (1977), 207–11; Alison Yarrington, Ilene D. Lieberman, Alex Potts, Malcolm Barker (ed.), 'An Edition of the Ledger of Sir Francis Chantrey R. A., at the Royal Academy, 1809–1841', *Volume of the Walpole Society* 56 (1991/2), 304–5.
23 *Morning Chronicle*, 23 May 1832. See also the proposals of the *Leeds Mercury*, 2 June 1832 for some 'durable monument' to be built 'with a subscription so general that the humblest Reformer in the land may contribute to it'.
24 *Morning Chronicle*, 12 June 1832; https://her.derbyshire.gov.uk/Monument/MDR8542 (accessed 19 February 2021); http://portal.historicenvironment.scot/designation/LB16944 (accessed 20 April 2021).
25 *Newcastle Journal*, 11 October 1834; Peter Brett, *The Grey Monument: The Making of a Regional Landmark* (Middlesbrough: University of Teeside, 2000).
26 British Library [hereafter BL], Place Collection of Newspaper Cuttings [hereafter Place Collection], Set 17, vol. 3, 23 June–15 December 1832, fos 15, 72, 88.
27 See, for example, the dinner to Althorp and Milton, *Northampton Mercury*, 30 June 1832.
28 *The Grey Festival* (Edinburgh, 1834).

29 Paul A. Pickering and Alex Tyrrell (eds.), *Contested Sites: Commemoration, Memorial and Popular Politics in Nineteenth-Century Britain* (Aldershot: Ashgate, 2004).
30 *Liverpool Mercury*, 8 June 1832.
31 *Aberdeen Journal*, 8 and 15 August 1832; *Aberdeen Press and Journal*, 8 February 1936.
32 Gordon Pentland, '"Betrayed by Infamous Spies"? The Commemoration of Scotland's "Radical War" of 1820', *Past & Present*, 201 (2008), 149–53.
33 Gordon Pentland, 'Scotland and the Creation of a National Reform Movement, 1830–1832', *Historical Journal*, 48, no. 4 (2005), 1019–21; J. H. Thomson, *The Martyr Graves of Scotland* (Edinburgh, n.d.), 249–50.
34 *Scotsman*, 19 May 1832.
35 *Pigot and Co.'s National Commercial Directory of the Whole of Scotland and of the Isle of Man 1837* (London, 1837), 230; *Lloyd's Register of British and Foreign Shipping 1832*, R nos 19 and 79.
36 *Caledonian Mercury*, 21 October 1833.
37 Ruth Mather, 'Remembering Protest in the Late-Georgian Working-Class Home', in *Remembering Protest in Britain since 1500: Memory, Materiality and Landscape*, ed. Carl Griffin and Briony McDonagh (Cham: Palgrave Macmillan, 2018), 139–40.
38 www.ancestry.co.uk (accessed 12 February 2021).
39 Durham University Library, Grey Papers, GRE/B40/12/12, Mackenzie to Grey, 6 September 1834.
40 *Parliamentary Debates*, 3rd ser., vol. 2, col. 490, Commons, 14 February 1832.
41 Wakefield, *Life of Thomas Attwood*, 209–14; A. E. Watkin, *Absalom Watkin: Extracts from His Journal, 1814–1856* (London, 1920), 163–4.
42 *Times*, 21 June 1832.
43 *Times*, 11 June 1832.
44 *Bristol Mercury*, 9 June 1832; *Chester Chronicle*, 8 June 1832.
45 Miles Taylor, 'Magna Carta in the Nineteenth Century', in *Magna Carta: The Foundation of Freedom, 1215–2015*, ed. Nicholas Vincent (London: Third Millennium Information, 2014), 136–53. For an example see the song 'The Barons Bold on Runnymede', BL, Place Collection, Set 17, vol. 3, 23 June–15 December 1832, f. 20.
46 *Scotsman*, 20 June 1832.
47 Linda Colley, 'The Apotheosis of George III: Loyalty, Royalty and the British Nation, 1760–1820', *Past & Present*, 102 (1984), 94–129; Stuart Semmel, 'Radicals, Loyalists, and the Royal Jubilee of 1809', *Journal of British Studies*, 46, no. 3 (2007), 543–69.
48 Nicholas Rogers, 'Crowds and Political Festival in Georgian England', in *The Politics of the Excluded, c. 1500–1850*, ed. Tim Harris (Basingstoke: Palgrave, 2001), 233–64.
49 *Chester Chronicle*, 8 June 1832. For excellent new work, which appeared too close to publication to be included in this chapter, see Timothy Jenks, 'The 1832 Reform Act and the Place of Illuminations in Late Hanoverian Political Culture', *English Historical Review*, 137, no. 589 (2023).
50 *Times*, 4 and 21 June 1832.
51 Alexander Somerville, *The Autobiography of a Working Man* (London: C. Gilpin, 1848), 156–8.
52 *Yorkshire Gazette*, 9 June 1832.
53 *Morning Post*, 12 June 1832.
54 *Leeds Mercury*, 2 June 1832.
55 *Southampton Herald*, 16 June 1832; *Liverpool Mercury*, 8 June 1832.

56 *Scotsman*, 20 June and 4 July 1832.
57 *An Account of the Origin of the Reform London Almshouses during the Mayoralty of Sir John Key, Lord Mayor of London. Instituted 1832* (London, 1835), iv; *Times*, 30 June 1832; *Examiner*, 16 September 1832.
58 BL, Place Collection, Set 17, vol. 3, 23 June–15 December 1832, fos 27, 97; *Times*, 30 June 1832.
59 See for example the celebration at Romford, *Chelmsford Chronicle*, 29 June 1832; National Archives [hereafter NA], HO52/17, f. 212, 'List of the Special Constables sworn the 12th, 13th, & 14th June by us the undersigned Justices of the Peace in and for the Town and Parish of Deal in Kent', 14 June 1832 and HO52/20, fos 136–7, Thomas Merriman to Lord Melbourne, 28 June 1832.
60 *Scotsman*, 28 July–18 August 1832.
61 *Aberdeen Journal*, 22 August 1832.
62 *Times*, 18 June 1832; *Morning Post*, 19 June 1832; Catherine Hall, *Macaulay and Son: Architects of Imperial Britain* (New Haven and London: Yale University Press, 2012), 162–74.
63 *Yorkshire Gazette*, 14 July 1832.
64 *Sheffield Independent*, 11 August 1832.
65 Mark Philp, 'Music and Movement in Britain, 1793–1815', *Journal of British Studies*, 60, no. 2 (2021), 403–15. See also idem, *Radical Conduct: Politics, Sociability and Equality in London 1789–1815* (Cambridge: Cambridge University Press, 2020), ch. 6.
66 William Tullett, 'Political Engines: The Emotional Politics of Bells in Eighteenth-Century England', *Journal of British Studies*, 59, no. 3 (2020), 555–81.
67 *North Devon Journal*, 21 June 1832.
68 *Scotsman*, 18 July 1832.
69 Mark Nixon, Gordon Pentland, and Matthew Roberts, 'The Material Culture of Scottish Reform Politics, c.1820–c.1884', *Journal of Scottish Historical Studies*, 32, no. 1 (2012), 46–9. For the Edinburgh banners see Helen Clark, *Raise the Banners High: The City of Edinburgh's Banner Collection* (Edinburgh: City of Edinburgh Museums & Galleries, 2001). For examples of 1832 banners reused in 1884 see *Dundee Courier*, 23 September 1884; *Leeds Mercury*, 13 October 1884.
70 *Glasgow Herald*, 12 June 1882.
71 *Sheffield Independent*, 9 June 1832.
72 *Scotsman*, 4 August 1832; *Aberdeen Journal*, 16 August 1832.
73 *Sheffield Independent*, 23 June 1832.
74 *Scotsman*, 20 June 1832; *A Brief Description of the Bungay Reform Festival* (Bungay, 1832), 14.
75 *Sheffield Independent*, 11 August 1832.
76 *North Devon Journal*, 21 June 1832.
77 BL, Place Collection, Set 17, vol. 3, 23 June–15 December 1832, fos 24, 71.
78 See, for example, the very detailed arrangements in *Brief Description of Bungay Reform Festival*.
79 See for example *Sheffield Independent*, 7 July 1832; *Yorkshire Gazette*, 14 July 1832. Kathryn Gleadle, *Borderline Citizens: Women, Gender and Political Culture in Britain, 1815–1867* (Oxford: Oxford University Press, 2009), ch. 5.
80 *Aberdeen Journal*, 8 August 1832 of processions at Huntly and Inverury.
81 For pioneering recent work focusing on political subjectivities of children in the period see Kathryn Gleadle, 'Playing at Soldiers: British Loyalism and Juvenile Identities during the Napoleonic Wars', *Journal for Eighteenth-Century Studies*, 38,

no. 3 (2015), 335–48; idem, 'The Juvenile Enlightenment: British Children and Youth during the French Revolution', *Past & Present*, 233 (2016), 143–84.
82 *Political Unionist*, 30 June 1832.
83 *Aberdeen Journal*, 29 August 1832.
84 *Leicester Chronicle*, 18 August 1832.
85 *Bristol Mercury*, 21 July 1832; *Aberdeen Journal*, 8 August 1832.
86 *Morning Chronicle*, 30 August 1832.
87 *Belfast News Letter*, 19 June 1832.
88 *Church Examiner and Ecclesiastical Record*, 7 and 14 July 1832.
89 NA, HO52/20, fos 118–22, Letter from James Tilby to Mr Nethersole and Mr Barrow, 29 July 1832.
90 BL, Place Collection, Set 17, vol. 3, 23 June–15 December 1832, f. 99.
91 Matthew Roberts, *Chartism, Commemoration and the Cult of the Radical Hero* (London: Routledge, 2019).
92 Henry Hunt, *(No. 11.) An Address from H. Hunt Esq., MP. to the Radical Reformers of England, Ireland, and Scotland, and Particularly Those of Cheshire, Lancashire, and Yorkshire, on the Measures of the Whig Ministers, since They Have Been in Place and Power* (London, 1831); idem, *Lecture on the Conduct of the Whigs, to the Working Classes, Delivered at Lawrence Street Chapel, Birmingham, on Wednesday, October 31st, 1831* (London, 1831).
93 *Poor Man's Guardian*, 23 July 1831.
94 *Bristol Mercury*, 7 July 1832; Steve Poole and Nicholas Rogers, *Bristol from Below: Law, Authority and Protest in a Georgian City* (Woodbridge: Boydell & Brewer, 2017), ch. 12.
95 *Bristol Mercury*, 21 July 1832.
96 NA, HO52/17, fos 201–2, Charles Pinney to Viscount Melbourne, 20 June 1832.
97 Poole and Rogers, *Bristol from Below*, 358–9.
98 *Morning Post*, 17 August 1832; *Standard*, 17 August 1832.
99 Katrina Navickas, *Protest and the Politics of Space and Place, 1789–1848* (Manchester: Manchester University Press, 2016).
100 J. C. D. Clark, *English Society, 1660–1832: Religion, Ideology and Politics during the Ancien Regime*, 2nd edition (Cambridge: Cambridge University Press, 2000), 554.

7

Living in stone or marble: The public commemoration of Victorian MPs

Kathryn Rix[*]

In 1847 the recently retired MP for Preston Peter Hesketh-Fleetwood attended the opening of schools built in his honour at Fleetwood, the Lancashire seaside town he had founded. Reflecting on the alternative forms this tribute could have taken, he remarked that 'he might have been able to have lived in stone or marble', would instead 'live in the hearts of the children educated in the schools'.[1] While Hesketh-Fleetwood had to wait until 2018 before a statue to him was unveiled, numerous other Victorian MPs were honoured in this way by their contemporaries, as part of what one newspaper described in 1872 as 'this absurd monument mania'. It observed that there seemed to be 'a hypochondriac fear lest our great men should be forgotten unless we erect a pile of masonry to their memory, or set up images of them in our streets'.[2] It was far from alone in highlighting the perils of 'statue mania'. The dubious artistic merits of Britain's public statues, particularly in London, attracted comment in the Commons on several occasions, with Lord Elcho asserting in 1862 that 'our public monuments and statues were egregious failures'.[3]

As these comments indicate, public commemoration through statues and monuments has long been a complex and contested process. This came into sharp relief in June 2020, when the 'toppling' of Bristol's statue of the seventeenth-century merchant and MP Edward Colston in protest at his links with the slave trade was swiftly followed by calls for the removal or re-evaluation of other memorials.[4] These included statues of Victorian MPs, notably William Gladstone and Robert Peel. The latter's statues in Manchester, Glasgow, Bradford, Preston and Leeds were among those targeted by petitions and protests, stemming in part from the views of Peel and his father on slavery.[5] Conversely, other MPs' statues received positive reappraisals. Todmorden's council ratified the laying of flowers at John Fielden's statue and passed resolutions in July 2020 noting 'with civic pride "Honest" John's untiring efforts on behalf of those least able to defend themselves', particularly his 'resolute and robust

---

[*] I would like to thank Philip Salmon, Henry Miller and Matthew Roberts for their comments on an earlier version of this chapter.

opposition' to compensating 'the "owners" of emancipated slaves'. A laminated notice with these resolutions was placed at the statue, with a view to installing a permanent plaque 'to reflect his achievements in a balanced way'.[6] The question of who is remembered in Britain's public sculpture also came under the spotlight a few years earlier when attention was focused on the paucity of statues honouring women. Those commemorated since 2016 in an effort to redress this imbalance include Mary Seacole, Millicent Fawcett, Emmeline Pankhurst and Nancy Astor.[7]

The memorialization of nineteenth-century politicians through public statues has already received scholarly attention. It has been examined within the broader history of Victorian sculpture, notably by Benedict Read and in regional studies published by the Public Monuments and Sculpture Association (PMSA).[8] A second strand has considered statues within the wider visual representation of politicians, which also included prints, portraits and pottery. Henry Miller's work has emphasized the significance which political likenesses attained between 1830 and 1880, a period which saw 'mass veneration of politicians and statesmen', and the part these images played in constructing political identities.[9] A third theme has been the role of statues in the creation of public spaces, particularly in northern England's growing industrial towns, where 'they became as much a part of the civic landscape then under construction as did town halls, law courts and market halls'.[10] The nineteenth-century politician whose statues have been most studied is Peel, whose death in 1850 is argued to have 'sparked off a burst of commissioning and raising public monuments that did much to make the portrait statue part of the grammar of public commemoration'.[11] Statues have featured in analysis of the popular images of Gladstone and Richard Cobden, and there has been research on monuments to the Duke of Wellington, George Leeman's statue at York and the role of statues in shaping Parliament Square as a political space.[12] While leading statesmen were most prominently honoured, monuments were used by radicals and reformers too, and Paul Pickering has examined the statue of the Chartist leader and Nottingham MP Feargus O'Connor.[13]

Aside from brief discussions by Miller and James Vernon there has, however, been little collective analysis of statues erected to nineteenth-century MPs whose names are now more obscure.[14] Yet these Victorian backbenchers made significant contributions not only to the business of parliament but to the localities they served. This chapter examines statues of MPs elected between 1832 and 1868 for constituencies in two major English regions, the North and the Midlands, for which a database has been compiled drawing on the History of Parliament's ongoing research, the PMSA's National Recording Project and a range of other sources, notably the newspaper press.[15] These regions include not only Lancashire's urban centres, generally regarded as leading the way in 'statue mania' as they honoured the Lancashire-born Peel, but also rural counties such as Herefordshire and Lincolnshire, and areas not covered by the PMSA, notably Yorkshire's West Riding.[16] Although these parameters have been used, some MPs included represented constituencies elsewhere for part of their career, some continued to sit after 1868 and some had moved to the Lords before being commemorated. This study focuses on statues erected for the purposes of public commemoration, excluding statues forming part of a wider scheme of exterior decoration on a building, those kept in private family hands, and other memorials, such as busts and funerary monuments. Statues within Westminster Abbey and the Palace of Westminster are also beyond its scope.

This chapter will assess which MPs received this highly visible recognition; why they were honoured in this particular form; and where, when and by whom these statues were erected, before exploring the 'afterlives' of these monuments.[17] In so doing, it rethinks the chronology of commemoration and considers key themes such as the connections between MPs and their constituencies, the civic functions of these monuments, and how the meanings of statues could change over time and in response to their site, shedding light on how statues were perceived by their instigators and have been received by the wider public since.

MPs' statues and the rationale for commemoration

Of the 843 MPs elected for constituencies in the North and Midlands between 1832 and 1868 (from a total of 2,591 MPs returned to Westminster in this period), fifty-six (15 per cent of this sample) had statues raised to them, with at least 108 statues erected in total, a figure which confirms prevailing perceptions of 'statue mania' among contemporaries and historians.[18] Seventeen were honoured more than once, including the five prime ministers in this group: Peel, Gladstone, Benjamin Disraeli, Lord Derby and Lord Salisbury. Peel, Gladstone and Disraeli, together with the anti-corn law campaigners Richard Cobden and John Bright, were each commemorated with more than three statues, venerated not only in constituencies they had represented but elsewhere in recognition of their national status.[19] Other leading figures also received national tributes, with statues in London to William Edward Forster (1890), marking his promotion of elementary education; Wilfrid Lawson (1909), for his efforts in the temperance cause; and Robert Stephenson (1871), remembered not as MP for Whitby but for his key role in developing Britain's railways.[20] However, analysing these fifty-six MPs collectively, it was their constituency connections which proved most significant in terms of commemoration: forty-two had a statue in a constituency they had represented, of whom thirty-one were only honoured in their constituencies.[21]

Those celebrated in their constituency had usually contributed to local affairs not solely as MP, but in a range of other capacities, including as employers, postholders in municipal government, magistrates, and, above all, major philanthropists. Derby's long-serving MP Michael Thomas Bass was honoured not only for his 'long and faithful Parliamentary services' but also 'his numerous and magnificent benefactions to the town'. His statue (1885) depicted him with plans for Derby's Free Library, one of many local institutions he had funded.[22] Unveiling a statue of the local manufacturer and former MP Edward Akroyd at Halifax (1876), the former mayor concluded his lengthy recitation of Akroyd's 'extraordinary liberality' – which included building two churches, founding the local rifle volunteer corps and establishing several educational institutions – by observing, 'Indeed I don't know what he has not done.'[23] Noting that 'the fitness of such a commemorative act depended upon the place, as well as upon the man', the sitting MP James Stansfeld lauded Akroyd as 'one of the main architects' of Halifax's fortunes and 'one of its worthiest representative citizens'. The reliefs on the pedestal of Akroyd's statue reinforced this message, depicting him in his roles as railway chairman, philanthropist and volunteer officer.[24] Such tributes reflected how deeply embedded many Victorian MPs were within their constituency's affairs and the central role they played within the civic sphere, irrespective of their record at Westminster. At Birkenhead David MacIver endorsed erecting a statue of his predecessor as MP, the shipbuilder John Laird, because 'no town ... owed so much to the energy, ability, and perseverance of a single man'.[25] Other employer-benefactor MPs similarly honoured included the carpet manufacturer Francis Crossley (Halifax, 1860); the hosiery manufacturer John Biggs (Leicester, 1873); the glass manufacturer John Candlish (Sunderland, 1875); the engineering magnate John Platt (Oldham, 1878); and the brewer Michael Arthur Bass (Burton upon Trent, 1911).[26]

It was not only in the growing industrial towns of the North and Midlands, however, that MPs' statues encapsulated a deep-rooted local connection. Rather than the employer-benefactor model, elsewhere older patterns of social and political relationships were foremost. At Chester, Richard Grosvenor, 2nd Marquess of Westminster, formerly MP for the borough and the county, was honoured by 'his tenants, friends and neighbours' as 'the generous landlord' and 'the helper of all good works', according to his statue's inscription (1869).[27] Also in the landlord-benefactor mould was William Duncombe, 1st Earl of Feversham. His statue (1871) was raised not in one of the major towns of his former North Riding constituency, but the small market town of Helmsley, close to his home at Duncombe Park. It was initiated by 'his tenantry and others', before developing into a wider county memorial.[28] While statues were more common in industrial towns than in rural counties such as Herefordshire and Shropshire, this was not straightforwardly a phenomenon of large towns and cities.[29] Helmsley, with a population of 1,437 when Feversham's statue was erected, was not the only small rural market town to commemorate an MP. Sleaford had 3,729 inhabitants when Henry Handley's statue was erected (1851), Cockermouth had 6,936 shortly before honouring the Earl of Mayo (1875) and Ormskirk 'barely 7,000' when it erected Disraeli's statue (1884).[30]

Strong local connections between the statue's subject and its location were not limited to the bond between constituency and representative. Six individuals were commemorated with statues in towns they had founded or played a major role in developing but not served as MP. The iron founder Henry Schneider (briefly MP for Norwich and Lancaster) was honoured at Barrow-in-Furness (1891), which he had been instrumental in developing as a modern industrial centre; the woollen manufacturer Titus Salt at Saltaire (1903), as well as in his Bradford constituency (1876); and the seventh (1901) and eighth (1910) Dukes of Devonshire – MPs for seats in Derbyshire and Lancashire respectively – at Eastbourne, which they had developed as a fashionable resort.[31] Two other town founders received belated recognition. Henry Pease had created the North Yorkshire resort of Saltburn-by-the-Sea while MP for Durham South in the 1860s. In 2002 a public art scheme funded a statue of him, which provoked local controversy due to its composition from scrap metal elements. In contrast, Hesketh-Fleetwood's bronze statue at Fleetwood (2018) more closely resembled the portrait statues erected by his contemporaries.[32]

Ties of birth and residence provided another reason why MPs were commemorated outside their constituencies, among them Bright in his native Rochdale (1891), Salisbury at Hatfield (1906), and the Oldham MPs John Fielden and William Cobbett in their respective birthplaces of Todmorden (1875) and Farnham (2016). While Fielden's statue was closely linked with his parliamentary achievements in securing the Ten Hours Act, Cobbett's, the only equestrian statue in this study, evoked his *Rural Rides* rather than his political career.[33] Other MPs were remembered beyond Britain, reflecting their involvement in Irish or colonial administration, among them George Howard, seventh Earl of Carlisle in Dublin (1870), where he was lord lieutenant; Henry Ward in Ceylon (1868), where he had been governor; and two former viceroys, Richard Bourke, sixth Earl of Mayo, and George Robinson, first Marquess of Ripon, honoured in India as well as at home.[34]

Embodying public virtues or a practical memorial: The forms and functions of commemoration

Despite the significant number of statues erected to politicians and others during the nineteenth century, there was persistent scepticism about the merits of memorialization, epitomized by Gladstone's assertion in 1866 that 'those who were worth being remembered were so without monuments' (although he did not demur when statues were raised to him, giving over twenty sittings to the sculptor for his 1870 Liverpool statue).[35] Yet the impulse to honour prominent local and national figures did not have to translate into a statue. Simon Morgan has shown the various ways in which public service could be acknowledged through testimonials, including illuminated addresses and gifts such as silverware during the recipient's lifetime.[36] Michael Arthur Bass quashed plans to erect his statue at Burton upon Trent to mark his generosity in providing a toll-free bridge but accepted a piece of silverware.[37] The presentation of portraits to MPs (or posthumously to their families) was another common tribute.[38] Even if a public monument was preferred, there were several alternatives to statues, from ornamental columns and obelisks to more utilitarian fountains and clock towers. While Herefordshire remembered George Cornewall Lewis's parliamentary services with a statue in Hereford (1864), his New Radnor constituents erected an Eleanor cross-style monument, and the temperance champion Wilfrid Lawson was appropriately remembered with a drinking fountain near his Cumberland home.[39]

However, as Miller's work suggests, political likenesses attained a 'remarkable popularity and cultural resonance' between 1830 and 1880.[40] The erection of statues in preference to other forms of tribute needs to be understood within the context of a polity increasingly used to seeing images of its representatives, whether in print or through material objects. As Donald Read has noted, 'the Victorians liked to have lasting physical reminders of their heroes, large statues in public and small artefacts at home'.[41] At Carlisle in 1844 – where a statue had recently been erected to Francis Aglionby MP, and where the format of a memorial to the county's lord lieutenant was under discussion – one newspaper opined that 'obelisks or columns are very well in their way' but had the disadvantage of 'conveying no idea of *character* to the mind'.[42]

Reports of statue unveilings routinely commented on whether the statue provided a good likeness; a key element was depicting the individual's character as much as their physical features. Samuel Morley's Nottingham statue, which showed him – as many MPs' statues did – giving a speech, was praised as 'full of character and force', while the *Liverpool Daily Post* applauded the features of Laird's Birkenhead statue which 'all tell as plainly as statuary can ... of the unrelaxing tenacity of purpose, which distinguished his career'.[43]

This capturing of the subject's qualities was particularly important because of the belief that statues could act as 'the permanent embodiment of public and private virtues', fulfilling 'an exemplary purpose' which was 'educative and instructive'.[44] Suggestions at Leeds that Edward Baines (senior) would be better commemorated by almshouses were rebuffed by one alderman, who insisted that if they wanted 'to induce the rising generation to imitate Mr. Baines's example, it must be done by a statue, or something of that kind, which people could look at'.[45] Although its position inside Leeds town hall made Baines's statue less visible to the public than an exterior location, its inscription left onlookers in no doubt about the qualities they should emulate, recording 'his integrity and perseverance, his benevolence and public spirit, his independence and consistency' and anticipating that 'posterity may know and imitate a character loved and honoured by his contemporaries'.[46]

The format of a proposed tribute was commonly the subject of public discussion, as at Birmingham, where Thomas Attwood's friends instigated a meeting after his death to consider 'erecting a statue, or founding a public institution'.[47] As in Baines's case, it was often suggested that a practical memorial was preferable to a statue, since, as the *Northern Echo* argued in 1874, 'few of them from their pedestals do the slightest conceivable good to the least living thing'.[48] The *Derby Mercury* claimed there was 'a very strong sentiment against wasting good money in an entirely useless statue' to honour Bass at Derby, with a convalescent home or hospital wing among the alternatives suggested.[49] The MP's own views could be invoked against a statue. Objectors to a statue of Morley at Nottingham argued that 'a man who has given a threefold refusal to the offer of a peerage does not want a statue'.[50] At Ripon, Lord Ripon and his wife had declined 'anything of a personal character' such as a statue for their golden wedding anniversary in 1901, preferring 'something for the benefit' of the locality, which had resulted in a recreation ground and nurses' home. There was therefore opposition to the council's decision to erect a statue after Ripon's death: one clergyman urged that 'something of a philanthropic nature such as Lord Ripon loved in his lifetime would be better'.[51]

Yet since their philanthropy was often a key reason for honouring an MP, it could be argued that practical memorials would merely replicate their efforts, whereas statues offered a different form of tribute. The committee which opted for a statue of Salt at Bradford in preference to 'an infirmary, tradesmen's home, alms-houses, or school' declared that any building would be just '*one* of many kindred institutions with which Sir Titus's name is associated, while the erection of a statue will much more *vividly* impress the traits by which his life is distinguished'.[52] Similar sentiments prevailed at Birkenhead, where Laird had already built churches, schools and a hospital. It was argued that a statue rather than another charitable project offered 'a form which would individualise the man'.[53]

Statues were by no means a cheap option: the costs of those considered here ranged from £376 for Aglionby's marble statue at Carlisle (1844) to over £5,000 for Gladstone's elaborate bronze memorial at Liverpool (1904), although between £1,000 and £2,000 was typical.[54] As this range indicates, there was, however, scope to cut one's cloth according to one's means. Whereas the £1,200 raised for Salford's Peel statue funded a bronze from the London-based Matthew Noble, those paying tribute to Peel at Preston, where subscriptions were more limited, economized by employing a local sculptor, Thomas Duckett, to carve a limestone statue for £620.[55] At Eastbourne the leading sculptor Hamo Thornycroft quoted £1,800 to £2,000 for the seventh Duke of Devonshire's statue in 1895. With around £600 raised by 1897, the cheaper alternatives of a clock tower or obelisk were mooted, but instead a different sculptor, Goscombe John, produced a slightly smaller statue for £1,050.[56] Not all projects came to fruition: neither Stockport nor Ashton-under-Lyne secured sufficient funds to erect statues of Peel.[57]

However, a building project such as almshouses, which would also entail future running costs far beyond the occasional maintenance needed for statues, was potentially much more expensive. The *Derbyshire Advertiser* noted that the convalescent home suggested to remember Bass at Derby 'would require a large sum annually for its maintenance'.[58] At Barrow-in-Furness a hospital wing was mooted instead of a statue of Schneider, but raising the estimated £5,000 was clearly unfeasible, given that the committee had to bargain the statue's sculptor down from £945 to £600.[59] Sunderland's suggested memorials to Candlish included a convalescent home, infirmary wing, scholarships or what the *Northern Echo* deemed 'the only absolutely bad' option, a statue. It argued that since Candlish was 'intensely practical as well as eminently benevolent', any tribute should share those characteristics, but predicted that this cheaper alternative would be selected by those who felt that they could 'hoist upon a pedestal some bronze hulk, bearing a resemblance, distant or otherwise, to the late M.P., and the thing is done'.[60]

Aside from the costs, selecting an alternative to a statue was fraught with other difficulties, not least agreeing on one project from the numerous options sometimes mooted. Having resolved in 1886 to erect Morley's statue, a chaotic meeting at Nottingham also saw a range of secondary projects proposed, including a memorial hall and almshouses, which had motions passed in their favour, and working-class scholarships, a hospital ward and a donation to the Young Women's Christian Association (all rejected). The *Nottingham Evening Post* cautioned against pursuing too many schemes, and in the event, with £1,500 subscribed, only the statue came to fruition.[61] While statue projects were usually presented as free from partisan feeling, some alternatives had the disadvantage of strong associations with one group or faction. There was controversy when it emerged that the (Anglican) National Society would control the schools chosen in preference to a statue honouring Hesketh-Fleetwood.[62] A carillon for Ripon cathedral was suggested as a cheaper alternative to a statue of Ripon, but the *Ripon Observer* was 'extremely doubtful' whether 'all sections of the community' would approve.⁶³ Those advocating practical tributes could potentially be mollified with the use of any surplus revenue for such purposes.⁶⁴

While objections to statues usually stemmed from a desire for more practical memorials, some cases saw outright opposition to honouring the individual concerned. As Paul Elliott has noted, moves to commemorate the Chartist leader O'Connor at Nottingham, where he had been MP, 1847–52, sparked a petition to the council protesting that 'there was nothing' in O'Connor's 'public character or principles' or 'his brief career in Parliament … to entitle him to be held up to favourable notice by the erection of a statue'. There were, however, also several petitions in favour of the statue, which the council agreed to accept as a 'work of art and not as at all identifying the council with [O'Connor's] political opinions'.⁶⁵ At a public meeting to discuss a monument to Robert Hall, who died suddenly less than two months after becoming Conservative MP for Leeds in 1857, some attendees argued that 'a statue was uncalled for', since Hall had not been involved with public affairs long enough to 'entitle him to a position equal to' Peel, Wellington or Baines, all recently honoured with local statues.⁶⁶ The Liberal *Leeds Times* conceded Hall's usefulness 'within his limited sphere of action' – he had been a well-regarded judge, including as Leeds's deputy recorder from 1842 – but denied that his services merited a statue, 'the highest reward of the state to its distinguished sons'. It suggested a bust or church memorial was more appropriate, arguing that if Hall received a statue, 'there would scarcely be a public man in Leeds who at his death would not be entitled to a similar honour'. However, a statue went ahead.⁶⁷

Reassessing the chronology of 'statue mania'

The decision to erect a statue could therefore be complicated and contested. Alongside the fact that statues offered a more visible and personal tribute, as well as potentially being cheaper than alternative proposals, 'statue mania' evidently played its part, as towns emulated each other in remembering leading citizens or national statesman in this way. The civic dimension to this will be discussed below, but first the timing of this process merits attention. Following Benedict Read's suggestion that 'Peel was the (unwitting) means whereby public statuary commemoration began to approach the prolific', other scholars have concurred that 'the fashion for erecting statues to politicians in Britain was largely created by [Peel's] premature death in 1850'.⁶⁸ The former prime minister, honoured above all for repealing the corn laws, was memorialized at an astonishing scale and speed, particularly in northern England. The first statue unveiling at Salford in May 1852 was followed by five more – Preston, Tamworth, Leeds, Bury and Montrose – in the next four months alone.⁶⁹

This form of commemoration became so prevalent that during an 1868 Commons debate on Carlo Marochetti's ill-fated London statue of Peel – considered so unsightly by MPs that it was melted down for the bronze to be reused for a fresh attempt by Matthew Noble – Lord Elcho claimed that 'a regular system of manufacturing public statues had grown up in this country'. He described how a sculptor would dress a stock figure, 'stuffed or not to suit the appearance of the person to be represented', in the subject's typical costume, take a cast and then model the head to put on top.⁷⁰ As a corollary of 'statue mania', what might be described as 'statue fatigue' already appeared entrenched by the mid-1860s, when the *Tavistock Gazette*'s London correspondent argued that commemorating Cobden with an educational project 'would be far preferable to a statue which would be inevitably unlike the man and unlike anything else, except some other stupid statue'.⁷¹ Arguing in 1870 for a practical tribute to Salt, the *Bradford Daily Telegraph* declared statues 'a public nuisance – they are, at most, a nine-days' wonder after they are unveiled'.⁷² The almost knee-jerk reaction of proposing a statue was ridiculed in the critic Coventry Patmore's essay 'Shall Smith Have a Statue?', which warned of the 'folly of having raised an abiding memorial of our possibly transient enthusiasm'.⁷³

Examining MPs' statues in the North and Midlands suggests that while Peel's death may have accelerated the process of commemoration through statues, this trend was already underway before 1850. The term 'statue mania' appeared at least as early as 1818, when a satirical work listed it alongside other 'manias', including 'pug mania', 'picture mania' and 'cameo mania', although whether its mention of 'statue mania' referred to private collections or public tributes was unclear.⁷⁴ Several examples can be advanced of pre-Reform MPs commemorated with statues in northern England prior to 1850, including George Canning (Liverpool, 1832), William Huskisson (Liverpool, 1847) and Daniel Sykes (Hull, 1833).⁷⁵ A week before Peel's death, Thomas Carlyle's pamphlet *Hudson's Statue* (referencing a failed attempt to commemorate the disgraced railway promoter and MP George Hudson) described the 'poor English Public' as 'exceedingly bewildered with Statues at present'.⁷⁶

Francis Aglionby, MP for East Cumberland – the first of the fifty-six MPs commemorated with a statue – died ten years before Peel. His sudden death in Carlisle's court house, where he was undertaking his duties as chairman of the Cumberland quarter sessions in July 1840, prompted fellow magistrates to instigate 'some suitable memorial or monument' to mark his 'long and useful services' in that role.⁷⁷ Appeals for subscriptions appeared in *The Times*, the *Morning Chronicle* and the county press, and by February 1841 it had been decided to erect a statue in the entrance hall 'within a few yards of where Major Aglionby fell and breathed his last'. Unlike the elaborate unveiling ceremonies accompanying later statues, it was placed there without fanfare in June 1844.⁷⁸ A few months later, in November 1844, there were reports that Hesketh-Fleetwood would be honoured with a statue, not by his former constituents but by Fleetwood's inhabitants in appreciation of the 'character' of their town's founder.⁷⁹ This was, however, one of three proposals, the others being a piece of silverware or, the chosen option, building schools. The *Fleetwood Chronicle*'s observation that 'nothing less than a statue can sufficiently mark the deep sense of the honourable gentleman's worth' indicated that, some years before Peel's death, statues were seen as the highest form of public accolade, although, in line with the utilitarian impulses seen elsewhere, it favoured establishing schools as 'living monuments' which would 'combine usefulness with ornament'.⁸⁰

Another MP for whom a statue was conceived (although not completed) before Peel's death was Henry Handley, who represented Lincolnshire South, 1832–41. A few months after his death in June 1846, it was decided to erect 'some suitable testimonial' in his native Sleaford; in June 1849, having raised £700, the committee advertised for designs 'for a pillar and statue'.[81] In contrast with the free-standing statues erected in most cases considered here, this early example was transitional in style: sixty-five feet high, it echoed 'the manner of Queen Eleanor's crosses', with Handley's statue at its lower level.[82] Although Sleaford's inhabitants were moved to act partly by Handley's 'premature death' aged forty-nine, this memorial also needs to be understood in its wider political context. While statue dedications were commonly accompanied by lengthy expositions of MPs' good works, the chairman of a dinner marking the statue's completion in April 1851 observed that 'there was no single great transaction in [Handley's] life that entitled him to this memorial', but still considered him 'the man in a million', citing his services as MP and as the Royal Agricultural Society's president (1841–2).[83] The timing of the decision to honour Handley's efforts 'in favour of the interests of Agriculture, not only in his place in Parliament, but in his private capacity' was significant, taken just a few months after the Commons voted to repeal the corn laws, by a meeting of 'landowners, farmers, and graziers' from this predominantly rural area.[84] Although a Reformer, Handley had put his constituency's concerns above party in 'resisting attacks upon the agriculturists' interest'.[85] As with the statues honouring Peel's role in corn law repeal, this was a monument not just to the man but to the cause he represented.

Although these early examples indicate that the significance of Peel's death should not be overstated when it came to honouring politicians with statues, the 1850s did mark a turning point, after which 'commemorative statues began to become a familiar part of the local streetscape'.[86] Table 7.1 shows the decades in which the 108 statues of the fifty-six MPs were unveiled or otherwise inaugurated, and the decade in which each MP was first commemorated.[87] On both measures, the 1850s to the 1910s appears as the key period of memorialization, peaking in the 1870s. While this study focuses on MPs elected between 1832 and 1868, if statues of MPs elected after 1868 are added (for northern and Midlands counties covered by the PMSA's volumes), this does not affect the overall pattern. It has been suggested that by the time of Queen Victoria's Diamond Jubilee, 'the prevailing mood turned against portrait statuary', with more practical projects preferred.[88] Although nineteen of the 108 statues were erected in the first two decades of the twentieth century (plus six of MPs from the later cohort), it should be noted that twelve of these were to just four individuals, with Gladstone alone accounting for five.[89] Yet there remained some appetite for this form of memorialization. Following the erection of a statue of the long-serving MP Francis Powell in 1910, the *Wigan Observer* suggested that Wigan should honour others who had 'played a great part' in its public life. The names it proposed – Nathaniel Eckersley and John Lancaster – were both former MPs and local benefactors.[90] The dramatic drop in the number of statues of 'worthy men' after the First World War has been linked to a decline in deference, as well as indicating other spending priorities in times of economic depression and post-war reconstruction.[91] When it came to MPs, it may also have reflected their changing social backgrounds and a different relationship with their constituencies, although this lies beyond this chapter's chronological scope.

In terms of the timing of commemoration, one notable finding which emerges from analysing these fifty-six MPs is the extent to which individuals were celebrated

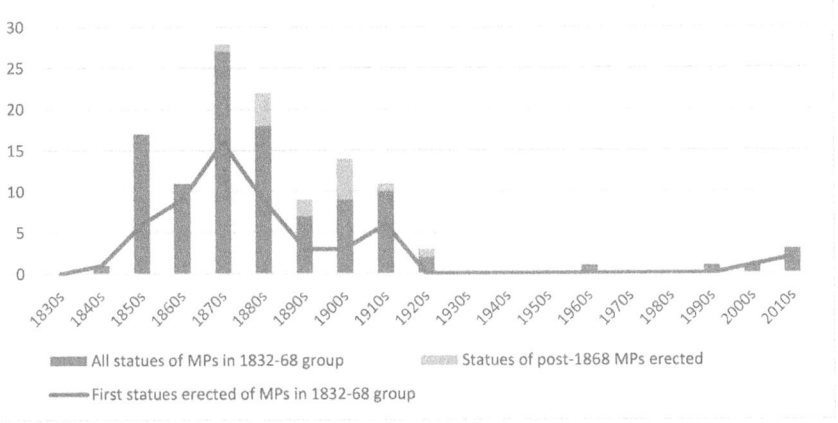

Table 7.1 Decades of erection of statues of MPs who sat for constituencies in northern England and the Midlands after 1832.

in their lifetime. Existing accounts have described this as a 'highly unusual honour', but although most statues in this study were indeed posthumous (typically instigated within a year of the subject's death), there were a significant number – a quarter of the group – where death was not the spur.[92] Of these fourteen individuals with statues proposed during their lifetimes, four had, however, died before the unveilings.[93] Gladstone was the living politician most honoured, with statues in his native Liverpool (1870) as part of its St. George's Hall pantheon; Manchester town hall (1879), where Charles Pelham Villiers (1877) and John Bright (1878) had received the same accolade; Bow (1882); and the City Liberal Club (1883).[94]

Honoured in St. George's Hall for both his national standing and his gift of a museum to Liverpool was the fourteenth Earl of Derby, with a statue instigated in 1867, although he died before its unveiling in 1869.[95] The first person commemorated with a St. George's Hall statue (1860) in his lifetime, William Brown, another former MP, was also recognized for large-scale philanthropy, following his gift of a library and museum.[96] The same rationale prompted statues of the second Marquess of Westminster (1869) and Crossley (1860) in the parks they had given to Chester and Halifax, respectively, although the former was initially reluctant about a statue and the latter protested that an illuminated address was sufficient appreciation.[97] Bass stymied plans in 1874 to mark his philanthropy and lengthy parliamentary service at Derby, arguing that 'a statue of a living man would be somewhat out of place in a locality which the original might be expected to frequently revisit'.[98] In contrast, Salt agreed not to publicize his objections to the Bradford statue proposed after his baronetcy in 1869.[99] Justifying this tribute, the committee's chairman declared it wrong that 'men of sterling worth and principle were first allowed to pass away, without any recognition by those with whose interest and welfare they were associated', although the *Knaresborough Post* was unconvinced, suggesting that

Bradford's inhabitants 'at least await for some time the verdict of posterity before they decide … who are great men and who are not'.[100]

In other cases, a significant moment in the MP's career provided the impetus. Akroyd's 'admirers' at Halifax decided that his Commons retirement in 1874 merited 'something more' than the illuminated address initially mooted.[101] Lengthy parliamentary service was the catalyst for the Birmingham Liberal Association's 1882 decision to erect Bright's statue to commemorate his silver jubilee as their MP, although having grumbled in his diary in 1875 when Manchester ignored his 'known aversion to statues' to commission its tribute, Bright was equally unenthusiastic about this later accolade.[102] The fiftieth anniversary of Powell's first election for Wigan generated plans for his statue in 1907. He not only wrote its inscription but spoke briefly at its 1910 unveiling, said to be 'only the second instance in England of a man being present at the unveiling of his own statue'.[103] The first appears to have been Mathew Wilson, honoured at Skipton two years after election defeat in 1886 ended his lengthy political career. He voiced his hopes that this honour would 'encourage another generation to devote their lives to the public service'.[104]

Statues and the civic identity of public space

Analysing why the Victorians wanted statues, Donald Read has outlined two key motivations, the 'moral purpose' Wilson alluded to, in which statues were 'a reminder of virtue and a source of inspiration', and 'a wish to ornament the new public places of their rapidly expanding towns'.[105] The latter impetus bolstered the case of those who preferred statues to utilitarian tributes. The *Derbyshire Advertiser* favoured a statue of Bass at Derby because the town was 'quite devoid of monuments of any description'.[106] Cumberland's lack of any 'public work of high art' was a 'reproach' which the *Carlisle Journal* felt would be redressed by the erection of Aglionby's statue, the first public statue in the county.[107] It drew an unfavourable contrast with Newcastle upon Tyne, and the same sense of civic comparison was evident at Birmingham, where the mayor noted at the unveiling of Attwood's statue that until recently 'no large town in the kingdom was more destitute of public ornaments than Birmingham'.[108]

Civic rivalry could clearly act as a spur to the erection of statues, as Gaunt has noted when it came to the Peel statues raised across the North and Midlands.[109] There was 'shame' in Villiers's constituency that Manchester had 'set us the example' in honouring him, and the same sculptor was swiftly commissioned in 1876 to produce another statue for Wolverhampton.[110] In a similar vein, Morley's former Nottingham constituents were encouraged to emulate Bristol's decision to erect his statue.[111] Commemorating local political notables could perform a variety of civic functions, for as Vernon has noted, it was 'the town that was celebrated as much as the individual, indeed the individual was celebrated as a product of the town'.[112] Unveiling ceremonies were therefore usually major civic events: when Platt's statue was unveiled at Oldham (1878), more than 10,000 people joined a procession which included 'borough and county magistrates, members of the town council and board of guardians, members of educational and other institutions, members of friendly and trades societies', and several mayors of neighbouring towns were present to witness Oldham's pride in its townsman.[113]

The role which outdoor public statues played in establishing 'the civic identity of public spaces' has been highlighted by several scholars.[114] As one of the most significant groups memorialized, MPs' statues were central to this. While some became part of indoor pantheons (as in Manchester town hall and St. George's Hall, Liverpool), most of those in this study stood outside. At Manchester, for example, Peel's statue in Piccadilly (1853) began the process of making this area into the town's 'principal public space'; later on, statues of Bright (1891) and Gladstone (1901) were among those which 'extended and consolidated' the 'important civic space' of Albert Square in front of Manchester town hall.[115] Erecting a statue in a particular site could help to shape and define that space, but this was a two-way process: the choice of location was one way to imbue statues with meaning. While a statue could provide a focal point for a new civic space, conversely, siting it in an established location could reinforce the accolade given to its subject. At Derby, despite incurring an additional £175 expense to divert the tramway terminus, the marketplace was chosen for Bass's statue as 'the finest open space in the town' and therefore 'the place of honour'. Concerns were raised that the 'scenes' and 'bad language' in the market would be disrespectful to Bass's memory, but, in a striking example of the belief that statues would encourage virtuous conduct, the *Derbyshire Advertiser* suggested that the statue's presence might 'exercise a moderating influence' over market-goers.[116]

Outdoor locations demanded statues on a larger, and therefore costlier, scale – £700 was quoted for an indoor (marble) statue of Schneider at Barrow-in-Furness, in contrast with £1,000 for an outdoor (bronze) statue – but had the advantage of greater prominence, visibility and ease of access, particularly for the working classes.[117] There were complaints that placing Aglionby's statue inside Carlisle's court house meant it was 'lost to the public'.[118] When a Liverpool statue for Samuel Graves was discussed, those proposing its inclusion in 'our local Walhalla' in St. George's Hall were countered by arguments that it deserved 'a more commanding site' in Lord Street because 'only a section of the community visit St. George's-hall'.[119] Given the perceived instructive function of statues, the more prominent the location, the better – at Leicester, one member of the memorial committee opined that placing Biggs's statue 'in a public thoroughfare' would be more 'calculated to improve the taste and the morals of the inhabitants'.[120] However, this was not simply a question of middle-class elites wishing to indoctrinate the working classes. The initial proposal that Villiers's statue be erected inside Wolverhampton town hall generated working-class objections. One correspondent to the local press suggested that tradesmen and workers withhold subscriptions until it was understood that the statue should not be 'a mere ornament of the Town Hall', while a works meeting urged that it should stand 'in some public thoroughfare where the great body of the people … might point proudly to it … as instancing their deep appreciation of long and faithful services'.[121] These arguments bore fruit, as the committee eventually agreed on a prominent outdoor site where several roads converged.[122]

The choice of site could also be used to reinforce the statue's civic significance. A key reason for locating Lewis's statue near Hereford's Shire Hall was that his 'connection with the county as well as the city would be implied'. The statue's inscription noted his ties to Hereford (as chief steward) and Herefordshire (as MP) alongside his ministerial posts but clearly demonstrated the salience of local civic identities by omitting to mention that he was latterly MP for New Radnor.[123] At Bradford, a site near the new town hall was chosen in preference to a park for Salt's statue, and the civic connection was underlined by emulating the building's stone and Gothic style in the statue's canopy. This location also had another effect on the statue's meaning, as it required the removal of stone alpacas flanking it on either side, symbolic of Salt's pioneering role in the commercial use of alpaca wool, in order to fit railings around it. His connections to Bradford as a large-scale employer were therefore less prominent than intended, although the statue did incorporate a plan of Saltaire.[124] The decision to erect Fielden's statue near Todmorden town hall not only exacerbated delays in its installation, as it languished in a warehouse for seven years awaiting the building's completion in 1875, but also added another layer of meaning to it.[125] Instigated in 1859 to honour Fielden's role in securing the Ten Hours Act, the statue drew subscriptions not only from Todmorden but from 'the Operatives of the Manufacturing Districts'.[126] It showed Fielden holding a copy of the act, referenced in the inscription, and his fellow factory reformer Lord John Manners unveiled it.[127] However, in coupling its unveiling with the inauguration of the town hall, which the Fielden family had bankrolled, it also became closely associated with Todmorden's civic identity and the Fieldens' benevolence.[128]

Statues and their subscribers: Commemoration and community cohesion

Alongside the choice of site, there were other opportunities to create the sense that statues belonged to the whole community. A handful of the statues considered here were funded by an individual, perhaps the most unusual being John Margerison, a Blackburn mill worker who bequeathed almost £3,000 in 1907 to commemorate his late employer William Hornby.[129] There were also projects with a partisan hue, such as Disraeli's statues at Ormskirk (1884), Chorley (1886) and Bolton (1887), erected by local Conservative associations or the Primrose League.[130] It was more common, however, for costs to be met by public subscription, with an emphasis on the tribute's cross-class and non-partisan nature. This was particularly the case when honouring figures who contributed significantly to their locality, which made it easier to put party aside and celebrate them in that light. At Halifax, where 7,000 people subscribed towards Akroyd's statue, it was reported that 'the project is receiving support from all classes, quite irrespective of party'.[131] The first public discussion of Bass's statue at Derby was said to have been attended by 'representatives of all classes of the community and all shades of politics', although such reports could not always be taken at face value, since a rival newspaper noted that only one Conservative spoke at this meeting.[132] Elsewhere, however, while one party may have instigated proceedings, efforts were made to stress cross-party support on the basis of the MP's services to their constituency. Local Conservatives reportedly contributed more than half the sum raised for Villiers's Wolverhampton statue by June 1876, and his fellow MP Henry Fowler insisted that 'what welded all parties of the borough together in recognition of the merits of Mr. Villiers was not so much his political as his parliamentary services in the every-day hard work of attending to its interests'.[133]

As well as seeking cross-party support, the middle-class elites who generally took the lead in such projects as part of their efforts at 'constructing, presenting and communicating civic identity' also endeavoured to engage the broader community.[134] The subscription list for Aglionby's statue in Carlisle was headed by donations of ten guineas, but arrangements were made for 'even the humblest admirers of Major Aglionby to contribute their mite'.[135] Those raising funds for Powell's statue at Wigan wanted their appeal to convey that it 'was not a matter of the classes only' but 'one for the whole town'.[136] Setting a limit (such as five pounds) on individual donations was one way of seeking to broaden the basis of fundraising. Mayo's Cockermouth statue, which set no limit, was funded by 144 donations of between five shillings and 75 pounds; in contrast, for Salt's Bradford statue, subscription sheets were sent to secretaries of friendly societies, as well as 'mills, sheds, and workshops'. It garnered 2,125 subscriptions, 'from the maximum, £5, to the child's 1d.'[137] Although doubts have been raised about how far workers felt pressure to contribute, there does seem to have been genuine working-class support in some cases at least.[138] At Leicester, where 1,070 of the 1,400 subscribers gave 'small sums', these working-class contributions proved decisive in enabling a statue of Biggs rather than a cheaper grave monument, while for Salford's Peel statue, the People's Monument Committee, composed of working men, raised just over a third of the £1,200 cost from 9,020 individuals.[139] Yet Terry Wyke has noted that within the rhetoric of class co-operation, class hierarchies remained intact, with unveiling ceremonies commonly organized along socially demarcated lines.[140]

One genuinely popular tribute was to the colourful and controversial Sir Robert Clifton at Nottingham. An enthusiastic gambler, he spent many years in France avoiding his debtors before his election in 1861 as an 'independent' Liberal, garnering Conservative and radical support due to his opposition to Nottingham's cliquish Whig leaders. His funeral, following his death from typhoid in 1869, aged just forty-two, drew 20,000 people.[141] In contrast with the usual public meetings convened by local elites for such purposes, Clifton's statue was initiated by his supporters in the Independent Society. The fund's treasurer was a coppersmith, William Pare, who noted that after Clifton's death 'he had been stopped by hundreds of people and asked, "Are you not going to erect a statue?"'[142] The project proved as contentious as Clifton himself. A 'bullock roasting' and associated festivities, whose profits were earmarked for the statue fund, generated less than five pounds, despite 1,800 people attending.[143] The original sculptor was dropped in 1873 after increasing his fee from £1,000 to £1,250.[144] With just £122 in the bank by 1875, Pare vehemently denied allegations of misappropriating funds.[145] After a last push for subscriptions, which, in an indication of the contributors' anticipated social backgrounds, could be left at not only the bank and newspaper office, but several pubs, a working men's club, grocer, butcher and bootmaker, enough was raised to commission a stone statue from W. P. Smith, assistant master of Nottingham's school of art.[146] Clifton's successor as candidate, William Seymour, had wanted it to have 'a good place ... in their great and splendid market-place', but Clifton's widow suggested a less contentious location facing the colliery Clifton had established.[147] The council granted this site in 1881, despite one councillor's protest, 'as one interested in the moral tone of the town', that they 'ought not to touch it'. However, the mayor accepted it on Nottingham's behalf when it was finally unveiled in 1883.[148]

The 'afterlives' of statues: From cultural reference points to landmarks

While the press reported in detail on debates surrounding the erection of statues and on their unveilings, far less attention was paid to how statues were regarded thereafter. The *Hereford Journal* suggested that 'after the first few days of novelty have exhausted their powers of attraction, the statue might as well be located in Siberia or the Sandwich Islands, for all that it is cared for or thought about', a prediction at odds with hopes that statues would serve as sources of moral inspiration or civic focal points.[149] In fact, statues attracted a range of formal and informal responses after their installation. Wyke notes their inclusion in local guidebooks 'as objects of civic import to draw to the attention of visitors'.[150] Such local pride remained in evidence at Todmorden forty years after the Fielden statue's unveiling, with visitors 'often conducted to the square to inspect the memorial and to have poured into their ears the old story which it was designed to perpetuate'.[151] Statues also became sites of private pilgrimage. In 1858 Lord Brougham detoured to Leeds to see the recently erected statue of 'his old friend' Baines, pronouncing it 'one of the most admirable portraits and statues he had ever seen', and Benjamin Wilson, a Chartist veteran, paid a similar homage to O'Connor's Nottingham statue nearly a quarter of a century after its unveiling.[152]

Statues were also incorporated into collective ceremonial. Despite being inland, Herbert Ingram's statue at Boston was deemed the most appropriate venue for an event naming the Skegness lifeboat in his honour, two years after the statue's unveiling.[153] Disraeli's statues saw regular tributes on Primrose Day (the anniversary of his death). At Liverpool in 1884 thousands 'made a pilgrimage' to see his statue, where 'workingmen and poor women' were among those depositing primroses, and ten bands paraded.[154] The laying of primroses at Disraeli's statues in Liverpool and Ormskirk was reported as late as 1939.[155] In contrast with these tributes, the primrose wreath placed on Skipton's statue of Wilson, a Liberal, on Primrose Day 1889 could have been dismissed as a prank but also reflected underlying tensions about the statue.[156] Its instigation at a meeting at the Bradford Liberal Club had riled local Conservatives, who – contrary to the cross-party harmony found in many memorials, and despite Wilson's strong local ties – objected that it was 'forced upon them' by 'the Bradford gentlemen'.[157] They even went so far as to secure a counsel's opinion that in granting the statue site, Skipton's local board was 'liable to an indictment for causing an obstruction to the highway', but did not pursue this.[158]

Other statues fêted on anniversaries included Bright's in Albert Square, Manchester, with wreaths laid on the centenary of his birth (1911) and twenty-fifth anniversary of his death (1914).[159] Ingram's Boston statue (1862) commemorated both his parliamentary services and his key role in providing a local waterworks, referenced in the figure pouring water at its base.[160] It was illuminated and decorated as the focus of celebrations for the waterworks' golden jubilee in 1899 and was similarly adorned on other anniversaries associated with Ingram, with 'the fountain … made to play', but by 1929 this custom had 'long since fallen into abeyance'.[161] While regular tributes dwindled over time, statues remained the site of one-off ceremonials. The centenaries of the deaths of O'Connor and Ripon were marked at their statues by the Nottingham Trades Council and the Ripon Civic Society in 1955 and 2009, respectively.[162] Some later tributes imbued statues with different meanings than initially intended. In contrast with the original emphasis on cross-party support for Villiers's Wolverhampton statue, a wreath-laying by Geoffrey Mander MP in 1932 was explicitly political, celebrating 'a century of Liberal representation'.[163] Statues were also treated less reverentially, from harmless pranks to more violent interventions. It was noted in 1946 that 'few public celebrations in Leicester pass without an informal "crowning"' of Biggs's statue, being adorned with a 'wartime firewatcher's tin hat' for Victory Day, and it was also the target of numerous student pranks and 'a thousand music hall jokes'.[164] The latter echoed the mentions of Clifton's Nottingham statue and Cobden's Manchester statue found in local pantomimes in the 1870s and 1880s.[165] At the 1880 election Ingram's Boston statue was targeted by 'Conservative roughs' who attempted to pull it from its pedestal, while in 1912 local suffragettes covered the fourteenth Earl of Derby's Preston statue in tar in protest at the sixteenth Earl's opposition to women's suffrage.[166]

It was evident that statues became cultural reference points within their locality. In an example of words being put into a statue's mouth which was not unique, a letter supposedly penned by Bright's statue was sent by the local workers' committee to the Rochdale press in 1914.[167] This was far from the only occasion on which this statue, unveiled in 1891, was referenced in local affairs. Its location near Rochdale town hall meant it became a key site for open-air speaking. At the January 1910 election, the Liberal MP Alexander Harvey noted that he was 'standing under the shadow of the great apostle of Free Trade', a doctrine he pledged to uphold.[168] It was not only politicians who invoked Bright's statue. In 1911 a policeman chose the motto on its pedestal – 'Be just and fear not' – as his pseudonym in a letter to the *Police Review*, urging the local watch committee to follow this principle when considering a rest day for the police, while this adage was also highlighted in a sermon to Rochdale's lads' brigade in 1914, fulfilling its creators' hopes that the statue could be used to inspire future generations.[169] Less in keeping with these aspirations, but equally interesting in demonstrating how statues became local reference points, was the 1923 comment by a man who refused to pay child maintenance that 'on the day he paid John Bright would step down from his monument'.[170]

Given their perceived roles in ornamenting and defining civic space, it is unsurprising that statues acquired more practical functions as local landmarks, with meaning becoming attached to the monument as much as its subject. Wyke has suggested that 'perhaps, after an initial flush of interest, many statues simply become part of the landscape … points of geographical rather than moral or historical orientation'.[171] Shifting perceptions of Biggs's statue were in evidence at Leicester. In 1925 the *Leicester Evening Mail* was dismissive of a local election campaigner who described it as 'an eyesore' and obstruction to traffic which should be removed, arguing that those who had been acquainted with Biggs regarded it 'with pleasure as an excellent representation of one of the best citizens Leicester ever possessed'. Leicester's council evidently concurred, deciding to recast the crumbling stone statue in bronze to ensure its continued existence in 1929.[172] In contrast, by 1949, when it was relocated for road improvements, it was the statue itself which had meaning as 'a Leicester landmark'. The newspaper now observed that 'John Biggs' statue is held in as much affection by the present generation as the man himself was a hundred years ago, so that many people do not like the idea of his leaving Welford-place'.[173] A similar attachment to the memorial rather than its subject was seen at Wigan, where Powell's bronze statue in Mesnes Park acquired a new layer of meaning, along with a well-polished foot, due to a long-standing ritual of rubbing its foot for luck, which inspired a 2013 song, 'Francis Powell's foot', by the local folk group Chonkinfeckle.[174]

The 'afterlives' of statues: Relegation, relocation and rehabilitation

While Powell's statue remains on its original site and was restored in 2010, other statues 'have suffered a great many indignities through alteration, neglect, decay or change of location'.[175] Wyke's comment about the increasingly frequent calls in early twentieth-century Manchester to 'banish the "monstrosities in stone trousers" from the city centre – statues of worthies who could not be named by many citizens' also applied elsewhere.[176] Just under half of the 108 statues in this study remain in their original positions. Only a handful have been completely removed, but several have been relocated more than once.[177] The debates surrounding these moves shed interesting light on changing perceptions of statues and are also significant given the impact a statue's location could have on its meaning.

Since statues' sites were commonly selected for their prominence, it is unsurprising that their occupation of this space has been reassessed. The statues of Disraeli in Liverpool, Laird in Birkenhead and Wilson in Skipton were all moved a short distance in the 1920s to enable the construction of war memorials, reflecting new priorities for commemoration in these important civic sites, although suggested moves for the same purpose of Cobden's Stockport statue and Candlish's Sunderland statue were not pursued.[178] However, the key reason for relocating statues, not only of MPs, but others, has been the remodelling of town centres to facilitate the expansion of public transport and motor traffic in the late nineteenth and early twentieth centuries. In an early example, the development of Bradford's tramways soon made the location of Salt's 1876 statue inappropriate. It saw a fatal accident in 1885 when an engine left the rails nearby and by the end of the decade was blackened with smoke from tram engines and had a cabmen's shelter erected behind it, which one alderman protested was 'not respectful' to Salt's memory 'or creditable to the town'.[179] There were objections to a proposed relocation to Peel Park, 'where no one would see it', according to one councillor, and in 1894 the borough surveyor was asked to draft plans to use space outside the town hall's west end 'as a site for the Salt statue and for public lavatories', hardly a more edifying prospect. Two years later, it instead joined the statue of another local notable, Lord Masham, in Lister Park.[180]

This was far from the only statue relocated from a central location to an outlying park, downgrading their earlier civic significance. The redevelopment of Oldham town centre in 1924 and a proposed bus station for Rochdale in 1933 saw the statues of Platt and Bright displaced from their positions of honour near the respective town halls to local parks.[181] Traffic collisions involving the central Birmingham statues of Attwood and Peel caused their relegation in the 1920s to Calthorpe Park, although neither remained there.[182] Attwood's statue moved in 1975 to Sparkbrook, where he had once lived, but suffered repeated vandalism and has been in storage since 2008. However, in an indication of evolving attitudes towards commemoration, when Attwood's great-great-granddaughter donated a new statue in 1993, Birmingham's council gave it a prominent site near the town hall.[183] Peel's Birmingham statue (1855) offers a prime example of how changing sites could affect a statue's meaning. It had already been moved once prior to its exile to Calthorpe Park, shifting a short distance in 1873 from its original location to Council House Square. At that point it lost its decorative railings featuring clusters of wheat, an important symbolic element connecting it with Peel's repeal of the corn laws. Its move in 1963 from the park to Edgbaston's police training college associated it instead with his foundation of the metropolitan police.[184] When the chairman of Birmingham Civic Society's Public Art Committee argued in 2019 for returning it to 'a place of civic prominence' in the city centre following the decision to relocate the college, he noted that the Edgbaston location was 'inapposite and tenuous', since the statue was erected to mark Peel's achievement in repealing the corn laws.[185]

One statue whose removal provoked considerable debate was Clifton's statue, never well-regarded by Nottingham's elite. When it was taken down in 1903, twenty years after its unveiling, to enable the building of a railway station, one local newspaper remarked that 'the wonder is that it was allowed to disfigure a prominent spot … for so many years'.[186] However, the statue's relegation to the corporation depot prompted heated discussion. Its detractors focused on its artistic failings, with one alderman claiming that its 'fearful ugliness' made it 'a positive disgrace to the town', views given extra fuel when the *Strand Magazine* featured it as having 'the worst pair of sculptured trousers in the kingdom'.[187] Its defenders, led by Alderman Bentley, asserted that 'it was not a question of ugliness or beauty of the statue', but a matter of principle. He considered its removal without the council's consent 'a gross insult to the working-classes' who had funded it and suggested that Morley's statue would not be so ill-treated. Other council members agreed that, irrespective of its artistic merits, they must 'keep faith with the people who erected it and put it in the care of the town'.[188] Protests by the 'few surviving subscribers' generated considerable popular sympathy, forcing the council to find a new site near the river Trent, where the statue arrived in December 1905.[189]

While in the early twentieth century some statues were dismissed as eyesores or obstructions, the early twenty-first century has seen their re-evaluation as assets for local heritage, triggering calls in several cases for reinstatement to their original prominent locations. Salford's statue of Joseph Brotherton, unveiled in Peel Park in 1858, has had a peripatetic existence: placed in storage in 1954 to make way for college buildings, sold together with Peel's statue to a private collector in 1969, purchased by Manchester's council in 1986 and erected by the river Irwell, before moving to Salford in 2012. It finally returned to Peel Park as part of the park's 2018 restoration 'to its former Victorian glory', according to Salford's mayor, who lauded the borough's first MP as 'a true reforming politician'.[190] Its rehabilitation continued with its inclusion in a 'Sound Sculpture Trail', which listed Brotherton's achievements, deeming him 'an all-round good bloke'.[191] Other relocations have also involved reconsideration of a statue's significance. In 2007 Pease's Darlington statue, moved in 1958 for road improvements, was returned to its original location, renamed Joseph Pease Place.[192] Its plinth featured four reliefs representing different aspects of Pease's life: his interest in education, parliamentary career, involvement in the abolition of slavery, and role in developing the Stockton and Darlington railway.[193] Its original unveiling (1875) coincided with the railway's golden jubilee, firmly connecting it with this theme.[194] In contrast, its 2007 unveiling, on the bicentenary of the abolition of the slave trade, foregrounded Pease's connection with the subsequent anti-slavery campaign. It was among forty English monuments and buildings whose listing schedules were enhanced to commemorate this anniversary. His record on this issue prompted the *Northern Echo* to comment in June 2020 that 'when statues are toppling on a daily basis, Darlington should say a word in praise of Mr Pease'.[195]

Elsewhere, while there have been bids for statues to return to their original sites, other priorities for commemoration have come to the fore. In 2007 it was mooted that Bright's statue should resume its initial location near Rochdale town hall. Echoing the civic rivalries which had characterized Victorian 'statue mania', one councillor remarked, not entirely accurately, that '[w]e must be the only town in the North West that does not have a statue of any of its great citizens in the centre'. After much debate, the costs and risks of damage in transit were considered too great. However, in 2016 Rochdale unveiled a statue of the entertainer Gracie Fields not far from where Bright's statue originally stood, helping to redress the lack of memorials to women.[196] Similar concerns were in evidence at Oldham, where there had been suggestions that Platt's statue return to its site near the town hall. Instead, when this public space was redeveloped in 2018, a statue of the suffragette Annie Kenney was erected, close to where Platt's once stood.[197] In the same year – the centenary of (partial) women's suffrage – members of the Bradford Civic Society were sympathetic to the idea of restoring Salt's statue to the town centre, thereby using 'our architecture and built environment … to celebrate the story of Bradford and create a strong civic identity', but agreed that 'money may be better spent on finding a way to honour one of the city's historic female figures'.[198] These debates demonstrate the ongoing significance attached to statues as civic monuments, but also reveal shifting priorities when it comes to who should be commemorated in the twenty-first century.

Conclusion

As Matthew Roberts has noted, much of the existing literature on commemoration 'has focused on nation-building, state-sponsored memory, war and genocide'.[199] In contrast, while there were some national tributes to major statesmen among the hundred plus statues considered in this chapter's regional case studies, the bulk of these projects were instigated at local level and most of those honoured were commemorated in their constituencies. A key theme which emerges in many cases is that these MPs were celebrated not simply for having represented these places at Westminster but for their wider contributions to local public life. The initial impetus may have come from the honouree's own party, and middle-class elites may have taken the lead in such projects, but the rhetoric which underpinned this civic veneration was commonly that of cross-class and cross-party co-operation. These efforts to set aside party when honouring these local notables resonate with Jon Lawrence's view that 'the "triumph of party", and of the party politician' in the half century after 1867 needs rethinking. As Daniel Craig and James Thompson have highlighted, the social elites who dominated nineteenth-century politics had shared beliefs and assumptions that cut across the party divide.[200] The commemoration of local political leaders through statues – with their associated civic, moral, educational and cultural functions – was one way of reinforcing some of their common values.

The geography and chronology of memorialization also require re-evaluation. The 1850s, with its flurry of statues to commemorate Peel, has widely been regarded as 'the crucial decade for statumania in the industrial towns'.[201] However, this study of MPs' statues indicates that this was not a phenomenon confined to large urban centres, with several statues in rural market towns or seaside resorts.[202] Significantly, the earliest projects for post-Reform MPs' statues considered here – at Carlisle and Sleaford – were in these smaller centres of population, and their instigation predated Peel's death. This suggests that one reason why Peel was so swiftly and widely honoured in this particular form was that statues were already regarded as the ultimate accolade. Finally, in analysing the impulse to pay tribute to leading local citizens and national statesmen in stone, marble or bronze, it is important to acknowledge persistent scepticism about the merits of memorialization, coupled with arguments for more useful forms of commemoration. Even those keen to erect statues became embroiled in debates over critical questions such as their siting. The meanings given to these statues by their Victorian creators have been overlaid with new ones over time, as statues have become civic landmarks, cultural reference points or, less positively, unwanted obstacles to modern development. In reassessing the role and significance of these monuments in the twenty-first century, it is important to understand their complicated histories in the nineteenth.

Notes

1 *Preston Chronicle*, 4 September 1847.
2 *Hamilton Advertiser*, 30 November 1872.
3 *Hansard*, 21 July 1862, vol. 168, c. 606.
4 M. Trusted, 'Preface', in *Toppling Statues. Papers from the 2020 PSSA Webinar Co-hosted by the Burlington Magazine,* ed. M. Trusted and J. Barnes (Watford: PSSA Publishing, 2021), 5.
5 BBC News website, 11 June 2020, 'Sir Robert Peel Statue Removal Calls "Targeting Wrong Man"', https://www.bbc.co.uk/news/uk-england-53005223; *The Herald*,

11 June 2020, https://www.heraldscotland.com/news/18512185.anti-racist-protesters-defiant-plan-topple-glasgows-peel-statue—despite-targeting-wrong-man/; https://repealpeel.wordpress.com/; https://www.examinerlive.co.uk/news/local-news/calls-removal-statue-sir-robert-18395273; https://www.lancs.live/news/lancashire-news/statement-after-calls-prestons-robert-18393543. All online sites were accessed on 4 January 2022.

6   Todmorden Town Council, Emergency Committee minutes, 1 July 2020, item 14 (accessed via https://todmorden-tc.gov.uk/meetings/). Planning permission for this plaque was sought in December 2021: Todmorden Town Council, Agenda for Development Committee meeting, 8 December 2021.

7   BBC News website, 7 July 2016, 'The Fight to Celebrate Great Women on Britain's Streets', https://www.bbc.co.uk/news/magazine-36707152; C. Criado Perez, *Invisible Women. Exposing Data Bias in a World Designed for Men* (London: Vintage, 2020), 11; UK Public Statues of Women database, pssauk.org/women/.

8   B. Read, *Victorian Sculpture* (New Haven: Yale University Press, 1982), chs. 5 and 6; https://www.vads.ac.uk/digital/collection/PMSA. See also G. Archer, *Public Sculpture in Britain. A History* (Norwich: Frontier, 2013), 121ff., J. Darke, *The Monument Guide to England and Wales* (London: Macdonald Illustrated, 1991), and for an earlier analysis, Lord Edward Gleichen, *London's Open-air Statuary* (London: Longmans, Green & Co., 1928).

9   H. Miller, *Politics Personified* (Manchester: Manchester University Press, 2015), 1–3, 9.

10 T. Wyke, 'Memorial Mania: Remembering and Forgetting Sir Robert Peel', in *People, Places and Identities: Themes in British Social and Cultural History, 1700s-1980s*, ed. A. Kidd and M. Tebbutt (Manchester: Manchester University Press, 2017), 78. See also J. Vernon, *Politics and the People. A Study in English Political Culture c. 1815–1867* (Cambridge: Cambridge University Press, 1993), 58–62; T. Wyke, 'Marginal Figures? Public Statues and Public Parks in the Manchester Region, 1840–1914', in *Sculpture and the Garden*, ed. P. Eyres and F. Russell (Aldershot: Ashgate, 2006), 85–97; S. Gunn, *The Public Culture of the Victorian Middle Class. Ritual and Authority in the English Industrial City 1840–1914* (Manchester: Manchester University Press, 2000), 50–4; K. Hill, '"Thoroughly Imbued with the Spirit of Ancient Greece": Symbolism and Space in Victorian Civic Culture', in *Gender, Civic Culture and Consumerism. Middle-Class Identity in Britain, 1800–1940*, ed. A. Kidd and D. Nicholls (Manchester: Manchester University Press, 1999), 105.

11 Wyke, 'Memorial Mania', 78. On commemorations of Peel, see also D. Read, *Peel and the Victorians* (Oxford: Blackwell, 1987), 294–301; R. Gaunt, *Sir Robert Peel: The Life and Legacy* (London: I. B. Tauris, 2010), 145–9; M. Stafford, 'Peel's Statue in Leeds – a First for Town and Country', *Leeds Art Calendar*, 90 (1982), 4–11.

12 M. Nixon, 'Material Gladstones', in *William Gladstone: New Studies and Perspectives*, ed. R. Quinault, R. Swift and R. C. Windscheffel (Farnham: Ashgate, 2012), 100–1; C. Wrigley, '"Carving the Last Few Columns out of the Gladstonian Quarry": The Liberal Leaders and the Mantle of Gladstone, 1898–1929', in *Gladstone Centenary Essays*, ed. D. Bebbington and R. Swift (Liverpool: Liverpool University Press, 2000), 244–5; A. Howe, *Free Trade and Liberal England, 1846–1946* (Oxford: Clarendon Press, 1997), 143–5; F. D. Munsell, *The Victorian Controversy Surrounding the Wellington War Memorial: The Archduke of Hyde Park Corner* (Lewiston and Lampeter: Edwin Mellen, 1991); H. Stedman, 'Monuments to the Duke of Wellington in Nineteenth-Century Ireland: Forging British and Imperial Identities', *Irish*

Geography, 46, no. 1–2 (2013), 129–59; H. Murray, 'A Case of Mistaken Identity: Hudson v. Leeman', *York Historian*, 23 (2006), 8–20; G. Hicks, 'Parliament Square: The Making of a Political Space', *Landscapes*, 16, no. 2 (2015), 164–81; S. J. Burch, 'On Stage at the Theatre of State: The Monuments and Memorials in Parliament Square, London' (PhD dissertation, Nottingham Trent University, 2003).

13 P. A. Pickering and A. Tyrrell eds., *Contested Sites. Commemoration, Memorial and Popular Politics in Nineteenth-century Britain* (Aldershot: Ashgate, 2004); P. A. Pickering, 'The Chartist Rites of Passage: Commemorating Feargus O'Connor', in ibid., 101–26. On radical commemorations, see also S. Poole, '"The Instinct for Hero Worship Works Blindly": English Radical Democrats and the Problem of Memorialization', *Patterns of Prejudice*, 54, no. 5 (2020), 503–12.

14 Miller, *Politics Personified*, 157–9; Vernon, *Politics and the People*, 58–62.

15 The counties covered are Cheshire*, Cumberland*, Derbyshire, Durham*, Herefordshire*, Lancashire*, Leicestershire*, Lincolnshire, Northamptonshire, Northumberland*, Nottinghamshire, Rutland*, Shropshire*, Staffordshire*, Warwickshire*, Westmorland*, Worcestershire* and Yorkshire. Those counties marked * are covered by the PMSA's published volumes, as is South Yorkshire (including Sheffield). For the PMSA's National Recording Project, see https://www.vads.ac.uk/digital/collection/PMSA.

16 Wyke, 'Marginal Figures', 85.

17 On the concept of 'afterlives', see D. Cherry ed., *The Afterlives of Monuments* (London: Routledge, 2014), 1ff.

18 The total number of MPs elected for constituencies in England, Ireland, Scotland and Wales between 1832 and the last by-election before the general election of 1868 is 2,591, according to the latest calculation of the History of Parliament's House of Commons, 1832–68 project: https://victoriancommons.wordpress.com/about/.

19 The MPs commemorated with more than one statue were Thomas Attwood; Richard Bourke, 6th Earl of Mayo (known as Lord Naas during his time in the Commons); John Bright; Spencer Cavendish, 8th Duke of Devonshire (Lord Cavendish/Marquess of Hartington); Robert Gascoyne-Cecil, 3rd Marquess of Salisbury (Lord Robert Cecil/Viscount Cranborne); Richard Cobden; Benjamin Disraeli; William Edward Forster; William Gladstone; George Howard, 6th Earl of Carlisle (Viscount Morpeth); George Robinson, 1st Marquess of Ripon (Viscount Goderich); Samuel Morley; Robert Peel; Titus Salt; Edward Smith-Stanley, 14th Earl of Derby (Edward Stanley/Lord Stanley); Frederick Stanley, 16th Earl of Derby (Hon. Frederick Stanley); and Charles Pelham Villiers. In addition, a reduced size copy of the statue of William Cavendish, 7th Duke of Devonshire (Lord Cavendish) at Eastbourne was subsequently given to the Fitzwilliam Museum, Cambridge, to mark his service as chancellor of the university: *London Evening Standard*, 14 February 1908.

20 J. J. Sexby, *The Municipal Parks, Gardens, and Open Spaces of London* (London: Elliott Stock, 1898), 266; *The Times*, 10 September 1906; *Daily News*, 17 January 1907; *Westminster Gazette*, 20 July 1909; *Newcastle Journal*, 18 June 1861; *Newcastle Daily Chronicle*, 5 December 1865; *Daily Telegraph & Courier*, 23 May 1871; https://historicengland.org.uk/listing/the-list/list-entry/1342041. Forster was also commemorated with a statue in his Bradford constituency (1890), but Lawson's family rejected proposals for a statue in his native Cumberland. Unless otherwise stated, the dates given in this chapter in relation to statues refer to the date of their unveiling (or installation, in cases where there was no formal unveiling).

21 This latter figure includes Thomas Attwood, who had the unusual honour of two statues in Birmingham (1859 and 1993), and Samuel Morley, remembered in both his Bristol (1887) and Nottingham (1888) constituencies.
22 *Derby Daily Telegraph*, 7 May 1884, 10 April 1885.
23 *Leeds Mercury*, 31 July 1876.
24 *Bradford Observer*, 31 July 1876; *Yorkshire Post*, 31 July 1876.
25 *Liverpool Mail*, 26 December 1874.
26 H. Miller, 'Biggs, John', J. Owen, 'Candlish, John', K. Rix, 'Crossley, Francis' and 'Platt, John', in *The History of Parliament. The House of Commons, 1832–68*, ed., P. Salmon and K. Rix (forthcoming); G. T. Noszlopy and F. Waterhouse, *Public Sculpture of Staffordshire and the Black Country* (Liverpool: Liverpool University Press, 2005), 39. Biggs, Candlish and Platt had also served their towns as mayor.
27 E. Morris and E. Roberts, *Public Sculpture of Cheshire and Merseyside (Excluding Liverpool)* (Liverpool: Liverpool University Press, 2012), 61.
28 *Yorkshire Gazette*, 13 April 1867; *Leeds Mercury*, 23 May 1867.
29 G. T. Noszlopy and F. Waterhouse, *Public Sculpture of Herefordshire, Shropshire and Worcestershire* (Liverpool: Liverpool University Press, 2010), xxi.
30 *The Census of Great Britain in 1851* (London: Longman, Brown, Green and Longmans, 1854), 181; *Supplement to the thirty-fifth annual report of the registrar-general of births, marriages and deaths in England and Wales* (HMSO, London: 1875), clxiv; J. Lewis ed., *Digest of the Census of 1871* (London: Edward Stanford, 1873), 161; *Burnley Express*, 13 September 1884.
31 D. A. Cross, *Public Sculpture of Lancashire and Cumbria* (Liverpool: Liverpool University Press, 2017), 133; *Huddersfield Chronicle*, 3 August 1874; https://historicengland.org.uk/listing/the-list/list-entry/113341; *Eastbourne Gazette*, 19 January 1898; *West Sussex County Times*, 29 October 1910. The eighth Duke of Devonshire was also among the leading statesmen honoured with a statue in London: *Westminster Gazette*, 19 March 1909.
32 *Northern Echo*, 30 June 2000, 15 December 2000, 22 February 2002, 21 March 2002, https://www.thenorthernecho.co.uk/news/7136347.sleepers-carved-railway-town/; https://www.thenorthernecho.co.uk/news/7122766.scrap-metal-art-town-splits-sculptures/; https://www.thenorthernecho.co.uk/news/7083660.letters-not-good-enough/; https://www.thenorthernecho.co.uk/news/7080589.go-ahead-controversial-works-art/; *Fleetwood Weekly News*, 9 May 2018, https://www.fleetwoodtoday.co.uk/news/sir-peter-celebrated-statue-unveiled-1032432.
33 T. Wyke, *Public Sculpture of Greater Manchester* (Liverpool: Liverpool University Press, 2004), 319; *Herts Advertiser*, 27 October 1906; *Manchester Courier*, 23 July 1859; *Haslemere Herald*, 9 September 2016, https://www.haslemereherald.com/article.cfm?id=113438&headline=Dame%20Penelope%20unveils%20Cobbett%20statue&sectionIs=news&searchyear=2016. The Cobbett statue is situated in the somewhat incongruous surroundings of the Churchill Retirement Living Complex, whose parent company donated £10,000 of the £50,000 cost.
34 Cross, *Public Sculpture of Lancashire and Cumbria*, 136–7; *Friend of India and Statesman*, 2 May 1867; J. P. Lewis, *List of Inscriptions on Tombstones and Monuments in Ceylon* (Colombo: H. C. Cottle, 1913), 337–8. Carlisle also had a statue erected by his tenants in Cumberland. Mayo had a statue in his Cockermouth constituency, as well as three statues in India: Cross, *Public Sculpture of Lancashire and Cumbria*, 160. Statues of Ripon, all by the same sculptor, were erected at Ripon (1912), Madras (1914)

and Calcutta (1915): *Voice of India*, 2 October 1909; *Englishman's Overland Mail*, 17 November 1910, 3 December 1914; *Ripon Observer*, 9 May 1912, 29 April 1915.
35 Viscountess Amberley's journal, 13 June 1866, in B. and P. Russell eds., *The Amberley Papers* (New York: W. W. Norton & Co., 1937), i. 512; Cavanagh, *Public Sculpture of Liverpool*, 280.
36 S. Morgan, 'The Reward of Public Service: Nineteenth-Century Testimonials in Context', *Historical Research*, 80, no. 208 (2007), 261–85.
37 *Dictionary of National Biography. Second supplement. Vol. I* (London: Oxford University Press, 1912), 108.
38 Miller, *Politics Personified*, 155–7.
39 Noszlopy and Waterhouse, *Public Sculpture of Herefordshire, Shropshire and Worcestershire*, 26–7; https://artuk.org/discover/artworks/monument-to-sir-george-cornewall-lewis-271854; Cross, *Public Sculpture of Lancashire and Cumbria*, 123.
40 Miller, *Politics Personified*, 1.
41 Read, *Peel and the Victorians*, 287.
42 *Carlisle Journal*, 6 July 1844.
43 *Nottingham Evening Post*, 12 October 1888; *Liverpool Daily Post*, 1 November 1877, cited in Morris and Roberts, *Public Sculpture of Cheshire and Merseyside*, 24.
44 Miller, *Politics Personified*, 159. See also Wyke, 'Marginal Figures', 93.
45 *Leeds Mercury*, 21 September 1850.
46 E. Baines Jun., *The Life of Edward Baines* (London: Longman, Brown, Green and Longmans, 1851), 368.
47 *Morning Post*, 28 March 1856.
48 *Northern Echo*, 23 April 1874.
49 *Derby Mercury*, 4 June 1884.
50 *Nottingham Evening Post*, 29 December 1886.
51 *Ripon Observer*, 28 March 1901, 14 October 1909.
52 *Bradford Daily Telegraph*, 10 May 1870.
53 *Liverpool Mail*, 26 December 1874. See also the decision of the memorial committee at Darlington to honour Pease with a statue rather than replicating his philanthropic endeavours: *Northern Echo*, 30 July 1874.
54 Cross, *Public Sculpture of Lancashire and Cumbria*, 148; Cavanagh, *Public Sculpture of Liverpool*, 175.
55 Cross, *Public Sculpture of Lancashire and Cumbria*, 107–8.
56 *Eastbourne Gazette*, 22 May 1895; *Eastbourne Chronicle*, 19 June 1897; *Derby Daily Telegraph*, 4 February 1899. John's statue was nine feet high rather than the ten proposed by Thornycroft.
57 Gaunt, *Sir Robert Peel*, 146.
58 *Derbyshire Advertiser and Journal*, 30 May 1884.
59 Cross, *Public Sculpture of Lancashire and Cumbria*, 132–3.
60 *Northern Echo*, 23 April 1874.
61 *Nottingham Evening Post*, 14 December 1886, 12 October 1888.
62 *Fleetwood Chronicle*, 4 January 1845, 15 March 1845.
63 *Ripon Observer*, 7 October 1909.
64 This was the case with Cobden's statue at Manchester, where some of the excess funds were used for a chair of political economy at Owens College, which his fellow MP Thomas Bayley Potter contended would be more in keeping with Cobden's views: Wyke, *Public Sculpture of Greater Manchester*, 125–6.

65 P. Elliott, 'Nottingham Arboretum's Oldest Figure: The Troublesome Statue of Feargus O'Connor', http://www.ng-spaces.org.uk/nottingham-arboretums-oldest-figure-the-troublesome-statue-of-feargus-oconnor/. See also Pickering, 'Chartist rites of passage', 114–19.
66 *Leeds Mercury*, 25 July 1857.
67 *Leeds Times*, 25 July 1857; *Leeds Mercury*, 18 July 1861. On Hall's career, see K. Rix, 'Hall, Robert' in Salmon and Rix, *House of Commons, 1832–68* (forthcoming).
68 Read, *Victorian Sculpture*, 107n.; Cross, *Public Sculpture of Lancashire and Cumbria*, xiv. On the 1850s as the decisive decade for shifting attitudes to public sculpture, see also Wyke, *Public Sculpture of Greater Manchester*, 3.
69 Cross, *Public Sculpture of Lancashire and Cumbria*, 108; Read, *Peel and the Victorians*, 298. Statues were also erected at Manchester (1853), Liverpool (1854), Cheapside, London (1855), Birmingham (1855), Bradford (1855), Glasgow (1859), Huddersfield (1873) and Parliament Square (1877): Read, *Peel and the Victorians*, 296, 298, 300; Cavanagh, *Public Sculpture of Liverpool*, 271.
70 Read, *Peel and the Victorians*, 296; *Hansard*, 25 June 1868, vol. 192, cc. 2140–1.
71 *Tavistock Gazette*, 13 April 1865.
72 *Bradford Daily Telegraph*, 10 May 1870.
73 C. Patmore, 'Shall Smith Have a Statue?', in *Principle in Art Etc.*, ed. C. Patmore (London: George Bell and Sons, 1889), 141.
74 Anon., *Prodigious!!! Or, Childe Paddie in London*, 3 vols. (London: W. Wilson, 1818), i. 194.
75 Cavanagh, *Public Sculpture of Liverpool*, 75, 150; J. J. Sheahan, *General and Concise History and Description of the Town and Port of Kingston-upon-Hull* (London: Simpkin, Marshall & Co., 1864), 503; *Hull Packet*, 1 November 1833.
76 T. Carlyle, 'Hudson's Statue', in T. Carlyle ed., *Latter-Day Pamphlets* (London: Chapman and Hall, 1850), 1–2. This pamphlet was dated 1 July 1850.
77 *Carlisle Journal*, 4 July 1840, 23 January 1841. The cause of his death was given as 'apoplexy'. He had been chairman since 1818: J. Owen, 'Aglionby, Francis Yates', in Salmon and Rix, *House of Commons, 1832–68* (forthcoming).
78 *Carlisle Journal*, 23 January 1841, 27 February 1841, 9 July 1842, 29 June 1844; Cross, *Public Sculpture of Lancashire and Cumbria*, 148.
79 *Newcastle Courant*, 8 November 1844.
80 *Fleetwood Chronicle*, 4 January 1845.
81 *Lincolnshire Chronicle*, 23 October 1846; *Stamford Mercury*, 1 June 1849. The eventual memorial cost nearly £1,000: *Stamford Mercury*, 25 April 1851.
82 E. Trollope, *Sleaford, and the Wapentakes of Flaxwell and Aswardhurn* (London: W. Kent & Co., 1872), 169. The memorial to William Duncombe, 1st Earl of Feversham, unveiled at Helmsley in 1871, was in a similar format.
83 *Lincolnshire Chronicle*, 23 October 1846; *Stamford Mercury*, 2 May 1851; *Journal of the Royal Agricultural Society of England* (1841), vol. 2, lxxxvi.
84 *Lincolnshire Chronicle*, 23 October 1846; *Stamford Mercury*, 23 October 1846.
85 *The Assembled Commons; or, Parliamentary Biographer* (London: Scott, Webster and Geary, 1838), 110; *Stamford Mercury*, 28 June 1850.
86 Noszlopy and Waterhouse, *Public Sculpture of Staffordshire and the Black Country*, xx.
87 Statues were typically unveiled within two to five years of the project being instigated.
88 Wyke, *Public Sculpture of Greater Manchester*, xi.
89 There were also three statues to Ripon, two to Salisbury and two to the eighth Duke of Devonshire.

90 *Wigan Observer and District Advertiser*, 12 November 1910.
91 Noszlopy and Waterhouse, *Public Sculpture of Staffordshire and the Black Country*, xx. On changing patterns of memorialization after the First World War, see also Hicks, 'Parliament Square', 172–3.
92 Wyke, *Public Sculpture of Greater Manchester*, 35. See also Cross, *Public Sculpture of Lancashire and Cumbria*, 131; Cavanagh, *Public Sculpture of Liverpool*, 173; and Wyke, 'Marginal Figures', 91. Taking the first statue erected to each of the forty-two MPs commemorated posthumously, thirty-four were initiated within a year of their death, three within two years and only five more belatedly.
93 These four were the fourteenth Earl of Derby, whose Liverpool statue was initiated before his death, Samuel Morley (Bristol), Sir Stafford Northcote (Exeter) and Lord Ripon (Madras and Calcutta). Morley and Ripon also had statue projects instigated after their deaths, at Nottingham and Ripon, respectively.
94 Cavanagh, *Public Sculpture of Liverpool*, 279; Wyke, *Public Sculpture of Greater Manchester*, x; *Pall Mall Budget*, 11 August 1882; *Pall Mall Gazette*, 14 December 1883.
95 Cavanagh, *Public Sculpture of Liverpool*, 277; *Liverpool Mercury*, 6 June 1867. Derby had sat in the Commons until 1844.
96 Cavanagh, *Public Sculpture of Liverpool*, 274; *Belfast News-Letter*, 17 October 1860.
97 Morris and Roberts, *Public Sculpture of Cheshire and Merseyside*, 61; *Leeds Mercury*, 3 September 1857; *Barnsley Chronicle*, 11 August 1860.
98 *Daily Telegraph*, 8 October 1874. He was commemorated with a statue after his death.
99 *Leicester Guardian*, 2 February 1870.
100 Barlo and D. Shaw (eds.), *Balgarnie's Salt, with Commentary and Additions* (Saltaire: Nemine Jevante, 2003), 215; *Knaresborough Post*, 15 August 1874.
101 *Leeds Mercury*, 31 July 1876.
102 *Birmingham Daily Post*, 8 June 1882; R. A. J. Walling ed., *The Diaries of John Bright* (London: Cassell and Company, 1930), 372 [entry for 13 July 1875], 504 [entry for 2 August 1883].
103 *Bradford Daily Telegraph*, 12 April 1907; H. L. P. Hulbert, *Sir Francis Sharp Powell Baronet and Member of Parliament: A Memoir* (Leeds: R. Jackson, 1914), 143–5; *Wigan Observer and District Advertiser*, 8 November 1910. Powell had been elected for Wigan in 1857 but had not represented it continuously, sitting for Wigan 1857–9, 1881–2 and 1885–January 1910, Cambridge 1863–8, and the Northern division of the West Riding 1872–4.
104 *Leeds Mercury*, 8 June 1888. Villiers had intended to attend the unveiling of his Wolverhampton statue in 1879 but was prevented from doing so by illness: R. Swift, *Charles Pelham Villiers: Aristocratic Victorian Radical* (London: Routledge, 2017), 212.
105 Read, *Peel and the Victorians*, 294.
106 *Derbyshire Advertiser and Journal*, 30 May 1884.
107 *Carlisle Journal*, 24 April 1841.
108 *Birmingham Journal*, 25 July 1857; *Illustrated London News*, 18 June 1859.
109 Gaunt, *Sir Robert Peel*, 147.
110 *Wolverhampton Express and Star*, 16 May 1876; *Manchester Times*, 20 May 1876.
111 *Nottingham Journal*, 8 September 1886.
112 Vernon, *Politics and the People*, 62.
113 *Manchester Courier*, 16 September 1878.

114 Wyke, 'Marginal Figures', 92. On this process in Manchester, Birmingham and Leeds, see Gunn, *Public Culture of the Victorian Middle Class*, 50–3.
115 Wyke, *Public Sculpture of Greater Manchester*, 3, 112.
116 *Derbyshire Advertiser and Journal*, 12 June 1885; *Derby Daily Telegraph*, 6 August 1885.
117 *Soulby's Ulverston Advertiser and General Intelligencer*, 15 August 1889. The 'colossal' scale usually used for exterior statues was 50% larger than life: G. T. Noszlopy, *Public Sculpture of Birmingham* (Liverpool: Liverpool University Press, 1998), xvi.
118 Cross, *Public Sculpture of Lancashire and Cumbria*, 148.
119 *Liverpool Weekly Courier*, 1 February 1873.
120 *Leicester Chronicle*, 27 April 1872, cited In T. Cavanagh and A. Yarrington, *Public Sculpture of Leicestershire and Rutland* (Liverpool: Liverpool University Press, 2000), 181.
121 *Wolverhampton Express and Star*, 18 and 24 May 1876.
122 *Wolverhampton Express and Star*, 24 October 1878.
123 *Hereford Times*, 17 October 1863; Noszlopy and Waterhouse, *Public Sculpture of Herefordshire, Shropshire and Worcestershire*, 26.
124 *Leeds Mercury*, 15 April 1872; *Bradford Observer*, 3 August 1874.
125 *Dublin Evening Mail*, 20 September 1865; *Todmorden Advertiser*, 4 September 1874; *Bradford Observer*, 5 April 1875. The statue, whose casting and erection had already been delayed by the difficult economic circumstances of the 'cotton famine', had arrived in Todmorden in 1868.
126 *Manchester Courier*, 23 July 1859; *Burnley Advertiser*, 20 August 1859.
127 *Daily News*, 13 November 1862; *Bradford Observer*, 5 April 1875.
128 *Manchester Evening News*, 2 March 1875. The Fieldens gave £40,000 for the town hall.
129 Cross, *Public Sculpture of Lancashire and Cumbria*, 25–6; *Cotton Factory Times*, 20 September 1907. Other statues funded by individuals included Gladstone at Bow (given by Theodore Bryant) and Albert Square, Manchester (funded by a legacy from William Roberts, a local architect and surveyor); Cobden at Bradford (for which a Bradford merchant, George Henry Booth, gave £1,000 to mark his retirement from business); and the unusual double statue of Charles Turner and his son in the Turner Memorial Home, Liverpool (funded by Turner's widow): *Pall Mall Budget*, 11 August 1882; Wyke, *Public Sculpture of Greater Manchester*, 22; *York Herald*, 5 October 1872; Cavanagh, *Public Sculpture of Liverpool*, 44.
130 Cross, *Public Sculpture of Lancashire and Cumbria*, 90.
131 *Edinburgh Evening News*, 31 March 1874.
132 *Derby Daily Telegraph*, 7 May 1884; *Derby Mercury*, 14 May 1884.
133 *Staffordshire Advertiser*, 20 May 1876; *Wolverhampton Express and Star*, 17 June 1876.
134 Wyke, 'Memorial Mania', 71.
135 *Carlisle Patriot*, 6 March 1841.
136 *Wigan Observer and District Advertiser*, 13 April 1907.
137 *West Cumberland Times*, 21 August 1875; *Bradford Observer*, 24 June 1870; *Yorkshire Post and Leeds Intelligencer*, 3 August 1874.
138 Wyke, 'Memorial Mania', 71.
139 *Leicester Journal*, 26 April 1872; Cavanagh and Yarrington, *Public Sculpture of Leicestershire and Rutland*, 178; Wyke, *Public Sculpture of Greater Manchester*, 195.
140 Wyke, 'Memorial Mania', 71–2.

141 J. Owen, 'Clifton, Sir Robert', in Salmon and Rix, *House of Commons, 1832–68* (forthcoming).
142 *Nottingham Journal*, 9 June 1869. On Pare, who died before the statue was completed, see *Nottinghamshire Guardian*, 7 March 1879.
143 *Nottinghamshire Guardian*, 24 September 1869, 15 October 1869; *Nottingham Journal*, 29 September 1869.
144 *Nottingham Journal*, 24 May 1873.
145 *Newark Herald*, 7 March 1874; *Nottingham Journal*, 19 May 1875, 31 October 1875.
146 *Nottinghamshire Guardian*, 6 July 1877, 4 May 1883; *Nottingham Journal*, 25 May 1883.
147 *Nottingham Journal*, 29 September 1869, 22 November 1869.
148 *Nottinghamshire Guardian*, 17 June 1881; *Nottingham Journal*, 25 May 1883.
149 *Hereford Journal*, 11 July 1863.
150 Wyke, 'Memorial Mania', 74. For an example, see the description and illustration of Joseph Brotherton's statue at Salford in G. Measom, *The Official Illustrated Guide to the North-Western Railway* (London: W.H. Smith and Son/Arthur Hall, Virtue and Co., 1859), 448.
151 *Todmorden & District News*, 7 March 1913.
152 *Sheffield Daily Telegraph*, 15 November 1858; B. Wilson, *The Struggles of an Old Chartist* (Halifax: J. Nicholson, 1887), 24.
153 *Illustrated Times*, 29 October 1864.
154 *Liverpool Weekly Courier*, 26 April 1884. On commemorations at the Disraeli statue in Parliament Square, see G. E. Buckle, *The Life of Benjamin Disraeli. Volume VI 1876–1881* (London: John Murray, 1920), 630–1.
155 *Liverpool Evening Express*, 19 April 1939.
156 *Craven Herald*, 27 April 1889.
157 *Batley Reporter and Guardian*, 7 August 1886; *Craven Herald*, 27 April 1889. Wilson lived nearby at Eshton Hall, had been the Skipton division's first MP, 1885–6, and had been chairman of the highway board and board of guardians, among other local roles: *Leeds Mercury*, 19 February 1887.
158 *Leeds Mercury*, 30 June 1888.
159 *Sheffield Daily Telegraph*, 17 November 1911; *Manchester Evening News*, 26 March 1914.
160 *Lincolnshire Chronicle*, 10 October 1862, 17 July 1863.
161 *Boston Guardian*, 15 July 1899; *Lincolnshire Standard and Boston Guardian*, 9 November 1929.
162 Elliott, 'Nottingham Arboretum's Oldest Figure'; https://riponcivicsociety.org.uk/2009/07/03/marking-the-marquess/.
163 *Staffordshire Advertiser*, 8 October 1932.
164 *Leicester Evening Mail*, 10 June 1946, 22 January 1949.
165 J. A. Sullivan, *The Politics of the Pantomime. Regional Identity in the Theatre, 1860–1900* (Hatfield: University of Hertfordshire Press, 2011), 125–6.
166 *Stamford Mercury*, 9 April 1880; Cross, *Public Sculpture of Lancashire and Cumbria*, 105. Violence at Ingram's statue had been averted in 1874 after the police removed a blue ribbon tied around its neck on the night a judge arrived in Boston to try an election petition: *Boston Guardian*, 13 June 1874.
167 *Rochdale Times*, 22 August 1914. For another example of this phenomenon, see the poem 'The New Fugitive Slave Law. Joseph Pease's (Bronze Statue) Remonstrance',

which presented Pease's Darlington statue as an opponent of this legislation: *Northern Echo*, cited in *The British Friend*, 1 November 1875.
168 *Rochdale Observer*, 15 January 1910.
169 *Police Review and Parade Gossip*, cited in *Rochdale Times*, 25 February 1911; *Rochdale Observer*, 6 May 1914.
170 *Manchester Evening News*, 9 March 1923.
171 Wyke, 'Marginal Figures', 95.
172 *Leicester Evening Mail*, 23 October 1925, 30 January 1929, 19 July 1930; Cavanagh and Yarrington, *Public Sculpture of Leicestershire and Rutland*, 180–1.
173 *Leicester Evening Mail*, 22 and 24 January 1949. After a brief sojourn in a council depot, the statue was installed in De Montfort Square in 1952. It returned to its original site in 1967 but was moved to a slightly different position in Welford Place in 1991: Cavanagh and Yarrington, *Public Sculpture of Leicestershire and Rutland*, 181.
174 https://historicengland.org.uk/listing/the-list/list-entry/1384493; Chonkinfeckle, 'Francis Powell's Foot', https://www.youtube.com/watch?v=6O46Lgx4z0s.
175 Heritage Fund news announcement, 1 October 2010, https://www.heritagefund.org.uk/news/mesnes-park-ps19million-lottery-funding-announced; Noszlopy, *Public Sculpture of Birmingham*, xxi.
176 Wyke, *Public Sculpture of Greater Manchester*, 7.
177 Two rare examples of statues which no longer survive are those of Cobden, formerly in Peel Park, Salford (1867), which was removed in 1954 to make way for college buildings, and whose whereabouts have been unknown since, and Peel's Huddersfield statue, removed from St. George's Square when it was in poor condition in 1949, of which only the plinth survives, in the garden of the Tolson Museum: Wyke, *Public Sculpture of Greater Manchester*, 52, 199; https://www.friendsoftolson.org.uk/formation-and-history/100-items-about-the-museum-and-huddersfield/21-to-30/.
178 Archer, *Public Sculpture*, 137; Morris and Roberts, *Public Sculpture of Cheshire and Merseyside*, 26; https://www.cravenherald.co.uk/news/19345357.nostalgia-moving-sir-mathew-wilson-statue-skipton-high-street/; Wyke, *Public Sculpture of Greater Manchester*, 346; *Shields Daily News*, 25 October 1921.
179 *Aberdeen Free Press*, 14 September 1885; *Sheffield Independent*, 19 September 1885; *Yorkshire Post and Leeds Intelligencer*, 12 April 1890.
180 *Shipley Times and Express*, 13 April 1889; *Wharfedale & Airedale Observer*, 12 October 1894, 6 March 1896; *Bradford Weekly Telegraph*, 2 May 1896.
181 Wyke, 'Marginal Figures', 90; Wyke, *Public Sculpture of Greater Manchester*, 285, 307; *Manchester Evening News*, 13 August 2007, https://www.manchestereveningnews.co.uk/news/local-news/no-sir-we-didnt-like-your-980351. The planned bus station in Rochdale was abandoned after a brief experiment, but Bright's statue had already been moved to Broadfield Park.
182 *Birmingham Daily Gazette*, 26 February 1925, 19 June 1925; *Westminster Gazette*, 3 March 1927.
183 Noszlopy, *Public Sculpture of Birmingham*, 30–1, 72–3; *Birmingham Mail*, 5 June 2008, https://www.birminghammail.co.uk/news/local-news/new-home-for-statue-of-brums-first-64367.
184 Noszlopy, *Public Sculpture of Birmingham*, 103–4. The statue's plinth remained in the park.
185 https://www.birminghamcivicsociety.org.uk/sir-robert-peel-statue/. In a similar vein, the Peel statue erected in Cheapside, London, in 1855 was moved to the police

college at Hendon in the 1950s: https://historicengland.org.uk/listing/the-list/list-entry/1249503?section=official-listing.
186 *Nottingham Journal*, 7 February 1903. For earlier criticisms, see *Nottingham Evening Post*, 14 December 1886.
187 *Nottingham Journal*, 7 July 1903; R. Graham, 'Trousers in Sculpture', *Strand Magazine*, xxvii, no. 157 (January 1904), 79–80. The *Nottingham Journal* referred to this article later that year: *Nottingham Journal*, 7 June 1904.
188 *Nottingham Evening Post*, 6 July 1903; *Nottingham Journal*, 7 July 1903.
189 *Lichfield Mercury*, 8 December 1905. Claims that Morley's statue would be better treated proved erroneous. It was replaced by a cheaper bronze bust in 1927 after being badly damaged when it fell off a lorry while being relocated from Theatre Square, where it was inconveniencing traffic, to Nottingham's Arboretum: *Nottingham Evening Post*, 28 September 1926; *Nottingham Journal*, 15 January 1927, 11 August 1927, 13 December 1928.
190 Wyke, *Public Sculpture of Greater Manchester*, 52; *Manchester Evening News*, 26 May 2018, https://www.manchestereveningnews.co.uk/news/greater-manchester-news/statue-much-loved-mp-returned-14703665.
191 https://www.diytheatre.org.uk/2021/05/sound-sculpture-trail-for-peel-park/; https://www.salford.gov.uk/media/396636/joseph-brotherton-scuplture.mp3.
192 P. Usherwood, J. Beach and C. Morris, *Public Sculpture of North-East England* (Liverpool: Liverpool University Press, 2000), 234; https://artuk.org/discover/artworks/monument-to-joseph-pease-17991872-308547/search/keyword:member-of-parliament-and-statue–referrer:global-search/page/1/view_as/grid.
193 Usherwood, Beach and Morris, *Public Sculpture*, 232–3.
194 J. S. Jeans ed., *Railway Jubilee at Darlington, September 27th and 18th, 1875* (Darlington: E. D. Walker, 1875), 19–20.
195 https://historicengland.org.uk/research/inclusive-heritage/the-slave-trade-and-abolition/legacies-of-slavery-and-abolition-in-listed-places/; https://historicengland.org.uk/listing/the-list/list-entry/1322930; *Northern Echo*, 13 June 2020, https://www.thenorthernecho.co.uk/history/18513980.proud-darlingtons-statue-joseph-pease/.
196 *Manchester Evening News*, 13 August 2007, https://www.manchestereveningnews.co.uk/news/local-news/damage-fear-rules-out-bright-1078532; *The Guardian*, 19 September 2016, https://www.theguardian.com/uk-news/2016/sep/19/our-gracie-comes-home-rochdale-salutes-gracie-fields-with-statue.
197 Wyke, *Public Sculpture of Greater Manchester*, 285; *Oldham Chronicle*, 14 December 2018, https://www.oldham-chronicle.co.uk/news-features/139/main-news/124818/emotions-run-high-as-beautiful-annie-kenney-statue-is-unveiled. In 2020 two Conservative parish councillors suggested that Platt's statue be relocated to his birthplace at Dobcross but drew opposition on cost grounds: *Saddleworth Independent*, 9 September 2020, https://saddind.co.uk/call-to-move-john-platt-statue/; *Oldham Times*, 22 September 2020, https://www.theoldhamtimes.co.uk/news/18738040.row-siting-statue-memory-industrialist-john-platt/.
198 *Telegraph & Argus*, 6 and 15 November 2018, https://www.telegraphandargus.co.uk/news/17202229.bradford-civic-society-debate-future-iconic-titus-salt-statue/; https://www.telegraphandargus.co.uk/news/17223828.civic-society-support-sir-titus-salt-statue-move—say-citys-female-heroes-recognised/.
199 M. Roberts, *Chartism, Commemoration and the Cult of the Radical Hero* (Abingdon: Routledge, 2020), xii.

200 J. Lawrence, *Speaking for the People. Party, Language and Popular Politics in England, 1867–1914* (Cambridge: Cambridge University Press, 1998), 59–60; D. Craig and J. Thompson *Languages of Politics in Nineteenth-Century Britain*, eds., (Basingstoke: Palgrave Macmillan, 2013), 10.
201 P. A. Pickering and A. Tyrrell, 'The Public Memorial of Reform', in Pickering and Tyrrell, *Contested Sites*, 13.
202 Evidence from beyond the regions which have been the focus of this chapter provides further support for this argument, with MPs' statues found in smaller towns including Devizes (honouring Thomas Sotheron-Estcourt, 1879) and Weymouth (Sir Henry Edwards, 1886): https://artuk.org/discover/artworks/thomas-sotheron-estcourt-18011876-statue-and-fountain-308111; *Illustrated London News*, 6 February 1886.

8

Peel's death as family tragedy: Remembering Sir Robert Peel in public and in private

Richard A. Gaunt*

The outpouring of public grief following the death of Sir Robert Peel (1788–1850), as the result of a riding accident in July 1850, and the myriad commemorative formats to which this gave rise, has formed a common reference point in recent considerations of the statesman's posthumous legacy.[1] Yet Peel's death was first and foremost a family tragedy. Using a hitherto neglected group of family papers, comprising personal responses to Peel's death, this chapter considers the extent to which the Peel family initiated, shaped and encouraged the process of posthumous valorization of Peel which took place in the aftermath of the tragedy. Sometimes, this was the direct consequence of the decisions and interventions which they made in the aftermath of Peel's death, but, at other times, it was a process which was outside their control. While historians have traced the individual routes by which communities across the industrial towns of the midlands and the north of England subscribed towards statues or named commemorative amenities (such as parks, towers and public baths) in Peel's memory, the extent to which this ran side by side with – or counter to – more private, family-focused memorialization has not previously been considered. Even before controversies regarding the appropriateness, siting and perpetuation of memorials to Peel emerged, during 2020, historians were aware that the process of commemorating Peel was fraught with difficulty, because it raised issues of civic pride and artistic taste as well as political controversy.[2] However, given that Peel's death is seen as having a particularly transformative effect upon the way in which public figures were commemorated and remembered in Victorian England, the absence of the personal, family voice appears striking.[3] By situating the immediate consequences of Peel's death in its family setting, this chapter helps to restore a sense of context to the wider process of civic and community-based public commemoration to which it gave rise and considers the extent to which these processes engaged, reinforced and interacted with one another.

* I am indebted to the great-great-grandson of Sir Robert Peel, who introduced me to the letter book (hereafter cited as Peel MSS) and allowed me to use it in this chapter. I am also grateful to the archivists at Surrey Record Office (Goulburn MSS) and Gloucestershire Record Office (Sotheron-Estcourt MSS) and to Allan Packwood, the Director of the Churchill Archives Centre, Churchill College, Cambridge (Enoch Powell MSS), for their assistance.

From Constitution Hill to the grave

On Saturday 29 June 1850, after attending a meeting of the Commissioners to the Great Exhibition between 11.00 am and 3.00 pm, Sir Robert Peel took his usual late-afternoon ride in central London. He was still breaking in a new horse, an eight-year-old which had been purchased at Tattersall's by Mr Beckett Denison earlier in the year. It later emerged that the horse had been sold by Sir Henry Peyton because of its unruly tendencies, but Peel was an experienced horseman and his new purchase had been ridden by Denison for three weeks before Peel took possession of it. With a groom in attendance, Peel called at Buckingham Palace, where he signed the visitors' book and made his way up Constitution Hill to Hyde Park Corner. Barely had he acknowledged one of Lord Dover's daughters, who was out riding, with a groom in attendance, when Peel's horse began to plunge, kick, swerve and ultimately throw its rider face downwards to the ground. The horse stumbled and fell, striking Peel's back with its knees. Two bystanders rushed to assist at the scene and were quickly joined by Dr Louis Foucart, a thirty-year-old surgeon from Glasgow, and Sir James Clark, the physician to Queen Victoria. A carriage was procured from Mrs Lucas of Bryanston Square and Peel was taken back to his home, 4 Whitehall Gardens, where he was initially laid on a sofa in the dining room.

From that point, until his death on Tuesday 2 July, Peel was attended by his family doctor of thirty years, Mr Hodgson; the leading surgeon, Sir Benjamin Brodie; Dr E. J. Seymour and Mr Caesar Hawkins, both of St George's Hospital, as well as Mr Shaw and Dr Foucart. Bulletins informing the public of developments began to appear on the gates of Peel's London home from 7.00 pm on Saturday evening, and this led, over the course of the next forty-eight hours, to the well-ordered gathering of hundreds of concerned people outside Whitehall Gardens, as they patiently awaited news of Peel's fate. By Tuesday, Peel appeared to be reviving, was able to walk (supported) for a time, and took some tea and broth. However, he deteriorated rapidly during the afternoon and lapsed into a coma from which he never recovered. At nine minutes past eleven in the evening, surrounded by three of his brothers (Lawrence, John and Jonathan); three of his sons (Frederick, William and Arthur); his son-in-law, Lord Villiers; his close political and personal friends, Sir Henry Hardinge and Sir James Graham; and his doctors, Peel died. He was sixty-two years old.[4]

'How to intrude upon private sorrow'

In the immediate aftermath of Peel's death, his Lancashire cousin, George, was moved to include an uncharacteristic piece of narrative in the commonplace book in which he recorded his financial expenditure: '29 June 1850. This evening about half past 6 on Constitution Hill London, Sir Robert Peel was thrown from his horse and most seriously hurt. He never rallied so as to give hopes of his recovery and died about 10 minutes past 11 on Tuesday evening the 2nd July. He was 62 last February.'[5] Though several family perspectives on Peel's death began to surface, in subsequent years, as the process of bringing the private correspondence, letters and diaries of distinguished Victorians before the public became a major publishing enterprise, a small but important body of material relating to the event remained shielded from public view. A group of approximately seventy letters of condolence, sent to Peel's widow, Julia (1795–1859), and their second son, Frederick (1823–1906), together with several published sermons and memorials generated by Peel's death, were gathered in a volume which bears the legend 'Hampton-in-Arden' on the cover and 'Sir Robert Peel, 1850' on its spine. The material was preserved by Frederick Peel, who lived at the manor house of Hampton in Arden in Warwickshire. Frederick was, according to the *Oxford Dictionary of National Biography*, 'the ablest intellectually of the Peel children, and, from his father's viewpoint, the most dependable'. He was also said to be his mother's favourite. Frederick quickly assumed a crucial role in coordinating family responses to his father's death. This was a matter of circumstance as well as preference. The new baronet, Frederick's elder brother, Robert (1822–95), was still abroad until the autumn of 1850, and his relationship with his parents was far worse than that between Frederick and his mother. Frederick, who was the Liberal MP for Leominster at the time of his father's death, burnished his family credentials still further when he was subsequently returned as MP for Bury, the ancestral birthplace of his father, between 1852–7 and 1859–65. In these circumstances, Frederick became the person to whom condolence letters were invariably addressed by correspondents and the key respondent on behalf of his mother. Meanwhile, legal matters arising from the disposition of Peel's estate were directed through Henry Goulburn, Peel's chancellor of the exchequer, who was one of his executors.[6]

'Nothing requires more delicacy than how to intrude upon private sorrow,' William Leech told Frederick on 18 July 1850. As Pat Jalland has argued, condolence letters, however formulaic their style and content, represent a crucial source of testimony as to the emotional register with which deaths (especially public deaths like that of Peel) were received by the Victorian public.[7] They offer a form of personal memorialization quite separate from the more public, institutionalized, expressions to be found in commissioned monuments and similar artefacts. The fact that the letter book was not deposited, along with the mass of Peel's personal and political correspondence, in the British Museum in the 1920s, gives an indication of their status as documentary testimony, insofar as the Peel family was concerned. After Frederick's death, the letter book descended through the line of Sir Robert Peel's youngest son, Arthur Wellesley Peel (1829–1912), to his son George. It was George who wrote the original entry on his grandfather for the *Dictionary of National Biography* and went on to publish *The Private Letters of Sir Robert Peel* in 1920. The vast bulk of the material in that edition was subsequently destroyed, as a result of wartime enemy bombing in 1941, but the letter book survived, and is now in the custody of George Peel's grandson. Though the papers were consulted by Norman Gash, while researching his two-volume *Life of Sir Robert Peel* in the 1950s, and some of them were subsequently used in that work, the larger part of the material generated by Peel's death has, until now, remained unused.[8]

Peel between death and the doctors

While most surviving letters offer condolences following Peel's death, a small number were written in the immediate aftermath of the accident when correspondents retained a hope that Peel would overcome his injuries. As Edward Clough Taylor, of Firby Hall in Yorkshire, wrote on 2 July, 'his convalescence will be hailed by very many in the county [sic] with joy and delight'. Among those enquiring after news before 2 July were family members such as Edmund Peel, political colleagues including John Young and notable citizens like Robert Lamond of Glasgow. Henry Brougham, a long-time political adversary-turned admirer, was less sanguine, confessing to Frederick on 2 July that he was 'alarmed by the accounts' which he had read. Others offered practical advice. On 1 July, Henry Willoughby recounted his experience of being in St George's Hospital for three weeks after a similar riding accident and noted that he had been treated by Caesar Hawkins who was now in attendance upon Peel. Willoughby recommended that Peel should be placed on a mattress which 'in an inclined position relieved all parts and did not press too much on any sore points'. This advice had already been taken; after his return home, Peel was placed on a patent water mattress, or hydraulic bed, which was raised onto the dining room table.[9]

Contemporary medical accounts, reinforced by later medical opinion, concluded that Peel had died as a result of fracturing several ribs under the left scapula, probably in consequence of his horse's collision with its rider after the fall. Peel had a comminuted fracture of the clavicle; fragments of bone had pierced the major blood vessels and may have introduced infection through the skin wound leading to broncho-pneumonia. Because of Peel's acute sensitivity to pain, his medical attendants maintained that it was not possible to examine his injuries more closely, or treat them more fully, before he died, while the admission of chloroform (which was still in its infancy) would probably have killed the patient, rather than cured him. Consequently, insofar as the doctors who attended him are concerned, 'if they failed to prevent a deterioration in the condition of their patient, it is unlikely that their treatment made the condition worse'.[10]

Few correspondents who wrote to Peel's family after his death were indelicate enough to comment on the precise circumstances attending the accident, or his medical treatment, though the 'old Harrow Boy' who sent a memorial verse in Latin on 17 July recalled that he had been thinking over Peel's accident at the precise moment that 'my mare slipped up and rolled over me – I employed a sleepless night in making the accompanying lines'. However, Charles Frederick Jephs, who claimed to have witnessed the accident, informed Frederick on 4 July that

> the account in the Times newspaper is quite wrong which states that Sir Robert retained the reins and that of [sic] consequence the Horse fell heavily upon him when in fact the animal did not fall at all but merely slightly stumbled previously

to Sir Robert leaving the saddle and was not at any time during the accident within 3 or 4 feet of the spot where Sir Robert fell.[11]

However, outside the family home, a lively controversy was conducted in the pages of *The Lancet* concerning Peel's medical treatment. The official account, attributable to Benjamin Brodie, recounted the medical facts but contextualized them with reference to family sensitivities. Most notable was the observation that 'from consideration to the feelings and express wishes of Lady Peel and her children, no examination of the body [had] taken place' after death.[12]

It was the lack of a post-mortem and coroner's inquest, as well as criticism of Peel's medical treatment, which subsequently attracted most attention. A letter from 'G.L.' acknowledged that an inquest at a corner's court was 'very painful to the feelings of the relatives' but thought that it was incumbent upon the family to have gone through it, nonetheless. John Langley also questioned the lack of a post-mortem and queried why the application of leeches to Peel's shoulder had been delayed so long after the accident. Such were the lingering doubts raised by his medical treatment that, a year after Peel's death, his literary executors, Edward Cardwell and Lord Mahon, asked Brodie for an authorized account, with the intention of publishing it. Brodie agreed a text with Seymour and Hawkins, which was largely consonant with that published in *The Lancet* at the time. The doctors maintained that their priority was to 'maintain circulation and diminish suffering' in the patient. Such was the nature of Peel's injuries, and so acute was his sensitivity to pain, that extensive bloodletting was considered impractical. The only thing which remained 'uncertain', given the lack of a post-mortem, was the 'exact position of the wound in the vein'.[13]

A less savoury postscript to Peel's medical care was provided by Dr Foucart, who had attended Peel from the time of his accident to his death. Foucart disputed the fee which he received from the family for his services, which he considered inferior to that given to his more distinguished colleagues. Foucart's complaint initially went to Peel's brother, John, before being referred to Goulburn. Foucart maintained that he had undergone eighty hours unwearied attendance on Peel and that this was followed, at Lady Peel's express request, by two days' constant attendance on the body, which he watched under lock and key until it was removed from Whitehall Gardens.[14] As a result of 'breathing the confined atmosphere poisoned by the effusion of decomposition', Foucart had subsequently been ill for six weeks, and in consequence 'my professional appointments and practice in Glasgow were for ever lost'. In seeking the family's support for his application as assistant surgeon in the East India Company, Foucart commented, 'I have sacrificed the whole of my worldly position and welfare for the sake of Sir Robert, surely it is not demanding too much that something be done for me'. Having failed to persuade Goulburn to augment his fee, Foucart proceeded to petition Lady Peel and the new baronet, in vain. Goulburn's growing irritation with Foucart was reinforced by Brodie, who was horrified to find that his name was being given as a referee for Foucart's pretentions. Foucart was described tartly by one correspondent as a man 'marked with the small-pox [who] dresses rather flashily', and his claims of family impoverishment are countered by the knowledge that his parents in Glasgow were 'well enough off to employ a live-in house servant' at the time of the 1851 census.[15]

Public funerals and private grief

On 3 July 1850, Joseph Hume moved that the House of Commons should adjourn as a mark of respect to Peel, who had served as a member of parliament for forty-one years; the motion received unanimous support.[16] Thoughts now turned to the proposal, fast gaining ground, for granting Peel a public funeral. In practical terms, a public funeral required a parliamentary resolution to sanction the use of public funds to meet the full costs. By contrast, private funerals, 'however extensive the popular interest, were ... the responsibility of relatives and executors, with decisions on matters such as policing being made on an *ad hoc* basis'.[17]

'I am ready for my own part to support a motion for a public funeral,' the Whig prime minister, Lord John Russell, told Sir James Graham on 3 July, 'if such be the wish of the friends and the family of Sir Robert Peel'. One such friend, Hardinge, was in no doubt about the matter – not only did the proposal do 'the Queen and Lord John credit. It must be in Westminster Abbey'. However, by the family's express desire, and in conformity with Peel's known wishes, a public funeral was declined. Instead, his committal was a private affair, and he was buried next to his parents at St Peter's, Drayton Bassett, on 9 July.[18]

Both the offer of a public funeral, and the family's decision to decline it, generated widespread praise, amplifying the emotions which Peel's death had begun to generate:

> The last and highest honour that a grateful country could offer – *a public funeral* – has been made ... and declined only in deference to feelings elevated far above human vanity and earthly pageantry. Obsequies devoid of parade and ostentation, and silent repose by the dust of his revered parents ... were his constant and last wish – his peculiar choice.[19]

Peel's determination that his final resting place should be 'in a quiet nook of an obscure country church' suggested a man devoid of worldly ambition – a fit example for others to emulate.[20]

However, the family's decision to decline a public funeral stimulated alternative methods for paying respects. On 3 July, Edward Buxton of Southwold had expressed the hope that 'a public funeral might be given to' Peel, as this would be 'cordially responded to by the great mass of the people'. In the absence of a national focal point for their grief, people across the country determined to mark their respects in alternative ways, including suspending all business, ringing the bells of churches muffled and hoisting flags at half-mast, at the time of Peel's funeral.[21]

In much the same way, Lady Peel's decision to decline all honours given in her husband's name reinforced the sense of his and, by extension, his family's selflessness. On 11 July 1850, Russell wrote to Lady Peel, advising her of Queen Victoria's wish to make her a Viscountess, 'as a mark of Her Majesty's appreciation of the eminent services rendered to the Crown and the nation by the late Sir Robert Peel'. Julia Peel responded that a paper in his own handwriting has just been given to me – in which he expressly desires – that no member of his family will accept (if offered), any title – distinction – or reward, on account of service he may have rendered in Parliament or in office … permit me to cherish obedience to the wishes of my dearly loved husband.[22]

In writing to Lady Peel, some days after this determination was made public, the writer Jane Loudon offered a 'humble tribute of admiration for your Ladyship's noble conduct in declining any other title than the one you at present honor, which indeed no additional honor could render more exalted'.[23]

The public recognition of Peel's merits, and the tragic circumstances which led to his death, coupled with an appreciation of his family's dignity in refusing to accept honours such as public funerals and titles, amplified the sense of his loss. As one correspondent remarked to Frederick, the 'privacy of his [father's] obsequies and the prohibition to his family against accepting those honours for themselves which he personally declined have indeed gilded his going down with a lustre all his own'. Even the fourth duke of Newcastle, who had differed from Peel on political matters, had spoken 'in warm praise of all that the newspapers reported of his funeral', for in such matters the duke opposed 'all expenditure beyond what is decent and becoming'.[24]

Similar sentiments were reflected in the healthy outpouring of sermonizing literature, religious texts and homilies which appeared over the course of succeeding weeks. This met the popular appetite for displaying public grief immediately while more permanent memorials were still in course of contemplation. Given the Victorian propensity to extract as much religious and symbolic meaning as possible from events of this nature, it is likely that this sermonizing would have happened in any event. However, the family's actions in declining all public honours made it desirable that communities should mark their respects in some way – and this invariably included a religious dimension.[25]

This explains the large number of sermons which were forwarded to Frederick, as a means of expressing condolences and respect, from different parts of the country. James Anderson, author of *The Dead Yet Speaking. A Sermon Preached in St George's Brighton, on the Sixth Sunday after Trinity, 1850. Being the Sunday after the Death of Sir Robert Peel* (1850), included published copies both for Frederick and his mother. Anderson was at pains to note that, if it should prove 'a needless aggravation of the agony of her trial, to present it to her, you will of course withdraw it. I leave it entirely to your discretion'.[26]

While most writers wrote in expectation of tacit approval, rather than active encouragement, others sought direct assistance with their work. Reverend John Tod Brown had already delivered the first part of his funeral sermon for Peel in Uxbridge when he wrote to Frederick on 15 July requesting help with its sequel:

You would favour me with any particulars not already known of the last moments of Sir Robert Peel (especially if possessing a religious tincture) which might be embodied in an effort intended at once to do honour to his memory and to profit those who survive. I beg to assure you that if you see fit to grant this request, I shall use the utmost caution and discretion both in reference to the particulars themselves and to the Source of my information.[27]

In making this appeal, Brown cited the precedents of Charles James Fox and William Pitt the Younger, whose final words were 'remembered when many lesser incidents are forgotten'. After Frederick declined this overture, Brown expressed the hope that he had not been 'offended at my freedom in addressing you as nothing could have been further from my intention than to give you any cause of displeasure'.[28]

The desire to extract every last ounce of detail from Peel's death bed denouement was widely shared. Within hours of Peel's demise, Prince Albert told Graham, 'We are so anxious to hear some details of the last moments of the dear friend and of the state of Lady Peel and his family that we should feel grateful, if you could come for a moment however painful the meeting must be for you.'[29]

The last dying speech of …

While the sanctity of the death bed was largely retained,[30] it was Peel's final speech in parliament which increasingly assumed talismanic status, not least because of the magnitude of the occasion upon which it was delivered. On Friday 28 June 1850, barely hours before the accident which cost him his life, Peel delivered his final speech in the House of Commons. It arose from J. A. Roebuck's motion on the government's conduct of foreign policy. Palmerston's actions in defending the rights of a British citizen, Don Pacifico, in Greece – which had already generated his famous 'Civic Roman Sum' speech – were countered in a lengthy speech by Peel. This was quickly turned into a pamphlet, priced at one penny, for widespread public circulation, while T. C. Hansard sought Frederick's assistance in ensuring that an accurate account of Peel's final words entered the official parliamentary record.[31]

Peel's last speech formed a common reference point for those who wrote expressing their condolences to the family. The Dean of Lincoln, Joseph Blakesley, adopted an exalted refrain, considering it

> the most noble specimen of impartial wisdom I know since the time of Thucydides [,] in that he has left a legacy to all public men in all nations: and I believe that its effect will be felt at once in every country of Europe. How few men have ever been allowed to end their career with such a climax as this![32]

It was for this reason, according to Blakesley, that Peel's death 'deserved beyond almost any on record the name of an euthanasia'. As Edward Clough Taylor remarked, in a similar vein, Peel had died before 'his splendid powers and extraordinary abilities had begun to fail'.[33]

Others drew a political reading from Peel's words which suggested that, had he lived, he would have openly embraced Liberalism. After Richard Cobden's death in 1865, his friend George Hadfield sent Frederick a letter which he had received at the time of Peel's death, and which contained Cobden's conviction that on questions in which I take a great interest such as the reduction of armaments, retrenchment of expenditure, the diffusion of peace principles etc. he had strong sympathies – stronger than he had yet expressed in favor of my views. Read his last speech again and observe what he said about diplomacy, and in favor of settling international disputes by reference to mediation instead of by ships of war.[34]

As one might expect, many of the condolence letters retained by Frederick were those which he received from Peel's political acolytes and supporters. Several correspondents suggested that the loss which had been sustained was not particular to those who shared his political views. Lord Jocelyn, who served as joint secretary to the board of control in 1845–6, believed that 'the loss although it will be felt deeply by many of us, is nothing to what it will be to the Country at large, who looked up to him in case of necessity as the only hand to guide the helm'. Spencer Walpole, the MP for Midhurst, expressed his sense that Peel's death was 'not merely a family but a national bereavement, which makes us almost a sharer in your sorrow'.[35]

Nor were expressions of grief confined to the generation which was associated with Peel's mature political career. Long-time Tory grandees, including the duke of Rutland and the 3rd marquess of Londonderry, also wrote to Frederick, the latter recalling that Peel 'cherished the memory and knew the value of my lamented brother [Lord Castlereagh, the foreign secretary who had committed suicide in 1822] and his recollection and appreciation of his career and services I never can forget'.[36]

However, it was the sense that Peel's political actions made him a statesman worthy of respect, irrespective of class, nationality or religion, which most clearly signalled the 'apotheosis' through which his public reputation had now passed.[37] Benjamin Brodie told Lady Peel that she had 'the sympathy of others in every class of society. I do not believe that in the memory of any living person there has ever been another occasion on which the loss of an individual has been so universally felt and deplored'. Edward Clough Taylor described Peel as 'ever my beau-ideal of a Statesman' and prophesied that 'the ever to be remembered name of Sir Robert Peel will shine in ages yet to come with undiminished splendour'. Meanwhile, B. T. Smith, of Tunbridge, referenced 'the unswerving disinterestedness and integrity, of one whose worth we all feel when it is too late, but which was not so generally acknowledged while his course was being run'.[38]

While the classless nature of tributes to Peel was widely referenced in condolence letters, so too was the impression that it was an event which transcended national boundaries. This was advanced as a cause for consolation, notwithstanding the family's private grief. Henry Dawson told Frederick that

> the departure of such a man is of course more deeply felt by his children but of such an illustrious one the whole world is a mourner and if grief when shared is lessened may the sorrow which all here render contribute to assuage in some slight degree the distress of your mother and her family.[39]

As G. S. Severn observed, Peel's family would have 'the universal sympathy of his friends of the Country and of the world'. Several expressions of condolence were received from across Europe, including the wife of Louis Philippe, the king of the French, the Hereditary Grand duke of Saxony, Tsar Nicholas I of Russia, and the duke of Montebello, a minister in the government of Francois Guizot of France.[40]

Meanwhile, Sir Henry Bulwer, writing from the United States, observed that Peel's 'rare abilities, and his still rarer devotion to his country's interests' meant that his loss was as keenly felt in America as it was 'throughout the civilized world'. Nor were these sentiments confined to those who shared Peel's political outlook. The king of Hanover, who (as the ultra-Tory duke of Cumberland) was a long-time political opponent of Peel, managed to express his admiration for Peel's 'amiable qualities as an individual and his talents as a Statesman' without venturing upon precise points of political difference.[41]

Monuments and memorials

Alongside private expressions of grief, the process of public commemoration of Peel gathered pace. On 12 July 1850, Russell moved in the House of Commons for a humble address to the queen, praying that she would 'give directions that a Monument be erected' to Peel in Westminster Abbey 'with an inscription expressive of the public sense of so great and irreparable a loss'. Goulburn kept Frederick informed of events, noting that 'nothing can have gone off better than Lord John Russell's proposal or more satisfactorily to us all'.[42] Ten days later, the first estimates of costs for the memorial – some £5,250 – were published.[43]

Events beyond Westminster were also advancing rapidly. On 3 July, John Potter, the Liberal mayor of Manchester since 1848, sent an address to Frederick, expressing the council's regret at the 'melancholy accident which has deprived England of one of her most distinguished Statesmen and Lancashire of one of her most illustrious sons'. Potter, who continued as mayor until 1851, was chairman of the memorial committee which oversaw the erection of Manchester's statue to Peel, which was unveiled by W. E. Gladstone in 1853.[44]

Likewise, Edmund Grundy, of the Wylde, sent Frederick a copy of the resolutions passed at a public meeting in Bury, which provided 'the mournful gratification of offering our sympathy and condolences on this afflictive dispensation'. The resolutions, which marked the start of the process which culminated in the unveiling of Bury's statue to Peel in 1852, commemorated the 'private excellencies of one who was as amiable in the domestic relations of life as he was exemplary in the discharge of his public duties'.[45]

Those writing on behalf of corporate bodies and the communities which they represented were at pains to express the classless quality of the reaction to Peel's death. William Baines, forwarding a resolution from Hull, told Frederick that it expressed 'the genuine feelings of every class among his constituents, from the highest to the lowest'. Likewise, William Beckett, of Kirkstall Grange near Leeds, observed:

I have been gratified in witnessing the sorrow that prevails here among all classes of people and in listening to the various expressions of regret which plainly indicate their belief that they have lost a true friend.[46]

A public meeting held at the Court House in Leeds had expressed its wish for a 'testimonial worthy of the occasion – each manufacturing establishment will appoint a Treasurer and canvass their own people'. The Mayor, Mr Bateson, subsequently informed Lady Peel that they had met together:

To consider in what way our affectionate esteem for the late Sir Robert Peel could be most effectually demonstrated, and with the concurrence of all ranks, parties, and classes, it was resolved, that a monument should be erected in memory of the illustrious statesman, whose untimely death we deplore, and that our sincere condolences should be tendered to yourself and your family, on the irreparable loss you have sustained.[47]

Though the motivation behind memorializing Peel in Leeds was, much as elsewhere in the industrial midlands and north, dominated by middle-class supporters of free trade, the element of civic pride was no less significant in these endeavours. It was telling that the Leeds meeting resolved to concentrate its efforts on establishing a local memorial rather than contributing to a national fund. This led, in 1852, to the erection of the first bronze memorial to Peel to be erected in the country.[48]

While these initiatives were communicated to Peel's family out of respect, other proposals, of a literary and artistic nature, required their formal approval. Several weeks before his death, Peel had given John Watkins permission to dedicate the biography of his father-in-law, Ebenezer Elliott, 'The Corn-Law Rhymer', to him. The book subsequently appeared, with a facsimile of Peel's letter of permission as a frontispiece and a memorial dedication, bordered in black ink:

This book derives a melancholy interest from the fact that one of the latest acts of the Right Honourable Baronet was an instance of his generous urbanity in granting permission that it should be dedicated to him. Elliott's memory will receive this posthumous honour; and the name of the Apostle of Corn-law Repeal will be linked in history with the Accomplisher of that great boon.[49]

Likewise, Charles Southey, son of the poet Robert Southey, had written to Peel at the time of his death, requesting permission to publish the correspondence in which he offered Southey a baronetcy and a pension. Following up the request subsequently, Southey assured Frederick that the correspondence would be 'honourable to the memory of both the writers'. The request was granted.[50]

Peel had been a leading patron of art, known for the magnificence of his private collection and his patronage of political portraiture, but he had sat for relatively few portraits during his lifetime. A week after his death, the artist Henry William Pickersgill wrote to Frederick informing him that he had a portrait of Peel 'my kind friend and patron' which he was 'most anxious to submit to you'. This was not the famous portrait of Peel in his prime, completed by Pickersgill earlier in his career, but another version, representing him in later life, in a similar pose but different clothes and accessories.[51]

Within ten days of this approach, the Conservative politician Thomas Grimston Bucknall Estcourt had agreed to buy the picture for 300 guineas. Pickersgill thought this well priced, 'considering the importance of the subject and the best extant [picture] since Sir Thomas Lawrence'. Estcourt agreed: 'I consider the likeness to be admirably portrayed [and] I am persuaded the picture will hereafter rank amongst the best works of British Artists.' Likewise, Charles Bathurst thought Pickersgill's likeness preferable because the portrait was 'not dandyish like Lawrence's'.

In contracting to purchase the portrait, Estcourt had in mind a scheme of memorialization closely connected with Peel's family. As he informed Goulburn on 18 July:

> In the absence of any other portrait taken at a late period of Sir Robert Peel's noble career, [the picture] would be to his widow, I conclude, invaluable, and if presented by his attached friends and admirers might be perhaps allowed to afford her some consolatory reflections.[52]

Having been invited to a meeting of Peel's friends and admirers, convened under Aberdeen's chairmanship on 23 July, to consider a suitable form of memorialization, Estcourt was in hopes that a subscription might be raised to underwrite the purchase of the picture, and he compiled a list of nearly ninety potential subscribers for this purpose. The list reflected the core of Peel's personal and political friends. However, difficulties arose when it became clear that Pickersgill was working on two competing canvasses of Peel; this, Estcourt feared, would undermine the 'unique and incomparable Treasure' which he had contracted to buy. He reminded Pickersgill that the purchase had been made specifically 'in order that it might be made available (as I intimated to you) by the friends and admirers of the lamented statesman, should they be disposed to present it to Lady Peel'.

While the original portrait was to have been presented to Julia, Estcourt also commissioned Henry Hering to publish an engraving for wider circulation. Hering reminded him of the need for swift action – 'I need scarcely tell you that there are a great many engravings of Sir Robert already in progress.' Pickersgill told Estcourt that his second canvas had been developed in response to the changing tastes of Victorian consumers, a position which Hering reinforced in defending Peel's portrayal in a frock coat. This would be 'much more acceptable to the public. I have found the dress coat universally objected to and I fear if we engrave our plate from your picture will be very much against the success of the publication'. Pickersgill's portrait, having been duly engraved, was subsequently returned to Estcourt, who put it on display in his family home, the idea for presenting it to Lady Peel having been overtaken by other memorial initiatives.[53]

Unbeknown to Estcourt, a family friend of more exalted status would take up the idea of presenting Julia Peel with a portrait of her late husband. Queen Victoria arranged for her favourite court painter, Franz Xaver Winterhalter, to produce a head-and-shoulders portrait of Peel. The picture was copied from Winterhalter's dual portrait of Peel and Wellington, in the royal collection, which was completed in 1844. By the queen's command, that portrait was published in an engraving by James Faed after Peel's death.[54] In forwarding the head-and-shoulders portrait to Julia, the queen recalled her 'dear, revered and ever to be lamented husband'. In reply, Lady Peel observed that the picture was the only portrait she possessed of her husband, and it was 'inexpressibly dear to my heart – which is indeed too truly desolate!'.[55]

The unmerry widow

The queen's gift reflects a key theme in the condolence letters which were sent to Julia and Frederick, in the weeks and months after Peel's death: concern for the health and well-being of his widow. Norman Gash observed that Julia's 'emotional nervousness had visibly increased' in the final years of Peel's life and that she was 'a little peculiar and unpredictable in her emotional reactions'.[56] On receiving news of Peel's death, the queen recorded her fears for 'poor Lady Peel, who is so delicate, so nervous, and who lived but for, and in him!'. Her concern had not lessened when she received a 'distressing account' from Hardinge, several months later: 'poor Lady Peel' was 'no better and cannot resign herself to her loss'. Moved by these accounts, the queen saw her in person a week later:

> It was a melancholy satisfaction to see the widow of this great and good man, whose loss is so irreparable to us all, and to try and say some soothing and comforting words to her. At first, she was dreadfully overcome, but she soon recovered and began to talk of her Husband, and his loss, her existence, all she had gone through and how great was her misfortune. The day of the fatal accident, he had been so well, and was so glad that he had made that speech [on Roebuck's motion]. Her eldest son, I fear is not kind to her, and most unsatisfactory, taking a very Radical line in politics etc. – but the other sons are very good to her. Lady Peel seemed much pleased at seeing me, and I think it did her good.[57]

However, when Julia saw Prince Albert, several months later, 'she quite broke down, for she had not yet seen him since poor dear Sir Robert's death', and her emotional state was a continued object of royal concern in subsequent years.[58]

As the queen's comments suggest, matters were not helped by Julia's poor relationship with her eldest son. To Goulburn, Julia complained that 'most of my sorrow lies at his door'. For his part, the new baronet told Goulburn – who acted as something of a mediator in these matters – that he and his elder sister, Lady Villiers, had been poorly treated by their mother. In trying to smooth these family difficulties over, Goulburn observed:

> I have always endeavoured to impress upon [your mother] that she must not expect from her children the same devotion which was paid to her by her late Husband nor be surprised or annoyed if her sons appeared to feel the loss which

they had sustained less constantly or acutely than she herself did … You must upon reflexion see how different is your position from that of your mother [and] how much she has to bear and to suffer of which you can form but an inadequate idea considering how much her suffering must be increased by any alienation [from you].[59]

Goulburn had a ringside seat in these family dramas, but most correspondents writing to the family in the aftermath of Peel's death could only recommend a recourse to religious teaching as the ultimate source of comfort in the years ahead. Lord Delawarr, whose elder brother Lord Cantelupe had recently died, told Frederick that it had 'pleased God to inflict a heavy blow upon [both] our Houses – doubtless for wise, although for our eyes hidden purposes'. B. T. Smith also expressed his empathy with Frederick, having recently lost 'a beloved father'. Smith told Frederick to 'build less on the sandy and shifting foundations of this world's honour and friendship, and to set one's faith more firmly in the unseen and imperishable. Sorrow soon passes into joy, when it works in us the peaceable fruits of righteousness'.[60]

Other writers drew on their family connection in recommending a 'humble submission' to the will of God. J. W. Faithfull, the Rector of Hatfield, ran a boarding school (The Parsonage), which had been attended by Frederick and his brothers. Faithfull recalled the 'warm affection and respect which you all felt towards a parent to whom you owe so much' and looked to God for 'the consolation which He alone can give. What He does we know not now, but we shall know hereafter'. Faithfull hoped 'that God will strengthen your faith, and confidence in His mercy, and enable you all, hereafter to say, "it is good for us that we have been in trouble"'.

W. M. Lally, the vicar of Drayton in Staffordshire, who counted the Peels among his parishioners, likewise attempted to counsel Frederick and Julia to

> regard <u>Death</u> in its <u>true</u> light, (as to the <u>Virtuous</u> <u>it</u> <u>is</u>) – and as, I trust, Sir Robert Peel <u>has found</u> it to be – 'the Gate of Heaven': <u>that</u> Gate thro' which <u>he has passed</u> from mortal, to <u>Im</u>mortal hours; and where he now waits to <u>receive her</u>, in God's good time, to be – as upon Earth she had always been – the happy Partner of his <u>honors</u>, and of his <u>love</u>. Only let her be <u>assured</u> that a Gracious God has <u>these Blessings in store</u> for her, and she <u>cannot fail</u> to receive comfort.[61]

The depth of Julia's grief made her widowhood a constant source of anxiety for her family and friends, and it was to Peel's closest political colleagues that she often turned for comfort. She expressed the depths of her grief in letters to Goulburn and requested visits from Graham whenever he was able to see her. These visits provided opportunities to awaken the memory of 'the bright, the happy past, and, too bitterly, the gloomy desolation of the present'. At the first Christmas after Peel's death, Graham attempted to comfort Julia, observing that 'these afflictions which it is so hard to bear are dispensations of the Father of all mercies, who uses them as the means of weaning us from this world and preparing us for a better'.[62]

It was Lord Aberdeen, Peel's foreign secretary, who best expressed the depth of the Peelites attachment to Lady Peel. He told Frederick at the end of July that he 'frequently almost forget the loss we have, all of us, sustained, when I think of her overwhelming wretchedness and desolation'. Nor was it merely

> as an object of pity that I think of her, struck down by a calamity that would touch a heart of stone; but also, with grateful feelings for years of kindness absolutely unvaried and uniform ... we may hope that time, if it [does] not bring relief, may yet so far regulate and modify her feelings as to render them endurable.[63]

Nor, for her part, had Julia renounced her interest in the fate of those who continued to be the standard-bearers of her husband's political creed. After the fifth duke of Newcastle defended the repeal of the Corn Laws, in speeches to his Nottinghamshire tenantry at the end of 1851, Julia wrote to him. Newcastle received the letter:

> [I]n the name of him whose approbation was to me the highest reward for any public act or exertion, and many days at post-hour I have felt, whilst I have been reading the letters of others, that there was <u>one</u> missing which in former days would have been the first despatched (and certainly the first read) to convey a few warm words of approval and encouragement. <u>He</u> is my Leader still, though invisible – I never take a step in public life without reflecting – how would <u>he</u> have thought of it [?].[64]

In much the same way, after Gladstone delivered his four and three-quarter hours budget speech, in April 1853, which built upon Peel's free trade measures of the 1840s, Julia wrote to congratulate him. Conscious of the compliment, Gladstone responded:

> I will not scruple to say that as I was inspired by the thought of treading, however unequally, in the steps of my great teacher and master in public affairs, so it was one of my keenest anxieties not to do dishonour to his memory, or injustice to the patriotic policy with which his name is for ever associated.[65]

Peel in public and private memory

Largely as a result of Queen Victoria's response to her widowhood, following the death of Prince Albert in December 1861, a stereotypical view has emerged of the histrionic Victorian widow, unable to face the reality of their altered situation. While some widows could demonstrate a form of 'chronic' or 'abnormal' grief, the Victorians did not – as Norman Gash observed – 'find the expression of fervid emotions unnatural especially in a bereaved widow'.[66] In the case of Julia Peel, much of the expression of that emotion remained concealed from public view, in private visits and personal correspondence, rather than being displayed ostentatiously before the public.[67]

In this respect, as this chapter has shown, while the boundaries between public and private commemoration of public figures were becoming blurred, at the time of Peel's death, they remained intact.[68] Decisions within the province of the family – such as whether to accept a public funeral or honours and distinctions on Peel's behalf – were driven by the known and express wishes of Peel himself. Other initiatives, such as the publication of Peel's words and, in some instances, his image, remained matters over which his family retained a degree of control. By contrast, communal acts of remembrance and the commissioning of public statues within newly crafted urban civic spaces were a process which was largely outside the family's influence – they were consulted and informed, rather than asked for approval. These collective acts of memorialization were complemented by a mass of personal choices by individual members of the public, which were only occasionally revealed to public view. Chief among these was the decision whether to display any of the widely available images, busts and artefacts of Peel within the privacy of the family home.[69] A vivid reminder of the tenacity with which Peel continued to be remembered in this way, even while his name was at a political discount, was recalled by Enoch Powell in 1982:

> I once had to call at a tenement cottage in a long terrace of similar houses in my old constituency in Wolverhampton. A pensioner opened the door to me, and as we stood talking, an object hanging by itself on the wall of the passage caught my attention. It was a little fame of gilded wood ornamented with carved ears of corn; and in the frame was a print of Sir Robert Peel. 'You take it', said my constituent, seeing how my eyes were glistening with interest. 'No,' I said, 'let him go on hanging there. He is in his right place' – in that industrial England for whose rise his life's work set the stage.[70]

In understanding the 'memorial mania' which encompassed both the 'remembering and forgetting' of Sir Robert Peel, over the two centuries after his death, an understanding of the familial and domestic context within which Peel's posthumous memorialization took place reminds us of the boundaries which continued to operate where public loss and private grief met.[71]

Notes

1 See, principally, Donald Read, *Peel and the Victorians* (Oxford: Blackwell, 1987), 266–304; Richard A. Gaunt, *Sir Robert Peel. The Life and Legacy* (London: I.B. Tauris, 2010), 143–60; Richard A. Gaunt (editor), *Sir Robert Peel. Contemporary Perspectives*, 3 vols. (Abingdon: Routledge, 2022).

2 Terry Wyke with Harry Cocks, *Public Sculpture of Greater Manchester* (Liverpool: Liverpool University Press, 2004). For a recent discussion, referencing Peel, see Dehn Gilmore, '"Preserving the Name Alive" versus "Getting About": Samuel Butler and the Problem of Memorial Sculpture', *Victorian Literature and Culture*, 50 (2022), 575–99.

3 John Wolffe, *Great Deaths. Grieving, Religion, and Nationhood in Victorian and Edwardian Britain* (Oxford: Oxford University Press, 2000), 157, acknowledges Peel's importance in respect of public attitudes but refers readers to Read's work, cited above. The familial context is best covered in Pat Jalland, *Death in the Victorian Family* (Oxford: Oxford University Press, 1996), although she does not mention Peel at all.

4   For these events, see Norman Gash, *Sir Robert Peel. The Life of Sir Robert Peel after 1830* (Harlow: Longman, 1986 edition), 697–701; J. S. G. Blair, 'Famous Trauma Victims. Sir Robert Peel', *Trauma*, 3 (2001), 187–90; A. G. W. Whitfield, 'Peel's Fall', *Annals of the Royal College of Surgeons of England*, 61 (1979), 158–60; Algernon West, *Recollections, 1832–1886*, 2 vols. (London, 1899), i, 61–2; Charles Stuart Parker, *Life and Letters of Sir James Graham, 1792–1861*, 2 vols. (London, 1907), ii, 110.
5   Papers of George Peel (in the author's possession), commonplace book, 30 March 1842–30, July 1867.
6   G. S. Woods, revised by H. C. G. Matthew, 'Sir Frederick Peel', *Oxford Dictionary of National Biography* (Oxford, 2004, online edition); Gash, *Sir Robert Peel*, xii, advances Frederick as Julia's favourite while noting that Peel himself favoured his third son, William (1824–55). For positive appraisals of Frederick, see Surrey Record Office, Goulburn MSS, 304/A2/13/5/10, Julia Peel to Goulburn, 4 November 1851; Queen Victoria's journal, 10 December 1850: http://www.queenvictoriasjournals.org (accessed 7 September 2022).
7   Jalland, *Death in the Victorian Family*, 8–12.
8   George Peel, *The Private Letters of Sir Robert Peel* (London, 1920); Richard A. Gaunt, 'Norman Gash and the making of *Mr Secretary Peel*' in D. W. Hayton and Linda Clark (editors), *Historians and Parliament* (Chichester: Wiley, 2021), 148–67; Norman Gash, *Mr Secretary Peel. The Life of Sir Robert Peel before 1830* (Harlow: Longman, 1985 edition), 676; Gash, *Sir Robert Peel*, 724. Material from the Peel MSS used by Gash in *Sir Robert Peel* includes an obituary article from *Chambers' Papers for the People* (705, n.5) and letters from the fifth duke of Newcastle and W. E. Gladstone (see n.64–5 below).
9   Peel MSS, Edward Clough Taylor to Frederick Peel, 2 July 1850; John Young to Frederick Peel, 2 July 1850; Robert Lamond to Frederick Peel, 1 July 1850; Henry Brougham to Frederick Peel, 2 July 1850; Henry Willoughby to Frederick Peel, 1 July 1850; Gash, *Sir Robert Peel*, 697–701.
10 Blair, 'Peel', 190; Jalland, *Death in the Victorian Family*, 77–97.
11 Peel MSS, 'On the Late Sir Robert Peel by an Old Harrow Boy', 17 July 1850; Charles Frederick Jephs to Frederick Peel, 4 July 1850. Also see the printed handbill containing Reverend T. Grinfield, *Tributary Verses to the Memory of the Right Hon Sir Robert Peel, Bart* (10 July 1850) with its lines: 'Oh, in the midst of life, we sink in death! How soon the steed may end the master's breath!'.
12 *The Lancet*, 6, 13 July 1850.
13 *The Lancet*, 13, 20 July 1850; T. Holmes, *Benjamin Brodie* (London, 1898), 173–4 and Appendix M. The original memorandum was dated 2 June 1851.
14 Peel's body was moved from his house in Whitehall Gardens to Euston Station on the evening of Friday 5 July, accompanied by Frederick, Hardinge, Graham, and Goulburn. Frederick accompanied it back to Tamworth, where it was taken to the family home at Drayton Manor: Gash, *Sir Robert Peel*, 715.
15 Goulburn MSS, 304/A2/13/5/9, correspondence file, including Foucart's letters to Goulburn of 22 November and 26 December 1850; 304/A2/13/5/11, Foucart to Sir Robert Peel and reply, 25 and 31 January 1851; https://www.glasgownecropolis.org/profiles/francois-foucart/ (accessed 2 September 2022).
16 Peel MSS, printed text of Hume's motion.
17 Wolffe, *Great Deaths*, 288.

18 Peel MSS, Russell to Graham, 3 July 1850; Hardinge's (undated) letter, in Parker, *Graham*, ii, 111.
19 Peel MSS, printed handbill incorporating text from the *Birmingham Journal*, 6 July 1850.
20 Peel MSS, *The Departed Statesman* (1850), issued by the English Monthly Tract Society. Peel is buried in the family vault inside the church.
21 Peel MSS, Edward N. Buxton to Russell, 3 July 1850; printed report (undated) of events at Hawkchurch, on the Dorset/Devon border.
22 Peel MSS, Russell to Lady Peel, 11 July 1850, and draft reply.
23 Peel MSS, Jane C. Loudon to Julia Peel, 16 July 1850. The letter has been annotated by an unknown hand to suggest it came from John Claudius Loudon (the garden writer) but, as Loudon died in 1843, it is from his wife (1807–58).
24 Peel MSS, John Tod Brown to Frederick Peel, 15 July 1850; University of Nottingham Manuscripts and Special Collections, Ne C 12430/1–2, Lord Lincoln to Edward Cardwell, 5 November 1850.
25 Jalland, *Death in the Victorian Family*, 17–38; Read, *Peel and the Victorians*, 283–4. A selection of this material can be found in Gaunt, *Contemporary Perspectives*, iii, 221–62, Including Joseph Arnould, *Memorial Lines on Sir Robert Peel* (London: Bradbury and Evans, 1850), a copy of which is in the Peel MSS.
26 Peel MSS, James Anderson to Frederick Peel, 26 July 1850; Gaunt, *Contemporary Perspectives*, iii, 228–37. Also see W. Thoms to Frederick Peel, 20 July 1850, forwarding Rev. John L. Adamson, *The Grave of a British Senator: A Sermon Preached on the Forenoon of Sabbath 14 July 1850 in St David's Church, Occasioned by the Death of Sir Robert Peel, Bart. Published by Desire of the Congregation* (Dundee, 1850), and W. H. Rowlatt to Frederick Peel, 1 August 1850, enclosing a manuscript extract from a sermon 'preached a fortnight ago'.
27 Peel MSS, John Tod Brown to Frederick Peel, 15 July 1850.
28 Peel MSS, John Tod Brown to Frederick Peel, 30 July 1850; John Tod Brown, *Funeral Sermon for Sir Robert Peel, Bart, Preached in Uxbridge Church on Sunday July 14 and 21, 1850* (London, 1850). The published version was dedicated to the duke of Buccleuch, who had resigned from Peel's cabinet over the repeal of the Corn Laws.
29 Peel MSS, Prince Albert to Graham, 3 July 1850; also in Parker, *Graham*, ii, 110; see the account of Peel's final days given by Graham in Queen Victoria's journal, 3 July 1850: http://www.queenvictoriasjournals.org (accessed 6 September 2022).
30 A request from the sculptor, E. H. Baily, asking for permission to make 'a cast from the face of your much-lamented Father' was swiftly declined: Peel MSS, E. H. Baily to Frederick Peel (undated, July 1850), annotated 'No'.
31 The Peel MSS contains both a printed notice of Roebuck's motion and Peel's detailed handwritten notes which formed the basis for his speech, as well as a copy of *Peel's Last Words* (London, 1850) and two letters from T. C. Hansard to Frederick Peel, 5 August, 4 September 1850. For the official report, see *Hansard Parliamentary Debates*, third series, cxii, 674–93 (28 June 1850).
32 Peel MSS, Joseph Blakesley to Frederick Peel, 9 July 1850.
33 Peel MSS, Edward Clough Taylor to Frederick Peel, 4 July 1850.
34 Peel MSS, George Hadfield to Frederick Peel, 14 April 1865, enclosing an extract from Richard Cobden to George Hadfield, 5 July 1850; for the complete letter, see Anthony Howe (editor), *The Letters of Richard Cobden*, 4 vols. (Oxford: Oxford University Press, 2007–15), ii, 217–18. For contrasting views of the speech, see Read, *Peel and the Victorians*, 284–6.

35 Peel MSS, Lord Jocelyn to Frederick Peel, 3 July 1850; S. H. Walpole to Frederick Peel, 3 July 1850; also see C. B. Adderley to Frederick Peel, 3 July 1850.
36 Peel MSS, Rutland to Frederick Peel, 2 July 1850; Londonderry to Frederick Peel, 7 August 1850.
37 E.g. for expressions of goodwill from the Jewish community, see David Salomons to Frederick Peel, 30 June 1850; Joseph Seborg, President of the Jews Orphan Asylum, to Frederick Peel, 12 July 1850.
38 Peel MSS, Benjamin Brodie to Lady Peel, 23 July 1850; Edward Clough Taylor to Frederick Peel, 4 July 1850; B. T. Smith to Frederick Peel, 10 July 1850; also see Brodie to Lady Peel, 25 September 1850, and Aberdeen to Lieven, 5 July 1850, in E. Jones Parry (editor), *The Correspondence of Lord Aberdeen and Princess Lieven, 1832–1854*, 2 vols. (London: Royal Historical Society, 1938–9), ii, 500.
39 Peel MSS, Henry Dawson to Frederick Peel (undated).
40 Peel MSS, G. S. Severn to Frederick Peel, 3 July 1850; Maria Amalia Teresa to [Frederick Peel?], 3 July 1850; Charles Alexander to Lady Peel, 14 July 1850; Nicholas I to Frederick Peel [12] July 1850; duke of Montebello to Lady Peel, 3 July 1850. Also see Lieven to Aberdeen, 7 and 15 July 1850, in Parry, *Aberdeen and Lieven*, ii, 500–2.
41 Peel MSS, Sir Henry Bulwer to Lady Peel, 16 September 1850; king of Hanover to Lady Peel, 17 November 1850. Bulwer went on to write *Sir Robert Peel. An Historical Sketch* (London: R. Bentley, 1874).
42 Peel MSS, Printed statement of Russell's resolution on 12 July 1850. The same evening, Goulburn moved the writ for a new election at Tamworth, one of whose seats was vacated by Peel's death.
43 Peel MSS, published estimate of costs, 25 July 1850. John Gibson completed the marble statue of Peel in Westminster Abbey; Martin Greenwood, 'John Gibson (1790–1866)', *Oxford Dictionary of National Biography* (Oxford, 2004, online edition): https://www.oxforddnb.com/ (accessed 6 September 2022).
44 Peel MSS, John Potter to Frederick Peel, 3 July 1850; Wyke, *Public Sculpture*, 111–13.
45 Peel MSS, Edmund Grundy to Peel, 16 July 1850, enclosing resolutions dated 10 July 1850; Wyke, *Public Sculpture*, 250–3; *Illustrated London News*, 18 September 1852.
46 Peel MSS, William Baines to Frederick Peel, 13 July 1850; William Beckett to Frederick Peel, 31 July 1850.
47 *Leeds Mercury*, 3 August 1850 (for the meeting); *Leeds Mercury*, 10 August 1850 (for the letter from Mayor Bateson to Lady Peel, 31 July 1850, and Frederick Peel's reply of 5 August 1850).
48 Melanie Stafford, 'Peel's Statue in Leeds – a First for Town and Country', *Leeds Art Calendar*, 90 (1982), 4–11.
49 Peel to Watkins, 29 May 1850 (facsimile) and dedication, in John Watkins, *Life, Poetry, and Letters, of Ebenezer Elliott, The Corn-Law Rhymer, with an Abstract of His Politics* (London, 1850).
50 Peel MSS, C. C. Southey to Sir Robert Peel, 2 July 1850; C. C. Southey to Frederick Peel, 17 July 1850. The correspondence was published in C. C. Southey, *The Life and Correspondence of Robert Southey*, 6 vols. (London, 1849–50), vi, 254–8.
51 Richard A. Gaunt, 'Robert Peel: Portraiture and Political Commemoration', *The Historian* (2012), 22–6; Peel MSS, H. W. Pickersgill to Frederick Peel, 10 July 1850; National Portrait Gallery, 3796.
52 Gloucestershire Record Office, Sotheron-Estcourt MSS, D1571 X40, Pickersgill to Estcourt, 19 July 1850; Estcourt to Henry Hering, 23 July 1850; Bathurst to Estcourt, 25 July 1850; Estcourt to Goulburn, 18 July 1850.

53 Aberdeen To Lieven, 23 July 1850, in Parry, *Aberdeen and Lieven*, ii, 503; Sotheron-Estcourt MSS, Estcourt's list of potential subscribers; Estcourt to Pickersgill, 27 September 1850; Hering to Estcourt, 24 September 1850. For the engraving, by George Raphael Ward, see Richard Ormond, *Early Victorian Portraits* (London: HMSO, 1973); British Museum, 1885,1114.39.

54 Peel MSS, *Criticisms on the engraving by Samuel Cousins, ARA of the late Right Honourable Sir Robert Peel, Bart, MP Painted by Sir Thomas Lawrence, PRA and of the engraving by James Faed of Field Marshal the Duke of Wellington, KG and the late Right Honourable Sir Robert Peel, Bart, MP painted by Winterhalter* (London, c.1850); Royal Collection, RCIN 404841 (1844); Oliver Millar, *The Victorian Pictures in the Collection of Her Majesty the Queen: Text* (Cambridge: Cambridge University Press, 1992), 288–90, 320–1.

55 Peel MSS, Queen Victoria to Lady Peel and reply, 20 May 1851. The portrait remains in the family's possession.

56 On Julia, see Gash, *Sir Robert Peel*, x–xv (quotes at xi).

57 Queen Victoria's journal, 3 July, 3 and 9 December 1850, 30 March 1851: http://www.queenvictoriasjournals.org (accessed 7 September 2022).

58 Queen Victoria's journal, 1 June 1852: http://www.queenvictoriasjournals.org (accessed 7 September 2022).

59 Goulburn MSS, 304/A2/13/5/10, Julia Peel to Goulburn, 7 October 1851; 304/A2/13/5/11, Sir Robert Peel to Goulburn and (draft) reply, 1 and 2 February 1851.

60 Peel MSS, Delawarr to Frederick Peel, 4 July 1850; B. T. Smith to Frederick Peel, 10 July 1850.

61 Peel MSS, J. W. Faithfull to Frederick Peel, 11 July 1850; W. M. Lally to Frederick Peel, 4 July 1850; also see Lally to Frederick Peel, 16 July 1850.

62 Goulburn MSS, 304/A2/13/5/10, correspondence from Julia Peel to Goulburn (1850–2); Peel MSS, Graham to Julia Peel, 17 August and 24 December 1850; the second letter is printed in Parker, *Graham,* ii, 117–18.

63 Peel MSS, Aberdeen to Frederick Peel, 31 July 1850. Also see Aberdeen to Lady Peel, 15 August 1850, in which he recommends her 'submission to the will of God'.

64 *The Duke of Newcastle and his tenantry. Speeches delivered by His Grace the Duke of Newcastle, to his tenantry, at the rent-audit for Michaelmas, 1851* (London: John Murray, 1852); Peel MSS, Newcastle to Julia Peel, 29 December 1851.

65 Peel MSS, Gladstone to Julia Peel, 20 April 1853. Also see Goulburn MSS, 304/A2/13/5/10, Julia Peel to Goulburn, 1 October 1852, commenting on Hardinge's elevation as commander-in-chief of the army following the death of the duke of Wellington.

66 Gash, *Sir Robert Peel,* xii; Jalland, *Death in the Victorian Family,* 230–50, 318–38; Elisabeth Darby, *The Cult of the Prince Consort* (New Haven CT, 1983).

67 These visits could sometimes generate their own form of commemoration; see Peel MSS, J. S. Harford to Lady Peel, 4 November 1851, enclosing his manuscript 'Lines on Lady Peel's much regretted departure' from Blaise Castle.

68 For later developments, see M. J. D. Roberts, 'The Deathbed of Lord Palmerston. An Episode in Victorian Cultural History', *Cultural and Social History*, 5 (2008), 183–96, and David Cannadine, 'War and Death, Grief and Mourning in Modern Britain', in *Mirrors of Mortality,* ed. Joachim Whaley (London: St Martin's Press, 1981), 187–242.

69 For growing access to 'Images of Fame', see Asa Briggs, *Victorian Things* (London: Batsford, 1988), 143–78.

70 Churchill College, Cambridge, Enoch Powell MSS, POLL 4/1/15 File 1, 'Speech at the Annual Dinner of the Peel Society, 22 October 1982'.
71 Terry Wyke, 'Memorial Mania: Remembering and Forgetting Sir Robert Peel', in *People, Places, and Identities: Themes in British Social and Cultural History, 1700s–1980s*, ed. Alan Kidd and Melanie Tebbutt (Manchester: Manchester University Press, 2017), 63–83; for Peel's declining political currency, over the course of the twentieth century, see Gaunt, *Contemporary Perspectives*, iii, 6–9.

9

'Whatever happened to all the heroes?': The monumental failure of British plebeian radicalism, c.1850–1920

Antony Taylor

The campaign around a memorial to commemorate the bicentenary of the Peterloo massacre in 2019 and the erection of a statue to Friedrich Engels in Manchester recovered from a rubbish heap in the Ukraine highlight the relative absence of memorials raised to commemorate the British radical past.[1] Most public monuments that commemorate nineteenth-century radicalism have been erected in the last fifty years as a project of recovery to remedy this absence.[2] Traditionally, British radicalism is characterized by the absence of official memorialization. In a background culture in Britain rich in commemoration, the rarity of physical reminders of the political reform movements of the nineteenth-century is striking. This, then, is a chapter about the absence, rather than the presence, of physical monuments to working-class reformers in Britain that engages with recent interest in designs for memorials that were either never realized or were vandalized and destroyed. Charting the failure of attempts to memorialize the Peterloo massacre, the collapse of projects to commemorate Chartism, and the amnesia around and neglect of the few monuments that do exist, this chapter catalogues the unsuccessful story of radical memorialization. It ranges across a variety of public, funerary, private and publicly constructed memorials and commemorative icons, pointing up failures, rather than successes, in attempts to highlight the absence of a visible public record of the history of plebeian radical struggle in Britain.

'Statuemania'

The later part of the nineteenth-century witnessed a period of frenetic monument building across Europe and North America. Described as 'statuemania' or a craze for memorialization, this frenzy of monument construction accompanied the emergence of modern nationalism and the nation-state and validated royal restorations in France, regime change, or the end to and resolution of conflicts. Here George L. Mosse's contention that such monuments represented 'a new style of politics ... based upon a secularized theology and its liturgy' still holds good.[3] As Maurice Agulhon noted, in France, the Third Republic witnessed the increasing public presence of busts and statuary celebrating Marianne and converting her image into an emblem of civic nationalism and pride.[4] Elsewhere in Europe statue construction was a particularly marked element in assertive and insurgent cultures seeking to carve out a coherent identity against the background of crumbling empires like the Austro-Hungarian empire before the Great War. Czech identity was especially dependent on monument-construction, drawing strength from the burial of prominent artists, writers and politicians in the National Cemetery in Vysehrad outside Prague, where their graves were characterized by opulent and excessive public statuary. Monuments celebrating the life and work of Jan Huss were also a marked feature of the Czech cultural renaissance.[5] Most of these monuments asserted the primacy of language, culture and letters. The Risorgimento in Italy witnessed the construction of a very large number of monuments, particularly in border areas like Trento abutting the Austro-Hungarian empire where the statue of Dante incarnated in stone the theme of the cultural inheritance of the Italian people and symbolized the region's innate Italian identity. To cement the role of the people, the design of the statue was subject to a popular consultation.[6] A similar process was at work in North America. There, myriad public memorials sought to impose unity in a fractured country after the divisions of the Civil War and asserted the values of Americanism and national self-confidence in the face of immigration, mass culture and the spread of the social problems associated with urbanization. In Philadelphia the shrine established to the Liberty Bell in Independence Hall carried connotations of nativism and anti-migrant sentiment.[7] As Erika Doss points out, in both Europe and North America there was always a 'laudatory' element to these public statues, emphasizing the individual achievements of those making breakthroughs in science, technology and the arts but ascribing the benefits to the community and to the nation.[8] In their merging of generic images of the people and national aspirations there were some lessons for British radicals here that placed the imprimatur of the people militant on the construction of monuments. These national memorials also demonstrated the constraints imposed on the construction of monuments where there was an absence of state, civic or party political funding.

The commemoration of movements of radical reform was an integral part of this tradition. The memorialization and commemoration of movements of radical reform and social protest were a potent element in European culture. Lynn Hunt has charted the move from the period of the French Revolution onwards towards the design of monuments emblematic of the people's struggle and created to embody a spirit of selfless toil, resistance and insurgency. These symbolic representations were less about representation and more about images of the collective and the whole.[9] Heroic, usually classical in precedent, and illustrative of the radical potential of the people, these monuments usually drew on classical designs for goddesses of liberty and noble, militant male nudes. Their design invoked classical traditions of slave revolts and the incarnation of the correct noble and martial virtues.[10] Transferred to North America via the emigration of European refugees, this tradition featured in the public commemoration provided by the Haymarket Martyrs monument in the former Waldheim (now Forest Home) Cemetery in Chicago. Designed by the German sculptor Albert Weinert and inspired by the homage to freedom that features in the verses of the Marseillaise sung by the martyrs, it depicts the goddess of liberty placing a laurel wreath on the brow of a prostrate worker.[11] Despite the origins of May Day, the international workers' holiday, in this commemorative experience, the memory of Haymarket failed to translate into the construction of permanent reminders of the event in Britain (or indeed anywhere outside the United States).[12] In a culture in Britain in which abstract ideas of liberty or freedom featured infrequently in the imagery of public statuary, there was little opportunity to mark moments of change with depictions of goddesses of liberty or heroic representations of freedoms gained, or dangers to the nation averted.[13] Most metaphoric allusions to the physical remains or to the survivals of working-class everyday life recorded the imprints of lower-class lives in the landscape or in their places of work. Here the representations were often of lives lived in quiet desperation or in unrelenting toil. Arthur Conan Doyle wrote of embattled communities in his Sherlock Holmes story of industrial sabotage, 'The Valley of Fear,' set in the mining industry in the United States against a backdrop of industrial detritus but based on British labour struggles, that 'the strength and industry of man found fitting monuments in the hills which he had spilled by the side of his monstrous excavations'.[14]

There were very few images of working-class people in positive roles in public statuary in Britain. Those that did exist were often seen as eccentricities or whimsey, notably the statue of the blind town crier, Joseph Howarth, 'Blind Joe', erected in Oldham in 1868.[15] Poets and balladeers from a humble background who received public recognition were usually depicted in bourgeois guise 'for admission into your post-mortem court of celebrities' as William Morris expressed it. Speaking to J. Bruce Glasier, Morris noted of the statue erected to Robert Burns in Glasgow in 1877: 'They've tried, don't you think, to make your ploughman poet look something of a fine gentleman, with his pigtail, his ribboned breeches and silver-buckled shoes.'[16] The top hat worn by 'Blind Joe's' statue in Oldham also speaks to a tradition of embourgeoisement of plebeian figures. A Chartist like Dr John Taylor from Ayrshire was memorialized only when the passage of time had softened the outlines of his political career and he could be remembered for his civic contribution alone. Taylor's statue, erected in Ayr in 1858 sixteen years after his death, recalled his contribution to freemasonry and municipal culture, rather than his political radicalism.[17] It was this deficiency in the accurate representation of real working people and their causes that Walter Cranc sought to remedy in his projected mural for an artwork in the Red Cross Street Hall, Southwark, where he asserted: 'we want a new calendar of the canonized. We want to familiarize the ploughman and the pedlar, the sailor at the helm and the weaver at his loom, with the heroism and glory, not of long ago, dead and buried saints and martyrs, but with the heroism and the glory of the saints and the martyrs of our own time'.[18]

A politics of absence

In the absence of 'holy places' in Britain where the spirit of protest might be invoked, most British radicals relied on pilgrimages to the shrines of liberty and freedom established in France at the Communards' Corner in the *Pere Lachaise* cemetery, at the Haymarket martyrs' monument in Chicago visited by the émigré radical Rudolf Rocker, resident in Britain, in 1913 and in Germany at the grave of Ferdinand Lassalle in Breslau, where a commemorative rally at his graveside was addressed by Fenner Brockway in 1932. Among the British delegates attending the International Workers' Congress in Paris in 1889 who laid flowers at the graves of the Communards was J. D. Nieass, 'the old Chartist whose thoughts naturally turned from 1871 to 1848'.[19] Such experiences provided opportunities for reflection and rumination on the power of the continuing struggle and the sacrifices made by others to the cause. Rocker wrote of his visit to the Haymarket Martyrs' Monument: 'I stood for a long time, thinking, silently beside their grave. Near by there was a fresh grave, with grass and wild flowers growing over it. It was the resting place of Voltairine de Cleyre who had died in Chicago on 6 June 1912. A remarkable woman. A rare spirit.'[20] Paradoxically, British radical heroes were commemorated in monumental form more often outside the British Isles than in Britain itself. The most potent reminder of Gerrard Winstanley, leader of the seventeenth-century Digger movement, was in Moscow where the obelisk in the Alexander Gardens, a monument set up in 1913 to memorialize three hundred years of Romanov rule, was renovated in 1921 as a monument to the precursors of the revolution, inscribing Winstanley, Thomas More and others in the pantheon of revolutionary thinkers.[21]

The British monumental tradition in radical culture is one grounded in the absence, rather than the presence, of radical remains, survivals and monuments to the fallen. For some radicals and founders of the Labour Party the monumental tradition in Britain was a reviled one that exalted religious intolerance, dogmatism and displays of arrant militarism over the unsung and unmarked resting places of ordinary soldiers 'shot at down' in the Great War for failure to fulfil their duty.[22] For most reformers their radical forebears and predecessors lived on in their work, rather than through pure acts of commemoration themselves. At a lecture to the Huddersfield Secular Society on the poetry of Ernest Jones, Mr Thomas Garbutt commented that 'the best monument that could be raised to the memory of this truly great man would be to place his works more extensively in the hands of the people'.[23] This was a very English tradition of the celebration of everyday radical careers, rather than the lauding of great events. William Kent, radical antiquarian and biographer, wrote: 'It is not, perhaps necessary that heretics should be commemorated by monuments, but they must be found graves.'[24] Such interest has provided a tradition among historians and the radical faithful of excavating or researching the burial places and absent spaces of memorialization for the displaced or missing remains of deceased radicals.[25] There were frequent laments to the forlorn and dilapidated grave sites of radical leaders like Major Cartwright in Finchley Cemetery; in some cases, as with the elaborate graveside memorial to Ernest Jones in Ardwick cemetery in Manchester, its existence had fallen out of radical memory altogether. The antiquarian Thomas Costley wrote: 'It is a great pity that the people of Salford have not erected a monument to his memory. It is sad to think that there is no monument, no statue – his name, his form almost unknown.'[26] 'Rex', an aged Chartist from Taunton interviewed in *The Social Democrat* in 1897, drew a comparison between Jones and Percy Bysshe Shelley as poets of the people who both lacked monuments.[27] *Reynolds' Newspaper* added to this refrain, asking 'where are the statues of Feargus O'Connor, Bronterre O'Brien, Sir Charles Wolseley and Samuel Bamford?' but was apparently unaware of the graveside monuments and statue dedicated specifically to Jones, Bamford, O'Brien and O'Connor.[28] W. T. Stead's complaint about the absence of a monument to commemorate the Chartists of 1848 also overlooked a pre-existing monument erected to the martyrs Sharp, Vernon and Williams, who died in prison that was still sufficiently well known in 1869 to provide a proposed rallying point for a march in honour of Ernest Jones after his death.[29] This theme of the retiring, unremarked hero, characterized by an absence of commemoration, is a constant in English radical culture (that also co-opted the traditions of Scottish and Welsh radicalism).[30] Frequently expressive of unsung and unremarked heroes and stalwarts of the reform struggle, it painted a narrative of the martyred dead, lying unrecorded and unmarked, but returned to the clay from whence they came with honour, after lives of quiet dedication and sacrifice. *Reynolds's Newspaper* wrote of popular adulation for national heroes in contrast to the relative anonymity of the radical paternalist, Robert Owen, sometimes seen as the father of socialism:

> [T]hey have created monuments to men who were but clay idols. But many of our greatest Englishmen, lovers of the people, martyrs to their cause, repose in their graves without records of brass or stone, their names even slipping out of a fading literature. The work of Robert Owen is its own monument and his name will presently emerge when the blatant din which drowns the deeds of our near contemporaries has subsided.[31]

Robert Owen did have a grave, a known resting place, a monument and, subsequently, a statue, at Newton in Montgomeryshire, and an obelisk in Kensal Green Cemetery, but it was testimony to the strength of this tradition that his place of interment was represented as 'an unmarked grave' unknown and unvisited, although the monument raised in 1863 at his grave remained a site of regular pilgrimage throughout the nineteenth century.[32] The disinterment and re-burial of the remains of the Bonnymuir martyrs executed after the 1820 rising, and the opening of their tomb in Sighthill burial ground in Glasgow in 1872, so that the remains of their transported comrade, Andrew White, might be interred with them, show the potency of this issue of recovering, comingling and reuniting the remains of the martyred dead.[33] The disembodied and disincarnate nature of radical remains, characterized precisely by the absence of spaces of mourning and commemoration, drew on a number of traditions, notably the absence of a place of burial for Tom Paine's bones, which became a radical cause celebre in its own right,[34] as well as overlapping with the Irish tradition of corporeal absence from home and fatherland. This tradition featured particularly in the 'mock funerals' surrounding commemorations in Ireland of the Fenian Manchester Martyrs, whose bodies were depicted as buried unmarked and unmourned in unvisited prison grounds located on foreign soil.[35]

Space, statues and public memorialization

This absence of plebeian memorialization is highlighted by the presence in British towns and cities of numerous municipal images designed to preserve intact the memory of middle-class reform movements like the Anti-Corn Law League, the anti-slavery movement and improving municipal reform crusades. Statues of aldermen and civic worthies became a commonplace in the town centres of northern and midlands cities in the nineteenth century, creating images of presiding 'city fathers' that superseded local political differences. As R. L. Greenall has commented, the statue of the first MP for the borough of Salford, Joseph Brotherton unveiled at Peel Park in 1858, in effect celebrated 'the rise of the borough with whose fortunes he had been so intimately connected, the arrival of their class, and the memory of the Anti-Corn Law League'.[36] The centrality of such images to the story of reform and improvement that typified the nineteenth-century cityscape has been noted by Patrick Joyce. He highlights the importance of public buildings, statues and monuments as physical incarnations of the liberal reforming spirit in liberalism's new urban heartlands.[37] In invoking a democratization of the urban experience, this tradition cemented liberalism at the heart of a narrative of freedom and individualism, consonant with the traditions of laissez-faire. These were crowded urban centres, where the proliferation of memorials and statues, later frequently with an imperial theme, began to squeeze out the possibilities for the construction of monuments that represented plebeian culture and the history of radicalism.[38] One correspondent in the *Manchester City News* bemoaned the numerous 'unsightly objects' that now littered Manchester city centre, lamented the prospects for more and highlighted the poor position of the statue of Oliver Cromwell 'dwarfed' by the cathedral and tramway wires.[39] Where radical memory is apparent in public statuary, it reflected liberalism's appropriation of the radical tradition and the Liberal party's utilization of central tropes of the radical past to portray liberalism as the culmination of a process of democratization and reform. The unveiling of a monument to Samuel Bamford, the Peterloo veteran, and author of *Passages in the Life of a Radical*, in Middleton in 1877, for example, provided the opportunity for a reflection on the overlaps between liberalism and radicalism, in which Bamford was depicted primarily as 'an early advocate of civil and religious liberty, freedom and parliamentary reform' in the inscription on the monument. For J. P. Hibbert, Liberal MP for Oldham, who presided at the ceremony, Bamford and his followers 'planted the seed we were reaping the fruits of and he hoped the fruits would be reaped for many generations to come'.[40] Often it was Liberal associations, donors and benefactors who held the funds necessary to memorialize the radical dead and to incorporate them into an avowedly liberal lineage. In Northampton, the construction of a statue to Charles Bradlaugh in 1894 was largely a Liberal affair, instigated by the local Liberal association and with an opening ceremony presided over by the Liberal MP for the borough, Sir Philip Manfield, and Liberal MP, F. A. Channing. At the unveiling, Bradlaugh was depicted as an embodiment of liberal values of self-improvement, education, hard work and self-worth. There was no mention of his republicanism or atheism, and for Manfield the true merits that emerged from his life were that his career provided 'a noble lesson in self-help which should encourage those who had to fight the battle of life and progress'.⁴¹ As Matthew Roberts has demonstrated, the contentious histories of the monuments erected to the Scottish Jacobin radicals in Nunhead Cemetery in London in 1851 and on Carlton Hill in Edinburgh in 1844 show that there was often little consensus around monument construction, and the Chartists were keenly aware of, and resistant to, Whig or Liberal attempts to appropriate plebeian radical memories of working-class protest.⁴²

Key events in radical and working-class history that stood outside the orbit of conventional liberalism remained, however, unrecognized or un-memorialized throughout the nineteenth and early twentieth centuries. As Paul Pickering has demonstrated, the expense of monument construction made statues difficult to build, and almost impossible to maintain, and there was often uncertainty about who, or what, was in the process of memorialization. Some, like Feargus O'Connor's statue in Nottingham, rapidly deteriorated after years of neglect.⁴³ From the period of the Chartist movement onwards, attempts to create a recognizable radical lineage that was set in stone usually failed. The monument to Henry Hunt in the grounds of the Rev. James Scholefield's chapel in Ancoats, Manchester, was only ever partially completed, and attempts to raise funds to erect a statue to William Cobbett came to nothing.⁴⁴ Where the memories of radical figures did survive, they did so through the medium of ephemera: commercial slipware for domestic use, handkerchiefs, wall plaques, cheap printed engravings and, above all, books and texts, described by Matthew Roberts as de facto 'monuments'.⁴⁵ Writing in the *National Reformer*, J. F. Haines lamented the absence from Britain's towns and cities of statues to radical heroes like Ernest Jones, Thomas Meagher and John Thelwall but proposed the recording of episodes in the lives of radical icons in spaces like radical clubs, controlled by the working-class reform movement itself: 'At present we might not be able to adorn our squares, streets or parks with freedom's heroes, but the various lecture halls that were being raised throughout the country by "our party" might be dedicated each to a hero, and the portico embellished with some episode in his life connected with his movement.'⁴⁶ A campaign to set up a statue to Ernest Jones in London came to nothing.⁴⁷ Without physical reminders or monumental survivals of radical heroes, a tradition of antiquarianism developed in radical circles in which premises, public buildings, places of business and the homes of the martyred dead were recorded by enthusiasts. These provided a potent 'monument to a movement' in the title of a pamphlet commemorating the Clarion House cycling club erected outside Newchurch-in-Pendle in Lancashire in 1912.⁴⁸ Richard Carlile retained a particularly devoted following who recorded sites connected with his career or launched plans for a Richard Carlile 'holy day', an irony that would not have been lost on one of the founders of the freethought movement. The smaller and more marginal such movements were (like the freethought movement) the more they sought to invest in the renovation and preservation of these accidental survivals.⁴⁹ The absence of a memorial to the Peterloo massacre in Manchester where the events of 1819 unfolded remained an important vacuum, depriving assemblies of radicals gathered to mark the events of the massacre of an appropriate shrine at which to pay homage to the fallen. As the *Daily Dispatch* noted at the time of the Peterloo centenary in 1919, the preservation of the memory of Peterloo remained largely an oral tradition: 'the memory of that day's happenings have ever been kept green on Labour and reform platforms and Peterloo is still quoted at public meetings' in a culture that was buoyed by the circulation of quasi-religious 'relics' or artefacts present at the day.[50] For some, the Free Trade Hall served in part as a reminder of the events of 1819. Writing of a women's suffrage demonstration in the hall in 1894, the *Labour Leader* imagined 'the ghosts of all those who have striven for freedom in that hall, and of those whose blood sanctified its site in 1819'.[51] Others aspired to something less tainted by memories of middle-class liberalism that might stand as a radical reproach to Toryism.[52] Three separate attempts were made to counter the liberal dominance of the memory of the massacre at sites that had connections to the events of post-Napoleonic War radicalism. In gatherings in preparation for anniversaries of the massacre from the seventieth anniversary in 1889 through to its centenary in 1919, attempts were made to variously set up a commemorative granite pillar or to renovate the obelisk dedicated to Henry Hunt's memory at Revered James Scholefield's chapel in Every Streets, Ancoats. In the event, nothing concrete materialized.[53] Moreover attempts to convert the vault under the Hunt memorial at Every Street chapel into a pantheon for fallen reformers resulted in the burial of five former Chartists only. The burials were halted after Scholefield's death in 1855 and the Hunt memorial itself was demolished in 1888.[54]

Imagining and constructing statues

Much radical monument fervour traded on the prospect of monuments that could never be constructed or were incapable of realization, a tradition that began with some of the projected and satirical designs for a monument to Peterloo.[55] At the height of the Boer War a correspondent to the Social Democratic Federation organ, *Justice*, proposed setting up a subscription for an imaginary monument in the Transvaal sympathetic to the interests of the Boer republics so that future visitors might read: 'This monument was erected by English, Scottish, Welsh and Irish residents from the British Isles ... as a tribute [as a] respect to the memory of the heroic dead of their own country who with the Boers fought and fell for the independence of the Orange Free State and the Transvaal.'[56] Transatlantic influences were also apparent in the imaginary and fantastical depictions of memorialization that circulated among radicals. The American author Ignatius Donnelly's populist novel of a rising in New York City, *Caesar's Column*, imagined an apocalyptic struggle between workers and employers resulting in widespread social disorder on the French revolutionary model. The novel culminates in the construction of a grisly monument to the rising comprising the bodies of dead plutocrats in Union Square sealed into a memorial column as permanent testimony to the sufferings of the population.[57] This image provided a satirical commentary on the cult of memorialization at the end of the nineteenth century, on the role of Union Square in New York for workers' demonstrations since 1882 and on the fashion for vertical build in New York. Less well known than in the United States, the novel received comment and some acclaim in Britain.[58]

The few successful radical monument constructions were the products of initiatives by bodies that could command revenue and were sufficiently integrated into working-class associational culture to raise appropriate funds through either existing budgets or subscriptions and appeals organized around the commemoration of locally significant individuals. Significant in such memorialization were trade unions, co-ops and temperance associations.[59] Writing in 1869, the former Chartist, George Julian Harney looked to both the trades unions and the co-operative movement, to commemorate the life and work of Ernest Jones: 'from the funds of trade unions and the profits of flourishing co-operative association(s) there ought to come free-will offerings and generous contributions to the funds for the family of Ernest Jones and also to a fund for erecting a monument over the remains of the lamented patriot and friend of the people'.[60] The strong miners and cotton operative associations were at the forefront of such campaigns, embedding trade union histories within local communities through the celebration of prominent trades unionists. In 1883 the Durham miners' unions successfully appealed for funds to raise a monument in Durham to Alexander Macdonald, one of the first two Lib-Lab working-men MPs elected to parliament in the 1874 general election. This was one of only a very small number of public memorials that carried the features of a working man on a public monument. His fellow MP, Thomas Burt, unveiling the statue commented:

[T]hat day they entered upon a new departure, and this was something amounting to a novelty almost in the ceremony. Statues had been erected to distinguished men, to heroes, to kings, to statesmen in cathedrals, cemeteries, and public places, but that day they were met to unveil and to do honour to a working man who was in every way worthy of it.[61]

Subsequently the activities of trades unions were central to the preservation and renovation of monuments, tombs and public statues that acted as the legacies of past radical campaigns. Meeting in Manchester in 1913, the Trades Union Congress donated money for a clean-up and a refurbishment of Ernest Jones's monument at his grave in Ardwick Cemetery, also laying a wreath in his memory.[62] Funds were also provided for the memorialization of local trades unionists, notably J. T. Fielding, an official in the local Cotton Spinners' Association, secretary of the Bolton Trades Council and the first working man to become a Justice of the Peace. The unveiling of his statue in Queen's Park, Bolton, attracted a procession of 20,000 people.[63] In addition, miners' union donations and a public subscription raising 35,000 individual contributions funded a graveside memorial to the Wigan miners' official, Ben Pickard, described as 'the *beau-ideal* of the miners' agent' at his funeral in Wigan Cemetery in 1887.[64] More tangential links to the development of trade unionism are revealed by the financial contribution of the Agricultural Labourers' Union to a statue of Joseph Priestly erected in Birmingham in 1874.[65] With dividends and budgets, the cooperative movement was in a good position to sponsor and finance commemorative monuments dedicated to the history of the movement. Funerals and the memorialization of pioneers of the movement were lavish affairs.[66] The ambiguities around the origins of cooperation also led to a search for a radical pedigree that resulted in the privileging of the Owenite inheritance within the co-operative movement. The one successful generic monument construction that revered the radical past and sought to create a living lineage and narrative of previous radical campaigns was the 1885 Kensal Green Reformers'

Monument in Kensal Green Cemetery, located next to a monument to Robert Owen and recording the contributions of notable figures to the radical platform, from Chartists like William Lovett to John Ruskin.[67] Updated and subsequently renovated by the cooperative movement, it emphasized the commitment of the individuals recorded on the monument to the 'associative idea' and saw in the cooperative ideal an anticipation of Tennyson's 'the federation of the world' and the League of Nations.[68] Intended as an antidote to Empire and Flag Days, the monument hoped to preserve memories of good deeds that had contributed to the sum of human happiness and improvement in stone: 'Positivists have their calendar of Great Men; the great religions have their days of memory for the saints and heroes; but democracy too often forgets.'[69]

Proxy memorialization

Recent literature on nineteenth-century culture has emphasized a spatial turn on the part of movements of radical protest.[70] Hoping to assert themselves in the new city and townscapes of industrial centres, advocates of platform politics sought places of congregation, protest and assembly. Frequently locked out of the public spaces, squares, town centres and parks by the civic and imperial monument mania of the mid-late nineteenth century, many radicals found themselves unrepresented in, or even alienated by, the new civic culture and set themselves in opposition to the monument design and creation of these years. Such sentiments were very marked in the radical press. Much radical ire was expended against the choice of figures and leaders memorialized in public places. *Reynolds's Newspaper* in particular expressed strong opposition to the upsurge in statue construction that characterized the decade of the 1850s, displaying hostility to the 'Wellington mania' that saw plans for a number of monuments commemorating the 'Iron Duke' that will 'soon be springing up like mushrooms around us'.[71] Deriding the expansive and excessive memorialization of Prince Albert and Sir Robert Peel after their deaths, the newspaper lamented the absence of similar memorialization to British literary and scientific figures 'who have conferred everlasting benefit and honour not only on their native country, but upon the whole human race'.[72] Responding to the proliferation of statues to Peel, the newspaper reported its concern that in towns where a monument to him was in process of construction, working people would be expected to contribute to a testimonial to defray the cost of the memorial as happened with some statues to Wellington where testimonials had been imposed: 'as a fitting tribute to the memory of a man who was ever ready at a moment's notice to turn the cannon's mouth or the bayonet's point against the industrial community'.[73] It made the same point about the construction of monuments to Prince Albert, asserting employer coercion against the workforce 'for the purpose of squeezing some of its hard-earned pence out of the pockets of the half-employed and half-famishing (sic) labour of the country'.[74] In regard to the Hyde Park statue of Albert, it declared it a 'forced monument' funded by reluctant and destitute contributors, which would in time fade into the background.[75] In the case of memorials to Sir Robert Peel, the paper also complained of the validation they gave to the 'new police', still seen in the 1850s as enemies of the community.[76]

Opposition to this new municipal and public symbolism and statuary took a variety of forms. The statues and memorials to civic fathers were often colonized, annexed or utilized as spaces of dissent during periods of radical protest, election disturbances or riot in a process that might be described as proxy memorialization. The centrality and conspicuous nature of these monuments made them natural gathering places for the expression of political protest. Here their original purposes were subverted and placed at the service of radical and reform causes. The statue of the Duke of Wellington in Norwich, for example, became an open-air venue for socialist public meetings addressed by William Morris from a wagonette in 1888; anarchists in Liverpool held their meetings around the podium of the Wellington statue there on Sundays in the 1890s.[77] Monuments to royalty were often colonized. The obelisk commemorating Queen Victoria's 1887 golden jubilee in front of Sheffield Town Hall became a 'Workers' University' in the 1890s: 'Its base was four-sided with several steps leading up to it and formed a convenient platform for speakers of all creeds … Socialists, Anarchists, Salvationists, Temperance speakers to mention only a few.'[78] During riots by the unemployed in Manchester in 1905, addresses, speeches and exhortations to political action were issued by the socialist orator Victor Grayson from the steps of the statue devoted to Queen Victoria in Piccadilly. Both Victoria's statue in Piccadilly and Albert's memorial in Albert Square became unofficial plinths for radical assemblage and acts of defiance against the authorities during the disturbances.[79] Elections often generated impromptu and spontaneous occupations of public statuary and monuments. In the 1859 general election, the independent radical candidate, Abel Heywood, running against the established Liberal party in Manchester, was castigated for addressing his supporters from the base of Sir Robert Peel's statue in front of the Royal Infirmary in Piccadilly, thereby converting it into a platform for their 'mob oratory'. Other accounts alleged that other 'destructives' 'would have clambered upon the head of Peel himself if they had been able'.[80] The issue haunted Heywood for some years and was recalled in the subsequent general election of 1865.[81] In such episodes the issue was the contestation of public space itself. Many of the spaces surrounding monuments were semi-sacred environments, sanctified by public use, ritual behaviour or historical memory of ancestral usage. In the context of nineteenth-century radicalism, the use of public space for demonstrations and riots often constituted a reoccupation of sequestered and plundered land. Trafalgar Square, in particular, was open to such narratives; a former site of struggles over the commons in the sixteenth century, and a place of popular entertainment and vagabondage, the square was depicted by radicals as a space of democratic inclusivity and participation where the paraphernalia and memorials of empire clashed directly with a remembered history of popular usage.[82] In the aftermath of riots in the square in 1887, Annie Besant's journal, *The Link*, commented: 'Our square still is, as it has been for years past, the open air Town Hall of the London democracy, sacred by many memories of claims to liberty spoken there, sacred by many memories of rights strenuously proclaimed there, sacred, most of all, by memories of blood lately shed there.'[83]

In the absence of icons and spaces where homage might be paid to the radical dead, radical culture was reliant on proxies, figures whose careers carried sufficient political and cultural weight to stand in for, or play the part of, the martyred departed.

These memorials might be regarded as substitute monuments, often dedicated to heroes whose stories resonated with reforming moments in Britain and that departed from their original purpose, serving an alternative function to the role originally ascribed to them by organizing committees and donors. In this way, some unlikely figures found their political pasts and monumental functions placed at the service of the radical platform and served the function of proxies for the radical martyred dead. Memories of the English Civil War were often invoked for this purpose, placing radicalism in touch with the Cromwellian and Puritan tradition of the 1640s and situating the parliamentary reform campaign in a broader narrative of opposition to tyranny, reaction and courtly excess. Monuments to battles and heroes of the parliamentary cause were often colonized by radicals. In 1875, at the prompting of Joseph Arch, the Agricultural Labourers' Union took advantage of the bicentenary of the Battle of Naseby to organize a march of 2,000 labourers to the memorial obelisk commemorating the site of the battle, where Arch cautioned, '[T]hey must, however, break the army of the tyrants by peaceable means.'[84] *Reynolds' Newspaper* saw Cromwell himself as one of the martyred heroes of the people, deserving of a major statue.[85] The statue built to his memory in Manchester by private subscription and unveiled in 1875, although an object of curiosity and a place of radical pilgrimage, was too controversial and too poorly situated at the approach to Exchange Station to provide a focus for demonstrations.[86] Despite exhortations that the statue was appropriate 'in this great city where the greatest movements in favour of progress had been carried on' fears that it would become a site of radical republican demonstrations failed to materialize and, instead, it stoked sectarian divisions in Manchester.[87] Stronger radical messages were encoded in the statue of William Wallace erected at Stirling Bridge. Completed in 1869 by a committee chaired by the ex-Chartist and Reform League member, John McAdam, it reflected his support for liberal nationalism in Europe, enthusiasm for the Italian Risorgimento and personal links to Garibaldi and the Hungarian nationalist, Lewis Kossuth. Both Garibaldi and Kossuth contributed to the construction of the monument. For McAdam, Wallace was a manifestation of an emergent national spirit in Scotland similar to the forces released by European liberal nationalisms.[88] His interest in Wallace was in a long tradition with links to the Chartist movement, where Wallace featured as a hero of amateur poetry submitted to journals like *The English Chartist Circular* and survived in late Victorian radical homilies as 'the forerunner of the Koskiuskos, Capodistrias, and Garibaldis of later times; he was the first soldier in Europe who fought not for a dynasty, but for a nation ... In Wallace democracy found its first great leader'.[89] As Matthew Roberts has pointed out, the proposed renovation and re-bronzing of Major Cartwright's statue in Cartwright Gardens, London, in 1842 by the Chartist movement were very much in this tradition, summoning up the spirit of Cartwright to assist the radical movement of the 1840s and asserting the statue's significance as 'the only one in London expressive of the principles contained in the People's Charter'.[90] Similar reverence was given to the statue of Richard Oastler, the factory reformer, in Bradford, erected in 1866 and depicted by the ILP on the eve of the Great War as an important part of the record of radical politics in the town.[91] Some monuments were wrongly represented or quite simply misidentified as sites with radical connections. The obelisk in Ludgate Circus in London described by Reg

Groves as a monument to John Wilkes was, in fact, a public street lamp erected when Wilkes was mayor and thus bearing his name, but with no radical implications. It was dismantled in 1950.[92]

Iconoclasm and the British radical tradition

Despite the strong alignment between memories of the English Reformation, Puritanism and the English radical tradition, attacks on statues, memorials and icons associated with iconoclasm and militant Protestantism barely featured as an aspect of the radical platform.[93] Indeed, statue desecrations were a minority tactic in British radicalism, depicted as an alien and un-British import in fantastical stories and shilling shockers that imagined the vandalism of public monuments under a future socialist state.[94] Attacks on statues during periods of heightened political emotion did occur in Britain but were seldom orchestrated or organized. An explicitly political motivation is apparent in attempts made on 31 August 1831 to topple the newly erected statue of William Pitt the younger in Hanover Square at the height of the reform bill crisis; on polling day in 1906 the newly elected MP for Stoke, Josiah Wedgwood, along with his brother Ralph, climbed the statue of his grandfather, Josiah Wedgwood the potter, opposite Stoke Station, to decorate it with the blue colours of the Liberal party.[95] Apart from such isolated events political motivation seldom featured in the recorded attacks against public statuary in London and the regional centres. Other desecrations of monuments were spontaneous actions or the work of individuals. The decapitation of James Wyatt's equestrian statue of Queen Victoria and mutilation of the accompanying statue of the Prince Consort in Regent's Park in 1859 were the lone actions of the former inmate of an asylum with mental health issues.[96] In the absence of statue daubings and vandalism at home, radicals often experienced a vicarious thrill at monument desecrations elsewhere in Europe: *Reynolds' Newspaper* was enthusiastic about the pulling down of Bonaparte's statue in the Place Vendome during the Paris Commune, labelling it as 'heroic' and a 'justifiable vandalism'.[97] Statue desecrations were emblematic of societies in crisis where there were significant ruptures in the existing social fabric, a breakdown of government or a moment of revolution. Some of these factors pertained in Ireland, where attacks on monuments and statues were more commonplace than in England, Wales and Scotland. Over the period 1870–1922 the statues of royal figures were systematically targeted in Dublin for their associations with the rituals of loyalism and were gradually removed or supplanted by statues to the rebels of 1798 and prominent nationalists and republicans in a process gathering pace with the formation of the Free State in 1922: statues to William III, George I and George II were among the casualties of this process.[98] The emphasis on destroying, ridiculing or toppling monuments in Ireland grew out of the circumstances of the Anglo-Irish Ascendancy and British rule, giving Irish republicanism a marked appreciation of the symbolism of monuments and statues as targets.[99] The damage dealt to statues in bombing attacks on British imperial and ceremonial buildings was deliberate, in the case of a dynamite attack on the Palace of Westminster in 1885 causing damage to the pedestals of statues of William IV and George IV.[100] Acts of iconoclasm in Britain occurred only where this tradition was imported into Britain by the presence of a significant Irish element in movements of protest. The strongest example of this is the community violence aspect apparent in the repeated vandalism of Gladstone's statue in Bow churchyard. Erected by Theodore Bryant with a compulsory exaction of one shilling from the wages of the predominantly Irish Bryant and May match girls, the hands of the statue were daubed with red paint during the 1888 strike at the match factory to symbolize the excessive and unjust nature of the levy.[101] Rumours that the hands of the statue were daubed with real blood circulated at the time. This bore some similarity to the painting and daubing of royal statues with green paint in Ireland. Annie Besant wrote in *The Link*: 'Later on they surrounded the statue – "we paid for it" they cried savagely – shouting and yelling and a gruesome story is told that some cut their arms and let their blood trickle on the marble paid for in very truth, by their blood.'[102]

Provisional memorialization

In the absence of monuments and recognized spaces in towns and cities that might serve as rallying points for radicals, reformers were forced back on improvised or impromptu memorials using natural features, prominent local landmarks and elements in the landscape that resonated with the memories of radical protest. These might be regarded as provisional memorialization, utilized in lieu of more solid places and spaces of remembrance. Such makeshift memorialization was commonplace for movements with few financial resources to fall back on and could be easily erased, leaving little evidence behind. In 1908 Alexander Stewart Gray, tribune of unemployed workers in northern cities, talked of invading the private land around St. George's Hill in Surrey where the first Digger settlement had been established and throwing up a mound adorned with a wreath of ivy in memory of Gerrard Winstanley.[103] This protest left no visible legacy. Provisional, ad hoc and proxy memorialization of space among radicals is especially marked with reference to trees. The reverence expressed by reformers for trees and the remnants of forests is a long-running theme, drawing on contemporary literary and cultural representations of forest life as a plebeian utopia. Struggles to save forests, like the campaign to prevent the enclosure of Epping Forest in East London, recalled traditional community dependence on forests.[104] Single trees were a surviving remnant of this enclave of freedom. This was an atavistic radicalism that drew on ancestral memories of the freedoms and liberation from constraints that characterized the imaginary history of the Middle Ages. The series 'The Working Man in History' that featured in the *National Reformer* began with idyllic glimpses of 'the merry greenwood' and allusions to Robin Hood. A subsequent article 'A Glimpse of Sherwoode' beginning 'Hurrah for the forest!' traded in images of merry parties gathered around the landmark Major Oak in the forest. This was a timeless vision of freedom dwelling among the boughs and the glades 'here in the forest with its memories extending back to the Caesars'.[105] The national romance with trees, particularly oak trees, and vision of them as providers of 'timber and tar' used in the design of warships existed in a radical incarnation in amateur poetry where their fragile position was seen as symbolic of a nation threatened by 'bishops, placemen and peers' conspiring to 'cut down this guardian of ours'. For some, the People's Charter was itself a metaphoric vessel: 'of stout old English oak were her timbers built'.[106] Such narratives constituted a working-class manifestation of the sentimental and nostalgic place within antiquarian literature reserved for trees connected with royal figures and major episodes in British history.[107] Passed down in radical culture through fanciful narratives of Arcadian and sylvan open-air life, the emphasis on trees also drew on images of trees of liberty imported from France during the revolution where they were sometimes depicted as 'monuments of insurrection' by critics and in an earlier expression that drew on British precedents, their role in the American Revolution.[108] Trees as rallying places for assembly and protest subverted the traditional emphasis on trees as markers for royal events.[109] This arboreal radicalism is apparent in the continuing belief that the history of parliament began with assemblages of Anglo-Saxons around trees, an idea much quoted in reform texts and speeches.[110] The planting of trees also symbolized moments of reform but could additionally subvert moments of loyalism. M. K. Ashby recalled the speech by the local vicar of Tysoe on the occasion of the 1887 royal jubilee in which he lauded 'the William and Mary elm, celebrating the coming of that man of peace, the Prince of Orange, the tree of constitutional liberty (the "Franchise Tree"); and now this sapling, the tree of loyalty'.[111] Trees connected up with the ephemeral nature of much British radicalism, representing impermanence and the transient. They provided effective, makeshift markers, especially when there were specific links with radical politics and places of assembly, used especially by rural political agitators, who gathered out of doors or in fields.[112] The Wellesbourne Oak in Warwickshire where Joseph Arch addressed the foundation meeting of the Agricultural Labourers' Union in 1872 was annually decorated and festooned with union jacks as a commemoration of the establishment of the Union; the so-called 'Martyrs' Tree', a sycamore on the green at Tolpuddle beneath which the trade union martyrs allegedly swore their illegal trade union oath in 1834, provided a rallying point for marches in memory of the men; a cutting from the tree was planted on the grave of James Hammett, the only martyr buried in English soil, in the 1980s.[113] There was a particularly strong association between trees and the history of peasant revolt. The Oak of Reformation on Mousehold Heath outside Norwich, from which Robert Kett, leader of the 1549 peasant rising, traditionally held court and dispensed justice, remained a place of strong radical associations for visiting reformers. Joseph Clayton, a member of the ILP and an amateur historian of the rising, highlighted its significance but acknowledged the difficulty of identifying the specific tree (or trees) used by Kett.[114] Especially significant was the reformers' tree, in Hyde Park, an old elm tree used to memorialize the 1866–67 reform bill protests, which was burnt down, vandalized and reduced to a stump but still operated as a place of radical assemblage into the 1880s.[114] Veneration of the oak tree as a symbol of liberty and justice persisted into the 1930s. In his homily to English liberties, *England, My England*, the Communist author Jack Lindsay lauded Kett's 'Oak of Reformation' as a 'symbol of the old liberties and rights of communal days; symbol of all that rejected the rule of competitive individualism and private ownership of the land'. In this reference to historical and inherited liberties, Lindsay drew affinities with the oak tree of Guernica where the Basque people traditionally sat in conclave, in a town that had been all but destroyed by a new tyranny under the guise of nationalism and Fascism.[115] The relevance of this tradition survived in the planting of the 'Addison Oak' to inaugurate the construction of the first inter-war council housing under the 1919 Addison act at the Sea Mills Estate in Bristol in June of that year. Here there were distant echoes of the displaced and supplanted peasantry of Albion whose rights and freedoms were restored through the new medium of state-sponsored housing.[116]

Conclusions

Plebeian radicalism in Britain has left few monumental survivals to mark its passing. All too often the co-joined history of radicalism and memorialization in Britain is about absence, quite as much as about presence. A number of campaigns highlighted the failure by radical reformers to construct, create or put in place monuments to the martyred dead. Some of the projected monuments imagined by radicals were never going to be built; others were neglected and forgotten. In this sense, the failure by campaigners throughout the nineteenth and twentieth centuries to construct a monument to Peterloo is typical of the broader silence towards past radical agitations evident in the lack of physical memorialization to platform radicalism during this period. A number of factors conspired to marginalize campaigns for monuments to reform and the protest movements they represented. The inherent poverty of many reform organizations, lack of available funds to maintain monuments, crowded municipal spaces and radicalism's dependency on the marginal and the transient pushed campaigns for monument construction out of the mainstream. With the exception of the trade union, temperance and co-operative movements which had resources to construct monuments, this left a vacuum in the internal culture of radical politics. Despite the overwhelmingly loyalist and patriotic nature of most public sculpture, few British working-men embraced acts of iconoclasm directly, although this practice became commonplace against British royal statues in Ireland. Rather, in the absence of monumental survivals, ad hoc and improvised methods of memorialization were resorted to by reform movements to preserve the physical survivals of a reforming lineage. This is apparent in provisional memorials to reform, notably the Reformers' Tree in Hyde Park. On occasion there was a resort to monuments erected to historical figures with radical connotations whose statues were conscripted into the cause of radical reform. Against a background of absence, the notion of the unmourned and unmarked radical saviour became central to reformers' perception of the radical hero.

Notes

1   Joseph Cozens, 'The Making of the Peterloo Martyrs, 1819 to the Present', in *Secular Martyrdom in Britain and Ireland: From Peterloo to the Present*, ed. Quentin Outram and Keith Laybourn (London: Palgrave, 2018), 48–50 and Tristram Hunt, '"Engels Comes of Age", *The Observer*, 8 November 2020, 50.

2   A memorial gravestone was erected to the memory of Dic Penderyn, leader of the 1831 Merthyr rising, in St. Mary's Churchyard, Aberavon, in 1966; William Lovett was given a plaque in Newlyn in Cornwall, unveiled by Michael Foot, and Neil Kinnock spoke at an event to erect a headstone on John Frost's previously unmarked grave in Bristol in 1986. Striking miners during the miners' strike of 1984-5 wanted to re-enact the Chartist march on Newport. See Gwyn Williams, *The Land Remembers: A View of Wales* (London: Futura Publications, Ltd., 1977), 185 and Dennis Johnson, 'Chartist History of the Red Rose', *The Guardian*, 10 October 1986.
3   George L. Mosse, 'Mass Politics and the Political Liturgy of Nationalism', in *Nationalism: The Nature and Evolution of an Idea*, ed. Eugene Kamenka (London: Edward Arnold, 1973), 39.
4   Maurice Agulhon, *Marianne into Battle: Republican Imagery and Symbolism in France, 1789-1880* (Cambridge: Cambridge University Press, 1981), ch. 1 and Eric Hobsbawm, 'Mass-Producing Traditions: Europe 1870-1914', in *The Invention of Tradition*, ed. Hobsbawm and Terence Ranger (Cambridge: Cambridge University Press, 1983), 271-2.
5   Pavla Statnikova, *Reflections on Vysehrad – a Short Guide* (Vysehrad: National Cultural Monument, 2005), 23-5 and Zdenek Vybiral, 'Hus in Historical Memory', in *Jan Hus: Courage to Think; Courage to Believe. Courage to Die*, ed. Jakub Smrcka, Blanka Zilynska, and Eva Dolezalova (Konstanz: Jan Hus Museum, 2015), 152-63. Hus was also a hero of British radicalism; see Charles Cockbill Cattell, *Martyrs of Progress: Being Historical Sketches of the Perils and Persecutions of the Discoverers and Teachers of All Ages and Nations* (London: Charles Watts, 1878), 10-11.
6   Giulia Mori, 'Un Applauso Interminabile: Trento e il Monumento a Dante. Storia di un Concorso', in *Non Ancora Italia: Temi Risorgimentali Dell'Arte in Trentino*, ed. Laura Dal Pra (Trento: Provincia Autonoma Di Trento, 2011), 69-88.
7   Charlene Mires, *Independence Hall in American Memory* (Philadelphia: University of Pennsylvania Press, 2002), chs. 4-5.
8   Erika Doss, *Memorial Mania: Public Feeling in America* (Chicago: The University of Chicago Press, 2010), 17-31.
9   Lynn Hunt, *Politics, Culture and Class in the French Revolution* (Berkeley: University of California Press, 1984), ch. 3.
10 Eric Hobsbawm, *Worlds of Labour: Further Studies in the History of Labour* (London: Weidenfeld and Nicolson, 1984), 83-102.
11 William J. Adelman, *Haymarket Revisited: A Tour Guide of Labor History Sites and Ethnic Neighbourhoods Connected with the Haymarket Affair* (Chicago: Illinois Labor History Society, 1976), 104-7 and 'The Haymarket Martyrs Tour', in *The Day Will Come: Honouring Our Working-Class Heroes, Stories of the Haymarket Martyrs*, ed. Mark Rogovin (Chicago: Illinois Labour History Society, 2011), 6.
12 Philip S. Foner, *May Day: A Short History of the International Workers' Holiday, 1886-1986* (New York: International Publishers, 1986), 25-6.
13 An exception to this is the 'Physical Energy' statue by G. F. Watts, erected in Kensington Gardens in 1906 as a monument to Cecil Rhodes, but really acting as a tribute to physical vigour and potency. The image featured on the Energen crispbread box: see John Whitlock Blundell and Roger Hudson, *The Immortals: London's Finest Statues* (London: Folio Society, 1998), 12.
14 Arthur Conan Doyle, 'The Valley of Fear', in *The Penguin Complete Sherlock Holmes* (London: Penguin Books, [1931] 1981), 819.

15 J. Vernon, *Politics and the People: A Study in English Political Culture, c.1815–67* (Cambridge: Cambridge University Press, 1992), 165.
16 J. Bruce Glasier, *William Morris and the Early Days of the Socialist Movement* (London: Longmans, Green and Co., 1921), 97. See for the unveiling of the Burns statue in Glasgow, *Reynolds's Newspaper*, 28 January 1877, 8.
17 W. Hamish Fraser, *Dr John Taylor, Chartist Ayrshire Revolutionary* (Ayr: Ayrshire Archaeological and Natural History Society, 2006), 9–11 and 88–90.
18 *The Link: A Journal for the Servants of Man*, 7 April 1888, 2.
19 *Justice*, 3 August 1889, 2. For demonstrations at the Communard Corner in Pere Lachaise Cemetery in Paris see Phillips Russell, 'In Memory of the Commune', *The International Socialist Review*, 15, no. 2 (1914), 69–71 and for demonstrations in memory of Lassalle, Fenner Brockway, *Inside the Left: Thirty Years of Platform, Press, Prison and Parliament* (London: George Allen and Unwin, 1942), 280.
20 Rudolf Rocker, *The London Years* (Nottingham: Five Leaves, [1956] 2005), 139. In the United States a tradition developed for socialist, trade union and Communist leaders to be buried around the monument. The ashes of Communist leader William Z. Foster were buried there after his death in 1961. See Edward P. Johanningsmeier, *Forging American Communism: The Life of William Z. Foster* (New Jersey: Princeton University Press, 1994), 351. Accounts of the Haymarket Martyrs' Monument stressed the vibrancy of the monument as a lived space, as opposed to the 'crumbling and neglected statue erected to the memory of the police who were killed at Haymarket': quotation from *The Free Commune* published in *Freedom*, 1 June 1899, 4.
21 John Gurney, *Gerrard Winstanley: The Digger's Life and Legacy* (London: Pluto Press, 2013), 1–3 and Enzo Traverso, *Left-Wing Melancholia: Marxism History and Memory* (New York: Columbia University Press, 2016), 64.
22 See Katharine Bruce Glasier on the Martyrs' Memorial in St. Andrew's Cathedral in *Labour's Northern Voice*, 26 November 1926, 2 and *The Herald*, 13 May 1916, 2.
23 *National Reformer*, 27 December 1874, 454, *Manchester Evening News*, 27 August 1877, 3.
24 William Kent, *London for Heretics* (London: Watts and Co., 1932), 59.
25 David S. Karr, 'The Embers of Expiring Sedition: Maurice Margarot, the Scottish Martyrs Monument and the Production of Radical Memory across the British South Pacific', *Historical Research*, 86, no. 234 (2013), 638–60.
26 Thomas Costley, *Lancashire Poets and Other Literary Sketches* (Manchester: Abel Heywood and Sons, 1897), 74. For a description of the dedication of the monument to Ernest Jones in Ardwick Cemetery, see the *Manchester Examiner and Times*, 10 April 1871, 4. The monument was quite elaborate but was still described as a 'humble tomb' by Dr Richard Pankhurst at a commemorative rally in Jones's memory, see *The City Jackdaw*, 14 March 1879, 136. For a radical pilgrimage to the grave of Major Cartwright in Finchley Cemetery, see the *Boston Guardian*, 21 July 1883, 5.
27 *The Social Democrat*, 1, no. 4 (1897), 99. In fact, Shelley does have a monument at University College, Oxford, unveiled in 1893.
28 *Reynolds' Newspaper*, 19 July 1896, 2. Bronterre O'Brien has a funerary monument at Abney Park Cemetery: see the *National Reformer*, 22 March 1868, 188. For O'Connor's funerary monument in Kensal Green Cemetery and statue in the Arboretum in Nottingham, see Paul Pickering, *Fergus O'Connor: A Political Life* (London, Merlin, 2012), 115.

29 W. T. Stead, 'A Plea for the Chartists', *Review of Reviews*, 17 (1898), 348–9 and *The Bee-Hive*, 13 February 1869, 1. For the monument to the 1848 Chartist martyrs see Paul A. Pickering, 'The Chartist Rites of Passage: Commemorating Feargus O'Connor', in *Contested Sites: Commemoration, Memorial and Popular Politics in Nineteenth-Century Britain*, ed. Paul A. Pickering and Alex Tyrrell (Aldershot: Ashgate, 2004), 101–26.
30 See Peter Mandler, *The English National Character: The History of an Idea from Edmund Burke to Tony Blair* (New Haven: Yale University Press, 2006), ch. 5.
31 *Reynolds's Newspaper*, 22 May 1887, 2.
32 See a debate about the condition of the monument on Owen's grave between G. J. Mantle and James Robertson, member of the Manchester Committee of the Owen Memorial Fund, in *The Commonwealth*, 22 December 1866, 1 and 29 December 1866, 1. For memorials to Robert Owen see *The Co-operative News*, 22 July 1899, 805 and for a commemorative gathering addressed by Ramsay MacDonald at New Lanark to the memory of Owen, see the *Labour Leader*, 13 June 1908, 374. Owen is also commemorated by a bust in the library of the International Labour Organization in Geneva donated in 1902 by 'the people of Wales': see Stirling Smith, *Robert Owen: Utopian Realist* (Manchester: Co-operative College, 1998), 38.
33 For the exhumation of the Battle of Bonnymuir Glasgow Martyrs see the *Northern Star*, 9 August 1846, 2 and for the funerary monument to the executed Hardie and Baird, and White's re-interment with them, see R. W. Finch, *My Lord They Are Printers* (London: CA&EP Branch, SOGAT '82, 1984), 53. The events of Bonnymuir were recalled in *The Labour Leader*, 21 April 1905, 34.
34 The fullest and most entertaining study of the fate of Thomas Paine's bones is a popular study by Paul Collins, *The Trouble with Tom: The Strange Afterlife and Times of Thomas Paine* (London: Bloomsbury, 2005), 31–84 but also see Paul A. Pickering, '"Grand Ossification": William Cobbett and the Commemoration of Tom Paine' in *Contested Sites*, ed. Pickering and Tyrrell, 52–80.
35 James McGill and Tom Redmond, 'The Story of the Manchester Martyrs', *North-West Labour History: Journal of the North-West Labour History Group*, no. 16 (1991/1992): 42–51.
36 R. L. Greenall, *The Making of Victorian Salford* (Lancaster: Carnegie Publishing, Ltd., 2000), 59 and Vernon, *Politics and the People*, 58–62. For Nonconformist monuments to anti-slavery crusaders, see J. R. Oldfield, '*Chords of Freedom*': Commemoration, Ritual and British Transatlantic Slavery* (Manchester: Manchester University Press, 2007), 56–87.
37 Patrick Joyce, *The Rule of Freedom: Liberalism and the Modern City* (London: Verso, 2003), ch. 4.
38 See the Boer War monument erected in St Anne's Square in Manchester in 1908 in the *Manchester City News*, 24 October 1908, 5.
39 *Manchester City News*, 13 August 1913, 5.
40 *Manchester Courier and Lancashire General Advertiser*, 8 October 1877, 6. The Bamford statue is also discussed in *The Co-operative News*, 30 December 1899, 1450.
41 *Northampton Herald*, 30 June 1894, supplement, 1 and the *Northampton Mercury*, 29 June 1894, 5.
42 Matthew Roberts, *Chartism, Commemoration and the Cult of the Radical Hero* (London: Routledge, 2019), 14–16.
43 Paul Pickering, 'The Chartist Rites of Passage: Commemorating Feargus O'Connor', in *Contested Sites*, ed. Pickering and Tyrrell, 101–26.

44 For the Scottish Martyrs' Memorial in Edinburgh, see Alex Tyrrell with Michael T. Davis, 'Bearding the Tories: The Commemoration of the Scottish Political Martyrs of 1793-94', in ibid., 25–51 and Roberts, *Chartism, Commemoration and the Cult of the Radical Hero*, 14–16.
45 Ibid., 9 and for ephemera as part of radical celebrity culture, S. J. Morgan, 'Material Culture and the Politics of Personality in Early Victorian England', *Journal of Victorian Culture*, 17, no. 2 (2012), 127–46.
46 *National Reformer*, 4 October 1874, 220.
47 *The Bee-Hive*, 13 February 1869, 1.
48 Stan Iveson and Roger Brown, *ILP Clarion House: A Monument to a Movement* (Preston: Independent Labour Publications, [1987] 2018), 21–44.
49 For buildings connected with Richard Carlile, see correspondence in the *National Reformer*, 22 October 1882, 283 and for a Richard Carlile day, the *National Reformer*, 8 February 1885, 148–9. A more recent expression of interest in radical premises and buildings relating to Carlile is Kent, *London for Heretics*, 33–6. For everyday survivals of radical history in houses, chapels and assembly halls, see Nick Mansfield, *Buildings of the Labour Movement* (London: English Heritage, 2013), 1–9.
50 *Daily Dispatch*, 16 August 1919, 3. For the role of 'memory keeping' in reference to Peterloo, see David Strittmatter, 'The Evolving Rhetoric of Peterloo, 1819–1919' in *Labour History Review*, 83, no. 3 (2019), 181–217 and for 'Peterloo relics', the *Manchester City News*, 10 December 1926.
51 *The Labour Leader*, 30 June 1894, 8. The historian Goldwin Smith also mentioned the role of the Free Trade Hall in memorializing Peterloo in a letter on public liberty in *The Bee-Hive*, 8 September 1866, 4.
52 Attempts to commemorate the events of Peterloo were at their most vigorous during periods of protracted Conservative rule and were often placed in a litany of complaints against the Tory party that included their support for the Pretender during the 1745 Jacobite rising; see the *Manchester Examiner and Times*, 5 January 1867, 4.
53 *Manchester Weekly Times*, 6 October 1888, 4, 20 October 1888, 2 and the *Manchester City News*, 16 August 1919, 2. For the Henry Hunt monument at Reverend Scholefield's Bible Christian Chapel in Ancoats, see V. I. Tomlinson, 'Postscript to Peterloo', *Manchester Region History Review*, 3, no. 1 (1989), 61–8. The memorial to the dead of the Pretoria pit disaster in Wigan in 1910, at a colliery owned by the Hulton family, might also be regarded as an implicit censure to the family for the role of the magistrate William Hulton in ordering the yeomanry to attack the crowd at Peterloo: see Paul Salveson, *The People's Monuments: A Guide to Sites and Monuments in North West England* (Manchester: Workers' Educational Association, 1987), 43.
54 Rob Hargreaves and Alan Hampson, *Beyond Peterloo: Elijah Dixon and Manchester's Forgotten Reformers* (Croydon: Pen and Sword, 2018), 212–13 and Navickas, *Protest and the Politics of Space and Place*, 192–3.
55 Gardner, 'William Hone and Peterloo', in 'Return to Peterloo', *Manchester Region History Review*, ed. Robert Poole, 23 (2012), 90–1.
56 *Justice*, 3 February 1900, 3.
57 Nicholas Ruddick, 'Introduction', *Caesar's Column: A Story of the Twentieth Century* (Middletown, CT: Wesleyan University Press, 2003 [1889]), xxxiv–xl.
58 There is a reference to *Caesar's Column* in *Land and Labour*, 1 September 1891, 6.
59 See for a monument commemorating the origins of the temperance movement in Preston, Alex Tyrrell, 'Preserving the Glory for Preston: The Campo Santo of

the Preston Teetotallers', in *Contested Sites*, ed. Pickering and Tyrrell, 122–47. Individual temperance advocates received their own funerary monuments, notably the monument in Wigan Cemetery raised by the teetotallers of Wigan and neighbourhood to the temperance advocate David Stuart (1814–66). See for Stuart, P. T. Winskill, *Temperance Standard Bearers of the Nineteenth-Century* 2 vols. (Manchester: Darrah Brothers, 1898), 472.

60 G. J. Harney, 'The Late Ernest Jones', *The Social Economist*, 1 July 1869, and for the co-operative movement's contribution to the Ernest Jones monument, *The Co-operator and Anti-Vaccinator*, 13 May 1871, 296.

61 *Reynolds's Newspaper*, 25 November 1883, 2.

62 *Labour Leader*, 28 August 1913, 10 and *The International Socialist*, 31 March 1917, 3.

63 *Cotton Factory Times*, 17 July 1896, 7 and Terry Wyke with Harry Cocks, *Public Sculpture of Greater Manchester* (Liverpool: Liverpool University Press, 2004), 213.

64 Quoted in Salveson, *The People's Monuments*, 33.

65 *National Reformer*, 9 August 1874, 81.

66 See the funeral of the former president of the Great and Little Bolton Co-operative Society, Samuel Taylor, in Tonge Cemetery in 1892 in F. W. Peaples, *History of the Great and Little Bolton Co-operative Society* (Manchester: Co-operative Wholesale Society, 1909), 467 and for the commemoration of cooperation, *Reynolds's Newspaper*, 3 March 1861, 8. For an example of a monument to a cooperative dignitary raised by public subscription see the monument dedicated to Joseph Smith (1841–83), assistant secretary to the Central Co-operative Board in Weaste Cemetery, Salford.

67 *National Reformer*, 13 September 1885, 167 and Kent, *London for Heretics*, 68–70.

68 W. Henry Brown, *Pathfinders: Brief Records of Seventy-Five Adventurers in Clearing the Way for Free Public Opinion* (Manchester: The Co-operative Union, Ltd., 1925), 45.

69 Ibid., 1.

70 See especially Katrina Navickas, *Protest and the Politics of Space and Place 1789–1848* (Manchester: Manchester University Press, 2016), 1–22. For further explorations of the importance of space and place for movements that were reliant on places of public assembly, see Thomas Lineham, 'Spatialising British Fascism', *Socialist History*, 41 (2012), 1–21.

71 *Reynolds's Newspaper*, 10 October 1852, 8.

72 Ibid., 27 April 1862, 3.

73 Ibid., 10 October 1852, 8.

74 Ibid., 27 April 1862, 3.

75 Ibid., 23 March 1862, 3.

76 Ibid., 21 July 1850, 4.

77 Reg Groves, *Sharpen the Sickle! The History of the Farm Workers' Union* (London: Merlin Press, [1949] 1981), 102 and Dennis Hardy, *Alternative Communities in Nineteenth Century England* (London: Longman, 1979), 180.

78 See the biography of Sheffield Communist party leader, George Henry Fletcher: Nellie Connole, *Leaven of Life: The Story of George Henry Fletcher* (London: Lawrence and Wishart, 1961), 7.

79 *Manchester Evening News*, 31 July 1905, 5.

80 *Manchester Courier*, 14 May 1859, 11 and 7 May 1859, 11.

81 *Manchester Examiner and Times*, 20 June 1865.

82 *Reynolds's Newspaper*, 27 November 1887, 1.

83 *The Link: A Journal for the Servants of Man*, 10 March 1888, 1.
84 *York Herald*, 16 June 1875, 3 and the *Northampton Mercury*, 19 June 1875, 6. There were further demonstrations at Naseby in 1878; see *The English Labourers' Chronicle*, 29 June 1878, 3.
85 *Reynolds' Newspaper*, 27 April 1862, 3.
86 See the guide to the statue erected 'on the spot where a skirmish took place between the royalists and roundheads – the first blood shed in the civil war', the *Life of Oliver Cromwell* (Manchester: Tubbs and Brook, 1875), 14.
87 See comments by Thomas Bayley Potter, MP for Rochdale, in the *Manchester Examiner and Times*, 2 December 1875, 6 and for criticism of the statue, *The Freelance*, 12 February 1875, 393–4 and the *Manchester Courier*, 1 December 1875, 5. The former Chartist, George Julian Harney, commented ironically on the divisive role played by the statue: see George Julian Harney, *The Chartists Were Right: Selections from the Newcastle Weekly Chronicle, 1890–1897*, ed. David Goodway (London: Merlin Press, 2014), 41–2. The statue of Cromwell in Warrington was also an object of sectarian tension: see Steve Cunniffe and Terry Wyke, 'The Curse of Cromwell: Warrington's Statue of Oliver Cromwell', *Northern History*, 46, no. 2 (2009), 245–59. For a contemporary view of the Cromwell statue in Warrington, see the *Warrington Dawn*, 1 January 1901, 11.
88 *Autobiography of John McAdam (1806–1883)*, ed. John Fyfe (Edinburgh: Scottish History Society, 1980), 79–81.
89 *Reynolds's Newspaper*, 11 November 1883, 3, *The English Chartist Circular*, 2, no. 61 (1842), 36, and Thomas Cooper's poem 'Chartist Song' in Thomas Cooper, *Poetical Works* (London: Hodder and Stoughton, 1877), 185–6. For Wallace as a hero of the ILP, see the *Labour Leader*, 19 October 1906, 337.
90 Quoted in Matthew Roberts, 'Chartism, Commemoration and the Cult of the Radical Hero c.1770–c.1840', *Labour History Review*, 78, no. 1 (2013), 14.
91 *Labour Leader*, 24 April 1913, 14. The British Fascist orator, Arnold Leese, mentioned the statue and claimed descent from Oastler; see Arnold Leese, *Out of Step: Events in the Two Lives of an Anti-Jewish Camel Doctor* (Guildford: the Author, 1951), 2. The political right also used monuments as rallying points; see the meeting in support of state-aided emigration of the unfit addressed by Arnold White at Cleopatra's Needle in London reported in *Justice*, 28 February 1885, 4.
92 Reg Groves, 'Wilkes and Liberty', *Labour Monthly*, 1 September 1930, 509–11. See for the 'Wilkes monument', Philip Ward-Jackson, *Public Sculptures in the City of London* (Liverpool: Liverpool University Press, 2003).
93 See T. D. Benson, *A Socialist's View of the Reformation* (London: Independent Labour Party, 1913), 2–14 and D. G. Paz, 'The Chartists and the English Reformation', *Bulletin of the John Rylands Library*, 90, no. 1 (2014), 25–47. See for the reverence by the Chartists for the Lollard tradition, Ernest Jones's speech on 'The State Church' in the *People's Paper*, 29 November 1856, 1.
94 See especially William Le Queux, *The Unknown To-morrow* (London: Wright and Brown, 1910), 46 and 187–8.
95 Leon Kuhn and Colin Gill, *Topple the Mighty* (London: Friction Books, 2005), 139–40 and Paul Mulvey, *The Political Life of Josiah C. Wedgwood: Land, Liberty and Empire* (Woodbridge: The Boydell Press, 2010), 14.
96 Kuhn and Gill, *Topple the Mighty*, 143–5 and *Reynolds's Newspaper*, 1 May 1859, 11.
97 Ibid., 21 May 1871.

98 See Donal Fallon, *The Pillar: The Life and Afterlife of the Nelson Pillar* (Dublin: New Island Books, 2014), chs. 3-4; Nuala C. Johnson, 'Sculpting Heroic Histories: Celebrating the Centenary of the 1798 Rebellion in Ireland', *Transactions of the British Institute of Geographers*, 19, no. 1 (1994), 78-93 and Maev Kennedy, 'Fallen Images Alter Idea of History', *The Guardian*, 18 May 1998, 9.
99 Guy Beiner, 'Fenianism and the Martyrdom-Terrorism Nexus in Ireland before Independence', in *Martyrdom and Terrorism: Pre-modern to Contemporary Perspectives*, ed. Dominic James and Alex Houen (Oxford: Oxford University Press, 2014), 109-31 and Robert Bevan, *The Destruction of Memory: Architecture at War* (London: Reaktion, 2006), 91-6.
100 *Reynolds's Newspaper*, 1 February 1885, 6.
101 For the background to this episode see Louise Raw, *Striking a Light: The Bryant and May Matchwomen and Their Place in History* (London: Bloomsbury, 2011), 150-1.
102 *The Link: A Journal for the Servants of Men*, 23 June 1888, 2.
103 Gurney, *Gerrard Winstanley*, 114.
104 Carl Griffin, 'Resistance, Crime and Popular Cultures', in *Forests and Chases of England and Wales c. 1500-1850: Towards a Survey and Analysis*, ed. John Langton and Graham Jones (Oxford: Oxford University Press, 2008), 49-54 and Mark Gorman, *Saving the People's Forest: Open Spaces, Enclosure and Popular Protest in Mid-Victorian London* (Hadfield: University of Hertfordshire Press, 2021), chs. 3-4 and 6.
105 *National Reformer*, 6 January 1867, 6-7 and 13 October 1867, 226-7. For trees associated with Robin Hood and the tradition of plebeian protest, see Brian Lund, *Robin Hood on Old Picture Postcards: A Selection of Picture Postcards Featuring the Legendary Figure and Places Associated with Him* (Nottingham: Keyworth, 2007), 14-15.
106 'Liberty Tree' in the *Western Vindicator*, 16 March 1839, 3 and W. Diack, 'The Story of the Chartists', *The Social Democrat*, 4, no. 4 (1900), 112.
107 See for a narrative that identifies the history of oak trees with the druids, King John and Julius Caesar, Major Hayman-Rooke, *Descriptions and Sketches of Some Remarkable Oaks in the Park of Welbeck in the County of Nottinghamshire* (London: J. Nichols, 1790), 5 and 17-18.
108 Hunt, *Politics, Culture and Class in the French Revolution*, 59 and Alfred F. Young, *Liberty Tree: Ordinary People and the American Revolution* (New York: New York University Press, 2006), ch. 8.
109 Trees were planted as affirmations of loyalty in both the 1887 and 1897 royal jubilees: see *Lloyd's Illustrated News*, 7 November 1897, 9.
110 G. J. Holyoake, *Public Speaking and Debate* (London: T. Fisher Unwin, [1866] 1893), 112.
111 M. K. Ashby, *Joseph Ashby of Tysoe 1859-1919: A Study of English Village Life* (Cambridge: Cambridge University Press, 1961), 125-6.
112 Joseph Arch, *From Ploughtail to Parliament: An Autobiography* (London: the Cresset Library, [1898] 1986), 97.
113 For the Wellesborne Oak, see *The English Labourers' Chronicle*, 21 May 1881, 5, and for the Tolpuddle Martyrs' Tree, Hilda Kean, 'Tolpuddle, Burston and Levellers: The Making of Radical and National Heritages at English Labour Movement Festivals', in *Heritage, Labour and the Working Classes*, ed. Laura Jane Smith, Paul Shackel and Gary Campbell (London: Routledge, 2012), 270-1; for the validation of the provenance of the Tolpuddle Martyrs' Tree, see Maev Kennedy, 'Tolpuddle Sycamore Did Shelter Martyrs', *The Guardian*, 15 July 2005, 7.

114 For the vandalism of the Reformers' Tree in Hyde Park, see Edward Owen, *Hyde Park Select Narratives, Annual Events Etc., during Twenty Years' Police Service in Hyde Park* (London: Simpkin, Marshall, Hamilton, Kent and Co., n.d.), 38–9 and for later meetings at the tree, *The Bee-Hive*, 25 July 1868, 1, the *National Reformer*, 30 May 1869, 349, the *National Reformer*, 10 August 1873, 81, the *Manchester Evening News*, 27 August 1877, 3.

115 Jack Lindsay, *England, My England: A Pageant of the English People* (London: Fore Publications, 1939), 21.

116 Brian Millett, 'The Bristol Tree Which Could Be Crowned the Best Tree in England', *Bristol Post*, 9 September 2019, https://www.bristolpost.co.uk/news/bristol-news/bristol-tree-could-crowned-best-3301162 (accessed 25 November 2022).

10

Making Martyrs: Contested histories and the British labour and Socialist movements' commemoration of the Dorchester labourers

Marcus Morris

When speaking at the annual Tolpuddle Martyrs Festival in 2018, the then Labour Party leader, Jeremy Corbyn, declared that the Martyrs were 'part of our national story … [and] part of our lives'.[1] The following year he noted how 'their struggle sowed the seed for the modern trade union movement and the Labour Party'.[2] In stressing the significance of the Martyrs in such a way, Corbyn was repeating the rhetoric of many of his predecessors, many other leading Labour figures and many in the wider labour movement, especially trade unionists. The annual festival attracts thousands and marks a key point in the movement's commemorative calendar, which, according to the organizers, 'reflects the spirit of those prepared to stand up and be counted, and for those just learning about its history … [and] is a joyful celebration of solidarity'.[3] The Martyrs' story has thus become a 'totemic moment of British social, rural, and labour history'.[4] In particular, it has become a foundational myth for the labour movement, occupying a central place in its historical memory and marking the 'beginning of a development leading to the trade unionism, left-wing attitudes and protest politics of today'.[5] The Martyrs' suffering and sacrifice should act as an inspiration to those in the movement, and their treatment an injustice to never forget. They are prominent and useful figures, but their mythologization is largely a construction of the 1930s by a movement in search of both a cause and a history.

Prior to the 1930s, the Martyrs were generally known as the Dorchester (or Dorsetshire) Labourers, with Tolpuddle invariably not seen as central to their identity or history. Their story could easily have faded through time. The Martyrs' actions and their impact were neither exceptional nor particularly long-lasting. They were not the first trade unionists and 'neither the adoption of trade unionism at rural Tolpuddle nor the judicial response was without precedent'.[6] Indeed, as Peter Jones has noted, 'they cannot even be said to have been particularly influential in the diffusion of union ideals in the countryside'.[7] As such, the Martyrs were not particularly obvious candidates for the pantheon of labour heroes, while their actions were not necessarily ones that sowed the seed for the trade union movement, later socialist organizations and the

Labour Party, as Corbyn suggested. That it would do this and that they would be designated 'martyrs' was primarily down to the actions of the Trades Union Congress (TUC) when commemorating their centenary in 1934.

The General Council of the TUC, and in particular its general secretary Walter Citrine, as Clare Griffiths has demonstrated, 'organized a huge effort to turn the movement's eyes on that part of the country, and to inspire the contemporary labour force to follow the lead of brave men a hundred years before'.[8] It was hoped that a divided and disillusioned movement, facing the challenges of a deep economic depression, failed episodes of direct action and struggling for members, would be provided with an exemplar of solidarity and sacrifice. It would act as a source of inspiration to and a rallying point for a beleaguered movement, giving it a shared (and constructed) narrative. The Martyrs were honoured in a way no other trade union or labour heroes had been before and it was hoped their story would become central to the history of trade unionism. The TUC's use and rebranding of this particular past, then, was a strategic decision and one that very deliberately romanticized the Martyrs' story. It also came at a moment of 'dramatic changes to the Labour Party's self-conception and self-presentation'.[9] Jeremy Corbyn's words above show that this strategy certainly met with a good deal of success. The story celebrated today, though, is one created at a particular moment in time to serve a particular purpose.

The events of 1934 were not entirely successful, but it would see thousands of trade unionists and others from the labour movement converge on Tolpuddle for a lavish gala festival, which was accompanied by a range of other activities and competitions. A grand procession and pageant were also held. It also saw the publication of *The Book of the Martyrs of Tolpuddle* by the TUC, a play (*Six Men of Dorset*) was performed, a medal struck, the sculptor Eric Gill designed a headstone for James Hammett (one of the Martyrs) and a shelter was erected next to the Tolpuddle Martyrs' Tree. Finally, six memorial cottages were built in the village to house the 'aged and the poor'. These cottages helped establish the village as a place of pilgrimage for visitors. It was during these commemorations that the Labourers were effectively rebranded as Martyrs by the TUC (though many would still refer to them during the festivities as the Dorchester Labourers). In effect, a series of traditions were invented that have been carried on well into the twenty-first century, which precluded or superseded other interpretations of the Martyrs' story.

The celebrations also had the effect of forming a memorial landscape in Tolpuddle, rather than other locations associated with their story. In part, this was deliberate. Citrine wrote in 1935 that he wanted 'to put Tolpuddle on the map in the real sense. It is now not on any of the road maps that I have seen'.[10] Creating this sense of place ensured a continued prominence as a site of heritage, a constant stream of visitors, and ensured it was part of the nation's radical landscape. As Hilda Kean has noted in her study of Tolpuddle and other labour festivals, moreover, such 'attempts to create a memory of a radical past within the nation have also resulted in the creation of memories of the commemorative events themselves as part of a radical political culture'.[11] Tolpuddle has thus also become a national celebration, part of a wider national history. To some extent this was the case in 1934 as well. It was in this context that Lloyd George (the former Liberal Prime Minister) would attend the commemorations. In addressing the crowds, he noted somewhat hyperbolically that 'we are here to commemorate one of the greatest and most triumphant struggles for human rights and liberty in this land, and it is meet and proper we should not miss the occasion at a time when human freedom is in greater peril than at any date in my lifetime'.[12] His words, alongside the TUC's actions, demonstrate how such festivals 'see people creating pasts needed for their own present and one which, in different ways, sustains them emotionally, as well as politically, in the present'.[13] The story of the Martyrs bequeathed by the 1934 celebrations then tells us more about the movement in the 1930s than it does about the Martyrs. It also illustrates much about the labour movement's and the Labour Party's relationship with the past.

Labour and history

There is a growing literature that examines primarily the Labour Party's, and the wider labour and socialist movements', use of history and their relationship with both their past and the nation's history more generally.[14] This has demonstrated that though the past is important more broadly to the labour movement and to the Labour Party in particular, there is at times a complicated or even antagonistic relationship with that past. H. M. Drucker has argued that 'the Labour Party has and needs a strong sense of its own past and of the past of the labour movement which produced and sustains it'. Moreover, he suggested that 'this sense of its past is so central to its ethos that it plays a crucial role in defining what the party is about to those in it'.[15] We can see this in both the 1934 commemorations of the Tolpuddle Martyrs and the ways in which their legacy is still celebrated. This strong sense of history has served a number of functions for the Labour Party and the wider movement.

A key function, as highlighted by Antony Taylor, is that these 'past stories of defiance, protest and dissent … provided an impetus to the rise of the Labour platform at both a national and local level'.[16] More than just providing a personal or emotional impetus, though, such stories were useful exemplars for the contemporary movement. As such, the movement's historical imagination has tended to centre on the inspirational leaders, pioneers and figureheads associated with these stories. In celebrating such figures, the Labour Party and wider movement have attempted to demonstrate a direct lineage to a radical tradition and radical political figures, which often was seen to stretch back to the late eighteenth century. This has served both an internal and external function. Externally, this claim to and place within an extended radical tradition in British history gave Labour politics a respectability, a longevity (given its infancy and relatively short history), and positioned it firmly within a British context. This was important given a standard trope for opposition groups was that the growth of such politics, and especially connected socialist ideas, was an importation of foreign ideas that were alien to British values and systems.[17] Internally, the appeal to this lineage has been used to suggest a shared history that promoted unity in the face of possible division.

Jose Harris has noted how 'Labour was always a broad coalition (changing in precise character over different periods) between trade unions, different brands of committed socialist, single-issue pressure groups, and (particularly after 1918) individual men and women interested in various kinds of ethical and practical reform'.[18] This coalition, moreover, is only broadened if we consider the wider movement and the diversity of connected groups and organizations. The function of history, therefore, has often been to reconcile these different groups and the different traditions that have led them to the movement. The aim has often been the creation of a shared narrative around a shared pantheon of labour heroes, which will act as a focus for party unity, and to also establish continuities (and downplay discontinuities) with a radical past. Often this shared narrative has been one of the inexorable rises of labour, which was regularly perpetuated by earlier historians of Labour. The TUC's promotion of the Martyrs clearly marked such an attempt, which also saw their story mythologized. Jon Lawrence has argued that such myths which 'Labour activists have internalized about their party's past have done much to shape their understanding of its present, and its future'. However, they 'have been constantly re-worked to draw lessons of contemporary relevance that support the ideological perspective of the myth-maker/historian'.[19] As such, the use of history within the Labour Party and the wider movement has never been without controversy.

History could provide unity, but it could also highlight the differences and focus existing tensions. It could act as a tool of exclusion as well as inclusion. With the past performing particular functions in particular contexts, there were (and are) competing myths and narratives that often reflected competing ideas about the party's and wider movement's place in the present in the face of a shifting opposition. The diversity and pluralism of traditions that have fed into the wider movement and the Labour Party also impact on the stories that need to be told and those that can be referenced (as we will see below with the Martyrs). As Martin Pugh has pertinently asked, given that the 'recruitment of [Labour] supporters came from diverse political backgrounds ... how far did the party offer something distinctive and how far something similar'?[20] Linked to this are questions around the old and the new in labour politics. Those seeking to modernize Labour have often questioned 'old Labour' and sought a break with the past. Indeed, Glen O'Hara and Helen Parr have argued that 'the constant striving for modernity, the stress on the future, and continual attempts to redefine both Labour and its policies, have always been at the heart of the party's history'.[21]

These studies have clearly demonstrated the importance of history to the Labour Party and how it often has a complicated relationship with its past. They are, though, mostly centred on the twentieth-century Labour Party, how it sees itself and the traditions that feed into its platform, rather than the wider movement and both its and the party's antecedents in the late nineteenth and early twentieth centuries. Moreover, they are centred on a broad conception of history and on the role played by competing histories or competing groups in that history. As such, this chapter builds on these studies but takes one particular history as its focus – the Tolpuddle Martyrs – and examines its development through the wider movement's history, exploring what this illustrates about the use of and place of history within that movement. As we have seen, the Martyrs were in many ways created to serve a particular purpose at a particular moment in time, taking on mythical status and becoming a unifying focal point. They have, in the words of Laura Foster, taken on 'malleable and mythological afterlives'.[22] This means their story and its changing place within the labour movement's history are illustrative of the mutability of labour history and of the discontinuities and continuities that marked different periods.[23] In this, their absence pre-1934 is as instructive as their celebrated presence after the centenary celebrations. This chapter, therefore, primarily examines the movement prior to the inter-war years, focusing on the direct antecedents to the Labour Party that emerged in the 1880s up until the First World War (mainly focusing on the leading socialist figures and organizations but also looking at other voices within this disparate movement), outlining the reasons why the Dorchester Labourers' memory was only occasionally invoked. These reasons and the use of the Martyrs' story more generally highlight the contested nature of the movement's past, the challenges in finding a common symbol or totemic figure, the importance of context, the need to accommodate and adapt to varied traditions, that ideas and people come in and out of the movement's story, and that there is a diverse and ever-changing pantheon of labour heroes.

The Martyrs' story, commemoration and history

In 1834, the six Martyrs were charged with swearing an illegal oath during an initiation ceremony for the Friendly Society of Agricultural Labourers. The society had been formed with the intention of resisting wage cuts and bargaining for better working conditions with local landowners. The six were held at Dorchester gaol (hence why they were remembered as the Dorchester Labourers) until their trial on 17 March 1834 at the county court in the town. The jury, made up of local landowners, found them guilty after being instructed to by the judge and the men were sentenced to transportation to Australia for seven years. After their transportation, the London Dorchester Committee was established to raise funds to support their families. Agitation against the convictions and sentences had begun even before they had left the country, with a public outcry over perceived injustice and support from high-profile radicals including Fergus O'Connor and William Cobbett. A campaign was launched to overturn the verdict and sentence, with an 800,000-signature petition demanding the Labourers' freedom presented to the House of Commons. Demonstrations were held, including one on 21 April 1834 where up to 100,000 would march through London to parliament in protest. This pressure resulted in the Home Secretary, Lord John Russell, granting conditional pardons in June 1835 and full pardons in March 1836.

Upon their return to Britain in 1837, the men were greeted as heroes, attending processions, meetings and dinners in their honour. The Dorchester Committee also obtained leases on two farms in Essex for the Martyrs (as a few now dubbed them) and their families. Their story did act as an inspiration from the outset. In particular, the account of the trial published by George Loveless (the leading Labourer), *The Victims of Whiggery*, became a mainstay at future Chartist meetings. Indeed, Tom Scriven has identified how 'from the outset, Chartism was intimately linked to the Labourers', noting that 'the People's Charter was in preparation during the summer of 1837' and through the Dorchester Committee they 'became close to many London radicals'.[24] Nevertheless, the Martyrs' influence would wane and it would be the Chartists who exerted a much greater influence on the rapidly growing labour and socialist movement and varied organizations that emerged in Britain from the 1880s. The Chartists, much more than the Martyrs, were the direct lineage that these later organizations highlighted. Antony Taylor has shown how the socialist groups of the 1880s and 1890s in particular saw themselves 'as the direct heirs to the Chartist movement' and that for many 'Chartism provided the starting point for an unfolding and organic struggle'.[25] The Social Democratic Federation (SDF), Britain's first avowedly Marxist party, thus declared that they were Chartism's 'legitimate heirs and successors', while its leader, H. M. Hyndman, believed he was 'reviving the Chartist organisation'.[26]

This celebration of a lineage that began with the Chartists meant that the Martyrs had been superseded in the movement's history by the very group that they had inspired. As such, they reflect the evolving nature of the movement, its use of history and its celebration of certain radical heroes. The Martyrs' waning influence demonstrated that even before the formation of the Labour Party, its immediate antecedents reflecting the mutable nature of the movement's history found their story had become less useful. Though now a foundational moment for Labour, for the groups that were founded in the 1880s and 1890s the Martyrs' story merely fed into the Chartists' story, which for them was the real foundational moment. Such foundational myths could clearly change depending on the movement's aims, needs and purpose in a particular moment. The Martyrs' story was a familiar one, hence Ramsay MacDonald purchasing a print of the Dorchester Labourers to be hung in the Labour Party's headquarters, but it often had a lesser standing than other stories or myths.[27] Some attempts were made in this period of growing labour and socialist agitation to celebrate and commemorate the Labourers, but these met with limited success and their story was seen to have much less relevance on the contemporary movement than the TUC may have suggested in 1934.

Two attempts to commemorate the Martyrs were co-sponsored by labour organizations in 1909 and 1912. In 1909, the 'movement for erecting a memorial to the six Dorset agricultural labourers' was led by 'the trade union and Parliamentary Labour leaders, the president of the Wesleyan Conference [the Martyrs were prominent Methodists], and other prominent persons'.[28] The memorial would consist of two cottages for poor and elderly agricultural workers. Speaking in support at a public meeting, Keir Hardie claimed that the Labour Party was 'carrying on the traditions of the life work of George Loveless … [whose] work consisted in striking off the fetters that bound workingmen and so enabled them to stand erect, looking the whole world in the face and requiring to cringe to no man'.[29] Such appeals were unsuccessful. They would be more fruitful in 1912 but still fell short of intended targets. The aim was to 'erect almshouses for labourers, and establish scholarships at Ruskin College, but in spite of every effort that has been put forth only a sum considerably less than £100 has been received'. Ultimately, only a memorial was erected, which was opened by the Labour Party leader, Arthur Henderson. However, he chose not to dwell on their impact on the labour movement, instead focusing on their religious background and the importance of the links between Christianity and labour.[30] As we shall see below, this would not have attracted many in the movement to the Martyrs. The failure of such commemoration attempts, meanwhile, illustrates their limited standing for many in the movement.

When the Martyrs' story featured, it did so in quite a limited fashion and with a foundational element different to that later attributed to it. For socialists, it tended to be viewed through the lens and language of class struggle. Hyndman thus considered 'the case of the six Dorchester labourers, one of the most infamous cases of tyranny in all the long record of class oppression'.[31] The primary focus was the punishment of the Martyrs and its perceived injustice, which spoke to the continued fight against the forces of authority. The SDF, for instance, played a very active role in free-speech campaigns in the 1880s and 1890s. One member of the SDF, John Spargo, suggested that 'nothing more disgraceful can be found in the annals of English industrial history than the terrible punishment meted out by the Whig Government … to the poor inoffensive Methodist-preacher labourers'.[32] This designation also illustrates a somewhat different and more contested perspective. The Martyrs' story was also used to highlight how 'the judges, juries, lawyers, and apparatus of the law's administration cannot be trusted … in the relations of employers and employed'.[33] They were also celebrated by some for suffering 'in the cause of liberty, justice and righteousness', with *Justice* proclaiming that their 'example should be a stimulus to our own and future generations'.[34]

The emphasis and rhetoric around the Martyrs' story often differed when discussed by the disparate elements of the movement, while it was often used to serve a different purpose. Where there were some similarities with the Martyrs' contemporary standing and that fashioned by the TUC in 1934 was in their influence on the trade union movement. They were often described as pioneers, with the *Labourer* glorifying their struggle as 'the first that assaulted the fort held by the oppressors of the workers'.[35] These 'trade union heroes', whose story was 'the best known episode of early Trade Union history', were presented by some as the starting point in the 'progress of Labour'.[36] As such, the Scottish socialist newspaper *Forward* argued that 'the burning indignation that arose throughout the country by the scandalous treatment of the Dorchester labourers gave an impetus to Trade Unionism which it might not otherwise have received'. Interestingly, though, this impetus was still couched in the terms of class struggle, with the paper describing it as 'one of the early attempts at class-consciousness'.[37] This was a rhetoric much less commonplace with the presentation of the Martyrs put forward by the TUC in 1934.

Such examples may suggest that the Martyrs' story was regularly invoked prior to the centenary celebrations, but this was not the case. They are largely absent from the list of historical figures celebrated in the late nineteenth and early twentieth centuries. As the *Wigan Observer* noted in 1904, 'whenever trade unionists are advocating the right of combination, and announcing the iniquity of judge-made law, we are reminded of the "six men of Dorset", and we are invited to follow their example'. However, the article goes on to suggest that 'who those six heroes were, or what they did, or how they suffered in freedom's cause, nobody seems to know'.[38] This could just reflect a general lack of historical awareness that some in the movement noted. Hyndman commenting that the British 'are too apt to forget their own history'.[39] He developed this further in *The Evolution of Revolution*, arguing that

> little is known in our country of the widespread democratic and Socialist agitation, which anticipated most of the social and political ideas that are often attributed to

foreigners. Even the names of the able, enthusiastic, self-sacrificing and persecuted leaders of the unceasing social and political propaganda, which stirred English society to its foundation, are forgotten; and, although they roused the spirit of revolt among the workers as it has never been roused since, the magnificent service they rendered is ignored.[40]

The *Labour Leader*, the newspaper of the Independent Labour Party (ILP), meanwhile, suggested that this applied to the movement's own history. It noted that 'a very full description of ... early Socialist writers in England has been given by more than one Continental historian, but we have no English account of these pioneers'. Indeed, 'all our English histories of Socialism are silent about these English Socialists'.[41]

As we have seen, though, with the veneration of the Chartist movement, a sense of history, the appeal to a particular historical radical lineage and the inheritance from particular historical figures, a sense of history was important to the movement. Alongside the Chartists for instance, the Martyrs' contemporary, Robert Owen, and the Owenist movement were often acclaimed as the first socialist movement and the origin of the term 'socialism'.[42] There was a genuine respect for many of these figures and in part this was an attempt to ensure that these 'English histories of Socialism' were remembered and their 'magnificent service' celebrated. This appeal to a British heritage, however, also served another important function. One of the most common criticisms of the labour and especially socialist movement at the end of the nineteenth and start of the twentieth centuries was that it was a Continental one, with socialism portrayed as an unsuitable set of foreign ideas. British socialists thus sought to legitimize and anglicize their socialism by playing on their heritage and British national characteristics, while embracing the politics of nostalgia. As such, an article from 1884 directly tackled the charge of foreignness, concluding that English socialism 'is native to the soil, and socialists of 1884 are but continuing the work which has been handed on from previous generations'.[43] Hyndman was therefore at pains to stress how they were 'the direct heirs of the ideas put forward at the beginning of the century by Robert Owen, Thomas Spence, William Cobbett, Thomas Hodgskin, Bray and others ... Bronterre O'Brien, Ernest Jones, Stephens, Oastler, Frost, Bull, Vincent O'Connor and many more'.[44]

There was a conscious and consistent appeal to a radical, native British heritage and tradition, of which the current movement was the most recent stage and one built on historical precedent. These British figures were often used then to legitimize the movement, demonstrate a political continuity with political movements of the past, with British national character, and to create a shared sense of identity and history that could bind a disparate (with regional/national as well as ideological divisions) movement together. As Paul Ward has highlighted, 'the interpretation of English history therefore entered into the symbolism and language of late nineteenth-century socialists and they used it in their day-to-day propaganda'. Keir Hardie was thus arguing that a socialist was one who sought 'to resuscitate a phase of British life which produced great and good results in the past'.[45] For many, this took the form of a direct appeal to an earlier age. The socialism of William Morris in particular and also Robert Blatchford (especially in the highly popular *Merrie England*), for example, harked back to an idealized and simply pre-industrial world, a Medievalism, which was built on historical precedent and was critical of the destructive forces of industrial Britain.[46]

Part of this look to an idealized past was about the search for new life, looking back to an older, pre-industrial England, when picturing what a future socialist society might look like. Such a past was preferable to any foreign example and helped counter the charges set out above.[47] Another tactic that relied on the past was the appeal to a series of great British democrats who had never advocated violence for revolutionary ends, thereby enhancing their own democratic reputation, adherence to native systems and further helping to rebuff the perceived unsuitability of their ideas to Britain. As one socialist was keen to point out, 'Social Democrats are not the wild, unreasoning subversionists of newspaper fiction, but are sober men and women who … are doing their best to enable England to pass in a peaceable and orderly fashion through the transition period to a better state of things'.[48] This was a movement that played on its own history, a wider radical history and key historical figures. However, although there was some celebration of the Tolpuddle Martyrs, they are a historical point of reference largely absent from the radical tradition invoked by the labour and socialist movement of the late nineteenth and early twentieth centuries, and also the early Labour Party. There are several key reasons for this, which reflect the wider tensions and challenges with using the past for the movement at this key moment of growth.

The Martyrs and the labour and socialist movements

Most contemporary histories of the labour and socialist movement were keen to stress the discontinuities between the movements of the 1830s and 1840s and those that emerged with the growth of socialism in the 1880s. Thomas Kirkup thus wrote that 'after the decline of the Owen agitation and of the Christian Socialist movement in 1850, socialism could hardly be said to exist in England'.[49] Max Beer went further, arguing that the period from the 1880s onwards was, though 'less stirring', 'of much more vital importance than of the foregoing periods'. It was 'the antiquities of socialist speculation and the childhood of Labour'.[50] The preceding movements were therefore of a different, less developed character to those that developed from the 1880s. In particular, they were less revolutionary (especially compared to Continental movements) and were, for leading socialist Belfort Bax, 'a flash in the pan, so far as revolutionary action was concerned, and hence could supply no starting-point for a revolutionary tradition'.[51] Such interpretations highlight a key reason why certain historical figures and movements such as the Martyrs were often absent from the histories and legacies that were celebrated by the movement that grew from the 1880s.

The discontinuities with the Martyrs, the context in which they were resisting and the distance of the modern movement from them meant that many perceived their actions and ideas as not relevant to the contemporary age. This distance from the past therefore coloured their relationship with it, and this extended to multiple other figures, organizations and movements. Beer suggested that 'between the years 1865 and 1885 Great Britain entered on a period of change. Thought was moving away from its old moorings. The rise of the working classes could no longer be denied; their influence on legislation and the wage-contract was visibly on the increase. They had obtained the franchise and the legislation of trade unionism'.[52] Given that the context had seemingly changed significantly, there was a question for many about the applicability of older ideas to the modern world and the modern movement. Ramsay MacDonald thus argued that 'we must explain and defend them [older ideas] with a different conception of Society in our minds, different formulae on our lips, and different guiding ideas for our activities'.[53] Theodore Rothstein, a member of the SDF, when writing about 'pioneers of the class struggle' – the Martyrs were not pioneers for Rothstein – noted that 'we must remember that these thinkers lived in a time when modern capitalism, with its machine industry, was very far from complete in its development'. For Rothstein, figures from the past might be celebrated, but the significance of their ideas should not be overplayed as they were invariably starting from a misunderstanding of the key issues in a different context.[54] Many in the movement, especially in the early twentieth century with the formation of the Labour Party, therefore saw recent developments as, in the words of Manny Shinwell, 'one of the great stages in the political evolution of this country'.[55]

The misunderstanding of key issues, it was suggested, often resulted from not being able to see the full picture or take a more holistic view. Ramsay MacDonald noted how those who had gone before had only seen either the economic side or the political side, and that 'Labour in politics must have a new outlook, a new driving force of ideas and a new standard of political effort' that embraced all sides.[56] It also resulted from the belief that their ideas had been 'supplanted by a doctrine of rights more accurate to the facts of social life'.[57] Older ideas, which the Martyrs reflected, were no more than 'an inspiration, a discovery of spiritual insight'; they 'could not be a scientific system of criticism, method or construction. The knowledge to make it so was not then available'.[58] The movement from the 1880s, especially across the socialist spectrum and inspired by Marxist thinking, saw itself as a 'scientific' one rather than an idealistic or utopian one. An article in *Justice* explained this key development: 'socialism has ceased to be ideal and utopian, and has become scientific and practical, because it is no longer only the noble aspiration of men who wish well to their kind, but at the same time a reasoned explanation of the social economical phenomena which we see around us'.[59]

The Martyrs (and their contemporaries) could ultimately only do so much given their context and the nature of development of the labour movement in the earlier part of the nineteenth century. As the ILP member William Stewart noted in relation to this period, 'after a long heroic struggle the old repressive combination laws had broken down. Trade Unionism had been legalized, an achievement in itself marking a big step in the advance towards liberty, but still only a step'.[60] Moreover, *Justice* argued that the ideas 'now preached among the nations *is* new, for the simple reason that it is the necessary result of the historical growth and economical development of the last hundred years'.[61] For many in the movement, then, there was a question about how you should celebrate something that was imperfect and where that should fit within the movement's historical narrative. There was still much advancement to be made, which led to questioning whether focusing on previous steps would limit further development. The context was also different in that the Martyrs' significance was primarily in the rural and agricultural setting, while the more modern movement centred on the urban and industrial. All of this meant that for many there could be a general hesitance when it came to celebrating historical figures, ideas and movements, and though there might be a lineage to such groups, their applicability to the current struggle was limited.

A further tension emerged in what the Martyrs stood for, or were seen to pioneer, which highlighted divisions within the movement that developed from the 1880s. As we have seen, the Martyrs were (and still are) often presented as founding fathers of the trade union movement who had suffered 'for loyalty to Trade Unionism'.[62] This link between the Martyrs and trade unionism was solidified and celebrated by the TUC in the 1930s, but this link was already established in the latter part of the nineteenth century. This for some in the movement, especially the socialist elements, was a problematic connection, as the support for trade unions varied significantly across the movement. At the beginning of the 1880s, moreover, many workers were not members of a trade union. It has been estimated that in 1880, for example, unions represented only 4 per cent of the occupied population, which suggested to many in the movement that forging links to unions would only have a limited significance in bringing about their wider goals.[63] Indeed, support for the unions seemed to be dwindling more generally. A letter to the *Pall Mall Gazette* noted that 'the trade unionists, however good the work may have been in the past, are now a small and dwindling minority of the labouring classes; that whereas 1,300,000 were represented at the [Trades Union] Congress of 1872 not 500,000 were represented at the Congress of last year [1885]'.[64] This questioned the applicability of the Martyrs' story once again. It also highlights a broader reason why these stories were contested or absent from the wider movement and why they could be as divisive as they were unifying.

The record of many trade unions, particularly those formed not long after the Martyrs' actions, was often criticized not only by those socialists opposed to their action but also those who were broadly supportive. As such, a story that celebrated such a legacy was not necessarily attractive to critics. Among a variety of criticisms, they believed that the unions were too often 'content to act in economic and social matters as if the wage-earning system doomed them to permanent subjection' and so 'divorced their activities entirely from politics'.[65] The SDF in its manifesto attacked the unions for 'representing only the merest fraction of the workers', for their lack of class consciousness and for making 'friends with the Mammon of Unrighteousness in the shape of the employing class'. Indeed, 'to the workers of the lower grades, and therefore to the majority of the workers, they are not even friendly', happy to make pacts while 'your less fortunate brethren are suffering and dying by your side'.[66] As John Burns argued, they were not 'moving in the interest of labour', did not want systemic change, and so were not 'expressing a desire to terminate a system that makes it possible for … crises to periodically recur'.[67] Trade unions were too often, according to the Socialist League, only 'looking for a small betterment' of their conditions and 'content to fight this question' only within 'sectional trades' unions'. They were neither class conscious nor willing to look for a better system, which meant for the League that 'it is a hopeless fight'.[68] Unions' intentions, then, were seen by some as incompatible with the modern movement and their history a questionable legacy to celebrate. Even Keir Hardie, who was broadly supportive of trade unionism, when asked who were the precursors to the movement, noted that 'Wycliffe, John Ball, Gerrard Winstanley, Sir Thomas More, Cardinal Manning and William Morris are the names that occur to me'.[69] It is noteworthy that apart from Cardinal Manning, who was instrumental in settling the 1889 London dock strike, none had any real connection to the unions.

The blame for the unions' limited outlook and associated aversion to proper social reform was firmly placed with their leadership. It was suggested that union leaders had consistently remained unconvinced of the need for political action independent of the two major parties. This clearly reflected the often-deep attachment that many had to the Liberal Party. As the Webbs noted, 'the assimilation of the political creed of the Trade Union leaders with that of the official Liberal part was perfectly sincere'.[70] Many felt, even if they were broadly supportive of trade unions, that it was impossible to work with such a collaborationist leadership, especially when across the movement it was their express intention to build alternatives to the two major parties. These leaders were 'compromisers, respecters of the powers that be, almost to a man'.[71] Theodore Rothstein thus concluded that the unions had a 'thoroughly middle-class ideology' and so it was 'no wonder that when at last a Socialist movement did arise in England [the 1880s] it found the trade unions already organized on a different basis, and has remained to this very day a thing apart from it'.[72] If the Martyrs were later celebrated by Labour members as pioneers of trade unionism, this was a unionism that many in the labour and socialist movement felt they stood apart from in the late nineteenth and early twentieth centuries. Moreover, such feelings were often reciprocated within the trade unions. Alastair Reid has highlighted how 'many trade unionists tended to be rather suspicious of the socialists, seeing them as deluded by unrealistic visions of the future'.[73] As the nature of the movement developed, then, so did the significance of different moments in its history, illustrating the mutability of the movement's history.

There was a similar tension in the Martyrs' connection to religion and particularly nonconformist traditions, which also highlighted divisions within the movement. There has been much written on the links between the labour and socialist movement that emerged in the 1880s, religion and nonconformism (especially Methodism).[74] Once again, though, there were quite different attitudes to such connections within the movement. When Arthur Henderson (as leader of the Labour Party) unveiled the 1912 memorial to the Martyrs after enjoying 'a cordial reception from the large number of Wesleyan Methodists ... who had gathered', as well as praising their impact on trade unionism celebrated their religious background. He argued that 'nothing could happen more wholesome to the future life of our country than the democratization of the forces of religion and the Christianising of the forces of democracy'.[75] He was not alone in making such a connection, while Methodists had been some of the principal adherents of celebrating the Labourers' legacy. The 1909 memorial movement, for instance, was headed up by the president of the Wesleyan Conference, while the Free Church Council were also heavily involved.[76] Indeed, they would focus on the Martyrs' religion as the chief reason why they were prosecuted. The *Holborn Review*, a Methodist periodical, noting in 1910 that the reason for their prosecution was not simply that 'the ruling classes most bitterly resented any combination', but because 'the leaders for such betterment were Nonconformists' the 'influence of the Established Church was against them'.[77] In this age of 'scientific socialism', many found such rhetoric to be incompatible with their version of socialism and the direction they believed the movement should be taking. In this context, then, the Martyrs were often absent as they were seen to stand for values that many felt should not be an influence on the movement, illustrating the challenge when adopting historical figures for a movement that spanned a wide political and ideological spectrum.

These differences within the broad movement point to the inchoate nature of it. This could be perceived as a strength of the movement; one correspondent to *Justice* wrote:

> With the growth of the Socialist movement and the diffusion of Socialist ideas, new thoughts, new sentiments, and even new forms of Socialism, make their appearance. In a movement like ours it is not possible, nor if it were possible would it be desirable, to secure absolute uniformity of thought and action. Diversity of thought and opinion leads to a discussion, discussion if carried on fairly and in a right and proper spirit is always productive of good.[78]

The history of the movement in the late nineteenth and early twentieth centuries, though, does not suggest that it was carried on 'in a right and proper spirit' or that it was 'productive of good'. Indeed, its inchoate nature, especially around what it stood for, could be a point of criticism for its opponents. As an article in *The Times* noted:

> One of the great difficulties in meeting Socialism [and the wider movement], or even in discussing it at all, is the extreme elasticity of its range, which extends from the Sermon on the Mount to the most ferocious gospel of hatred and destruction. Its forms are so numerous and its doctrines so indeterminate and variable that it is always possible to evade a plain issue and escape criticism by abandoning one formula and substituting another.[79]

One socialist wrote that 'there was, as I remember an almost total failure to agree what "Socialism" meant in terms of a concrete, specific, political practice'.[80] Such division or lack of a unified ideological understanding was a key factor in the Martyrs' absence prior to the 1930s, and more generally in the challenges that emerged when the movement attempted to use history as a unifying force. To find groups, ideas, moments or histories that could be celebrated across and appeal to this diverse movement thus represented a key issue for those in the movement. Antony Taylor has suggested that this was in part overcome by embracing 'a highly mixed tradition, sufficiently broad to span the spectrum of left opinion and to encompass a range of stories from different perspectives about the national past'.[81] The Martyrs show that these traditions and historical narratives were not fixed, and neither were the leading characters always the same in the movement's myths and stories.

Labour's contested histories

The Tolpuddle Martyrs' story and its history within the wider labour and socialist movement's history highlight much about the wider movement's relationship with the past. Labour history is a mutable one, and this changing relationship with the past is illustrated particularly well through the relationship to one group. The Martyrs may now be a foundational myth for the Labour Party and trade unionism that is celebrated annually, but as we have seen this was a creation of the TUC in the 1930s and their status was somewhat different among antecedent groupings and organizations. Their story was known, and their achievements praised, but they did not occupy such a central role as pioneers of the movement. This was primarily because their story was not seen as applicable to a more modern and 'scientific' movement, but it also reflected the multiple divisions across this diverse movement on various issues. The celebration and adoption of labour heroes was not a linear process. Instead, this is a story of adaption and accommodation, with different histories privileged or downplayed in different moments. The labour movement has thus commemorated its history, key moments and important figures in ever-changing ways, as internal pressures and the pressure exerted by a diverse opposition alter within constantly shifting contexts.

Literature on the movement's and specifically the Labour Party's use of history and relationship with its and the nation's past has demonstrated that it is important to the movement, serving a number of functions. It has highlighted that this relationship, though, is often complicated and at times even antagonistic. In widening the scope this chapter, in part through looking primarily at the years prior to the formation of the Labour Party, has further developed our understanding of the use of history by the wider movement. By examining the relationship to one historic group it shows that their absence from the historical narrative is as illustrative as their presence, reinforcing the notion that the movement's story is not one of continuous historical development, with the discontinuities as important as the continuities. The use of history was an important tactic for the wider movement, but the particular histories being used changed depending on their relationship to the present, the associated ideologies and the required purpose. History could focus existing tensions, as with the Martyrs prior to the 1930s, as much as it could be a unifying force, which was the hope in the 1930s. The Martyrs' mythical status was useful for the TUC, but the perceived impact and significance of their story seemed to matter much less to the movement that emerged in the 1880s. This reinforces the contested nature of the movement's past, its mutability, the challenges in finding common symbols or totemic figures, the need to adapt to a variety of often competing traditions and ideas, and the need to accommodate an every-changing narrative.

Notes

1. https://www.youtube.com/watch?v=oV-P7WMt2c4 (accessed 12 January 2022).
2. https://twitter.com/jeremycorbyn/status/1152928444445057024 (accessed 12 January 2022).
3. https://www.tolpuddlemartyrs.org.uk/festival/2021 (accessed 19 January 2022).

4   Carl J. Griffin, 'The Culture of Combination: Solidarities and Collective Action before Tolpuddle', *The Historical Journal*, 58, no. 2 (2015), 444.
5   Clare Griffiths, 'From "Dorchester Labourers" to "Tolpuddle Martyrs": Celebrating Radicalism in the English Countryside', in *Secular Martyrdom in Britain and Ireland: From Peterloo to the Present*, ed. Quentin Outram and Keith Laybourn (Cham: Palgrave Macmillan, 2018), 78.
6   Griffin, 'Culture', 478.
7   Peter Jones, 'The Tolpuddle Martyrs Museum and Related Sites', *Labour History Review*, 67, no. 2 (2002), 226. See also David Englander, 'Tolpuddle: The Making of Martyrs', *History Today*, 34, no. 12 (1984), 47–50.
8   Clare Griffiths, 'Remembering Tolpuddle: Rural History and Commemoration in the Inter-war Labour Movement', *History Workshop Journal*, 44 (1997), 146.
9   Laura Beers, *Your Britain: Media and the Making of the Labour Party* (Cambridge, Mass.: Harvard University Press, 2010), 2.
10 Quoted in Griffiths, 'Dorchester', 62.
11 Hilda Kean, 'Tolpuddle, Burston and Levellers: The Making of Radical and National Heritages at English Labour Movement Festivals', in *Heritage, Labour the Working Class*, ed. Laurajane Smith, Paul Shackel and Gary Campbell (Abingdon: Routledge, 2011), 269.
12 *Aberdeen Journal*, 9 July 1934.
13 Kean, 'Tolpuddle', 272.
14 For example, see Jon Lawrence, 'Labour – the Myths It Has Lived By', in *Labour's First Century,* ed. Duncan Tanner, Pat Thane and Nick Tiratsoo (Cambridge: Cambridge University Press, 2000); C. V. J. Griffiths, 'History and the Labour Party', in *Classes, Cultures and Politics: Essays on British History*, ed. C. V. J. Griffiths, J. J. Nott and W. Whyte (Oxford: Oxford University Press, 2011), 282–301.
15 H. M. Drucker, 'Conservative Socialism: Antihistorical Materialism in the British Labour Party', *International Political Science Review*, 1, no. 3 (1980), 324.
16 Antony Taylor, '"The Pioneers of the Great Army of Democrats": The Mythology and Popular History of the British Labour Party, 1890–1931', *Historical Research*, 91, no. 254 (2018), 723.
17 For a fuller discussion of this need to domesticize socialist ideas see Paul Ward, *Red Flag and Union Jack: Englishness, Patriotism and British Left, 1881–1924* (Woodbridge: Boydell Press, 1998).
18 Jose Harris, 'Labour's Political and Social Thought' in Tanner, Thane and Tiratsoo, *Labour's*, 9.
19 Lawrence, 'Labour', 341–2.
20 Martin Pugh, *Speak for Britain! A New History of the Labour Party* (London: Vintage Books, 2011), 8–9.
21 Glen O'Hara and Helen Parr, 'Conclusions: Harold Wilson's 1964–70 Governments and the Heritage of "New" Labour', *Contemporary British History*, 20, no. 3 (2006), 487.
22 Laura C. Forster, 'The Paris Commune in the British Socialist Imagination, 1871–1914', *History of European Ideas*, 46, no. 5 (2020), 615. Thomas Paine provides a similar example, see Marcus Morris, '"The Neglect of Paine Seems Particularly Strange at the Present Political Juncture": Explaining British Socialists Relationship to Paine, c.1884–1914' in *The Legacy of Thomas Paine in the Transatlantic World*, ed. M. Morris and S. Edwards (London: Routledge, 2018), 133–49.

23 For the continuity versus discontinuity debate see Eugenio Biagini and Alastair J. Reid, 'Currents of Radicalism, 1850-1914', in *Currents of Radicalism: Popular Radicalism, Organised Labour and Party Politics in Britain, 1850-1914*, ed. Eugenio Biagini and Alastair J. Reid (Cambridge: Cambridge University Press, 1991), 1-19; E. H. H. Green (ed.), *An Age of Transition: British Politics 1880-1917* (Edinburgh: Edinburgh University Press, 1997); Neville Kirk, *Change, Continuity and Class: Labour in British Society, 1850-1920* (Manchester: Manchester University Press, 1998); Richard Price, *British Society 1680-1880: Dynamism, Containment and Change* (Cambridge: Cambridge University Press, 2009).
24 Tom Scriven, 'The Dorchester Labourers and Swing's Aftermath in Dorset, 1830-8', *History Workshop Journal*, 82, no. 1 (2016), 13.
25 Antony Taylor, '"The Old Chartist": Radical Veterans on the Late Nineteenth- and Early Twentieth-Century Political Platform', *History*, 95, no. 320 (2010), 462.
26 *Justice*, 1 August 1903; H. M. Hyndman, *The Record of an Adventurous Life* (London: Macmillan, 1911), 273.
27 *Aberdeen Post and Journal*, 1 August 1927.
28 *The Times*, 8 February 1909.
29 *Labour Leader*, 28 May 1909.
30 *Western Gazette*, 31 May 1912.
31 H. M. Hyndman, *The Historical Basis of Socialism in England* (London: Kegan Paul Trench & Co., 1883), 282.
32 *South Daily News*, 1 September 1899.
33 *London Daily News*, 28 March 1906.
34 *Justice*, 17 November 1921.
35 *Labourer*, July 1917.
36 *Daily Herald*, 24 May 1912; *Communist*, 9 July 1921.
37 *Forward* (Glasgow), 2 April 1921.
38 *Wigan Observer*, 9 January 1904.
39 Hyndman, *Historical*, 228.
40 H. M. Hyndman, *The Evolution of Revolution* (London: Grant Richards, 1920), 295.
41 *Labour Leader*, 5 July 1907.
42 Thomas Kirkup, *A History of Socialism* (London: Adam and Charles Black, 1906), 3.
43 *Justice*, 19 April 1884.
44 H. M. Hyndman, *Socialism and Slavery* (London: SDF, 1890), 4.
45 Ward, *Red*, 34.
46 See Jan Marsh, 'William Morris and Medievalism', in *The Oxford Handbook of Victorian Medievalism*, ed. Joanne Parker and Corinna Wagner (Oxford: Oxford University Press, 2020); Ruth Kinna, *William Morris: the Art of Socialism* (Cardiff: University of Wales Press, 2000).
47 Ward, *Red*, 22, 26. For more on this new life, see Stephen Yeo, 'A New Life: The Religion of Socialism in Britain, 1883-1896', *History Workshop*, 4 (1977), 5-56.
48 *The Times*, 24 October 1887. For further discussion of this see Graham Johnson, 'Making Reform the Instrument of Revolution: British Social Democracy 1881-1911', *Historical Journal*, 43, no. 4 (2000), 977-1002.
49 Kirkup, *History*, 327.
50 Max Beer, *A History of British Socialism: Volume 2* (London: G. Bell and Sons, 1929), 195.
51 E. Belfort Bax, *Reminiscences and Reflexions of a Mid and Late Victorian* (New York: Thomas Seltzer, 1920), 126.

52 Beer, *History*, 279.
53 J. Ramsay MacDonald, *Socialism and Society* (London: Independent Labour Party, 1908), 122.
54 *Justice*, 14 September 1912.
55 Griffiths, 'History', 286. This notion of political evolution has also informed some of the key historiography, for example Ross McKibbin, *The Evolution of the Labour Party, 1910–1924* (London: Oxford University Press, 1974).
56 J. Ramsay MacDonald, 'Introduction', in *J. Keir Hardie: A Biography*, ed. William Stewart (London: National Labour Press, 1921), xxi.
57 MacDonald, *Socialism and Society*, 157.
58 J. Ramsay MacDonald, *The Socialist Movement* (London: Williams and Norgate, 1911), 203.
59 *Justice*, 3 April 1886.
60 Stewart, *Hardie*, 61–2.
61 *Justice*, 3 April 1886.
62 *Daily Citizen*, 16 February 1914.
63 John Callaghan, *Socialism in Britain* (Oxford: Basil Blackwell, 1990), 14.
64 *Pall Mall Gazette*, 22 September 1886. These figures may be exaggerated, but there was a significant drop. John Callaghan has suggested a fall from 594,000 in 1874 to 381,000 in 1880. Callaghan, *Socialism*, 14.
65 Hyndman, *Evolution*, 315.
66 *Justice*, 6 September 1884.
67 *Justice*, 24 January 1885.
68 Socialist League, *Strikes and the Labour Struggle* (London: Socialist League, n.d. [mid-1880s]).
69 Taylor, 'Pioneers', 728.
70 Sidney and Beatrice Webb, *The History of Trade Unionism* (London: Longmans, Green and Co., 1920), 374.
71 H. M. Hyndman, *Further Reminiscences* (London: Macmillan, 1912), 102.
72 *Justice*, 21 September 1901.
73 Alastair J. Reid, 'Labour and the Trade Unions' in Tanner, Thane and Tiratsoo, *Labour's*, 225.
74 For example, see K. D. Brown, 'Nonconformity and the British Labour Movement: A Case Study', *Journal of Social History*, 8, no. 2 (1975), 113–20; Mark Bevir, 'The Labour Church Movement, 1891–1902', *Journal of British Studies*, 3, no. 22 (1999), 217–45; Peter Catterall, 'The Distinctiveness of British Socialism? Religion and the Labour Party c.1900–1939', in *The Foundations of the Labour Party*, ed. Matthew Worley (Farnham: Ashgate, 2009), 131–52; Liam Ryan, 'Nonconformity and Socialism: The Case of J. G. Greenhough, 1880–1914', *Historical Research*, 95, no. 258 (2019), 771–89.
75 *Western Gazette*, 31 May 1912.
76 *The Times*, 9 February 1909; *Labour Leader*, 28 May 1909.
77 'The Story of the Tolpuddle Martyrs', *Holborn Review*, 1910, 45.
78 *Justice*, 6 April 1895.
79 *The Times*, 7 January 1909.
80 T. A. Jackson, *Solo Trumpet* (London: Lawrence and Wishart, 1953), 52.
81 Taylor, 'Pioneers', 728.

11

Magna Carta, memory diplomacy, and the use of the past in Anglo-American relations, c. 1915–65

Sam Edwards

In the summer of 1957, on meadows that slope gently towards the Thames, a large crowd gathered to dedicate a monument to a much-mythologized moment from the medieval past. Carved with the legend 'To Commemorate Magna Carta, Symbol of Freedom under Law', the monument – a columned pagoda surrounding a central pillar of stone – was the first such structure in Britain dedicated to this pivotal historic event. But it was neither the work of locals nor that of the British government; rather, it had been initiated and funded by the American Bar Association (ABA). To this extent, the monument performed a subtle appropriation, drawing a line between Runnymede and Washington; Magna Carta and the Declaration of Independence; Britain and the United States. As Lord Evershed explained in his speech at the dedication ceremony:

> The principles enshrined in Magna Carta were regarded as their birth right by American colonists. These same principles, and in many cases the terms of the articles themselves, exercised a profound effect upon the constitutions of the states of the Union and also upon the Federal Constitution itself, notably the Fifth and Fourteenth Amendments.[1]

This was by no means the first occasion that Americans had staked a claim to the events of 1215. As Harry Dickinson has shown, 'during the War of Independence a number of American Patriots had used the example of the English barons using force to compel King John to accept the terms of Magna Carta to justify their own resort to arms against what they regarded as Britain's oppressive and arbitrary polices adopted since the early 1760s'.[2] For many colonists, therefore, the signatories at Runnymede provided both inspiration and justification for their own act of rebellion against the 'tyranny' of George III, an unsurprising development given that many colonial authorities had in fact incorporated Magna Carta into their laws in the decades before the outbreak of hostilities.[3] Little wonder that in the immediate aftermath of the American victory, and as Lord Evershed's dedication speech implied, Magna Carta remained influential. Key parts – especially Clause 39 (which declared that no government is above the law)

– were duly incorporated into various new state constitutions, and the document also emerged as an influential touchstone for the Federal Constitution, ratified in 1789.[4]

Towards the end of the nineteenth century, this long-running investment in Magna Carta found further encouragement in a contemporary diplomatic development – the Anglo-American 'rapprochement'.[5] Prompted by shifting geopolitical realities together with various domestic concerns, this period saw many Anglo-American cultural and political elites confidently declare themselves members of a single 'Anglo-Saxon' family, a racialized world view which duly secured particular prominence in new forms of 'memory diplomacy'. While not called this at the time, Brian Etheridge's phrase nicely captures the essence of the endeavour: a type of inter-state activity based around instrumentalizing history and at times centred on carefully choreographed acts of commemoration.[6] It proved an especially popular method for cultivating Anglo-American relations in the years around the First World War and often involved what Erick Goldstein has called a 'sub-structure' of various non-state actors: writers, journalists, philanthropists, retired statesmen, municipal and provincial elites.[7] In the hands of such 'unofficial' diplomats history was an invaluable resource, one that might be trawled for episodes, events and even individuals that could be 'used' to show the deep roots of the assumed transatlantic racial bond. Magna Carta was one such 'event'; indeed, of all the various histories mined for meaning by twentieth-century memory diplomats Magna Carta had a unique resonance and utility. After all, this was a document popularly understood to offer an assertive 'Anglo-Saxon' retort to the tyrannies of the Norman Yoke, and so it was peculiarly responsive to the racial and cultural assumptions informing the turn of the century 'rapprochement'. As such, this chapter traces the twentieth-century history of Magna Carta's use within Anglo-American memory diplomacy. From the document's 700th anniversary in 1915, to the ways in which it was 'used' during and after the Second World War, to its repurposing and redeployment during the Cold War, Magna Carta emerged in the twentieth century as a powerful 'vector' – that is, a 'conduit' – for the commemoration of Anglo-American connection and comradeship.[8]

Unlike much previous scholarship, therefore, the chapter's focus is not the details of Magna Carta's presence or enduring legacy in US legal doctrine and constitutional history.[9] Instead, it considers how the ancient document has been *instrumentalized* within the discourses and dynamics of transatlantic relations, and to this extent it contributes to recent work examining the eight-century-long mythologization of Magna Carta.[10] In doing so, the chapter identifies two distinct phases of activity. The first, from *c*.1915 to *c*.1940, saw the document used by elements within the Anglo-American patrician class to assert the idea of underlying 'Anglo-Saxon' ties binding the United States and UK into (as they saw it) a single, and indissoluble, whole. During the second phase, *c*.1940–65, this fundamental assumption continued, but the diplomatic discourse subtly shifted, with overt appeals to a racialized past now increasingly replaced by the broader (and ostensibly less exclusionary) idea that Magna Carta enshrined the values of the 'English-speaking peoples', values which in turn secured new significance in the era of Cold War ideological confrontation. At its broadest, therefore, examining commemorations of Magna Carta helps us to better understand some of the contrasts *and* continuities within twentieth-century Anglo-American relations, especially regarding the transition from the Edwardian era of racial 'Anglo-Saxonism' to that of the Cold War 'Special Relationship'.

Race, rapprochement and memory diplomacy

The 'use' of Magna Carta within Anglo-American memory diplomacy has roots in a key development at the turn of the twentieth century, the 'great rapprochement'. For historian Bradford Perkins, this was a period – c.1880–1920 – in which many of the disputes that had lingered between London and Washington since the Revolution were finally resolved. Among these were the questions of the continued British presence in North America (in Canada, but also in the Pacific Northwest), the details of trade and the economic relationship (sometimes tense, as during the American Civil War), as well as the more general issue of British rights and responsibilities in the western hemisphere, claimed by President Monroe in 1823 as an exclusive American sphere of influence in which the encroachments of European empires were decidedly unwelcome. The 1896 settlement of the Venezuela Boundary dispute is an oft-cited marker. Remarkably, and in implicit recognition of the perceived legitimacy of the Monroe Doctrine, the British government accepted American arbitration over the borders of a South American imperial possession.[11]

In part, this new departure in the Anglo-American relationship was informed by shifting geopolitical realities, especially the rise of Imperial Germany and also of a modernizing Japan, developments which were perceived by many British and American elites as representing a threat to the established order. In a new world of supposedly hostile and upstart rivals, therefore, London and Washington drew closer together. Such closeness was also aided by everything from the burgeoning economic ties of transatlantic trade and investment, to the emergence of a shared literary culture, to the familial connections forged through marriage and migration. As Dana Cooper has shown, this was an era in which more than one aristocratic family sought to rejuvenate their dynasty with an infusion of American genes and money.[12] Crucially, though, another driving force informing the realpolitik of the rapprochement was a newly powerful and pervasive *idea* – Anglo-Saxonism.

This idea had a deep and diverse well-spring and an unusually long history. In sixteenth-century Britain, where it first emerged in recognizable form, Anglo-Saxon 'texts provided evidence of nationhood, nationality, and historical lineage', something which offered invaluable support for contemporary Protestantism.[13] Put differently, the Anglo-Saxon past offered a viable 'indigenous' history to those keen to break free from the rule of Rome. Unsurprisingly, such ideas had peculiar resonance among those nonconformists later drawn to settlement in the New World. In this sense, Anglo-Saxonism (not unlike small pox) travelled with the early settlers on their perilous journey across the storm-tossed Atlantic, subsequently becoming especially apparent in the work of the Virginia Company of London, in the activities of Captain John Smith, and in the 'Christianography' (that is, the theologically informed world view) of early New England. As Michael Modarelli has shown, the 'myth of American Anglo-Saxonism' might therefore be traced back to this initial moment of colonial transplantation.[14]

In the years that followed Anglo-Saxonism secured still greater prominence in American thought and culture. By the eighteenth century, it was particularly noticeable in the writings of figures such as Thomas Jefferson and, later, informed the increasingly intense arguments over questions of government and taxation which brewed in the 1760s and 1770s. Indeed, for Jefferson, Saxon 'liberty' was an American inheritance and thus the thirteen colonies constituted 'the new ground upon which the Saxon race would be revived'.[15] By the time the American Revolution broke out such thinking provided an invaluable resource. Here was the means to justify the rebellion against British rule while nonetheless declaring a continuity with – and respect for – the past. The colonists, like their Saxon forebears, were simply loyal Englishmen contesting the rule of a foreign tyrant (with the Hanoverian George III now standing in for the Norman King John).[16]

It was in the late nineteenth century, however, that transatlantic Anglo-Saxonism entered a significant new phase, now becoming explicitly racialized.[17] This was a development shaped by a veritable cocktail of contemporary factors. In Britain, the ongoing debate over Irish Home Rule inspired an 'othering' impulse among some elements of the British political establishment, one which claimed fundamental differences between 'Anglo-Saxon' and 'Celt'.[18] In the United States, a similar impulse emerged in the era of so-called 'new immigration', with an increasingly virulent nativism asserting that the arrival of 'alien' peoples and cultures – especially from southern and eastern Europe – represented a potentially lethal threat to the Anglo-Saxon body politic.[19] At the same time, the consolidation of racial segregation likewise amplified this Anglo-Saxonism; indeed, it powerfully shaped both the legislation and violence that so defined the Jim Crow system. Elsewhere, this appeal to a pseudo-scientific language of racial difference and exclusion was also energized in both countries by an age of imperial conquest and colonization. In North America, influential ideas of Anglo-Saxon 'manifest destiny' legitimated the violence inherit in Westward expansion while in Britain a similarly aggressive programme of territorial expansion together with the constitutional successes of the so-called white dominions (especially in terms of their establishment of institutions of law and governance) powerfully bolstered elite investment in Anglo-Saxonism.[20] Subsequent events at the very turn of the twentieth century only further intensified such thinking. In 1898, as the United States went to war with Spain, none other than Rudyard Kipling called on Americans to shoulder the 'white man's burden' while just a few years later, when the British Empire was embroiled in its own Imperial war, many American elites likewise offered London their racially coded solidarity. In short, by the first decade of the twentieth century 'articulate Englishmen and Americans at all levels of society declaimed about the supposed racial affinity of their two countries and described Great Britain and the United States as natural allies because of the racial bond'.[21]

In the decade before the outbreak of the First World War, therefore, racial Anglo-Saxonism emerged as the dominant discourse informing Anglo-American political culture, something that in turn shaped newly emerging forms of 'memory diplomacy'. As already noted above, this was a type of 'unofficial' diplomatic endeavour involving various cultural and political elites and often centred around the purposeful commemoration of transatlantic ties and connections. Two widely anticipated anniversaries are suggestive of how acts of memory diplomacy provided a powerful platform for contemporary Anglo-Saxonist thinking: the Centennial of the Treaty of Ghent (1914) and the Mayflower Tercentenary (1920).[22]

The Treaty of Ghent formally ended the War of 1812, the last occasion during which the United States and UK had been in conflict, and so the centennial was seen by many Anglo-American elites as an invaluable opportunity to celebrate the 'ties that bind'. Interest in marking the anniversary first emerged in around 1911–12 with the establishment of two parallel committees, one on each side of the Atlantic. By 1914, these committees had developed a full programme of ambitious events due to culminate in December 1914 with a grand ball and ceremony in Ghent itself. But the outbreak of war in Europe intervened, and so the various plans and projects were postponed. With Allied victory in 1918, however, interest returned, and in relatively quick order two linked projects, both first conceived back in 1914, were realized: a statue of Abraham Lincoln at Westminster (1920) and another of George Washington overlooking Trafalgar Square (1921). At the dedication ceremonies for both, orators gave full vent to contemporary Anglo-Saxonism. At the dedication of the former, the key American in attendance, Elihu Root (a former secretary of state) declared that Lincoln was 'of English blood' while Prime Minister David Lloyd George confidently asserted that the Great Emancipator had the 'best-known historical face in the Anglo-Saxon world'.[23] Similar sentiment recurred a year later at the dedication of the Washington statue. This time, the lead American speaker, Dr Smith, President of Washington and Lee University, remarked that Washington's English ancestry spoke of the 'common racial kinship' linking the United States and Great Britain, while Lord Curzon, the foreign secretary, happily accepted the statue of Washington by declaring it celebrated him as a 'great Englishman'.[24] Predictably, the very same racial assumptions shaped the Mayflower Tercentenary of 1920, the occasion marking the 300th anniversary of the arrival in the 'New World' of the so-called Pilgrim Fathers. Once again, ceremonies were performed on both sides of the Atlantic, and for all those involved – politicians, philanthropists, parish priests and town worthies – the migration to North America of seventeenth-century protestant separatists was defined as powerfully indicative of the deep-rooted ties binding the two branches of the 'Anglo-Saxon' family. For instance, the US Tercentenary Commission welcomed one new memorial to the Pilgrim Fathers as an expression of 'the abiding friendship of the Anglo-American people', while one British commentator similarly found in this memorial – erected at Immingham in north Lincolnshire – a powerful statement of Anglo American 'kinship'.[25] Such ideas reveal the overarching discursive context in which transatlantic elites also outlined plans for yet another much anticipated anniversary, one uniquely well-able to accommodate contemporary Anglo-Saxonist obsessions – the 700th anniversary of Magna Carta, in 1915.

Magna Carta and Anglo-American relations: From Anglo-Saxonism to the special relationship

Although signed six hundred years prior to the establishment of the United States, Magna Carta nonetheless developed a distinctive presence in American culture. By the eighteenth century some of its ideas and assumptions were institutionalized in state and federal constitutions as well as in specific constituents therein, perhaps most notably the Supreme Court. Here was Jefferson's 'Saxon inheritance', an idea he acquired from deep reading into the celebrated legal scholarship of Sir Edward Coke, for whom Magna Carta was foundational.[26] And Jefferson was not alone – many others of the revolutionary generation likewise found in Magna Carta the means to contest the rule of parliament and king, ideas subsequently carried into the early republic.[27]

To an extent, this was but one feature of a broader American investment in the middle ages, with a particular form of medievalism becoming so entrenched in nineteenth-century American culture that 'neo-Gothic castles and cathedrals adorned the country's landscape, medieval inspired literature and art filled its homes, and its citizens admired imagery, institutions, and ideals purportedly drawn from a chivalric and martial past'.[28] It was a very similar situation in Britain, where the medieval past likewise loomed large in the Victorian present. As one scholar has succinctly put it, this medievalism

> lay at the root of new laws and social policies. It changed religious practices. It deeply coloured national identities. And it inspired art, literature, and music that remains influential to this day. Sometimes driven by nostalgia, but also often progressive and future-facing, this wide-reaching movement, which reached its peak during the reign of Queen Victoria, looked back to a range of different peoples and historical periods spanning a thousand years, in order to inspire and vindicate cultural, political and social change.[29]

Such medieval 'nostalgia' – apparent on both sides of the Atlantic – was thus a central part of the backdrop against which Magna Carta now emerged not simply as constitutional guide or inspiration but, rather, as a diplomatic conduit or 'vector'.

A book published in 1880 is indicative of this developing trend. The work of American legal scholar J. C. Wells, and written with 'American citizens' principally in mind, the book provides an exhaustive history of Magna Carta, from its thirteenth-century origins to its nineteenth-century legacies. Indeed, a full half of the volume – over 200 pages – examines Magna Carta's significance to 'constitutional civil liberty', from its earliest arrival in the colonies through 'to the centennial year of American independence' (just a few years previous, in 1876).[30] A very similar commemorative appropriation is apparent in the volume produced by another American lawyer a few years later, in 1900, a volume in which the author – Boyd Barrington – celebrates Magna Carta as an event of compelling interest to 'all of the Anglo-Saxon race'.[31] Elsewhere, in 1897 none other than W. T. Stead, a particularly committed transatlantic 'Anglo-Saxonist', was even contending that June 15 – the date on which Magna Carta was signed – should be established as a day to celebrate the unity of the 'English-speaking race'.[32] But it was the International Magna Charta Day Association (IMCDA) formed in 1907 by Canadian-born James Hamilton that actually took on the task and in doing so most clearly marks the emergence of a new interest in explicitly *using* the events of 1215 for contemporary transatlantic diplomacy.[33] As Donald MacRaild, Sylvia Ellis and Stephen Bowman have shown, the IMCDA saw in Magna Carta the means to develop a 'worldwide Anglo-Saxon patriotism', and thus a key objective was to have

15 June officially designated as 'interdependence day', that is, a day to celebrate the ties of history that bound the United States and UK into what Charles Dilke had famously called in 1868, *Greater Britain*.[34]

The activities of the IMCDA combined with a contemporary obsession for commemorative pageantry duly ensured there was also keen interest in marking the 700th anniversary of the signing of Magna Carta in 1915. A General Committee was established in 1914 to organize the occasion, and its members included an array of Anglo-American cultural, political and religious leaders, including figures such as Lord Bryce (a former British ambassador to the United States with a well-known affection for US constitutional history) and C. H. Firth, the president of the Royal Historical Society. The stated intention of this committee was to organize a suitably impressive gathering at Runnymede. Much like the centennial of the Treaty of Ghent, however, the outbreak of war in Europe meant that this 'proved not desirable, nor indeed possible'.[35] Britain was too busy defending Magna Carta's underlying principles 'through force of arms', while the United States remained neutral. It was thus American entry into the conflict which led to the only significant *transatlantic* commemoration of Magna Carta to emerge around the 700th anniversary: a collection of scholarly essays published in 1917. The volume's preface includes a special consideration of the significance of 1215 to Americans, explaining that

> the charter of 1215 was the starting point of the constitutional history of the English race, the first link in a long chain of constitutional instruments which have moulded men's minds and held together free governments not only in England but wherever the English race has gone and the English tongue is spoken. The Bill of Rights was in the thoughts of those who framed the first Constitutions of Massachusetts and Virginia when the North American colonize renounced their allegiance to the British Crown; and much of the document of 1689 was incorporated into those constitutions. From them the old provisions, largely in the original words of the Great Charter, passed into the Federal Constitution of the United States when it was drafted in 1787 and adopted, with the first ten amendments, in 1788 and 1791.[36]

Such were the claims made on Magna Carta in the midst of the First World War, claims also asserted in a dedicated chapter elsewhere in the same volume. Indeed, for the author of this chapter, H. D. Hazeltine, a key significance of the document signed by King John in 1215 concerned its subsequent 'imperial history' – that is, its export abroad – 'the most important phase' of which 'was its effect upon the constitutions and laws of the American colonies and of the Federal Union that was established after their War of Independence'.[37] As Hazeltine went on to explain, 'the Englishmen who settled in America in the seventeenth century inherited all the preceding ages of English history', and so '[t]o them belonged Magna Carta and the Common Law'.[38]

This increasingly familiar idea that Magna Carta was a dual Anglo-American 'inheritance' received still further rehearsal in the immediate post-war period. In November 1918, a gathering of dignitaries in London saw one American offer a story of familial connection, one with roots in the meadows at Runnymede. As he explained it, 'the men who declared America independent in 1776 were the heirs in title of those who brought Charles I to the scaffold, who created the first parliament after the Battle of Evesham, and who wrung by force of arms from King John the Great Charter of our Liberties'.[39] Similar followed in 1921, with the London *Times* declaring – on American Independence Day – that the United States and Great Britain both 'derive their conceptions of social order from the same source', and this was 'the Great Charter of 1215'.[40] Hardly surprising, then, that President Woodrow Wilson's vision for a post-war 'League of Nations' identified it as the 'World's Magna Carta'. The British committee set up to support the drafting of the League's 'Covenant' even included among its number Lord Bryce, former Chair of the 1915 Commemoration Committee (and author of the forward to the 1917 volume of Magna Carta essays).[41] Within just a few years, though, changing geopolitical circumstances meant that these transatlantic celebrations of Magna Carta increasingly lost some traction (although the IMCDA nonetheless persisted in their activities through to the Second World War).

By the middle of the 1920s, in fact, the Anglo-American relationship hit a rocky patch as new tensions emerged regarding the details of the post-war peace as well as over naval disarmament.[42] The Washington Naval Conference of 1921–22 is a useful marker, for while agreement was eventually reached regarding the relative strength of the United States Navy and the Royal Navy this was not before some significant disputes and the associated emergence of mutual distrust.[43] In the United States, too, this was an era of a resurgent popular Anglophobia which encouraged many Americans to look across the Atlantic and see not an Anglo-Saxon 'brother' but, rather, a different cliché – perfidious Albion. Those wily British propagandists, bankers and manufacturers who had encouraged a naive and innocent American public to support the global war effort were singled out for particular criticism, with one infamous publication later labelling such figures the *Merchants of Death* (1934).[44] Together with the fallout over the League of Nations, such thinking ensured that the interwar period was less conducive to celebrations of deep-rooted Anglo-American connection.[45] At the same time, developments at Runnymede itself encouraged a rather more 'national' narrative, particularly after 1931, when the site was gifted to the nation by the owner, Lady Fairhaven, and then taken into the care of the National Trust.[46] Notably, for instance, the major commemoration held at Runnymede in 1934 – a large-scale pageant involving 5,000 performers – was entirely focused on British history, from the arrival of the Roman Legions through to the return home of victorious redcoats in 1816 (after vanquishing Napoleon). There was no space here, it seems, for even a brief nod to the Mayflower Compact or to the American Constitution.[47] It was not until the decades' end, therefore, as global tensions once again ramped up, that *transatlantic* interest in the utility of Magna Carta as commemorative 'vector' resurfaced.

Early signs of this renewed interest can be found in 1937 when the 150th anniversary of the Federal Constitution was widely celebrated in the United States, an occasion that led more than one British observer to note approvingly the links between the 'great Charter' of 1215 and the text ratified in 1789.[48] Two years later, the First Order of Virginians celebrated the 320th anniversary of legislative assembly in the colonies as marking the earliest beginnings of an 'American Magna Charta'.[49] But it was during the 1939 New York World's Fair that Magna Carta once again took centre stage in the commemoration of Anglo-American brotherhood. In the British Pavilion, for instance, the 'principal exhibit' was the 'Lincoln copy of Magna Carta', with the London *Times* pointedly reminding their readers that the 'whole economy of the United States – its independence of character and its liberty – rests as surely as the British structure upon the meeting on those fields by the Thames seven centuries ago'.[50] The same idea was powerfully asserted by the very manner in which Magna Carta was displayed. It was the focal point of the Pavilion's 'Hall of Democracy' in which 'the story of the evolution of Parliament and the struggle for full individual freedom is told in a way that will appeal to American minds'.[51] The *New York Times* sets the scene well, explaining that an

> elaborate canopy suggests the heraldry of the Middles Ages. There is a raised dais on which might have once been set the throne of a king. For the first time citizens of the New World look upon the Great Charter, concluded in the year 1215 and now brought across the sea to New York.[52]

And this was a journey with real contemporary significance, for as the *Times* continued, '[a]n urgent significance lurks in the crabbed calligraphy of the Latin script. Magna Carta is the birth certificate of democracy, and free peoples are staking millions of lives, billions of money, on a covenant that they consider to be essential to their pursuit of happiness'.[53] Indeed, such was Magna Carta's perceived significance that at the fair's end some Britons suggested that a copy should be left permanently in the United States, for Americans 'may be considered to have some right in a document of our race'.[54]

The outbreak of war in September 1939 rather forced the issue, and the Lincoln copy of Magna Carta was indeed transferred into American care, albeit only for 'the duration'.[55] It was given 'refuge' by the Library of Congress, with the British Ambassador, Lord Lothian, reminding Americans that the ancient text had 'played its part … in the inspiration of the American War of Independence, in the framing of the Constitution, and in Abraham Lincoln's struggle to "preserve the Union"'.[56] Significantly, this was sentiment with which the president, Franklin Delano Roosevelt, was eminently comfortable, explaining during his third inaugural in January 1941 that the 'democratic aspiration is no mere recent phase in human history. It is human history. It permeated the ancient life of early peoples. It blazed anew in the middle ages. It was written in Magna Carta'.[57] Speaking to a crowd of over 100,000, and all too aware that the democratic way of life was just then being 'assailed' on all sides, FDR even explained the exact path through which this medieval document had arrived into the American present. It is, he sermonized, 'written into our Mayflower compact, into the Declaration of Independence, into the Constitution of the United States, into the Gettysburg Address'.[58]

Even before the United States entered the war, therefore, Magna Carta had already re-emerged as a crucial touchstone in Anglo-American relations, much as was the case – albeit it briefly – in 1915. But there was also now a subtle shift in emphasis and meaning. Gone was the explicitly racialized discourse of the early twentieth century celebrating Magna Carta as 'Saxon inheritance'; such language was pushed beyond the pale by the violent racism inherent in Nazism and Fascism. In its place, therefore, came celebrations of the shared ideas, institutions and values of the 'English-speaking peoples', a phrase which in fact had become increasingly popular in transatlantic diplomatic discourse from the 1920s onwards.[59] Crucially, though, this was a discursive transition which Magna Carta could readily accommodate, for as we have seen such thinking had long been implicit to perceptions of the document in the transatlantic world. In this sense, the changing circumstances of the 1940s simply required a shift in emphasis; away from celebrations of Magna Carta as expressive of an inherent 'Anglo-Saxon' capacity for self-government towards instead a reading which emphasized that ideas of liberty, law and governance were the great and enduring gifts of the 'English-speaking peoples' to world history.

Perhaps unsurprisingly, no one saw the power and utility of this reading of Magna Carta better than Winston Churchill, the most famous 'Anglo-American' of the twentieth century. Indeed, when he became Prime Minister in 1940 Churchill already had a long track record in 'using' history to cultivate a certain idea of transatlantic connection. As early as July 1918, for instance, he had happily celebrated 4 July in Britain with a speech to the 'Anglo-Saxon Fellowship' (a transatlantic organization) in which he offered a rather Jeffersonian take on the origins of the Revolution. As Churchill explained it to an audience that included senior US military figures, Britons were now 'glad … that an English colony declared itself independent under a German King'.[60] This was of course perfect grist to the mill given the campaign then being waged by the Anglo-American militaries against the Kaiser's Germany. By the time of the next war, therefore, Churchill was well equipped – in rhetorical terms – to seek increased American support via a politically expedient appeal to the past. Take, for instance, the way he welcomed Congressional approval of the Lend-Lease Act, legislation which provided essential munitions and material for the British war effort. Clearly aware of FDR's recent Inaugural, Churchill pointedly celebrated Lend-Lease as a 'new Magna Carta' which 'proclaims by precept and example the duty of free men and free nations, wherever they may be, to share the responsibility and burden of enforcing them'.[61]

Magna Carta remained a recurrent reference point in the months that followed, especially any time Anglo-American diplomats wanted to assert the existence of common interests. Thus, at a London dinner in June 1941 the American ambassador to the Allied governments in exile 'paid tribute' to Britons and applauded their 'bravery' and 'determination to maintain the principles of justice, liberty and the rights of free men, as expressed in Magna Carta'.[62] Across the Atlantic, meanwhile, a similar gathering in New York saw one speaker assert American 'sympathy' for Britain before reminding the gathered crowd that the United States and Great Britain were 'linked … through the ideals embodied in the Declaration of Independence and Magna Carta'.[63] A few months later, Magna Carta day itself was marked at St. John's Cathedral in New York with 'prayers' identifying the ancient text as the 'cornerstone of liberty'.[64] Little wonder that by the summer of 1941 the American Ambassador to the Court of St. James was happily telling a group of British teachers during a goodwill tour that their counterparts in the United States 'had many ways of interesting young people' in the 'history of their own country', but there was always one underlying consistency: they 'began really with Magna Carta and the Bill of Rights'.[65]

It was in the joint Anglo-American declaration of war aims, however, that this instrumentalization of Magna Carta received perhaps its fullest wartime expression. For the document outlining these aims, signed on the decks of a Royal Navy warship moored off the coast of Newfoundland, was called, very deliberately, the Atlantic *Charter*. Reporting on the momentous occasion, one American paper even declared that the document signed by Churchill and FDR in August would very likely 'rank in world significance with the signing of Magna Carta at Runnymede and the adoption of the Constitution of the United States'.[66] And for Churchill, while some of the Charter's clauses were a subject of concern (especially Clause Three with its anti-colonial tenor), there was at least some comfort to be had in how he had identified 'America firmly with Britain's cause'.[67] Moreover, Magna Carta persisted as a recurrent subject of attention for the remainder of the conflict, often being name-dropped to assert the legitimacy of the Anglo-American cause and, elsewhere, deployed as a synonym and shorthand for the idea that deep ties of history and sentiment bound together the 'English-speaking peoples'. In spring 1943, for instance, Senior American air force officers were the guests of honour at a special anniversary commemoration at Runnymede, while a year later the celebration of St. George's Day similarly included a ceremony at Runnymede featuring a detachment from the US military (who gifted a flag to be hung in the nearby church of Egham).[68] At the war's end, these activities even helped shape yet another 'Charter', that of the United Nations, a document which Secretary of State John Foster Dulles welcomed as a 'Greater Magna Carta'.[69]

This sustained transatlantic investment in Magna Carta – apparent across the conflict – ensured that it retained cultural traction as the war gave way to peace. In fact, the shifting geopolitical circumstances of the immediate post-1945 period gave such investment new impetus, with Magna Carta redeployed in the early Cold War and often by increasingly high-profile diplomatic actors. See, for instance, the way in which the recently elected Prime Minister Clement Atlee moved quickly in 1945 to reassure Americans that they had nothing to fear from his ostensibly 'socialist' government. As Atlee explained it during a trip to Washington, the Labour Party stood firmly 'in line with those who fought for Magna Carta and Habeas Corpus, with the Pilgrim Fathers and the Declaration of Independence'.[70] They were good allies, in other words, should there be any future showdown with the tyranny beyond the Urals.

But it was the man Atlee defeated in the General Election of 1945 – Winston Churchill – who most firmly staked a claim to Magna Carta and in doing so established it as a central component of his overriding post-war project, the establishment of an Anglo-American 'special relationship'. The key moment occurred in March of 1946 during a speech Churchill delivered at Westminster College, in Fulton, Missouri. Invited to attend the college's graduation ceremonies by President Harry Truman, and in doing so provided with an invaluable platform to deliver his views on the worsening global situation, Churchill famously declared that an 'Iron Curtain' had descended from 'Stettin in the Baltic to Trieste in the Adriatic'. And in response, therefore, he called for a 'special relationship' between the British Empire and the United States, an idea that must be built, he asserted, on their 'joint inheritance' of the 'great principles of freedom and the rights of man'. For Churchill, these were principles recorded in 'Magna Carta, the Bill of Rights, the Habeas Corpus, trial by jury, and the English common law', and which achieved 'their most famous expression in the American Declaration of Independence'.[71] Such was Churchill's idea for a 'special relationship', a phrase which duly entered the lexicon of transatlantic diplomatic discourse. In the years that followed, Churchill took every opportunity to further develop this theme. For instance, his multi-volume *History of the English-Speaking Peoples* (1956–58) gives special attention to the events 'on the great meadow at Runnymede', and in Volume 1 – subtitled *Birth of a Nation* – he paints an evocative scene of a 'handful of resolute men' (the Barons) forcing the King to acknowledge the limits of his power by signing those 'Articles' subsequently 'used as the foundation of principles and systems of government of which neither King John nor his nobles dreamed'.[72] In the fourth and final volume, meanwhile, subtitled *The Great Democracies*, Churchill develops this further, spending significant time exploring some of these very 'systems', most notably in the United States.[73] Elsewhere, in his *History of the Second World War* (1954), Churchill uses a full chapter to trace the signing of the Atlantic Charter, a joint Anglo-American declaration he describes as of 'profound and far-reaching importance' (and thus almost on a par – at least in his mind – with Magna Carta).[74]

Churchill's appropriation of Magna Carta found a receptive audience in Cold War America. In 1947, and after having granted it asylum for the duration of the war, an original copy of the document was even included on the 'Freedom Train' which toured the country and which soon 'became caught up in the emerging ideological struggle with communism'.[75] The train's sacred cargo brought together the text sealed at Runnymede with famous Americana, including the Mayflower Compact, the Declaration of Independence and the Gettysburg Address.[76] But the most notable Cold War-era effort to 'use' Magna Carta both to defend American liberties *and* cultivate transatlantic connection can be found in the activities of the ABA.

Originally established in 1878, the ABA had 26,000 members by the end of the 1920s and it would continue to grow across the twentieth century. Like many in the American legal system, the association's leadership had long asserted that their profession's roots lay in England, a commitment inspired by the role of English Common Law in the early period of colonial settlement as well as by the fact that many of the signatories of the later Declaration of Independence were Alum of the Inns of Court in London. In the era of Anglo-American 'rapprochement' this entrenched Anglophilia encouraged the association to develop a close rapport with British counterparts, and so it was that in 1924, following an invitation from the bar and Law Society of England, that the ABA took the decision to hold their annual meeting in London. One thousand lawyers crossed the Atlantic, including most of the Supreme Court justices as well as judges from all forty-eight states. They were hosted to dinner by British friends who took every opportunity to celebrate the ties of affection, sentiment and law which united what Srdjan Vucetic has called the 'Anglosphere'.[77] Three decades later, in 1957, the ABA returned to London for a second visit.

If the 1924 trip was an impressive occasion, the 1957 tour was still more so, involving over 3,000 American lawyers. Once again, they were treated to ceremony, pageantry and oratory, but this time at the centre of the ABA's second British 'pilgrimage' was the dedication of a monument at Runnymede, funded by subscriptions from their members and intended to celebrate 'Magna Carta as the ultimate bulwark against communism'.[78]

Unveiled on a warm July day and before a crowd of 4,000, the monument was designed by Sir Edward Maufe of the Royal Academy and consisted of a neoclassical and columned pagoda made of white Portland Stone, at the centre of which was a stone pillar carved with the words 'To Commemorate Magna Carta – Symbol of Freedom Under the Law'.[79] The first such structure of its kind erected at Runnymede, it marked, said the ABA's outgoing president, E. Smyth Gambrell, the 'birthplace of sovereign power administered within the limits of judicial process and according to the law of the land'. And for Gambrell, therefore, the distant events of 1215 had profound significance for the modern United States, as the key principle of Magna Carta – 'that no-one shall be above the law' – was subsequently '[t]ransplanted to the virgin soil of a new world'. To this extent, explained Gambrell, the 'spirit of this place [Runnymede] breathed in every American colony'. A familiar recounting of American history followed, one which identified the War of Independence as the result of the 'royal veto of the provisions of Magna Carta' and thus an event which reminded the world that 'Anglo-Saxons will govern themselves'.

As such language suggests, there was more than a hint of the old Anglo-Saxonism in Gambrell's address; indeed, at one point he went so far as to claim that in the 'English-speaking peoples' is a 'common blood line, comingling Celt and Saxon, Dane and Norman, Pict and Scot'.[80] But, compared to the rhetoric of the immediate post-1918 period, such explicitly racialized language was now displaced by a more general Cold War-era appeal for the English-speaking peoples to defend liberty from 'tyranny'. As Gambrell declared in his rousing conclusion, '[i]n the Fellowship of free men that knows no limits of race or creed or land or time, let us be rededicated to the service that lies to our hands, mindful that those who defend liberty and justice anywhere defend it everywhere'.[81] Similar ideas punctuated the speeches of others. One visiting American lawyer declared that the idea of Magna Carta 'stirs the Anglo-American pulse like a battle cry against oppression and liberty',[82] while the association's president-elect, Charles S. Rhyne, claimed that 'every American citizen would be less than he is but for the privileges of Magna Carta'.[83] Back in Britain, meanwhile, the London *Times* confidently asserted that 'difference between what the monument represented and what Communism represented was freedom under law – the acknowledgment that there were moral limitations on civil power'.[84]

It was during the special dinner held at Guildhall on 31 July, however, that this theme received its most assertive articulation at the hands of, once again, Winston Churchill. The dinner in question was hosted by the British Law Society and it drew to a formal close the ABA's second 'pilgrimage' to Britain. The occasion was carefully choreographed so as to impress the society's American guests, and the latter seem to have been rather taken by the 'memorable experience' of dining in the 'great, vaulted, cathedral-like Guildhall'.[85] But the 'high-point', at least according to the *Journal* of the ABA, was a 'brilliant fifteen-minute address' by the 'old lion' during which the former Prime Minister pointedly lingered on the key idea informing the ABA's visit: that it was from Britain that the United States derived 'the Common Law, the tradition of Magna Carta and the heritage of freedom under law'. Indeed, as Churchill explained it in a history lesson that was apparently 'interrupted by round after round of applause': 'Between Magna Carta and the formulation of the American Constitution, we in

Britain can claim authorship of the whole growth of the English common law'.[86] Much like he also asserted in the multi-volume history published just a year later, these were the 'ties of intellect and spirit' which gave the 'English-speaking peoples' their essential unity. Thus, just a year after the Suez Crisis, perhaps the episode most damaging to the post-war 'special relationship', here was Churchill reminding a room full of influential Americans of the debt they owed to their English heritage.

This was an idea which secured still further elaboration a few years later during yet another memorial dedication. This time, however, the structure – a stone surrounded by trees and pasture – was dedicated not to the distant events of 1215 but to a celebrated individual recently struck down in his prime: President John F. Kennedy, assassinated in 1963. As one evocative press description put it, beyond the memorial (designed by Sir Geoffrey Jellicoe):

> a more formal path of Portland stones leads to two seats dug into the hill. Some of the stone comes from the Roach Bed at Portland and shows the remains of oysters that lived 75 million years ago. Some fine old thorn trees surround the paths, and a good specimen of an American Oak was found to be near the stone. An American scarlet oak, which holds its leaves all winter, has been planted in the memorial enclosure, and will eventually give shade to the stone.[87]

For the organization responsible – the Kennedy Memorial Trust (KMT) – Runnymede was an eminently suitable location for this act of homage. After all, JFK had a long-running affection for Britain going back to the days when his father was ambassador to the country in the late 1930s. He was a keen admirer of Churchill and had developed a close rapport with Prime Minister Harold Macmillan, who was in fact a distant relation. His sister, 'Kick' Kennedy, was buried in an English churchyard (Edensor in Derbyshire), and his brother, Joe Jr., had been killed in the sky above Suffolk when his aircraft exploded during a wartime mission. And JFK was, of course, a man whose White House was compared to the court of King Arthur's Camelot.[88] Where better than Runnymede to commemorate this twentieth-century 'knight', especially as 1965 was also the 750th anniversary of the document's signing?[89] Equally important, at least according to his eulogists at the dedication ceremony, the slain president was a defender of Western liberties and hence Runnymede was a place where his memory would keep good company. As the Queen put it in her address, Kennedy 'championed liberty in an age when its very foundations were being threatened on a universal scale'. This was clearly a sentiment with which Dean Rusk, the American Secretary of State, heartily agreed. Accepting the memorial on behalf of President Johnson, Rusk remarked that it would remind those who came to pay their respects 'of the common dedication of the British and American peoples to the cause of human liberty'.[90]

That said, and as Robert Cook and Clive Webb have shown, not all Britons seem to have agreed with such lofty oratory, and indeed such had been the general apathy to the KMT's 1964 public appeal for funds that the government of Harold Wilson was forced to step in and make right the shortfall.[91] Even once it was unveiled the memorial seems to have been met with ambivalence in some quarters and outright hostility in others. It was subject to occasional vandalism, defaced, and at one point a small explosion very almost rent it asunder.[92] Nonetheless, if its local reception was not quite what the KMT had hoped, their choice of location remained fitting given the structure's ultimate point and purpose – to pay homage to President Kennedy but in a manner which also allowed for the celebration of the 'special relationship'. And as we have seen, over half a century of transatlantic investment in Magna Carta had made Runnymede the perfect place.

Conclusions

In the early twentieth century, after two decades of diplomatic 'rapprochement', Anglo-American elites began investing their time, energy and money in an emerging form of 'informal' inter-state activity: memory diplomacy. In line with what amounted to a contemporary obsession with historical anniversaries, these unofficial diplomats – the IMCDA, writers, journalists and historians – turned their attention to any event or episode which might be made to accommodate the political, cultural and indeed racial underpinnings of their world view. At root, theirs was an 'Anglo-Saxonist' vision which celebrated imagined ties of blood and biology between Americans and Britons. The 1914 centenary of the Treaty of Ghent – which ended the War of 1812 – drew their attention, for this was an opportunity to celebrate 100 years of peace between the United States and Great Britain. It was marked with statues in London commemorating two American presidents, Washington and Lincoln, both of whom were claimed as 'Anglo-Saxons' whose ancestry indisputably tied them to England. Another anniversary, this time of the Mayflower sailing in 1920, similarly encouraged public pronouncements regarding the 'racial' connections assumed to bind together America and England.

But the pre-eminent vehicle for the celebration of such 'Anglo-Saxon' solidarity was a document sealed by King John near the banks of the Thames in 1215 – Magna Carta. Here was an assertion of Anglo-Saxon liberties in the face of a foreign tyranny (the Norman Yoke), and so here was an historical episode eminently useable by transatlantic Anglo-Saxonists. And use it they did, an appropriation powerfully aided by the fact that Magna Carta had already established an influential position in American culture both before and after the Revolution. Early colonists had used it to inform the constitutions they wrote; revolutionaries like Thomas Jefferson deployed it to legitimate their rebellion against the rule of George III; American legal scholars found in it – and in English Common Law more broadly – the intellectual bedrock necessary to the development of American jurisprudence in the early republic. All this ensured that Magna Carta was peculiarly well-able to accommodate the demands and assumptions informing Anglo-American memory diplomacy. From the formation in 1907 of the Magna Charta Day Association, to the 700th anniversary in 1915, to the careful placing of the Lincoln copy in the British Pavilion at the New York World's Fair, Magna Carta emerged in the first half the twentieth century as a powerful commemorative 'vector' for ideas of Anglo-American connection. The Second World War only further energized this, especially as more high-profile diplomatic actors now got in on the act: FDR purposefully referenced it in his inaugural and it was similarly 'present' in how his British counterpart, Winston Churchill, received news of Lend-

Lease. Little wonder that it would go on to shape the very articulation of Anglo-American war aims – outlined in the Atlantic Charter of 1941 – as well as informing the ideas and institutions shaping the post-war world, most noticeably the 'Charter' of the United Nations.

It was in a powerful post-war diplomatic discourse authored by, once again, Winston Churchill that Magna Carta found itself most explicitly reused: the 'special relationship'. Gone, though, were references to 'Anglo-Saxon' qualities; in their place came the idea that the document sealed at Runnymede in 1215 was expressive of the genius of the 'English-speaking peoples'. In doing so, Magna Carta was also repurposed for a new mission – the defence of the West against the 'tyranny' of Communism. This was certainly the view of the ABA, committed by principle and practice to the idea of 'freedom before the law'. Hence why they funded and erected a monument at Runnymede, dedicated in the summer of 1957 with a full quota Anglo-American pageantry. Hence, too, why just a few years later a semi-official British organization chose the same site for a memorial to a murdered American president, John F. Kennedy. Here was a man who had heroically defended Western liberties in the face of potential nuclear Armageddon – the Cuban Missile Crisis – and here, too, was a man who many contemporaries celebrated in death as knightly, chivalric and indeed 'Arthurian'. Where better to commemorate him than upon meadows once trod by the Knights of Yore? Kennedy's memorial stands there still today, carved with words from his 1961 inaugural declaring his commitment to the 'survival and success of liberty'. It is an 'acre' of England 'given to the United States of America by the people of Britain', and it reveals an important chapter in how Magna Carta was used across the first half of the twentieth century as vehicle and vector for the cultivation of Anglo-American comradeship.[93]

Notes

1. The Right Honorable Lord Evershed, 'The Magna Carta Memorial Ceremonies: Runnymede, Sunday, Afternoon, July 28', *American Bar Association Journal*, 43, no. 10 (October 1957), 903.
2. Harry Dickinson, 'Magna Carta in the American Revolution', in *Magna Carta: History, Influence and Context: Papers Delivered at Peking University on 800th Anniversary of Magna Carta*, ed. Lawrence Goldman (London: Institute of Historical Research, 2018), 99.
3. Credance Sol, 'Exploring the Magna Carta and Governmental Immunity Doctrines: The View from the United States', in *The Rights and Aspirations of the Magna Carta*, ed. Elizabeth Gibson-Morgan and Alexis Chommeloux (London: Palgrave Macmillan, 2016), 67.
4. Sol, 'Exploring the Magna Carta and Governmental Immunity Doctrines: The View from the United States', 67.
5. Bradford Perkins, *The Great Rapprochement: England and the United States, 1895–1914* (New York: Atheneum, 1968).
6. For 'memory diplomacy', see Brian Etheridge, 'The Desert Fox, Memory Diplomacy, and the German Question in Early Cold War America', *Diplomatic History*, 32,

no. 2 (2008), 207–38. See also M. Todd Bennett, 'The Spirits of '76: Diplomacy Commemorating the US Bicentennial in 1976', *Diplomatic History*, 40, no. 4 (2016), 695–721.

7   Erick Goldstein and Melanie Hall, 'Writers, the Clergy, and the "Diplomatization" of Culture: The Sub-structures of Anglo-American Diplomacy, 1820–1914', in *On the Fringes of Diplomacy*, ed. Anthony Best and John Fisher (London: Ashgate, 2011).

8   See Nancy Wood, *Vectors of Memory: Legacies of Trauma in Postwar* Europe (Oxford: Berg, 1999).

9   The significance of Magna Carta to American legal thinking has been much discussed. See, for example, Sol, 'Exploring the Magna Carta and Governmental Immunity Doctrines: The View from the United States' (65–88) and Geraldine Gadbin-George 'UK Supreme Court versus US Supreme Court: Modern Use of Magna Carta' (39–64) in Gibson-Morgan and Chommeloux, *The Rights and Aspirations of the Magna Carta*; Christopher J. Rowe, 'The American Bar Association Looks to England, 1924 and 1957', *American Journal of Legal History*, 61, no. 4 (2021), 385–415; A. E. Dick Howard, 'Magna Carta's American Adventure', *North Carolina Law Review*, 94, no. 5 (2016), 1413–22; Nicholas P. Miller, '"A Second Magna Charta of Highest Liberties": American Freedom, and the Heritage of the Magna Carta', *Journal of Church and State*, 60, no. 3 (2017), 426–48.

10 For the 'use' and 'mythologization' of Magna Carta see, for example, Nic Vincent, *Magna Carta: Origins and Legacy* (Oxford: Oxford University Press, 2015); Nic Vincent, *Magna Carta: The Foundation of Freedom, 1215–2015* (London: Third Millennium, 2014): Peter Coss, 'Presentism and the "Myth" of Magna Carta', *Past and Present* (2017), 227–9; John Baker, *The Reinvention of Magna Carta, 1216–1616* (Cambridge: Cambridge University Press, 2017), esp. 442–51; Ralph Turner, *Magna Carta* (Abingdon: Routledge, 2003), esp. 208–25; David W. Saxe, 'Magna Carta and the Exercise of Transnational in the Twenty-First Century', in Udo Hebel, *Transnational American Memories* (Boston: De Gruyter, 2009), 425–45.

11 Perkins, *The Great Rapprochement*; Edward P. Crapol, 'From Anglophobia to Fragile Rapprochement: Anglo-American Relations in the Early Twentieth Century', in *Confrontation and Co-operation: Germany and the United States in the Era of World War I, 1900–1924*, ed. Hans-Jurgen Schroder (Oxford: Berg, 1993), 13–32.

12 Dana Cooper, *Informal Ambassadors: American Women, Transatlantic Marriages, and Anglo-American Relations, 1865–1945* (Kent, OH: Kent State University Press, 2014).

13 Michael Modarelli, *The Transatlantic Genealogy of American Anglo-Saxonism* (Abingdon: Routledge, 2019), 39.

14 Modarelli, *Transatlantic Genealogy of American Anglo-Saxonism*, 54–5.

15 Ibid., 172–91; Stanley R. Hauer, 'Thomas Jefferson and the Anglo-Saxon Language', *PMLA*, 98, no. 5 (1983), 880.

16 See Michael D. Hattem, *Past and Prologue: Politics and Memory in the American Revolution* (New Haven: Yale University Press, 2020), 76, 78; Eric Foner, *Tom Paine and Revolutionary America* (New York: Oxford University Press, 1976), 76.

17 For transatlantic Anglo-Saxonism, see Srdjan Vucetic, *The Anglosphere: A Genealogy of a Racialized Identity in International Relations* (Stanford: Stanford University Press, 2011); Reginald Horsman, *Race and Manifest Destiny: The Origins of American Exceptionalism* (London: Harvard University Press, 1981); Anna Martellone, 'In the Name of Anglo-Saxondom, for Empire and Democracy: The Anglo-American Discourse, 1880–1910', in *Reflections on American Exceptionalism*, ed. David K. Adams and Cornelius A. Van Minnen (Keele: Keele

University Press, 1994), 83–96; Paul A. Kramer, *The Blood of Government: Race, Empire, the United States, and the Philippines* (Chapel Hill, NC: University of North Carolina Press, 2007); Stuart Anderson, *Race and Rapprochement: Anglo-Saxonism and Anglo-American Relations, 1895–1904* (Rutherford: Fairleigh Dickenson University Press, 1981); Duncan Bell, *Dreamworlds of Race: Empire and the Utopian Destiny of Anglo-America* (Princeton: Princeton University Press, 2020).

18 Lewis P. Curtis, *Anglo-Saxons and Celts: A Study of Anti-Irish Prejudice in Victorian England* (New York: University of Bridgeport, 1968), 1–16.

19 See John Higham, *Strangers in the Land: Patterns of American Nativism, 1860–1925* (New Brunswick, NJ: Rutgers University Press, 1995).

20 See Horsman, Race and Manifest Destiny; John C. Mitcham, *Race and Imperial Defence in the British World 1870–1914* (Cambridge: Cambridge University Press, 2016); Marilyn Lake and Henry Reynolds, *Drawing the Global Line: White Men's Countries and the International Challenge of Racial Equality* (Cambridge: Cambridge University Press, 2012).

21 Stuart Anderson, 'Racial Anglo-Saxonism and the American Response to the Boer War', *Diplomatic History*, 2, no. 3 (1978), 222.

22 For more detailed discussion of the Treaty of Ghent anniversary, see Sam Edwards, '"A Great Englishman": George Washington and Anglo-American Memory Diplomacy, c.1890–1925', in *Culture Matters: Anglo-American Relations and the Intangibles of 'Specialness'*, ed. Robert M. Hendershot and Steve Marsh (Manchester: Manchester University Press, 2020), 158–88; Sam Edwards, '"From Here Lincoln Came": Anglo-Saxonism, the Special Relationship, and the Anglicization of Abraham Lincoln, c.1860–1970', *Journal of Transatlantic Studies* 11, no. 1 (2013), 22–46.

23 *The Times*, 24 July 1920.

24 *The Times*, 1 July 1921.

25 *Hull Daily Mail*, 1 August 1924, 5. For further details regarding this memorial, see Sam Edwards, 'Towards a Local History of Anglo-American Relations: Commemorating the Pilgrim Fathers on the Humber, c.1918–1925', *Britain and the World*, 15, no. 2, (2022), pp. 142–167. For more general discussions of the Pilgrim Fathers in American and transatlantic memory, see Erick Goldstein, 'Diplomacy in the Service of History: Anglo-American Relations and the Return of the Bradford History of Plymouth Colony, 1898', *Diplomacy and Statecraft*, 25, no. 2 (2014), 26–40; John Seeyle, *Memory's Nation: The Place of Plymouth Rock* (London: University of North Carolina Press, 1998); Udo Hebel, 'Historical Bonding with an Expiring Heritage: Revisiting Tercentenary Festivities of 1920-21', in *Celebrating Ethnicity and Nation: American Festive Culture from the Revolution to the Early 20th Century,* ed. Jurgen Heideking, Genevieve Fabre and Kai Dreisbach (Oxford: Berghahn, 2001).

26 Baker, *The Reinvention of Magna Carta*, 335–409.

27 See Hattem, *Past and Prologue*, 76, 78.

28 Tison Pugh and Susan Aronstein, *The United States of Medievalism* (Toronto: University of Toronto Press, 2021), 10. See also Kathleen Verduin, *Medievalism in North America* (Cambridge: D. S. Brewer, 1994).

29 Joanne Parker and Corinna Wagner, *The Oxford Handbook of Victorian Medievalism* (Oxford: Oxford University Press, 2020).

30 J. C. Wells, *Magna Charta: Or, the Rise and Progress of Constitutional Civil Liberty in England and America; Embracing the Period from the Norman Conquest to the*

Centennial Year of American Independence (Des Moines: Mills and Company, 1880).
31   Boyd Barrington, *The Magna Carta and Other Great Charters of England with an Historical Treatise and Copious Explanatory Notes* (Philadelphia: William J. Campbell, 1900).
32   See Bell, *Dreamworlds of Race*, 298–9.
33   The IMCDA was not the only organization established around this time in an effort to 'use' Magna Carta for the celebration of transatlantic connection. In 1909 it was joined by the National Society Magna Charta Dames and Barons, one of a number of American 'ancestral' organizations founded at the turn of the century.
34   Donald MacRaild, Sylvia Ellis and Stephen Bowman, 'Interdependence Day and Magna Charta: James Hamilton's Public Diplomacy in the Anglo-world, 1907–1940s', *Journal of Transatlantic Studies*, 12, no. 2 (2014), 140–62; Charles Dilke, *Greater Britain: A Record of Travel in English-Speaking Countries* (London: Macmillan, 1868).
35   Henry Elliot Malden, *Magna Carta Commemoration Essays* (London: Royal Historical Society, 1917), xix.
36   Ibid., xiii.
37   Ibid., 180.
38   Ibid., 181.
39   *The Times*, 19 November 1918.
40   *The Times*, 4 July 1921.
41   See Hugh A. Tulloch, *James Bryce's American Commonwealth: The Anglo-American Background* (Woodbridge: Boydell Press, 1988).
42   See David Woodward, *Trial by Friendship: Anglo-American Relations 1917–1918* (Lexington: University Press of Kentucky, 1993); B. J. C. McKercher, *Anglo-American Relations in the 1920s: The Struggle for Supremacy* (London: Macmillan, 1991), 3; Donald J. Lisio *British Naval Supremacy and Anglo-American Antagonisms, 1914–1930* (Cambridge: Cambridge University Press, 2014).
43   Lisio *British Naval Supremacy and Anglo-American Antagonisms, 1914–1930*.
44   H. Englebrecht and F. C. Hanighen, *The Merchants of Death* (New York: Dodd, Mead and Co., 1934).
45   *The Times*, 6 May 1919.
46   *The Times*, 12 April 1932.
47   *The Times*, 29 May 1934; 8 June 1934; 11 June 1934.
48   *The Times*, 17 September 1937.
49   D. M. MacRaild et al., 'Interdependence Day and Magna Charta', 142.
50   *The Times*, 10 April 1939.
51   *The Times*, 2 May 1939.
52   *The New York Times*, 21 May 1939.
53   Ibid.
54   *The Times*, 23 August 1939; see also 21 August 1939.
55   *The Times*, 29 November 1939; *The New York Times*, 29 November 1939.
56   *The Times*, 29 November 1939.
57   *The Times*, 21 January 1941.
58   *The Times*, 21 January 1941.
59   See Peter Clarke, 'The English-Speaking Peoples before Churchill', *Britain and the World*, 4, no. 2 (2011), 203.

60 Winston Churchill, 'Independence Day 1918', Churchill Archives, CHAR 9/56.
61 *The Times*, 13 March 1941.
62 *The Times*, 4 June 1941.
63 *The Times*, 5 June 1941.
64 *The New York Times*, 16 June 1941.
65 *The Times*, 22 July 1941.
66 The Atlanta Constitution, quoted in *The Times*, 16 August 1941.
67 David Dimbleby and David Reynolds, *An Ocean Apart* (London: Hodder and Stoughton, 1988), 136.
68 *The New York Times*, 16 June 1943; *The Times*, 24 April 1944.
69 *The New York Times*, 26 June 1945.
70 *The Times*, 14 November 1945.
71 Winston Churchill, 'The Sinews of Peace' speech, Westminster College, Fulton, Missouri, 5 March 1946: The Sinews of Peace ('Iron Curtain Speech') – International Churchill Society (winstonchurchill.org) (accessed 24 March 2022).
72 Winston Churchill, *The History of the English-Speaking Peoples: Volume I, The Birth of Britain* (London: Cassell and Co., 1956), 199.
73 Winston Churchill, *The History of the English-Speaking Peoples: Volume IV, The Great Democracies* (London: Cassell and Co., 1958).
74 Winston Churchill, *The Second World War: Volume Three, The Grand Alliance* (London: The Reprint Society, 1952), 354.
75 E. Foner, *The Story of American Freedom* (London: Papermac, 2000), 250.
76 Ibid.
77 Vucetic, *The Anglosphere*.
78 Rowe, 'The American Bar Association Looks to England, 1924 and 1957', 391.
79 See E. Smyth Grambrell, Lord Evershed, Charles S. Rhyne, and Hartley Shawcross, 'The Magna Carta Memorial Ceremonies: Runnymede, Sunday, Afternoon, July 28', *American Bar Association Journal*, 43, no. 10 (October 1957), 900–7.
80 Ibid.
81 Ibid.
82 *The Times*, 29 July 1957.
83 *The New York Times*, 29 July 1957.
84 *The Times*, 29 July 1957.
85 See The Law Society's Dinner at Guildhall in London, July 31, *American Bar Association Journal*, 43, no. 10 (October 1957), 911.
86 Ibid., 914–15.
87 *The Times*, 8 May 1965.
88 See Pamela S. Morgan, 'One Brief Shining Moment: Camelot in Washington, DC' in Verduin, *Medievalism in North America*, 185–211.
89 One feature of the 750th anniversary was the publication of a short booklet outlining Magna Carta's historical significance, with an introduction provided by none other than Chief Justice of the United States Supreme Court Earl Warren. See *The New York Times*, 11 June 1964.
90 *The Times*, 15 May 1965.
91 For details about the Kennedy memorial, see Robert Cook and Clive Webb, 'Unravelling the Special Relationship: British Responses to the Assassination of President John F. Kennedy', *The Sixties: A Journal of History, Politics and Culture*, 8, no. 2 (2015), 186–90.

92 Ibid., 188.
93 The ABA remains invested in Runnymede and in the memorial unveiled in 1957, and they have returned on several occasions, including in 1985, 2007 and 2015. Notably, not all Britons were actually happy to give the land to the United States, and even the National Trust had 'reacted angrily' to this suggestion. See Cook and Webb, 'Unravelling the Special Relationship: British Responses to the Assassination of President John F. Kennedy', 188.

12

Remembering British rule: The uses of colonial memory in Hong Kong protest movements, 1997–2019

Mark Hampton and Florence Mok[*]

On 1 July 1997, the People's Republic of China (PRC) assumed control of Hong Kong, which for a century and a half had been administered as a British Crown Colony. Hong Kong Island and Kowloon had been formally ceded to Great Britain between 1841 and 1860, as the spoils of war, and might, in principle, have continued as British territories in perpetuity. But the New Territories, leased to Britain in 1898 for ninety-nine years, accounted for the vast majority of the colony's land mass, and the infrastructures of the ceded and leased areas had been interwoven to such an extent that separating them was not feasible. The PRC made it clear in the early 1980s that it intended to take the occasion of the expiring lease to reclaim the entire territory, and by 1984 the Sino-British Joint Declaration had formalized the terms of the 1997 'handover'. In order to assuage anxieties of Hong Kong people about their incorporation into a regime that many of them, or their parents, had fled; to help China absorb a richer, more globally integrated territory; and to allow Britain to make a graceful exit amidst widespread charges that it was abandoning its loyal subjects, the diplomats agreed upon the principle of 'One Country. Two Systems'.[1] Under the agreement, Hong Kong's political and economic system would remain separate from that of the PRC for a period of fifty years, until 2047, and Hong Kong would be ruled by Hong Kong people with significant autonomy. Six years later, in 1990, the PRC ratified the Basic Law, the document that would serve as Hong Kong Special Administrative Region (SAR)'s 'mini-constitution'.

Yet the SAR arrangement did not resolve all potential conflicts, and it opened new ones. In particular, the Basic Law called for the Hong Kong government to enact a national security law, while also pledging the gradual introduction of democratic election of the Hong Kong government by universal suffrage. Both of these would, after

---

[*] The work described in this chapter was substantially supported by a grant from the Research Grants Council of the Hong Kong Special Administrative Region, China (Project No. LU13601415). In addition, we are grateful to Ronnie Yim for research assistance.

1997, become the subject of mass protests – the former because of popular opposition to such a law and the latter because of dissatisfaction with the slow pace of democratization as well as the particular interpretation Beijing gave to election by universal suffrage. Moreover, in the intervening years between the Joint Declaration and the change of sovereignty, the 1989 Tiananmen Square protests and their suppression had alarmed Hong Kong people and temporarily turned the PRC into an international pariah. At the same time, the British state made it clear that, in transferring the territory of Hong Kong it was also transferring its people: they would not have the right of abode in the UK. Hong Kong's last colonial governor, Chris Patten, introduced significant electoral reform that, as seemed likely, Beijing would simply reverse in 1997. To the more cynically minded, Patten's pro-democracy measures, adopted only on Britain's way out the door, constituted an exercise in public relations and legacy-building; to the PRC, they constituted an attempt at subverting Beijing's authority in the post-colonial era. At the time of the change of sovereignty, British and US commentators warned that 'the world will be watching' to ensure that the PRC honoured its treaty agreements.[2] The Prince of Wales pledged, in his speech during the 'handover' ceremonies, that the UK would 'maintain its unwavering support for the Joint Declaration'.[3] Despite this rhetoric, however, it seemed likely that Hong Kong people themselves would have to negotiate the practicalities of the SAR's relationship to China.[4]

This chapter examines five large-scale protest movements or demonstrations in post-handover Hong Kong, all of which focused on aspects of the relationship between the territory and the Chinese nation-state: (1) the 1 July march in 2003 against implementation of a national security law, (2) the Protest against Moral and National Education Reforms in 2012, (3) the Umbrella Movement in 2014, (4) the Mong Kok Civil Unrest in 2015 and (5) the Anti-Extradition Bill Protests in 2019 (and their subsequent evolution into a list of 'five demands' including full democratization). All of these emerged from local concerns about the Hong Kong 'way of life' or impending 'mainlandization'. Yet the discourse employed in these movements, particularly the 2014 and 2019 ones, frequently invoked the British colonial legacy. Such uses of historical memory contain their share of irony, not least because appeals to a 'usable past' tended to grow as actual historical memory waned; the protesters, including many of their leaders, were disproportionately young, and the movements in the 2010s included many people who would have had no personal recollections of the colonial era. In addition, the appeal to the colonial era could be jarring in the case of protests specifically calling for universal suffrage, given the lack of democratic institutions during the colonial era. Indeed, if there was a colonial legacy that could withstand historical scrutiny, arguably it was less about British democracy than the fact that, in suppressing the 2019 protests, the largest under consideration here, both the government and the police force employed measures originally developed by the colonial state.

History and memory

Historical memories play an important role in shaping a society's collective identities. Similar sociopolitical values, cultures and languages derive from shared historical roots and past experiences are the foundation for identity formation in any communities. Historical memories also shape one's political orientations and attitudes. As John Tosh has pointed out, 'Our political judgements are permeated by a sense of the past, whether we are deciding between competing claims of political parties or assessing the feasibility of particular policies. To understand social arrangements, we need to have some sense of where they have come from.'[5] However, history is not the same as memories. History as a discipline emphasizes the differences that exist between the past and the present. When analysing the past, context should be taken into consideration and anachronism should be avoided.[6] Unlike history, memories' existence is always linked with people's present consciousness. In other words, it is 'not the past that produces the present'; instead, it is 'the present that produces the past, through an effort of the creative and analytical imagination'.[7] Memories are also far from fixed or infallible – people forget and change their focuses from time to time.[8] Therefore, in Michael Bentley's words, history should be 'precisely non-memory, a systematic discipline which seeks to rely on mechanisms and controls quite different from those which memory triggers and often intended to give memory the lie'.[9]

It is common that a society's historical memories do not reflect history accurately. While such distortion can simply be the results of false recollection, often it is a conscious and deliberate action to serve contemporaries' political, economic and social needs. This is particularly common in political discourse, where historical memories are employed to sustain a sense of legitimacy, suppression and injustice, and solicit popular support for social movements and political campaigns. A similar phenomenon can be observed in post-1997 Hong Kong, where historical memories were highly selective and inaccurate, sometimes even fabricated. In particular, it is noticeable that some politicians, activists and protesters started painting a rosy picture of Hong Kong's colonial past; by the late 2010s there was a growing sense of colonial nostalgia. Above all, the narrative that rule of law was a British legacy which contributed to Hong Kong's stability and prosperity was widely propagated.[10] For example, in 2018, Yau Wai-ching, pro-independence activist and former legislative councillor, suggested that under Beijing's interference, 'concepts such as civil liberties and the separation of powers, which people held dear under the relatively enlightened rule of British, are being abandoned'.[11] In 2019, when the Extradition Bill was proposed, former Governor Chris Patten also argued that the law would 'remove the firewall between Hong Kong's rule of law and the idea of law which prevails in communist China' – 'an idea of law where there aren't any independent courts, where the courts and the security services and the party's rule, which are sometimes pretty obscure, are rolled all together'.[12] Ray Wong, an activist that advocated Hong Kong independence, similarly believed that if the law was passed, 'the legal system in Hong Kong will be destroyed'.[13] All these statements imply that under the principles of rule of law, Hong Kong had enjoyed judicial independence and freedom of expression throughout the colonial era.

However, this narrative downplays both the extent to which 'rule of law' was a discourse of colonial governmentality[14] and the extent to which the colonial state often honoured it in the breach. Judicial independence and separation of power were not consistently practised during the colonial era. For example, Christopher Munn pointed out that Hong Kong's criminal justice system in the nineteenth century was intrusive and racially discriminatory.[15] As Carol Jones has noted, even well into the post-war era, effective restraints on state power were absent in Hong Kong's legal system.[16] During the 1967 riots, the rule of law concept was seriously compromised when the colonial state invoked twelve Emergency Regulations, which granted the colonial government the right to trial without public proceedings, deport and detain.[17] In addition, the colonial state often imposed restrictions on freedom of speech and press. For example, in 1952 and 1956, with the support of London, the colonial government ordered the suspension of a number of left-wing newspapers and arrested their publishers, editors and printers on the ground of 'publishing seditious publications'.[18] Most importantly, these narratives downplay the relatively little progress made towards democratization before 1997. After the Second World War, Hong Kong remained an 'unreformed colonial polity' amid decolonization in Asia and Africa. The Legislative Council primarily consisted of unofficial members that were appointed by the governor. The members of the Executive Council were appointed either by the Queen or the governor.[19] These professional and business elites largely represented 'a restricted class in society'.[20] Despite the introduction of democratic reforms after 1984, direct election was never implemented before the handover of Hong Kong.[21] The Urban Council which had elected unofficial members only possessed a limited executive power.[22] Before 1983 its electoral franchise was extremely narrow, opened merely to people who were qualified by income, education or professions.[23] There is evidently a mismatch between memories and history. Nevertheless, does this gulf that separate historical truth from social memories always exist? When did people start invoking colonial memories to pursue their political agenda? And how did the society's collective memories on British colonialism in Hong Kong change over time?

The National Security Law (2003)

The first major protests against the government of the new SAR came in response to the Tung Chee-hwa administration's 2003 proposal of a national security law. The change of sovereignty had coincided with the Asian financial crisis, beginning in July 1997, and although Hong Kong was not the hardest hit territory, both its currency and its stock market had come under sharp speculative pressure, leading to large-scale intervention by the Hong Kong Monetary Authority in both markets.[24] Following recovery from this crisis, a late 2002 outbreak of Severe Acute Respiratory Syndrome (SARS) in neighbouring Guangdong spread to Hong Kong by March 2003, killing nearly three hundred people in the territory within a few months. It was against the backdrop of this public health emergency that the national security law, first gazetted in February, was debated.

According to legal scholar Michael C. Davis, whose Article 23 Concern Group helped to launch the protests, the group reacted not so much to enacting such a law, which after all the Basic Law's Article 23 required but the 'rather draconian' draft bill including, among other things, search and seizure power for the police and the banning of organizations in Hong Kong that were banned in mainland China. In addition, the attempt to push the law through quickly, with minimal debate, exacerbated public concern.[25] Ultimately an estimated half a million protesters joined a 1 July protest against the proposed law; in response Tung initially pledged to pass a less severe version but by September had announced the proposed law's withdrawal, promising it would be reintroduced later after public consultation. Eighteen months later, Tung resigned as chief executive mid-way through his term.

Protest discourse around this legislation centred largely on human rights or the hope for an evolution towards full democracy, with little reference to the British colonial legacy. Those references to Britain that did occur merely contrasted the formal position of a colony responsible to a democratic government with that of a SAR beholden to a one-party state. For example, the Hong Kong Federation of Students argued that the time was not yet right for national security legislation because the PRC had not yet implemented a democratic government; the implication was that China was gradually evolving towards a Western-style political system and that when that happened, such legislation for Hong Kong would be appropriate.[26] Similarly, Margaret Ng, a Legislative Councillor from the Civic Party, argued that draconian laws under the colonial government were ultimately checked by the fact that the governor was responsible to a democratically elected parliament in Britain.[27] University of Hong Kong legal scholar Albert Chen Hung-yee contrasted the colonial government's practice of public consultations with the Tung administration's failure to do so.[28] Other critics explicitly denied any attachment to British colonial rule, even affirming commitment to Chinese sovereignty, insisting only on Hong Kong people's commitment to attaining democracy, and interpreting the large-scale march as a clear demonstration of this commitment.[29]

The Moral and National Education Reforms (2012)

In October 2010, on the heels of the 2008 Beijing Summer Olympics and amidst widespread perceptions that China's government had responded more effectively than most to the global financial crisis, Chief Executive Donald Tsang announced the coming implementation of a compulsory 'moral and national education' curriculum, to be implemented in primary schools in 2012 and secondary schools in 2013. This curriculum would replace an existing 'moral and civic education' curriculum. In Carol Jones's description, activities 'were to include understanding the Basic Law, supporting the national sports teams, singing the national anthem and appreciating Chinese culture and ideas, such as filial piety, broadmindedness and solidarity'. Aimed explicitly at encouraging Hong Kong people's subjective identification with the Chinese nation and national government, this policy did not emerge out of nowhere but indeed grew out of efforts made since the handover to foster Chinese national identity in the territory.[30] In an even broader context, this new curriculum can be placed within a longer tradition of teaching Chinese history and Confucian culture in colonial Hong Kong, a practice that Law Wing Sang has linked to the promotion of a Confucian-based 'collaborative colonial power'.[31] Government ministers defended the curriculum against charges of indoctrination, insisting that it was merely an innocuous and reasonable attempt to instil patriotism. The Education Bureau's April 2012 guidelines articulated the aim of promoting 'Chinese virtues', placing this aim as well as mention of the 'nation' in a series of geographic imaginaries ranging from the family to local society to the global or universal, in effect downplaying the patriotic element through subsumption.[32] Indeed, official pronouncements effectively likened the curriculum to the sorts of syllabi on offer in countries around the world.

Regardless of intent, a population already sceptical of 'mainlandization' was not inclined to give the government or the proposed curriculum the benefit of the doubt. Both an ongoing concern about Beijing's long-term intentions, and a population wary of the transformation of the territory's economy and neighbourhoods by mass tourism, parallel trading and immigration, formed a backdrop to this proposed reform. Two points stand out about the ensuing protest movement. First, unlike the 2003 protests, the ones against the curriculum reform were spearheaded by very young people, notably the fourteen-year-old Joshua Wong who, in May 2011, co-founded Scholarism.[33] This new generation of activists would subsequently be leading participants in the 2014 Umbrella Movement. Second, with the coming of a new generation of activists also came increasing reference to and nostalgia for the late colonial era. A July 2012 poll of students, co-organized by the New Youth Forum and the Cross-Strait Exchange Association, found that slightly more than half of them had favourable impressions of the colonial rule of which they had no personal memories. Among the qualities attributed to British rule were that it was 'more democratic' than the SAR and that the British had made decisions in the long-term best interest of the territory. The survey also noted frankly that, compared to students in Taiwan or Macau, the students were the worst-informed about historical facts, but one of its organizers, Andrew Ng Wai-ming (then a second-year student in economics and finance), insisted that this did not justify the planned national education course.[34] Around the same time, as Scholarism made preparations for a 29 July 2012 march that ultimately attracted some 90,000 participants, the question of whether those who waved the colonial flag in protest were welcome at the march came up for discussion in the Hong Kong Golden Forum. Scholarism's official response was that they would not exclude such demonstrations but would prefer a banner reading 'No Brainwashing' to the colonial flag, as it was more directly relevant.[35]

In late August, some fifty members of Scholarism began to occupy the park beneath government headquarters, with three engaging in a hunger strike. What began as a three-day occupation turned into an indefinite one, and over the course of ten days, tens of thousands of protestors participated in the demonstrations. With the controversy still raging on National Day (1 October), more than forty protestors reportedly waved colonial flags outside the Hong Kong Liaison Office, the agency representing the PRC government in Hong Kong.[36]

The Umbrella Movement (2014)

By 2014, there was still little progress towards democratic constitutional reform; many even argued that there was a political regression. In the executive-led political system, department heads, judges and government officials remained 'constitutionally more powerful than most presidents in the world'.[37] Under Article 74 of the Basic Law, legislators could only propose bills that 'do not involve public expenditure, political structure, or operation of the government', and the chief executive's approval was also needed. Besides, the size of the electoral franchise had not been expanded but reduced by new regulations such as proportional representation, which, in an atmosphere of growing distrust, were perceived as an erosion of Hong Kong's autonomy.[38] Such 'political disenfranchisement', along with Beijing's attempt to redefine 'high degree of autonomy' and reassert the primacy of one country over two systems and increased social distrust, had led to serious discontent among Hong Kong Chinese, who perceived the 'rule of law' and 'freedoms' as their core values.[39]

In August 2014, the National People's Congress announced the '31 August Decision', which outlined that the Hong Kong chief executive candidate needed to be demonstrably patriotic. In the chief executive election in 2017, candidates were required to obtain support from more than half of the members in the 1,200-person nominating Election Committee. The elected candidate needed to obtain final approval from the Chinese government. The development of universal suffrage in the Legislative Council also required Beijing's approval.[40] Many Hong Kong Chinese perceived these changes as an attempt to pre-screen chief executive candidates and, by extension, a deprivation of their own political rights. The decision soon sparked off a series of street protests ultimately known as the Umbrella Movement.

During the movement, some protesters demanded British intervention. For example, in the 'Hong Kong-United Kingdom Reunification Campaign', which was organized by an online Facebook group with more than 13,600 followers, the Supreme Court Road in Admiralty was occupied and demands were made that Britain 'fulfill her duty to Hong Kong'.[41] A protest organized next to the British Consulate General in Hong Kong in October included a similar request. These protesters urged the UK Prime Minister to respond to 'the revolution' which 'has broken out in Hong Kong' and to keep the British Consulate General open for 24 hours a day, providing 'asylum and humanitarian aid to Hong Kongers'. The protesters warned that if the Consul General refused to respond to their demands, they might escalate their actions and organize another sit-in or hunger strike.[42] Some students and teachers even tried to seize the opportunity to petition British Parliamentarians when they visited Hong Kong.[43]

These requests illustrated a prevailing belief that Britain still bore responsibility to safeguard Hong Kong people's political rights. For example, a secondary school student argued that 'British did sign the Sino-British Joint Declaration so she should take half responsibility of Hong Kong'.[44] Another protester, Miss Ching, also believed that it was 'Britain's responsibility to monitor China's implementation of the agreements'.[45] Protesters articulated that these were legitimate demands as 'Hong Kong was transferred from the United Kingdom to China without Hong Kongers' consent'. Now that they were in danger, the British government was obliged to 'fulfil her duty of Hong Kong and her people', 'declare the Sino-British Joint Declaration void' and reclaim Hong Kong.[46]

These demands were also underpinned by the beliefs that the colonial government had been more democratic than the SAR government and had laid down a more open and accessible political framework. For example, in an article, activist Joshua Wong implied that the rule of law was a British legacy, which, under the Sino-British Joint Declaration, should be preserved:

This meant that Hong Kong, an international metropolis, proud of its freedoms and openness, could be part of China but run separately under the principle of 'One Country, Two Systems'. Hong Kong could enjoy rights that came from the maintenance of its core values of judicial independence and separation of powers, as well as the implementation of universal suffrage after the handover in 1997, working finally toward the ultimate aim of democratic self-governance.[47]

Louis Leung Ka-kit articulated a similar notion:

> Despite the arbitrariness of the colonial government, accountability was ensured under the manner of democratic political system. Today, the One Country is a closed autocracy. The communist government never take the difference of the Two Systems seriously. Hong Kong people have been increasingly upset since the handover. The Umbrella Revolution represents an outbreak of the accumulated stress of many years.[48]

By arguing that the rule of law is a British legacy which was guaranteed under the Sino-British Joint Declaration, activists and politicians could justify their social movements and legitimize their political demands. Through depicting the colonial government positively, they could also portray the current regime as a regressive and autocratic government, soliciting support from various social groups in the society.

The Mong Kok Civil Unrest (2016)

The Umbrella Movement however did not lead to the implementation of universal suffrage. Instead, the People's Central Government imposed more control over Hong Kong. There was increased distrust towards the Chinese government. For example, in 2015, about 40 per cent of the informants in the University of Hong Kong's Public Opinion Programme indicated that they did not trust the Beijing government.[49] Escalated state-society tensions also led to the formation of localist political parties that advocated Hong Kong's secession from China. Some of these newly formed parties encouraged the use of militant resistance tactics, such as the Hong Kong Indigenous and the Hong Kong National Party.[50] The changing political culture among the younger generation was evident and could be observed in the 2016 Mong Kok Civil Unrest.

The Mong Kok Civil Unrest was first triggered by the Food and Environmental Hygiene Department's (FEHD) attempt to drive away and arrest hawkers that set up stalls in the street without license in Mong Kok on the Chinese New Year Eve. Traditionally, their presence had been tolerated.[51] Many activists therefore viewed the FEHD's action as an encroachment of Hong Kong's local culture, an example of mainlandization or mainland-inspired gentrification.[52] On 8 February, activists such as Lau Siu-lai and members of the Hong Kong Indigenous started advocating people to back the hawkers. More than 300 people gathered in Mongkok and tried to stop the hawker crackdown.[53] Soon, the police intervened and the incident was turned into a confrontation between the activists and the police. A disturbance subsequently broke out. Protesters blocked the roads and set fire to rubbish bins. In response, police opened fire to disperse them. At the end, at least 130 people were injured and 61 people were arrested.[54] The government categorized the civil unrest as a 'riot' but refused to set up an independent inquiry to investigate its causes.[55]

After the riots and arrestment, colonial memories were again invoked in the public discourse. Chip Tsao, a pro-Britain columnist and writer, made the following comment:

> During British colonial era, the colonial government, which was good at governance, would show exceptional mercy and compassion to grassroots especially at festivals like Lunar New Year in time of economic decline. Selling fishballs without a license cannot be mentioned with selling drugs. It does violate law, but it is not criminal …. Time to reminisced about the good old days of British colonial era …. You can tell the difference at a glimpse between the universal humanity of the West and the implementation of power of petty small-minded Chinese.[56]

Ivan Choi Chi-keung, Senior Lecturer in the Chinese University of Hong Kong, also compared responses of the SAR government to the Mong Kok incident to that of the colonial government in 1967:

> In fact, the colonial government has conducted an independent commissioned investigation after the 1966 riots and publish *Kowloon Disturbances 1966: Report of Commission of Inquiry*. In the report, both direct and indirect causes were studied, such as political, economic and social factors …. The colonizers in the past was more open-minded than today's SAR government. Half a century ago, the colonial government was open enough to carry out an independent investigation on riots and achieve a conclusion that the riots were rooted from social factors. After half a century, SAR government refused to do so because of the criminal investigation to be conducted by the police. Wasn't the criminal investigation also conducted in 1966? Is the governance of Hong Kong upgraded or degraded? It is not hard for the reader to have an answer.[57]

These expressions of positive colonial memories were powerful statements which politicians and activists could use to mobilize the public. By portraying the supposedly exploitative colonizers as more 'benevolent' than the Chinese regime, one can show how authoritarian the latter is. Such rhetoric also justified the need to engage in resistance movements and set up an independent commission of inquiry.

The Anti-Extradition Bill Protests in 2019

In February 2018, Chan Tong-kai, a Hong Kong national, murdered his girlfriend in Taiwan and returned to Hong Kong. Arguing that the absence of formal extradition agreement between Hong Kong and Taiwan meant there was no way to extradite Chan for trial, the Hong Kong government proposed to amend the existing law to allow extraditions of suspects to Taiwan and mainland China. Many Hong Kong Chinese were sceptical about the government's motives, arguing that a specific criminal charge was being exploited in order to introduce a wholesale challenge to Hong Kong's autonomy. Many articulated a worry that China's judiciary system, completely different from Hong Kong's, would be unable to guarantee fair and transparent trials. The weekend before the Extradition bill was to be introduced into Legislative Council, a peaceful mass demonstration protested against it, and on the day it was to be introduced, 12 June, protestors disrupted proceedings, preventing the Legislative Council from meeting; the police responded with large quantities of tear gas, and the Police Chief denounced the disruption as a 'riot', a term that had significant legal consequences. On 16 June, the day after the bill was 'suspended' (but not formally withdrawn); the protest was joined by about 2 million people, an unprecedented scale in Hong Kong history.[58]

Space does not permit a detailed recounting of the events of the second half of 2019. A few points should be highlighted, though. First, the protest movement was effectively leaderless, relying on social media up-voting and down-voting to reach a consensus on strategies and tactics. Leaders familiar from 2014 were frequently quoted in the media, but they had no control over the movement. Second, the events escalated in a spiral, as protestor anger at police repressive tactics led to increasingly disruptive actions, such as obstruction of transportation networks and destruction of property owned by those deemed sympathetic to the government or the PRC. At the same time, what had begun as a single-issue protest evolved into 'five demands', as indicated at the beginning of the chapter. Third, the movement rejected the 'occupy' model of 2014, instead, echoing Hong Kong-born film star Bruce Lee, determining to 'be water', emphasizing fluid movement from one location to another around the territory. Fourth, the forum-based consensus carefully weighed what degree of disruption would be tolerated by society without alienating those sympathetic, but uncommitted. Fifth, a clear distinction existed between those who participated in the peaceful marches, usually earlier in the day, and the harder core who engaged in more disruptive tactics and engaged with the police directly, often deep into the night. Yet despite this distinction, participants in social media forums insisted on maintaining a unity of purpose, while others who sympathized but did not get involved directly supported the movement through donations. Sixth, government of Chief Executive Carrie Lam largely delegated response to the political crisis to the police, who used repressive tactics, in many cases against secondary school students. In addition, massive quantities of tear gas were unleashed. For some five months the protests raged, particularly in the evenings and weekends, before reaching a crescendo in mid-November. The coming of the Covid-19 pandemic in early 2020, and the implementation of a National Security Law – instigated by Beijing, not, as attempted in 2003, by the Hong Kong government – in mid-2020, formed a decisive conclusion to the anti-Extradition protests. At the same time, some of the most visible anti-government protestors left Hong Kong, many of them to the UK which, unlike in the 1990s, now opened a path to residency for holders of the British National Overseas passport.[59]

The discourse of the 2019 protests shared some similarities with previous movements. Many netizens glorified colonial governance in forums such as LIHKG by comparing the colonial government with the Beijing government. In a 'leaderless' and evolving protest movement, most discussions centred on strategies and tactics, both for maximizing the disruption to the government and thus increasing the cost of not meeting the 'five demands', and for persuading public opinion, both locally and globally (above all in the United States and UK). However, sprinkled within this discourse came reflections not merely of what kind of society Hong Kong should become following a successful movement, but comparisons of the present with the colonial past – one that most frontline protestors would have had little (if any) personal memory.

One June 2019 discussion responded to a post asking participants to share their memories of the colonial era. Those responders identifying as having been born in the mid-1980s or later tended to idealize the colonial period. For example, a netizen claimed, incorrectly, that few protests happened during the colonial era because 'the governance of the colonial government in Hong Kong was so good'. The 'only single huge protest' that happened in British Hong Kong was in fact 'against the massacre in Beijing Tiananmen Square'.[60] A netizen named Kok Kok went so far as to praise Chris Patten as 'Hong Kong's father' and suggested that 'since the colonial era is gone, the governance of Hong Kong is worser year by year due to the competence of the Chinese government'.[61] Others believed that Hong Kong Chinese were largely protected by 'the British flag' during the colonial era but now lived under 'the Tyranny of a Police State'.[62] Colonial nostalgia was can also be observed in the actual protests. In particular, colonial flags were repeatedly used by some activists to represent Hong Kong's core values, freedom and equality before law.[63] Some protesters even advocated Hong Kong's return to Britain:

> The Extradition Bill proposed by the Chinese government and the Hong Kong SAR government devastatingly erodes human rights and freedom enshrined in Hong Kong. It severely violates the principle of 'One Country, Two Systems' as stated in the Sino-British Joint Declaration and the Basic Law ... We strongly stand against the Extradition Bill! We urge the UK to take effective measures to protect all British Nationals and Hong Kong citizens living in Hong Kong. The Chinese outrageously breached the Sino-British Joint Declaration, we thus urge the United Kingdom to take proper solutions and take Hong Kong![64]

Others offered nostalgic memories that had less to do directly with governance than with quality of life. For example, one contrasted the prosperity of the 1980s and 1990s with the economic struggles in more recent years; one mentioned increased pollution since the handover, and another, incredibly, found in the colonial past an attractive alternative to the materialism of the current period.[65] These types of nostalgia effectively conflated British rule with late-industrial economics, an era when the post-1978 opening of China offered new opportunities for Hong Kong entrepreneurs but had not yet thoroughly transformed Hong Kong into a service-oriented post-industrial economy. They also obscured the fact that many Britons themselves mourned similar loss since the late 1970s.

At the same time, others challenged both the accuracy and the usefulness of appeals to an idealized colonial era. For instance, an article in *Lausan* pointed out that these memories were only 'myths of our colonial past' and questioned 'how can there be an "erosion of rights and freedoms" if we never actually had them'. It argued that 'British colonialism is often remembered fondly for reforms implemented by Governor Murray MacLehose administration in the 1970s'. However, for most of the colonial era, Hong Kong Chinese 'could not be elected to the government' and 'their efforts to strike and protest were repeatedly suppressed'. The public therefore should recognize 'the current movement as a struggle to make space for democratic futures beyond not only Beijing's authoritarianism, but also the constricting frameworks prescribed by colonial governance' were increasingly propagated.[66] Older commentators in particular pointed out that those idealizing British rule had little knowledge of its actual practice. One pointed out (accurately) that the governor was appointed by Britain without local consultation, mentioned a colonial-era protestor who had been imprisoned for distributing flyers, and, hyperbolically, claimed that colonial-era Hong Kong Chinese were slaves distinguished only by being treated better than those across the border.[67]

Conclusion

It would be an overstatement to say that the protest movements in Hong Kong since 1997 have been preoccupied with the colonial legacy or with Hong Kong's post-colonial relationship with Britain. Other discourses were more important, for example appeals to human rights or the importance of Cantonese. In addition, the argument of this chapter is, of necessity, suggestive rather than conclusive. Yet an examination of the discourse offered by protestors against either the policies of the Hong Kong government or, in 2019, against the government itself, and articulations of discontent with the direction of the society more broadly, suggests that, as the colonial era receded from lived experience – and especially as a new, politically active, generation emerged that had little or no personal memories of that period – protest discourse increasingly turned to the colonial era for a usable past. Given the disjunction between the actual character of the colonial period and the self-governing future many protestors advocated, this is more than a little curious. Beyond the incommensurability of colonial reality and contemporary memory, it is more than a little ironic how closely protestors' discourses about the late colonial era mirrored those explicitly created by the colonial government as a strategy for creating a non-democratic legitimacy, especially in the 1970s.[68] In other words, discourses that opponents of the late-colonial government would have surely found unconvincing and self-serving justifications had been, by 2019, co-opted by opponents of an SAR government that displayed significant continuities with its predecessor.

One may speculate as to the reason. Historians have often found protest movements backward looking in their rhetoric, particularly the more radical they became: for example 1760s Massachusetts anti-British colonists appealing to 'historic rights of Englishmen' or British radicals in the age of the French Revolution appealing to an older 'popular constitutionalism'.[69] These discourses imply that a current government or ruling elite has disrupted a more desired, previously existing, state of affairs, and they call for a 'revolution', in J. C. D. Clark's terms, meaning a return to an earlier state.[70] The generation of protestors that emerged in the wake of the 2012 proposed curriculum reforms was more alienated from Beijing than the leaders of the 2003 protest movement had been. Yet an appeal to Hong Kong's past against twenty-first-century arrangements is, of necessity, an appeal to the colonial past. Arguably the invocations of British rule or nostalgia for the colonial era say less about any approbation of the British than a lack of an alternative usable past.[71]

Notes

1 The PRC's leadership also intended 'One Country, Two Systems' as a model for Taiwan's incorporation within China.
2 See e.g. Margaret Thatcher, Speech at International Herald Tribune Conference (the future of China), 14 October 1996, https://www.margaretthatcher.org/document/108367 (accessed 17 May 2021); James R. Sasser, U.S. Ambassador to China, Address to the Asia Society, Washington, DC, 4 March 1997, https://1997-2001.state.gov/regions/eap/970304_sasser_china.html (accessed 17 May 2021).
3 'Words of a Prince and a President: Continuity, Change and Assurances', *New York Times*, 1 July 1997, 8.
4 For the historical context of Hong Kong's relationship with mainland China, see John M. Carroll, *The Hong Kong-China Nexus* (Cambridge: Cambridge University Press, 2022).
5 John Tosh, *The Pursuit of History* (London and New York: Longman, 1984), 2.
6 Ibid., 9–11.
7 Geoffrey Cubitt, *History and Memory* (Manchester and New York: Manchester University Press, 2007), 31.
8 Tosh, *The Pursuit of History*, 2.
9 Michael Bentley, *Modern Historiography: An Introduction* (London: Routledge, 1999), 155.
10 Steve Tsang, 'Commitment to the Rule of Law and Judicial Independence', in *Judicial Independence and the Rule of Law in Hong Kong*, ed. Steve Tsang (Hong Kong: HKU Press, 2001), 1; Ming Chan, 'The Legacy of the British Administration of Hong Kong: A View from Hong Kong', *China Quarterly*, 151 (1997), 567; John D. Wong and Michael H. K. Ng, 'Introduction: Negotiating the Legitimacy of Governance', in *Civil Unrest and Governance in Hong Kong: Law and Order from Historical and Cultural Perspectives*, ed. John D. Wong and Michael H. K. Ng (London and New York: Routledge, 2017), 2; Carol A. G. Jones, *Lost in China? Law, Culture and Identity in Post-1997 Hong Kong* (Cambridge: Cambridge University Press, 2015); Michael C. Davis, *Making Hong Kong China: The Rollback of Human Rights and the Rule of Law* (Columbia: Columbia University Press, 2020); John D. Wong, 'Constructing the Legitimacy of Governance in Hong Kong: "Prosperity and Stability" Meets "Democracy and Freedom"', *The Journal of Asian Studies*, 81, no. 1 (2022), 1–19.
11 Yau Wai-ching, 'Opinion: Democracy's Demise in Hong Kong', *The New York Times*, 16 September 2018, https://www.nytimes.com/2018/09/16/opinion/politics/democracys-demise-in-hong-kong.html.
12 'The Last Fight for Hong Kong: Activists Gear Up over Extradition Law', *The Guardian*, 7 June 2019, https://www.theguardian.com/world/2019/jun/07/the-last-fight-for-hong-kong-activists-gear-up-to-protest-extradition-law.
13 Ibid.

14 See Patrick Joyce, *The Rule of Freedom: Liberalism and the Modern City* (London: Verso, 2003), 240–57, for this point in the context of the Raj.
15 Christopher Munn, *Anglo-China: Chinese People and British Rule in Hong Kong, 1841–1880* (Richmond: Curzon Press, 2001).
16 Carol Jones and Jon Vagg (eds.), *Criminal Justice in Hong Kong* (Abingdon: Routledge, 2007).
17 Ray Yep, '"Cultural Revolution in Hong Kong": Emergency Powers, Administration of Justice and the Turbulent Years of 1967', *Modern Asian Studies*, 46, no. 4 (2012), 1014.
18 Chi-kwan Mark, 'Everyday Propaganda: The Leftist Press and Sino-British Relations in Hong Kong, 1952–67', in *Europe and China in the Cold War*, ed. Janick Marina Schaufelbuehl, Marco Wyss and Valeria Zanier (Boston and Leiden: Brill, 2008), 151–71.
19 George B. Endacott, *Government and People in Hong Kong, 1841–1962: A Constitutional History* (Hong Kong: Hong Kong University Press, 1964), 230–4.
20 Ibid., 234.
21 Lo Shiu-hing, *The Politics of Democratization in Hong Kong* (London: Macmillan, 1997), 90–3.
22 Ian Scott, 'Bridging the Gap: Hong Kong Senior Civil Servants and the 1966 Riots', *Journal of Imperial and Commonwealth History*, 45, no. 1 (2017), 138; Norman Miners, *The Government and Politics of Hong Kong* (Hong Kong: Oxford University Press, 1975), 156.
23 Ibid., 157.
24 Anindya K. Bhattacharya, 'The Asian Financial Crisis: An Evaluation of Market Intervention Policies by Hong Kong Regulators', in *Asian Financial Crisis Financial, Structural and International Dimensions (International Finance Review)*, ed. J. J. Choi, vol. 1, (Bingley: Emerald Group Publishing Limited, 2001), 293–303.
25 Davis, *Making Hong Kong China*, 30–1.
26 'Forums Were Held One after Another; HKFS Proposing Position Paper against the Article 23', *Apple Daily*, 19 October 2002. (相繼舉行論壇聲討法 學聯擬立場書反廿三條,《蘋果日報》, 2002年10月19日。).
27 'Margaret Ng: July 1 March Is the Result of the Violent Legislation', *Ming Pao Daily News*, 7 September 2003. (〈吳靄儀:七一大遊行 粗暴立法後果〉,《明報》, 2003年9月7日。).
28 Albert Chen Hung-yee, 'A Defining Moment in Hong Kong's History', *South China Morning Post*, 4 July 2003.
29 Wong Hong, 'Democratic-Reunification Returns to Democracy', *Apple Daily*, 2 July 2003. (黃洪:〈民主回歸回歸民主〉,《蘋果日報》, 2003年7月2日。); 'The Road to Political Reform', *South China Morning Post*, 26 December 2003.
30 Jones, *Lost in China?*, 233–5 (quotation 235). For the context of the 2012 controversy, see Paul Morris and Edward Vickers, 'Schooling, Politics and the Construction of Identity in Hong Kong: The 2012 "Moral and National Education" Crisis in Historical Context', *Comparative Education* 51 (2015), 305–26. On the wider question of Hong Kong identity, see Catherine S. Chan, 'Culture and Identity', in *Hong Kong History: Themes in Global Perspective,* ed. M. K. Wong and C. M. Kwong (Singapore: Palgrave Macmillan, 2022).
31 Law Wing Sang, *Collaborative Colonial Power: The Making of the Hong Kong Chinese* (Hong Kong: University of Hong Kong Press, 2009). See also Flora L. F. Kan, *Hong Kong's Chinese History Curriculum from 1945: Politics and Identity* (Hong

Kong: Hong Kong University Press, 2007); Gregory P. Fairbrother, *Toward Critical Patriotism: Student Resistance to Political Education in Hong Kong and China* (Hong Kong: Hong Kong University Press, 2003); Grace Ai-Ling Chou, *Confucianism, Colonialism, and the Cold War: Chinese Cultural Education at Hong Kong's New Asia College, 1949–63* (Leiden: Brill, 2012).

32 Curriculum Development Council, Moral and National Education Curriculum Guide (Primary 1 to Secondary 6), April 2012, https://www.edb.gov.hk/attachment/en/curriculum-development/moral-national-edu/MNE%20Guide%20(ENG)%20Final_remark_09102012.pdf (accessed 1 December 2021). Reflecting the success of the protests against the curriculum, the document's title page notes that the government formally shelved the guide on 8 October 2012.

33 Ada Lee, 'Scholarism's Joshua Wong Embodies Anti-national Education Body's Energy', *South China Morning Post*, 10 September 2012, https://www.scmp.com/news/hong-kong/article/1032923/scholarisms-joshua-wong-embodies-anti-national-education-bodys-energy (accessed 20 December 2021).

34 Jennifer Ngo, 'Colonial HK Freer, Say 51pc of Students', *South China Morning Post*, 20 July 2012, https://www.scmp.com/article/1007283/colonial-hk-freer-say-51pc-students (accessed 20 December 2021).

35 'Should the Group of People Who Wave Colonial Flags Join the March Organized by Scholarism on 29 July?' HK Golden Forum, 19 July 2012, https://forum.hkgolden.com/thread/3846348/page/8. (7月29日,學民思潮遊行,香港旗團出唔出? 香港高登討論區, 2012年7月19日。).

36 'Waving Colonial Flags to Protest against CCP's Interference on Hong Kong', *Apple Daily*, 2 October 2012. (〈揮港英旗抗議中共插手治港〉,《蘋果日報》, 2012年10月2日。).

37 Ma Ngok, *Political Development in Hong Kong: State, Political Society ad Civil Society* (Hong Kong: Hong Kong University Press, 2007), 59.

38 Ibid., 117; Lee Ching Kwan, 'Take Back Our Future: An Eventful Sociology of the Hong Kong Umbrella Movement', in *Take Back Our Future: An Eventful Sociology of the Hong Kong Umbrella Movement*, ed. Lee Ching Kwan and Sing (Ithaca, NY: Cornell University Press, 2019), 5.

39 Ibid., 6–7.

40 *The National's People Congress's Decision on Universal Suffrage for HKSAR Chief Executive Selection*, New China News Agency, 31 August 2014.

41 Details for this campaign can be found on their Facebook page: https://www.facebook.com/pg/HongKongandUKreunite/about/?ref=page_internal.

42 'Occupy Supreme Court Road in Admiralty! We Demand the UK to Fulfil Her Duty to Hong Kong!', Hong Kong-UK Reunification Campaign Facebook Page, https://www.facebook.com/events/1492905177636343/. Similar events were also held on 14 October 2014; details can be found on the event page of Hong Kong-UK Reunification Campaign Facebook page, https://www.facebook.com/events/384093601748256/. A statement made by an occupier during the event, 21 October 2014, https://youtu.be/kcDkVKlZcbA.

43 'Netizens' Appeal for Occupying the British Consulate-General Hong Kong' ('網民籲佔領英駐港領事館'), *Apple Daily*, 10 November 2014; 'DSE Student Calls on Occupying the British Consulate-General Hong Kong' ('DSE男籲佔英領館 退學瞓身抗爭'), *Apple Daily*, 11 November 2014.

44 'DSE Student Calls on Occupying the British Consulate-General Hong Kong'.

45 'Netizens' Appeal for Occupying the British Consulate-General Hong Kong'.
46 See the Facebook page of Hong Kong-UK Reunification Campaign.
47 Joshua Wong (translated by Melody Andrea Chuh), 'Self-Determination Is the Only Solution for Hong Kong', *Time*, 24 September 2015, https://time.com/4042269/hong-kong-self-determination-occupy-umbrella-revolution/.
48 Louis Leung Ka-kit, 'Pedantry and Cynicism' ('迂腐與犬儒'), *Ming Pao*, 30 October 2014.
49 'On the Whole, Do You Trust the Beijing Central Government?', Hong Kong University Public Opinion Programme (2015).
50 See Ying-ho Kwong, 'The Growth of "Localism" in Hong Kong: A New Path for the Democracy Movement?', *China Perspectives*, 3 (2016), 64.
51 Kam C. Wong, *Public Order Policing in Hong Kong: The Mongkok Riot* (Cham: Palgrave Macmillan, 2018), 4.
52 Tai Wei Lim and Tuan Yuen Kong (eds.), *Studying Hong Kong: 20 Years of Political, Economic and Social Developments* (Singapore: World Scientific, 2018), 203.
53 'The Localists Called on 300 People to Support Hawker In Hong Kong, Police Fired Two Shots' ('本土派號召300人旺角撐小販警開兩槍'), *Apple Daily*, 9 February 2016; 'Teacher Siu-lai Was Arrested' ('小麗老師被捕'), *Standnews*, 8 February 2016.
54 'Mong Kok Riots: Police Arrested 61 Men and Women for Their Involvement in the Riots' ('旺角騷亂:警引用參與暴動罪61男女被捕'), *Apple Daily*, 9 February 2016.
55 'Shots Fired and Bricks Thrown: Hong Kong Tense after Mong Kok Mob Violence on First Day of Lunar New Year', *South China Morning Post*, 9 February 2016, https://www.scmp.com/news/hong-kong/law-crime/article/1910845/shots-fired-and-bricks-thrown-hong-kong-tense-after-mong.
56 Chip Tsao, 'One Nite in Mongkok: Monologue of Logic and Memory' ('旺角黑夜–邏輯和記憶的獨白'), Chip Tsao's Facebook Page, 10 February 2016, https://www.facebook.com/tokit.channel/photos/a.288915521180978/1021150711290785.
57 Ivan Choy Chi-keung, 'Studying Social Factors Means "Glorifying" Riots?'' ('探究社會基礎就是「美化」騷動?'), *Ming Pao*, 18 February 2016.
58 Florence Mok, 'Hong Kong Protests: How Did We Get Here?', *Diplomat*, 21 June 2019.
59 Yew Lun Tian and William James, 'UK Offers Hong Kong Residents Route to Citizenship, Angering China', *Reuters*, 29 January 2021, https://www.reuters.com/article/uk-hongkong-security-britain-china/uk-offers-hong-kong-residents-route-to-citizenship-angering-china-idUSKBN29Y0Q1.
60 'Ministry of Foreign Affairs: During British Colonial Era, Did Hong Kong Residents Have the Freedom for Street Protest?', Lihkg Forum, 25 July 2019, https://lihkg.com/thread/1362869/page/2.
61 Kok Kok's Twitter, 1 May 2020, https://twitter.com/lowsalarygirl/status/1256020460682113024.
62 Daphne315's Twitter, 27 August 2020, https://twitter.com/DaphnePoyee315/status/1298704777652482048.
63 Hong Kong-UK Reunification Campaign Facebook Page, 2 July 2019, https://www.facebook.com/HongKongandUKreunite/posts/2491098420935418; 'Flagging Patience: Colonial Emblems Divide Opinion at Hong Kong Protests', *Hong Kong Free Press*, 1 August 2019, https://hongkongfp.com/2019/08/01/flagging-patience-colonial-emblems-divide-opinion-hong-kong-protests/; Holmes Chan, 'Explainer: The Conflicting Messages behind Protesters' Use of the Colonial Hong Kong Flag',

64 'Stand against the Extradition Bill! Return Hong Kong to the UK!', Hong Kong-UK Reunification Campaign Facebook Page, 10 June 2019, https://www.facebook.com/HongKongandUKreunite/posts/2451649004880360.

Hong Kong Free Press, 13 July 2019, https://hongkongfp.com/2019/07/13/explainer-conflicting-messages-behind-protesters-use-colonial-hong-kong-flag/.

65 'I Was Born in the 80s; Let Me Tell You about the 13 Years of Colonial Era in My Memory (我係一個80年代出世既人, 等我講下我記憶中嗰十三年英屬香港)', 4 June 2019, LIHKG, https://lihkg.com/thread/1185989/page/1; https://lihkg.com/thread/1185989/page/4.

66 Yehua, 'Hong Kong's Former Colonizers Cannot Be Our Saviour', *Lausan*, 3 March 2020, https://lausan.hk/2020/hong-kongs-former-coloniser-cannot-be-our-saviour/?fbclid=IwAR2zuwBbq8JVx9oMgHID8rfAQ_AK2bYJehwNR0JbggoSTjSm8OUqRVm_ZW8.

67 Kelvin Yeung: Hong Kong Has No Separation of Powers (楊潤雄:香港並非三權分立), 31 August 2020, LIHKG, https://lihkg.com/thread/2182244/page/3.

68 Suzanne Pepper, *Keeping Democracy at Bay: Hong Kong and the Challenge of Chinese Political Reform* (Rowman and Littlefield, 2007); Mark Hampton, *Hong Kong and British Culture, 1945–97* (Manchester: Manchester University Press, 2016), 131–59; Florence Mok, *Covert Colonialism: Governance, Surveillance and Political Culture in British Hong Kong, c. 1966–97* (Manchester: Manchester University Press, 2023).

69 Michael Zuckert, 'An American Paradox: Natural Rights and the American Revolution', in *Human Rights and Revolutions*, ed. Jeffrey N. Wasserstrom, Greg Grandin, Lynn Hunt, and Marilyn B. Young, 2nd edition (Rowman & Littlefield, 2007), 65–82; James Epstein, *Radical Expression: Political Language, Ritual, and Symbol in England, 1790–1850* (Oxford: Oxford University Press, 1994), 3–28.

70 J. C. D. Clark, *Revolution and Rebellion: State and Society in England in the Seventeenth and Eighteenth Centuries* (Cambridge: Cambridge University Press, 1986).

71 Indeed, for this very reason, left-wing activist Tony Wong critiques the slogan 'Restore Hong Kong'. Wong, 'This Is Not Restoration: Notes on a Protest Slogan', in *Reorienting Hong Kong's Resistance: Leftism, Decoloniality, and Internationalism*, ed. Wen Liu, J. N. Chien, Christina Chung, and Ellie Tse (Basingstoke: Palgrave, 2022), 3–14.

Index

Adams, Gerry 81–3
adherents 20, 41, 67, 70–1, 228
affective asceticism 106
Aglionby, Francis 143–5, 147, 150–1, 153
Agricultural Labourers' Union 201, 204, 207
Akroyd, Edward 141–2, 150, 152
almshouses 129, 144–5, 222
American Bar Association (ABA) 235, 246–7, 250, 255 n.93
American Revolution 22, 207, 238
Amyot, Thomas 25
Anderson, James, *The Dead Yet Speaking. A Sermon Preached in St George's Brighton, on the Sixth Sunday after Trinity, 1850. Being the Sunday after the Death of Sir Robert Peel* 177
Anglicans 15, 17, 28, 38, 41, 46, 73, 145
Anglo-American relationship 9, 236–7, 239
  and Magna Carta 239–49 (*see also* Magna Carta)
  memory diplomacy 236–9
Anglo-French 70
Anglo-Irish Treaty of December 1921 69, 83
Anglophobia 83, 242
Anglo-Saxonism 10, 207, 236–49
Anglosphere 246
anti-Catholicism 20, 25. *See also* Catholics/Catholicism
Anti-Corn Law League 198
antiquarian/antiquarianism 196, 199, 207
anti-slavery movements 53, 158, 198
Arch, Joseph 204, 207
ascetic radicalism 104–6
Ashton-under-Lyne National Charter Association 102, 108
Atlantic Charter of 1941 245–6, 250
Atlee, Clement 245
Attwood, Thomas 123, 126, 144, 150, 157, 162 n.21

Baily, E. H. 188 n.30
Baines, Edward 144, 146, 154, 180
Bamford, Samuel 197–8
baptism, political 121, 126–7, 131, 133
Barry, Tom 82, 91 n.108
Basic Law 257, 260–2
Bass, Michael Arthur 143, 145, 150–2
Battle of the Boyne 20
Baume, Pierre 107
Beer, Max 225
Beith, R., 'Spirits of the Mighty Dead' 102
Belfast (Good Friday) Agreement 86
Besant, Annie 203, 206
Biggs, John 142, 151, 153, 155–6
Bill of Rights 16, 18, 23–4, 27–8, 131, 244–5
Birmingham Civic Society's Public Art Committee 157
Birmingham Liberal Association 150
Birmingham Political Union 123, 126
Black Lives Matter, protesters of 1
'Blind Joe,' Oldham 195
Boer War monument 200
Bonnymuir martyrs 197, 211 n.33
Bradford Civic Society 158
Bradford Liberal Club 154
Bradlaugh, Charles 198
Bright, John 141, 143, 149–51, 154–5, 157–8, 168 n.181
Brotherton, Joseph 157–8, 198
Brown, John Tod 177–8
Brunswick Clubs 20
Bryant, Theodore 206
Burgess, Thomas 46
Burke, Edmund 15, 19, 78, 104
  Reflections on the Revolution in France 17, 104
Burns, Robert 99, 195
Burt, Thomas 201
busts 141, 146, 169 n.189, 186, 194, 211 n.32. *See also* statues; monuments

Butt, Isaac 77
Byron 97, 99

Callaghan, John 233 n.64
Canning, George 20, 147
canons 2–4, 6, 47, 68, 76–7, 84
   constructing 78–80
   and Troubles 81–3
Carlile, Richard 107, 199, 212 n.49
Carlyle, Thomas 78
   Hudson's Statue 147
Cartwright, John 22, 24–5, 116 n.82, 132, 196, 204, 210 n.26
Catholic Emancipation 20, 28, 72
Catholics/Catholicism 20, 71–2, 77, 80–1, 84
Catholic Stuarts 5
celebratory regime 16–18
Chantrey, Francis 124
Chartism/Chartists 5–7, 24–5, 28, 49–50, 80, 85, 93–110, 111 n.1, 112 n.7, 114 n.50, 115 n.61, 116 n.82, 193, 196–7, 199–202, 204, 221–2, 224
children, role of (in celebrations) 131–2
China
   Beijing 10, 258–9, 262–3, 266, 268
   Hong Kong (*see* Hong Kong)
Christian Socialist movement 225
Churchill, Winston 244–50
   destruction of statue 1
   The Great Democracies 246
   History of the English-Speaking Peoples 246
   History of the Second World War 246
Citrine, Walter 218
civic identity of public space 150–2
Civil War 69, 71, 76, 194, 204, 237
Claim of Right 18
Cleave, John 107
Clifton, Robert 153, 155, 157
Cobbett, William 6, 93, 96–8, 102–3, 105, 110, 116 n.82, 143, 199, 221
   accusation against 113 n.22
Cobden, Richard 7, 140, 147, 155–6, 163 n.64, 166 n.129, 168 n.177, 178
Cole, Charles, *The Spirit of Wat Tyler* 98
collective memory 2–4, 12 n.17, 16
Collins, Michael 82–4

Colston, Edward, destruction of statue 1, 11, 139
commemoration 1–4, 8–11, 17, 19, 26, 54, 68, 93, 95, 100, 102, 108, 110, 114 n.35, 121, 123–30, 139–40, 146–8, 158–9, 171, 185, 193–4, 196–7, 201, 207, 218, 222, 236, 241, 243
   and community cohesion 152–4
   forms and functions of 143–6
   MPs' statues and rationale for 141–3
   public 8, 139–40, 171, 180, 194
Communism 246–7, 250
Confucian 261
Connolly, James 81–2, 85
conservatives/conservatism 6, 15, 18–22, 25, 27, 69, 104, 129, 152–5, 212 n.52
constitutional nationalists 77–8, 85
co-operative movements 201–2, 208
Cooper, Thomas 98, 100–1, 107
Corbyn, Jeremy 217–18
cotton famine 166 n.125
counter-revolution 21, 81, 104
critical heritage studies 2. *See also* heritage
Cromwell, Oliver 27, 198, 204, 214 n.87
Cross-Strait Exchange Association 262
Cuban Missile Crisis 250
Curtis, William 19
Czech identity 194

Dafis, Dafydd (of Castell Hywel) 37–9, 48–9
   'Chwyldroad Ffrainc' (The French Revolution) 50
   Telyn Dewi (Dewi's Harp) 50
Daniel O'Connell's Repeal Association 69, 72–3
Davies, David 40–1, 43, 48, 53
   The Influence of the French Revolution on Welsh Life and Literature 53
Davis, Thomas 69, 73–5, 77–80, 83–5
   literary nationalism 75
   'Tone's Grave' 73
dead generations 2, 78
Declaration of Independence, American 235, 243–6
Declaration of the London Whig Club (1795) 20

Declaration of the Loyalty of the Town of Sheffield (1972) 21
Defence of the Realm Act 85
democratic legitimacy 68
democratization 35, 198, 228, 258, 260
de Valera, Éamon 70, 83
Dillon, James Blake 73
Disraeli, Benjamin 141–2, 152, 154, 156, 167 n.154
Dissenters 15, 17, 25, 35, 38–9, 41, 44, 46, 49, 53. *See also specific dissenters*
Doheny, Michael 74, 80
Donnelly, Ignatius, *Caesar's Column* 200
Dorchester Committee 221
Dorchester Labourers (Tolpuddle Martyrs) 9, 217–18, 221–3
Duffy, Charles Gavan 73
Dugdale, William 109
Duke of Wellington 140, 203

Earl Grey Tower 124
Easter Rising of 1916 68–9, 78, 80–2
Edwards, Thomas (Twm o'r Nant) 43
elites 2, 4, 7, 9, 43, 93, 110, 153, 236–9, 249, 260, 268
  elite memorialization 122–4
  middle-class 151, 153, 159
Elliott, Ebenezer, 'The Triumph of Reform' 131
Emergency Regulations 260
emigration 41–2, 48, 194, 214 n.91
Emmet, Robert 71–2, 77, 80, 84, 98–9, 101–3, 114 n.50
emotions 7, 94, 106, 110, 112 n.10, 183, 185, 205
England 5, 18, 20–1, 96, 106, 122, 126–7, 140, 146, 150, 205, 224–5, 228, 249
English Chartist Circular 98, 114 n.47
English Common Law 246, 248–9
Enlightenment 7, 22, 36, 38, 94, 104, 106, 108–10
equality 24–5, 38, 71, 267
Estcourt, Thomas Grimston Bucknall 182
Europe/European 9, 22, 27, 45, 47, 50–1, 67, 193–4, 204–5, 238–9
Evans, Alcwyn C. 42
  History of Carmarthen 44

Evans, Christmas 48
Evans, John James
  Dylanwad y Chwyldro Ffrengig ar Lenyddiaeth Cymru (The Influence of the French Revolution on Welsh Literature) 53
  Morgan John Rhys a'i Amserau (Morgan John Rhys and His Times) 53
Evans, Thomas (Tomos Glyn Cothi) 37, 39–40, 43–5, 47–9, 51, 53
  death anniversary of 52
  'La Marseillaise' as 'Cân Rhyddid' (The Song of Liberty) 51
  Trysorfa Gymmysgedig 44
Evans, Titus (of Machynlleth) 41
Extradition Bill (2019) 259, 266–7

Faithfull, God. J. W. 184
Famine 75
'Famous Guerrilla Leaders' series 82
Farish, William 99
Fascism 208, 243
Federal Constitution 235–6, 240–2
Fenian Brotherhood 69, 74
Fenian Manchester Martyrs 197
Fenians/Fenianism 68, 74–7, 80–1, 84, 89 n.51
festivals and jubilees 129–32
Fielden, John 139, 143, 152, 154
Fielding, J. T. 201
First Reform Bill 28
Fishguard invasion of 1797 38, 41
Fitzgerald, Edward 98–9, 101
forced monument 202
Foster, William Z. 210 n.20
Fox, Charles James 22, 28, 178
  History of the Early Part of the Reign of James II 23
France 4, 15, 17–18, 25, 50, 72, 77, 122, 153, 193–4, 196, 207
"Franchise Tree" 207
Franklin, Benjamin 97
Fraternal Democrats 23
Free Church Council 228
Freedom Train 246
freethought movement 107–8, 199
Free Trade Hall 200, 212 n.51
French affinity 77, 89 n.66

French Revolution 4–5, 15–18, 20–3, 25–7, 36, 39, 41, 43, 51, 53, 71–3, 93, 104–7, 126, 194, 200, 268
French Wars (1793–1815) 129, 133
Friendly Society of Agricultural Labourers 221
Frost, John 109, 209 n.2

Gaelic League movement 78–9, 85
Gagging Acts 21, 95
Gambrell, E. Smyth 247
Gammage, R. G. 99
Garibaldi, Giuseppe 204
General Election of 1918 70
genocide 2, 74, 158
George III 20, 38, 40, 235, 238, 249
George, Lloyd 218
Gettysburg Address 243, 246
Gillray, James, *Life of William Cobbett* 113 n.33
Gladstone, William 7, 139–40, 143, 145, 148–9, 151, 166 n.129, 180, 185, 206
Glorious Revolution of 1688 2, 5, 15–18, 21, 27
  conservative appropriation of 18–20
  displacement of 25–7
  and radicals 23–5
Godwinism 25
Godwin, William 95, 104, 106, 110, 112 n.16, 117 n.92
Gonne, Maud 77
Gorsedd Beirdd Ynys Prydain (Assembly of the Bards of the Isle of Britain) 37–8, 43, 45–6, 54
gospel 48, 79, 84, 229
Gothic style 105, 109, 152
Goulburn, Henry 173, 175, 180, 182–4
'Greater Magna Carta' 245
Great Repeal Bill 121
Green, Alice Stopford 71
Griffith, Arthur 68, 70, 83–4
guerrilla memorialization 1, 69
Gunpowder Plot 26–7

Habeas Corpus 27, 245
Haines, J. F., *National Reformer* 199
Halbwachs, Maurice 16, 23, 26
Hall, Robert 146

Hammett, James 207, 218
Handley, Henry 142, 147–8
Hanoverian regime 17–18, 23
Hardie, Keir 222, 224, 227
Hardy, Thomas 25, 27, 95, 98, 114 n.47
Harney, George Julian 98, 100, 105, 201, 214 n.87
Harvey, Alexander 155
Haydon, Benjamin 122–3
Haymarket Martyrs monument, Chicago 194–6, 210 n.20
Hayter, George, 'The House of Commons,1833' 123–4
Hazeltine, H. D. 241
Hazlitt, William 96–7
hegemony, Anglican 15, 28
Henderson, Arthur 222, 228
heritage 1–3, 6–7, 20, 28, 93–4, 98, 100–1, 106, 109–10, 157, 218, 224, 247–8. *See also* intangible heritage
Herrmann, Rachel 55 n.3
Hesketh-Fleetwood, Peter 139, 142, 145, 147
Hetherington, Henry 107
Heywood, Abel 107, 203
history
  historical consciousness 68, 70, 87 n.9, 87 n.25
  Labor Party and 219–21, 230
  of labour and socialist movement 225–9
  Martyrs' story, commemoration and 221–5
  and memory 3, 5–6, 9, 15, 26, 28, 29 n.9, 258–60
Hobson, Bulmer 84
Holberry, Samuel 100–1, 113 n.32
Holy War of 1798 74
Home Rule/Home Rulers 68, 77–8, 238
Hong Kong 257, 259–60
  Food and Environmental Hygiene Department (FEHD) 264
  Hong Kong Federation of Students 261
  Hong Kong Monetary Authority 260
  protests (*see* Hong Kong protest movements)
  Public Opinion Programme 264
  Special Administrative Region (SAR) 257, 260–3, 265, 268

Hong Kong protest movements 9–10
  Anti-Extradition Bill Protests (2019) 258, 265–8
  Mong Kok Civil Unrest (2015) 258, 264–5
  against Moral and National Education Reforms (2012) 258, 261–2
  against National Security Law (2003) 258, 260–1, 266
  Umbrella Movement (2014) 258, 262–4
Hong Kong-United Kingdom Reunification Campaign 263
Horsley, Samuel 38–40, 43
House of Brunswick 19, 24
Hughes, Brendan 81
Hull Working Men's Association 110
Hunt, Henry 24, 102, 105, 108, 126, 132, 199–200
Hutton, Hugh 123
Hyndman, H. M. 222–4
  The Evolution of Revolution 223–4

iconoclasm 1, 205–6, 208
immortality 80, 97, 101–3
Imperial Germany 237
Independent Labour Party (ILP) 49, 224
Independent Society 153
Ingram, Herbert 154–5, 167 n.166
intangible heritage 2, 12 n.9. *See also* heritage
International Labour Organization 211 n.32
International Magna Charta Day Association (IMCDA) 240–2, 249, 253 n.33
invention of political tradition 1–4, 6, 9–10
Ireland 5, 20, 30 n.31, 38, 67–79, 84–6, 121, 127, 205–6, 208. *See also* Irish republicanism
Irish Citizens' Army 78, 81
Irish Free State 69, 85
Irish People newspaper 75, 83
Irish Republican Army (IRA) 69–71, 81, 86
Irish Republican Brotherhood (IRB) 69–70, 73–80, 83
Irish republicanism 6, 67–72, 76, 79, 81–6. *See also* Ireland; republicanism

Irish Revolutionary Brotherhood. *See* Irish Republican Brotherhood (IRB)
Irish Volunteers 69, 71, 79

Jacobin/Jacobinism 5–6, 25–7, 39, 42, 50, 54, 95, 97–8, 199
Jacobite 16, 18, 20, 27, 212 n.52
James II 15, 21
Jefferson, Thomas 238, 244
  Saxon inheritance 240, 243
Jenkins, R. T. 53
Jones, David (Welsh Freeholder) 40, 42–3, 49
Jones, Ernest 98, 100, 196–7, 199, 201, 210 n.26
Jones, Hugh (of Llangwm), Interludes 49
Jones, John (Jac Glan-y-Gors) 37, 48–9
  Seren tan Gwmmwl (A Star under a Cloud) 41, 43, 49
Jones, William (of Llangadfan) 37, 41, 49, 100–1
Joshua Wong 262

Kennedy, John F. 248–50
Kennedy Memorial Trust (KMT) 248–9
Kensal Green Cemetery 197, 201–2, 210 n.28
Kent, William 196
Kett, Robert 207
Kickham, Charles 75, 77, 80
Kossuth, Lewis 204

Labour Party 9, 45, 49, 217–19, 222, 225–6, 245
  and history 219–21, 230 (*see also* history)
Laird, John 142, 144, 156
Lalor, James Fintan 78–80, 83, 85
League of Nations 202, 242
Lend-Lease Act 244, 249–50
liberalism 178, 198–200
Liberal Party 198, 203, 205, 228
'Library of Ireland' history series 73
Lincoln, Abraham 239, 243, 249
  Lincoln copy of Magna Carta 243, 249
Lindsay, Jack 207
The Link 203, 206
literary nationalism 75
literary separatism 75, 77, 80, 84

literary tourism 100
Locke, John 71
London Corresponding Society (LCS) 23, 25, 27, 94, 96, 98
London Democratic Association 100, 105
London Dorchester Committee 221
London Working Men's Association (LWMA) 98, 105–7
Lord Brougham 47, 154
Lord Bryce 241–2
Lord Elcho 139, 146
Lord Evershed 235
lost generation 5, 36–7, 41
Loveless, George 221–2
Lovett, William 105–6, 202, 209 n.2
loyalty/loyalism/loyalists 5, 18–22, 24, 36–7, 40–1, 48, 54, 81, 96, 129, 133, 205, 207, 227
Luby, Thomas 75, 77, 80

Macaulay, Catherine 122
  History of England from the Accession of James I to That of the Brunswick Line 15
Macaulay, Thomas Babington, *History of England* 16, 28
MacDonald, Ramsay 222, 226
Mackenzie, Peter 125–6
Mackintosh, James, *History of the Revolution in England in 1688* 22
Magna Carta 2, 9–10, 24, 124, 127, 131, 235–6, 239, 250, 254 n.89
  and Anglo-American relations 239–49
  Clause 39 235
  Lincoln copy of Magna Carta 243, 249
  memory diplomacy 236–9
Magna Charta Day Association 9, 249
Maguire, Tom 86
'mainlandization' (Hong Kong) 258, 262
Manfield, Philip 198
man worship 105, 118 n.103
'Martyrs of Liberty' 99
Marxist 222, 226
Mary Reform 121
Mayflower Compact 242–3, 246
May, Theresa 121
McAdam, John 204
McGuinness, Martin 82
Medievalism 54, 225, 240

memorialization 1–2, 4, 7–8, 10, 93, 121–2, 132–3, 140, 159, 182, 186, 193, 196, 199–203, 208
  elite 122–4
  guerrilla 1, 69
  practical memorials 143–6
  provisional 206–8
  proxy 202–5
  public 124–6, 194, 198–201
Methodism 228
militant republicanism 76–9, 84–5
Mitchel, John 70, 73–4, 77–81, 83–5
  History of Ireland 74
  Jail Journal 68, 74, 84
  The Last Conquest of Ireland (Perhaps) 74
mock funerals 197
Monroe Doctrine 237
monuments 7, 10, 125, 139–41, 193–4, 198–9, 201, 204, 207–8, 210 n.26, 213 n.59, 213 n.66, 214 n.91, 235, 246–7, 250. *See also* busts; statues
  destruction of 1–2
  forced 202
  imaginary 200
  monument mania 125, 139, 202
  public 124, 139–40, 143, 193, 201, 205
Morganwg, Iolo. *See* Williams, Edward
Morley, Samuel 162 n.21, 169 n.189
Morris, William 195, 203, 224
Morus, E. Ben (Myfyr Teifi) 49
multi-sensory celebrations 130
Murray, George 39–40

national celebrations 126–9, 218
nationalism 5–6, 68, 70, 75–9, 81, 84, 104, 193–4, 204, 208
nationality 72–3, 79–80, 84, 179, 237
National Library of Wales 51–2
National People's Congress 263
National Political Union 96, 132
National Society Magna Charta Dames and Barons 253 n.33
natural right 16, 23–4, 68, 73, 77–8
neo-Fenian Dungannon Clubs 71
neo-Fenians 77
neo-Jacobins 100, 105
neo-Romanticism 84

New Poor Law 102–3
New Youth Forum 262
Nonconformists/nonconformism 36, 38, 45, 228–9, 237
Nora, Pierre 3, 10
North America 193–4, 237–9
Northern Echo 144–5
Northern Ireland 69–70, 81–2, 86
Northern Star 23, 98–9, 102, 109
Nottingham Trades Council 155

Oastler, Richard 105, 204
O'Brien, Bronterre 105–6, 197, 210 n.28
O'Connell, Daniel 69, 72–3, 88 n.40
O'Connor, Arthur 100–1
O'Connor, Feargus 100–1, 105–6, 111 n.1, 140, 146, 154–5, 197, 199, 221
Ó Faoláin, Seán 71
O'Hagan, Des 81–2
Old IRA 82
O'Leary, John 75–7, 80
O'Mahony, John 74, 80
O'Malley, Ernie 84
Owen, Geraint Dyfnallt 52, 112 n.16
Owen, Robert 197, 202, 211 n.32, 224–5

Paine, Thomas 2, 6, 15–17, 23, 27, 45, 52, 71, 93, 95–8, 100, 102–3, 106, 110, 114 n.33, 116 n.82, 197, 211 n.34
  'Bill of Wrongs and Insult' 15, 24
  birthday commemoration of 114 n.35
  The Constitution Produced and Illustrated 24
  Rights of Man 17, 26
pan-British 126–7, 129
pantheons/pantheonism 1–2, 4, 6–7, 9, 19, 27, 38, 69, 83, 93–5, 97–104, 106–7, 110, 113 n.32, 116 n.82, 151, 220–1
  paper pantheon 2, 6, 93, 99, 110, 111 n.2, 116 n.82
Pare, William 153, 167 n.142
Parnell, Charles Stewart 77–8, 85
Parnellite campaign 77
Patmore, C., 'Shall Smith Have a Statue?' 147
Patten, Chris 258–9

Pearse, Patrick 69–71, 78–81, 83–6, 158
  'Ghosts' 78–80
Peel, Frederick 173–4, 177–81, 183–4, 187 n.6
Peel, George, *The Private Letters of Sir Robert Peel* 173
Peel, Julia (Lady Peel) 173, 175–7, 179, 181–5
Peel, Robert 7–8, 102, 139–40, 145–8, 150–1, 153, 157, 159, 168 n.177, 168 n.185, 171, 202–3
  accident and death (caused by horse) 172
  condolences (letters of condolence) 172–4, 179–80, 183
  final speech in parliament 178–80
  grief of Lady Peel 183–5
  medical treatments (criticism of) 174–5
  monuments and memorials of 180–3
  in public and private memory 185–6
  public funeral 176–8, 187 n.14
Penderyn, Dic 209 n.2
People 75–6
People's Charter 204, 207, 221
People's Monument Committee 153
People's Republic of China (PRC) 257, 261–2, 266
Peterloo Massacre 100–2, 126, 132, 193, 199–200, 208, 212 nn.51–2
Pettit, Philip, *Republicanism: A Theory of Freedom and Government* 86 n.2
Pickersgill, Henry William 181–2
Pigott, Charles, *Political Dictionary* 24
pilgrimages 73, 82, 100, 154, 195, 197, 204, 210 n.26, 218, 246
Pilgrim Fathers 239, 245, 252 n.25
Pitt and Grenville Acts. *See* Gagging Acts
Pitt Club of Nottingham 19
Pitt Dinner, London Tavern (1815) 19
Pitt, William 17, 19–20, 38, 43, 178, 205
  and Iolo Morganwg 39
  Reign of Terror 26, 35, 45
Platt, John 142, 150, 169 n.197
plebeian radicals/radicalism 9, 199, 206, 208
political philosophy 68, 71, 74, 78
political silencing 5–6, 35, 37, 43–5, 54

Political Unions 122–3, 127, 129–30, 132–3
posthumous 2, 4, 6–8, 23, 94–7, 99, 102–3, 110, 112 n.16, 117 n.84, 171, 186
Potter, John 180
Powell, Francis 148, 150, 153, 156, 165 n.103
practical memorials 143–6
Price, Richard 15, 17, 21–3, 37, 40, 95, 104
   Discourse on the Love of Our Country 22
Priestley, Joseph 17, 39–40, 44, 95, 201
Primrose League 152
Prince Albert 178, 183, 185, 202
The Proclamation of the Irish Republic 78, 81–2
Protestants/Protestantism 19–20, 28, 71–3, 81–2, 84, 125, 237
protest movements in Hong Kong. See Hong Kong protest movements
Provisional Army Council 86
Provisional Irish Republican Army (PIRA) 68–70, 75, 81–3, 85–6, 87 n.12, 91 n.108
provisional memorialization 206–8
proxy memorialization 202–5
public memorialization 124–6, 194, 198–201
Public Monuments and Sculpture Association (PMSA) 140, 148
public sphere 4, 9, 54, 93, 104, 110
Puritans/Puritanism 9, 27, 52–3, 117 n.92, 204–5

Queen Victoria 47, 148, 182–3, 185, 203, 205

race/racism 10, 236–41, 243, 247, 249, 259
radicals/radicalism 5–7, 9, 15–18, 24–8, 35–7, 41, 44–5, 47–54, 69, 83, 85, 91 n.112, 93–8, 101–5, 107, 110, 114 n.51, 118 n.117, 126, 132, 193–200, 202–8, 218–19, 268
   ascetic 104–6
   Glorious Revolution and 23–5
   iconoclasm and 205–6
   plebeian 9, 199, 206, 208

radical Enlightenment 7, 94, 104, 107, 112 n.12
radical Romanticism 94
rational/rationalism 104, 109, 117 n.92, 128–9
Read, Benedict 140, 146
rebels/rebellions 68, 71–2, 74–8, 80, 83, 93, 98–9, 205, 235, 238, 249
Redmond, John 77–8
Reeves, John 18–19
Reform Act of 1867–8 7
Reform Acts of 1832 7, 25, 32, 121, 126, 131–3
Reformers' Tree 207–8
reform movement 36, 38, 125, 127–9, 133, 193, 198–9, 208
religious sectarianism 70, 72–3
remembrance, cultures of 1–2, 4, 6, 9, 21, 94, 122
'Renewed by the Reformers of Avondale at the passing of the Reform Bill – ANNO DOMINI 1832' 125
Repealing the Act of Union 70, 72
republican authenticity 82, 86
republicanism 6, 24, 49, 51, 67–72, 74, 76–7, 81–2, 84–6, 99, 198, 205. See also Ireland; Irish republicanism
Revolutionary Nationalists 77
Revolution Clubs 18
Revolution Principles 15, 18–20, 28
Revolution Settlement 15, 17, 20, 24–5, 28
Revolution Society 17
Reynolds, G. W. M. 100
Rhys, Morgan John (Morgan ab Ioan Rhys) 37, 41–3, 47–8, 53
Richards, William (of Kings Lynn) 37, 41–2, 44, 49
   Cwyn y Cystuddiedig as *The Triumph of Innocency* 44
   History of Lynn 44
   Trysorfa Gymmysgedig 44
Ripon Civic Society 155
Robert, Thomas, *Cwyn yn erbyn Gorthrymder* (A Complaint against Oppression) 43
Rocker, Rudolf 196
Rodgers, Daniel 70

Romanticism/Romantics 6–7, 16, 36, 93–4, 97–106, 108–10, 114 n.39
   difficulties of defining 111 n.3
   and emotion 112 n.10
romantic memory 6, 106
Romantic Studies 6, 94, 102, 106, 110, 112 n.9
Rossa, Jeremiah O'Donovan 80
Rothstein, Theodore 226, 228
Rousseau, Jean-Jacques 83, 110
Royal National Eisteddfod of Wales 46
Russell, John 176, 180, 221
Russell, William 21, 27
Ryan, Desmond 80, 84

Salt, Titus 142, 144, 147, 149, 152–3, 156, 158
Saxon inheritance 240, 243
Schneider, Henry 142, 145, 151
Scholarism 262
Scholefield, James 199–200
Scotch Martyrs 98–9, 114 n.47, 212 n.44
Scotland 18, 20, 126–7, 129, 204–5
The Scotsman newspaper 129
sectarian/sectarianism 46, 70, 72–3, 75–6, 81, 84, 204
sentimentalism 104, 106
separatism/separatist tradition 6, 68, 78–81, 83–5
   constructing 68–72
   framing 73–6
   past rebellions 76–8
sermons 15, 17–18, 155, 173, 177
Shan Van Vocht periodical 77
Shaw, Francis 68
Shelley, Percy Bysshe 99–100, 104, 110, 197, 210 n.27
   Frankenstein 109
   Queen Mab 109
Sinn Féin 70, 81, 83, 85–6
   History of Republicanism 82
Sino-British Joint Declaration 10, 257, 263–4, 266
Smith, B. T. 179, 184
Smith, Goldwin 212 n.51
Smith, Joseph 213 n.66
Social Democratic Federation (SDF) 200, 222–3, 226–7

socialism 81, 112 n.12, 197, 224–6, 229
Socialist League 227
social memory 2–3, 12 n.17
Society for Constitutional Information 17
Society of United Irishmen 68, 70, 73
Sound Sculpture Trail 158
Southey, Robert 99, 181
   Wat Tyler 100
sovereignty 15, 71–2, 247, 258, 260–1
Speeches from the Dock 76–7, 84
statuemania 1–2, 8, 139, 141, 158–9, 193–5
   reassessing chronology of 146–50
statues. *See also* busts; monuments
   and civic identity of public space 150–2
   cultural reference and landmarks 154–6
   decades of erection of statues of MPs 148–9
   destruction of 1–2, 11, 139
   imagining and constructing 200–2
   MPs' statues and rationale for commemoration 141–3
   practical memorials 143–6
   relegation, relocation and rehabilitation 156–8
   and subscribers 152–4
St Enda's school, Dublin 78, 80
Stephens, James 74, 80
Stephens, Thomas 45

Taliesin ab Iolo 45–7
Tan War 82
Taylor, John 195
Taylor, Tony 110
Teifi, Dafydd Glan 43
Ten Hours Act 143, 152
Thelwall, John 6, 25–6, 37–8, 94–9, 102–3, 107, 111 n.5, 112 n.7, 113 n.28, 116 n.82, 117 n.92, 199
Thomas Liberty Broad 126
Thornhill, William Pole 124
Tiananmen Square protests (1989) 258, 267
'To Commemorate Magna Carta, Symbol of Freedom under Law' 235, 247
Tolpuddle Martyrs 9, 207, 217–20, 225, 230

tombs 103, 197, 201, 210 n.26
Tone, Theobald Wolfe 69, 71–4, 77–85
   An Argument on Behalf of the Catholics of Ireland 71–2
   death of 72
   Letters 84
   Life of Theobald Wolfe Tone 72
   visit to Panthéon, Paris 83
Tory/Tories 5, 15–21, 27–8, 123, 128, 200
Trades Union Congress (TUC) 201, 218–20, 222–3, 227, 230
   The Book of the Martyrs of Tolpuddle 218
trade unions/unionism 9, 49, 54, 201, 207–8, 217–19, 223, 226–8, 230
tradition and memory 3, 10
transatlantic 9, 69, 200, 236–42, 244–6, 249, 253 n.33
transcendent 101, 108
Treasonable and Seditious Practices 21
Treaty of Ghent (1914) 239, 241, 249, 252 n.22
trees, planting of 207
trial by jury dinners 17, 25–7
Troubles 69, 81–3
Tung Chee-hwa 260–1
Turner, Charles 166 n.129

Unitarian/Unitarianism 39–40, 43, 45–6, 48, 50, 52–3, 147, 150
United Irish League organization 78
United Irishman newspaper 74, 75
United Irishmen 71–8, 81, 84, 98
United Irish movement 69, 71, 73, 83
United Nations 245, 250
the United States 4, 9, 69–70, 74–6, 210 n.20, 235–6, 238–9, 241–5, 247, 249–50, 255 n.93, 267

vandalism 157, 205–6, 248
Villiers, Charles Pelham 149, 151–2, 155, 165 n.104
Vincent, Henry 108–10, 119 n.120
violence 20, 41, 45, 67–70, 72, 76, 78, 81–3, 85, 105, 167 n.166, 225, 238
   republican violence 70
   revolutionary violence 73, 88 n.40

Volney, C. F. 7, 94, 104–10, 119 n.120
   Ruins; or a Survey of Revolutions of Empire 53, 107–9
Voltaire 83, 110

wage-earning system 227
'Waiting for the Times; the Morning after the Debate on Reform, 8 October 1831' 122
Wales 5–6, 18, 35–41, 43–4, 47, 49, 53–4, 95, 97, 127, 205
Wallace, William 4–5, 204
War of Independence (1919–21) 69, 71, 82, 84
Washington, George 97–8, 105, 114 n.38, 239, 249
Washington Naval Conference of 1921–2 242
Watkin, Absalom 126
Watkins, Joshua 42
Watson, James 107, 109
Watts, G. F. 209 n.13
Whig Reform Bill (1831) 96, 132
Whigs/Whiggism 5, 7, 15–23, 26–8, 125, 199, 223
   Foxite Whigs 19, 22
   Walpolean Whigs 19
White, Hayden
   historical past 23, 31 n.49
   practical past 5, 16
White, Henry 23
Wilkes, John 205
William III 19–20, 27–8, 205
Williamite 18–20, 28
William IV 124, 127, 205
William of Orange 5, 17, 21, 23, 26–7
Williams, Edward 37–8, 43–7, 49, 51
   'Breiniau Dyn' (The Rights of Man) 43, 49
   death anniversary of (homage) 52–3
   'Gwawr Rhyddid' (The Dawn of Liberty) 50
   Iolo Morganwg a Chywyddau'r Ychwanegiad (Iolo Morganwg and the Poems of the Appendix) 52
   'Iolo Morganwg and the Romantic Tradition in Wales' 52, 54
   and Pitt 39

Williams, Hugh 98, 100
Williams, Robert, *Enwogion Cymru. A Biographical Dictionary of Eminent Welshmen* 47–9
Willoughby, Henry 174
Wilson, Mathew 150
Winstanley, Gerrard 196, 206
Winterbotham, William 17–18
Winterhalter, Franz Xaver 182–3
Wolfe Tone memorial, Dublin 78
Wollstonecraft, Mary 95, 104–6, 117 n.96
    Vindication of the Rights of Men 104

working-class 8–9, 20, 45, 54, 96–9, 105, 113 n.32, 118 n.117, 145, 151, 153, 157, 193, 195, 199–200, 207, 225
'The Working Man in History' series 206
Wyvill, Christopher 21–2

Yeats, W. B. 77, 80
Y Gell Gymysg (The Mixed Cell) 44, 48
Young Ireland/Irelanders 69, 73–7, 79, 81, 83, 85

www.ingramcontent.com/pod-product-compliance
Lightning Source LLC
Chambersburg PA
CBHW071809300426
44116CB00009B/1248